SAINT BENEDICT
and
HIS TIMES

St. Benedict
(Perugia. San Pietro)

SAINT BENEDICT

and

HIS TIMES

BY

HIS EMINENCE

ILDEPHONSE CARDINAL SCHUSTER, O.S.B.

Archbishop of Milan

TRANSLATED BY

GREGORY J. ROETTGER, O.S.B.

Monk of St. John's Abbey

WITH A PREFACE BY

RIGHT REV. ALCUIN DEUTSCH, O.S.B.

Abbot, St. John's Abbey

IMPRIMI POTEST

✠ Balduinus Dworschak, O.S.B.

Abbas Sti Joannis Baptistae

Collegeville, Minn., July 18, 1951

NIHIL OBSTAT

William Fischer, S.T.D.

Censor Librorum

IMPRIMATUR

✠ Joseph E. Ritter ,

Archiepiscopus

Sancti Ludovici, die 9 mensis Julii, 1951

In obedience to the decrees of Pope Urban VIII and other sovereign Pontiffs, the writer declares that the graces and other supernatural facts related in this volume as witnessing to the sanctity of Servants of God other than those canonized or beatified by the Church, rest on human authority alone; and in regard thereto, as in all things else, the writer submits himself without reserve to the infallible judgment of the Apostolic See, which alone has power and authority to pronounce as to whom rightly belong the Character and Title of Saint or blessed.

This Arouca Press edition is a reprint of
the book originally published in 1951
by B. Herder Book Co.

ISBN: 978-1-989905-46-3 (pbk)
ISBN: 978-1-989905-47-0 (hardcover)

Cover design by
Michael Schrauzer

Preface

For the past fourteen centuries the giant figure of St. Benedict has cast its shadow over Western civilization. Like the mustard seed of the Gospel parable, Monte Cassino, the cradle of the Benedictine Order, grew and ramified, until the great tree embraced all of Christian Europe to such an extent that a certain period of history is aptly spoken of as the "Benedictine centuries."

Following upon the tremendous upheavals that marked the invasions of the barbarian hordes and the downfall of the Roman Empire, Benedictine monachism was the instrument God chose not only to bring the faith to the young and vigorous peoples of the North, but also to transmit to them the best of the cultural inheritance of ancient Greece and Rome.

To St. Benedict and to Monte Cassino the great monastic foundations of medieval France, England, Germany, and Switzerland looked back as to their common origin and paid their deepest respect and reverence to the great Patriarch. Even in the darkest of times, Monte Cassino stood out like a mighty lighthouse, shedding its beneficent light upon all that came within its orbit.

Tragic it is beyond words that in our own days this monument to religion and peace and culture should have fallen victim to the hands of the destroyer. Whether the blame for the destruction of that famous pile ultimately falls to this side or to that makes little difference. With this catastrophe goes a far deeper consideration. Is it perhaps a presage of the future, of black ages of a new and horrible barbarism stalking about the face of the earth—a negation of what Monte Cassino and Western civilization stood for? God forbid!

And yet, should such times come, who knows but that divine Provi-

vii

dence may not again employ Benedictine monachism to bring the light of God's truth and a Christian way of life to the neo-pagan generations, as He did after the gigantic cataclysm of Rome's downfall?

In any event, recent decades have seen a remarkable renaissance of Benedictinism. In the year 1880, then regarded as the fourteenth centenary of the Patriarch's birth, the Benedictine Order had shrunk to small dimensions. Since that time, however, despite two World Wars, it has grown and prospered. In the United States alone, twenty-two abbeys of Black Monks count well over two thousand members.

Throughout the world an interest in the Rule of St. Benedict and in the monastic family as an ideal of Christian life has been developing in past years. The sage precepts of St. Benedict's monastic code, though written originally for the men of the sixth century, by reason of the genius inherent in that Rule are equally applicable to the modernity of the twentieth century, and perhaps more necessary than ever if Christian civilization is to survive.

Despite the importance of St. Benedict in the history of the Church and of the world, we know extremely little of the man as such, for example, the dates of his birth and death, family relationships, contacts with popes and other great men of his time: details with which the modern biographer is mightily concerned. He himself left no written monument except his Rule for Monasteries. Apart from that, we possess the collection of miracles of St. Benedict found in the second book of St. Gregory's *Dialogues*. More than this brief sketch the medieval mind did not seek. Indeed, the Rule served as a kind of biography for the ancients, since St. Gregory wisely remarks that the Patriarch could not have lived otherwise than he taught. Wherefore the Rule is for all the admirers of St. Benedict a most precious heritage, because of the wise precepts it contains and also because it reflects so clearly the spirit and the mentality of the great saint.

Using the *Dialogues* of St. Gregory as the point of departure, Cardinal Schuster, one of the outstanding scholars of our age, has fitted St. Benedict into the times in which he lived. With the immense fund of knowledge—historical, juridical, liturgical, archeological, and literary—at his disposal, the author is peculiarly suited to invest the rather sketchy outline of St. Benedict with flesh and bones. Like the true disciple of the great Patriarch that he is, His Eminence professes that this work was one to which he devoted himself with special pre-dilection. And he has succeeded well.

It affords me particular pleasure to prefix these few words to His Eminence's book. Ever since the days, decades ago, when we were students together at the Collegio di Sant'Anselmo in Rome, I have had great admiration for the deep learning and the deeper spiritual-ity of this great follower of St. Benedict. Despite the worries and cares which the government of the great diocese of Milan, particu-larly in these latter years, has heaped upon its shepherd, he has still found time in his busy days to devote to learned pursuits. His present book, though written from a scholarly background, has a popular appeal. Its translation fills a definite lacuna, since no other major biography of St. Benedict is available in the English language at the present time. May its pages serve to bring the great Patriarch to the knowledge of an ever-increasing number of admirers; may the perusal of this work stir up many so that they "may strive to love what he loved and practice what he taught."

✠ Alcuin Deutsch, O.S.B.
Abbot, St. John's Abbey

that this work was one to which he devoted himself with special pre-
dilection. And he has succeeded well.

It affords me particular pleasure to prefix these few words to His
Eminence's book. Ever since the days, decades ago, when we were
students together at the Collegio di Sant'Anselmo in Rome, I have
had great admiration for the deep learning and the deeper spirituality of this great follower of St. Benedict. Despite the worries and
cares which the government of the great diocese of Milan, particularly in these latter years, has heaped upon its shepherd, he has still
found time in his busy days to devote to learned pursuits. His present
book, though written from a scholarly background, has a popular
appeal. Its translation fills a definite lacuna, since no other major
biography of St. Benedict is available in the English language at the
present time. May its pages serve to bring the great Patriarch to the
knowledge of an ever-increasing number of admirers; may the perusal
of this work stir up many so that they "may strive to love what he
loved and practice what he taught."

✠ Alcuin Deutsch, O.S.B.
Abbot, St. John's Abbey

Contents

St. Romanus gives the habit to St. Benedict
(Florence. Basilica of San Miniato)

Subiaco. Convent of St. Scholastica

Subiaco. Views of the Sacro Speco

xviii

Subiaco. Basilica of the Sacro Speco monastery

St. Benedict rolls naked in the thornbushes

Subiaco. Apse of the lower church

St. Benedict miraculously recovers the iron blade
(Sacro Speco)

Cassino and Monte Cassino

Monte Cassino from the northeast

After the first bombing

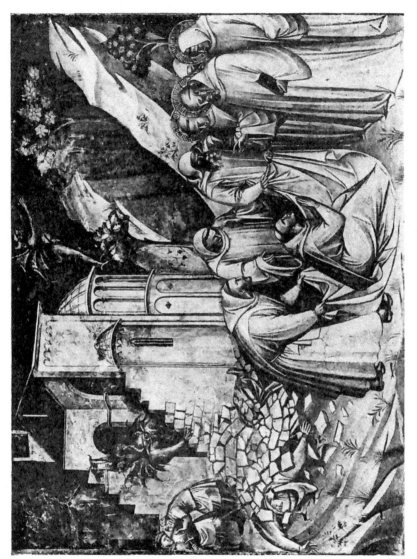

St. Benedict restores to life the monk buried under a wall

(Florence. San Miniato)

Two hundred sacks of flour miraculously supplied
(Monte Oliveto)

Last supper of St. Benedict and St. Scholastica together
(Subiaco. Sacro Speco)

Death of St. Benedict
(Monte Cassino)

Monte Cassino. Airview

After the bombardment (February 15, 1944)

Monte Cassino. Entrances

Monte Cassino. Cloister of Benefactors

Monte Cassino. Central nave of basilica

Monte Cassino. Choir and high altar after the first bombing.

Monte Cassino, Choir (1692)

Monte Cassino. Crypt of the basilica

Monte Cassino. Crypt of the basilica

CHAPTER I

The Sources

WITHOUT a doubt, as far as the older historians were concerned, the question of the sources of the life of St. Benedict did not present itself in the same light as it does to us.

In centuries past, when the individual was normally circumscribed by a definite field of action and when means of communication were limited, living memory and local tradition quite sufficed to preserve the record of his life. On the other hand, for the public, the eternal child, it was enough to see reproduced on the pages of a written biography the general outlines of the person in question, leaving perhaps to the artist a little more liberty to add decorative details.

Even with regard to men of outstanding fame, their biography generally came years after their death. This happened at Rome with regard to St. Gregory; in the ninth century John the Deacon finally wrote his life. The same thing was true of St. Ambrose at Milan; there no one thought of writing even the briefest biography of him. Had not St. Augustine, in Africa, concerned himself about the matter, by entrusting it to Paulinus, formerly a notary of the Milanese Church, today we should know very little about the life of the great bishop of the metropolis of the Italian Province, or we should have to content ourselves with Greek sources.

So it was also with St. Benedict. None of the popes, statesmen, bishops, or saints who came in contact with him during the eighty years of his life ever thought of setting down in writing even the least biographical note. And that is not all. The very monks of Subiaco and Monte Cassino, just as they did not bother to transcribe the various ecclesiastical or pontifical documents relating to the foundation of their respective monasteries, so likewise they showed no concern about handing on to future monastic generations the story of their Master.

By great good fortune the Lateran monastery of St. Pancratius was close to the Caelian Hill and the paternal house of St. Gregory the Great; this circumstance favored the relations of the future Pope with the immediate disciples of St. Benedict. From the sum total of the great Pope's literary production, it is easy to see that his monastic vocation thrived greatly during the pleasant years of his youth in the domestic walls on the *Clivus Scauri,* by reason of the spiritual intimacy with his saintly mother, his aunts, who all were elevated to the honors of the altar, and above all by his frequent intercourse with the first abbots and monks of Monte Cassino.

It is certainly not going too far to assert that Gregory may have personally visited the places sanctified by the life and miracles of St. Benedict. Otherwise it is difficult to understand how, in the second book of the *Dialogues,* he could give so much local color to his narrative, attributing great importance to the slightest topographical details: things that would be of interest only to one who was well acquainted with the places and the disposition of the buildings that witnessed the events he undertakes to describe. Another man would have been satisfied with generalities.

Nevertheless St. Gregory did not wish to write a life or a story of St. Benedict in the modern fashion. He might have done so. But as he himself declares in a letter to Bishop Maximilian of Syracuse,[1] in the *Dialogues* he intended to gather a kind of *floretum*—so many centuries before the *fioretti* of St. Francis!—of the most striking miracles of the bishops and monks who then shone in Italy by their holiness: *"Aliqua de miraculis patrum, quae in Italia facta audivimus, sub brevitate scribere."* Hence Gregory systematically passes over chronological or biographical matters when they are not connected with the miracles, which were exclusively of interest to him.

So, likewise, although dedicating an entire book to St. Benedict, he omits all chronological data (when he was born, how long he lived,

---

[1] *Epist.,* Bk. II, no. 51.

in which year and under which consul he died). Not that the Pope considered such matters unimportant; but he regarded them as out of place in a simple collection of *fioretti* or miracles, which was not intended to be a biography. The second book of the *Dialogues* takes that part of the story of St. Benedict for granted. It was written in the spirit of the world of the sixth century.

But Gregory does not close his eyes to the rules of good criticism. We are reassured on this point by his juridical training and mentality, as well as by the habits acquired in the prominent political positions he held before he became a monk. After Pelagius I had ordained him a deacon in St. Peter's, he spent several years as *apocrisiarius* or apostolic nuntius at the imperial court of Byzantium. If there was a man who would not swallow whole the tales that were told him, it was certainly Gregory, accustomed to doubt, to sift and to weigh both his own words and those of others.

As a matter of fact, his narratives, written for the purpose of fostering piety, are based primarily on direct testimony, which he is always at pains to cite. Sometimes he gives the exact words of his informants; at other times he faithfully puts down their meaning.[2] Whoever has become acquainted with the austere juridical mentality of St. Gregory as manifested throughout the fourteen books of his Letters cannot desire a better guaranty of historical seriousness and sincerity.

I have said that in the *Dialogues* St. Gregory did not wish to compile biographies of saints, but only to report their miracles. Since, however, marvelous happenings run through the warp and woof of the life of St. Benedict, the *fioretti*, for us, supply the place of a biography, because miracles were strewn wherever he passed. Gregory seems to take a special delight in them. In the other three books of the *Dialogues* he devotes at most one or two chapters to the different saints; to St. Benedict, on the other hand, he dedicates the entire second book.

In the kind of preface by which the great Pontiff introduces the *fioretti* of St. Benedict, he begins by declaring expressly that he does not intend to give a complete story, since he did not go to the trouble

---

[2] *"Per singula quae describo, quibus haec auctoribus mihi comperta sunt, manifesto. Hoc vero te scire cupio, quia in quibusdam sensum tantummodo, in quibusdam vero et verba cum sensu teneo. Quia si de personis omnibus ipsa specialiter verba tenere voluissem haec rusticano uso prolata stylus scribentis non susciperet. Seniorum valde venerabilium didici narratione quae narro"* (Dial., Bk. I, Prologue).

of discovering everything that in one way or another might have reference to his hero. "I have not been able to learn all he did, but the few things that I am about to relate, I had from four of his own disciples."

For us it is unfortunate that Gregory, because of the abundance of the material, chose to omit, as he declares, many other details concerning St. Benedict with which he was acquainted. He wrote for a generation almost contemporary with his hero, at a time, namely, when the living tradition could easily supply the many lacunae of his account. "It would give me much pleasure, Peter, to relate many other things about this venerable abbot, but I must pass over a number of them because I must speak of the deeds of other holy men also." [3] Ours the loss, and we must deplore the slenderness of this only source, when, on the other hand, it might have been so ample. But so it is. St. Benedict's generation has transmitted to us only the *fioretti* gathered by St. Gregory.

I must make one exception in favor of Mark the Poet, who, in a brief ode on the holy Patriarch, presents himself as one of his disciples at Monte Cassino. Later we shall examine those verses, though they add little to Gregory's narrative.

In the centuries immediately following, no one gave himself the trouble to gather the popular traditions concerning St. Benedict that were current in Rome, at Subiaco, and in the Campania. Hence, in writing the story of St. Benedict, all we can do is to put the *fioretti* in their historical framework, to explain them as best we are able, and to interpret their historical and juridical data in the light of the imperial and canonical sources. That is precisely the purpose of these pages.

For whom did St. Gregory originally intend this book? We can immediately answer that question by citing the words of the author on the point: "The brethren who live with me urge me strongly to relate in brief some of the miracles of the Fathers of which I have learned in Italy, for which undertaking I greatly need the help of your charity." [4]

The monks and the ecclesiastics attached to the private apartment

[3] *Dial.*, Bk. II, chap. 36.
[4] John the Deacon, *Vita S. Gregor.*, Bk. IV, no. 75; *Epist.*, Bk. II, no. 50.

of the Pope in the Lateran palace, who led a quasi-conventual life with him, induced the saint at length to put in writing these edifying anecdotes in the lives of the holy Fathers concerning whom they discoursed so frequently in common.[5]

We are acquainted with the names of some of the monks who lived with Gregory: Peter the Deacon; the notaries Aemilian and Paterius; Abbot Maximilian, later bishop of Syracuse; Augustine and Mellitus, afterward bishops and apostles of England; Marinianus, who in his turn became metropolitan of Ravenna; Claudius, abbot of Sant'Apollinare in Classe; and another Claudius, abbot and superintendent of a hospital in Jerusalem.[6]

As may be seen, they were all persons distinguished by their culture and the excellence of their virtue; they were the kind of men Gregory wished to have at his side, in order to prepare them personally for the most arduous tasks of the episcopal office. All these monks, who came from St. Andrew's, already followed the Rule of St. Benedict. Hence we can easily divine the reason why St. Gregory dedicated the entire second book of the *Dialogues* to the life of the Patriarch of Cassino.

This biography of St. Benedict without a doubt represented a kind of manual of the spiritual life for the community of the Lateran, while the Rule continued to gain ground on all sides and to become public property. Without further ado Gregory himself refers his readers to an examination of it.

The highly cultured circle to which the story of St. Benedict was originally addressed justified the diligence which Gregory exercised in repeatedly indicating his sources and his witnesses. We need only refer to this circumstance, that, while the Pope was dictating his narratives to Peter the Deacon, Abbot Bonitus and his monks were scarcely a hundred yards away to check the accounts. In the group of jurists, theologians, and men who were being prepared for the government of the Church, writings unworthy of the place simply would not have been tolerated. As a matter of fact, on one occasion, when Abbot Claudius had the hardihood to copy the scriptural comments

---

[5] "*Videbantur passim cum eruditissimis clericis adhaerere Pontifici religiosissimi monachi; et in diversis professionibus habebatur vita communis.*"
[6] *Ibid.*, Bk. II, no. 11.

of St. Gregory rather negligently, the author immediately disowned the edition which had not been authorized by him.

As a result, after the death of Claudius, the Pope instructed his nuntius to the exarch of Ravenna to go immediately to Sant'Apolli-nare in Classe, to demand of the monks all the notes of the abbot, and to send them to Rome, that thus they might effectively be taken out of circulation. The author complained that his former pupil "put down in his own way what I, because of my illness, could not write; when it was read to me, I discovered that the sense of my words had been greatly changed." [7]

The notary Paterius was more circumspect. Before publishing an anthology of Gregory's biblical comments, he requested the author's approbation. By reason of this literary scrupulosity, as John the Deacon informs us, several works of St. Gregory were consigned to the flames without ever being published; in the ninth century some still lay unedited in the archives of the Lateran: *"Ante succensa sunt quam edita . . . sicut reliqua ipsius opera quae nunc in Sancta Romana Ecclesia retinentur adhuc sub custodia, ne penitus vulgarentur."*

Gregory gave another example of his historical exactitude and his literary probity. At Rome a certain Oriental monk, Andrew by name, after altering a Latin version of Eusebius of Thessalonica, had also put out, under the name of the Pope, a Greek version of sermons supposedly preached by him.

The Pontiff took the matter very seriously. After searching out and destroying all these literary falsifications, he submitted the whole affair to a Roman council, which pronounced an anathema against the falsifier.[8] These occurrences serve as a guaranty for the authenticity of Gregory's story of the Patriarch of Monte Cassino.

At the beginning of his narrative concerning St. Benedict, Gregory cites four major sources of information, though he does not say whether they were oral or written: "I have not been able to learn all he did, but the few things that I am about to relate, I have from four of his own disciples: from Constantine, a very venerable man, who succeeded him in the government of the monastery; Valentinian, who for many years presided over the monastery at the Lateran; Sim-

---

[7] *Ibid.,* Bk. VI, no. 70.
[8] *Epist.,* Bk. XII, no. 74.

plicius, who was his second successor; and finally, Honoratus, who is still the abbot of the monastery in which Benedict first lived." At the Lateran the Pope knew several other monks educated at Monte Cassino by the Patriarch; but he cites only the primary authorities, with whom he had been acquainted from his youth.

As is evident, they are first-class witnesses, since they are successors of the Patriarch himself in the government of his two most important monasteries.

All that we know of the second abbot of Cassino, Constantine, is contained in the words: *"reverentissimo valde viro,"* [9] a title which Gregory gives only to high-ranking prelates, and not even always to bishops. This implies that he considered Constantine a worthy successor of his master. Besides there is the *valde*, unusual in Gregory's formal style, but for which he must have had a good reason. Unfortunately we do not know the reason.[10]

[9] According to strict classical usage, *reverentissimus* was a passive title of praise, attributed generally to youths between the ages of three and sixteen. Occasionally we find: *fratri reverentissimo*. Cf. *Raccolta di scritti in onore di Felice Romarino*, pp. 696 f. ("Vita e Pensiero").

In the *Liber diurnus Romanorum Pontificum* the title of *reverentissimus* is given to the archbishop of Ravenna, and in general to more distant bishops. Other bishops are called *dilectissimi*.

[10] Constantine, who apparently enjoyed considerable prestige in Rome, where he was called *reverentissimus valde vir*, cannot have governed the community of Cassino later than 560. St. Gregory was about twenty at that time. The question arises, where he became so well acquainted with Constantine as to number him among the four principal informants about the life of St. Benedict. Perhaps on the frequent visits of the son of Gordian to the Lateran monastery he may have met the successor of St. Benedict when he made an occasional trip to Rome. But these casual conversations of the youth with the abbot scarcely suffice to give him the important place among the witnesses that Gregory assigns to him. Another solution is possible.

It was customary among the more devout families of Rome, especially those of the patrician class, to receive as their guests the monks and prelates who came to the city on business. This was done even by the paralytic Servulus, who begged at the door of St. Clement's. Thus St. Athanasius, St. Jerome, St. Thomas of Farfa, and others found ready hospitality in Rome in the palaces of Marcella, Paula, and others.

It is consequently possible that the *reverentissimus valde vir*, Constantine, was the welcome guest of Gordian in his *domus* on the *Clivus Scauri*. This would explain more easily the special respect which Gregory shows him by the addition of *valde* to the customary *reverentissimus*.

St. Gregory himself intimates that his monastic vocation went back precisely to those early years, and later, at Constantinople, he told Bishop Leander as much. His vocation manifested itself in adolescence, but originally he thought it prudent to hide it from his parents, and so he undertook the various offices to which he was successively promoted in accordance with the norms of the *cursus honorum* then in vogue. Even in the midst of the world he was already a monk.

Concerning Valentinian, on the other hand, we know a little more. Apparently he came from the Campania, and before ruling the Lateran community of St. Pancratius had led a monastic life at Monte Cassino. We know that a brother of his was accustomed annually to go on a pilgrimage to Monte Cassino in order to be blessed by the Patriarch and to visit Valentinian. Gregory does not tell us the name of this brother; but he assures us that, despite his lay garb, his soul was deeply religious. Most likely he lived in a village not far from Cassino, because on these annual pilgrimages, by leaving his house early in the morning, he usually arrived fasting at Monte Cassino by dusk.

When, during the years 593–594, Gregory busied himself with dictating the *Dialogues* to Peter the Deacon, he speaks of Valentinian as no longer living. How long had he been dead? We do not know, but from the way he is mentioned among the witnesses, the impression arises that his abbatial activity in Rome preceded chronologically that of Simplicius, who is named afterward and who was the third abbot of Monte Cassino. About the year 560, Simplicius prepared a special edition of the *Regula monasteriorum*, which till then had remained in the archives of Cassino during the exile of Pope Vigilius at Constantinople.

Now, if the long abbatial tenure of Valentinian at the Lateran falls between the government of Constantine and Simplicius at Monte Cassino, we cannot set its beginning earlier than 545, in which year Vigilius was taken to Constantinople. In the absence of the Pope, certainly the founding of a monastery in his city was out of the question.

At the same time it does not seem right to put off the rule of Valen-

---

This situation lasted till the death of his father: *"Diu longeque conversionis gratiam distuli, et postquam caelesti sum desiderio efflatus, saeculari habitu contegi melius putavi"* (*Moral.* I; *Epist. ad Lean.*). During this period he became acquainted with Constantine, who died soon after.

Gregory continues: *"Aperiebatur enim mihi iam de aeternitatis amore quid quarerem: sed insolita me consuetudo devincerat, ne exteriorem cultum mutarem. Cumque adhuc me cogeret animus praesenti mundo quasi specietenus deservire . . . tandem cuncta sollicite fugiens, portam monasterii petii."*

In the fifteenth homily on the Gospels, Gregory relates the story of the paralytic Servulus, who, despite the fact that he lived on alms, nevertheless practiced a generous hospitality: *"Scripturae sacrae sibimet codices emerat, et religiosos quosque in hospitalitate suscipiens, coram se legere sine intermissione faciebat."* At his death there was present, besides the guests and pilgrims, a monk of the monastery of St. Andrew: *"Cui rei monachus noster interfuit."*

tinian till about 560; by then Pope Pelagius I was in a position to dominate the strong opposition of clergy and people against him in Rome. At that time Simplicius was abbot of Monte Cassino, and Valentinian certainly preceded him in the abbatial office. Hence nothing remains except to place the *"anni multi"* of his rule at the Lateran between 545 and 570.

Concerning Abbot Simplicius we know little more than the name and the fact that he was a priest. Nevertheless he must have been a person of some importance, because he brought out the first edition of the Rule and saw to its diffusion. As a matter of fact, a poet of the eighth century attributed to him merits comparable to those of the Patriarch of monks:

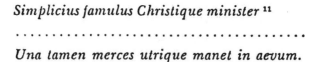

Simplicius famulus Christique minister [11]

. . . .

Una tamen merces utrique manet in aevum.

Honoratus, abbot of Subiaco, was certainly the only one of Gregory's four informants who was still alive in 593 and 594. But he must have been quite old if his master was dead about forty years. When, about 529, Benedict left Subiaco, Honoratus could scarcely have been more than twenty. Unless he went to Subiaco later, when, possibly, St. Benedict sent him thither from Monte Cassino as successor to St. Maur.

This aged abbot of Subiaco seems to be a most diligent and conscientious witness. As a matter of fact, when Gregory relates the interview between the Patriarch and Sabinus of Canosa during the siege of Rome, he tells us that he received his information from Honoratus, and he in his turn—since there is question of events that occurred at Monte Cassino—duly attests that these things were related to him by the brethren of Cassino, and that he was not a direct witness. All

---

[11] Victor of Capua in the *Codex Fuldensis* also signs himself: *Victor famulus Christi et eius gratiae episcopus Capuae.* Near Aricia in Latium an inscription of the fifth century has the following:

HIC REQUIESCIT FAMU(*lus Dei*)
PRESBI(*ter*) CUIUS ANNI F(*uerunt*)
P M LXXX DEPOSITUS IN (*pace*)
V C CONS

While the title *Dei famulus* designates simply an ecclesiastic or a monk, Simplicius' rank in the hierarchy is clearly indicated by *"XPI que minister."*

of which goes to show what great importance was attached to the veracity of the sources and the exactness of their testimonies. "Although Honoratus, his disciple, from whose report I have learned these things, admits that he did not hear them from the lips of the man of God himself, he bears witness that the brethren had told him" (chap. 15).

Occasionally the papal biographer cites other minor sources, namely:

a) The *"vir illustris Antonius"* relates the miracle of the elephantiasis that was healed (chap. 26). He was evidently a personage of some importance and held official positions.

b) The monk Peregrinus of the following chapter *"narrare consueverat"*—hence he resided in Rome, perhaps in the Lateran monastery—the miracle of the thirteen gold pieces which were found on the grain to satisfy the needs of a poor merchant.

c) The monk Exhilaratus, who afterward rose to be a prelate of high repute in the pontifical court, is the relator of the miracle described in chapter 18.

d) Similarly, Pope Pelagius I and many other religious men inform Gregory of the embassy of St. Benedict to the monk Martin on Monte Cassino.[12]

e) Other disciples of St. Benedict tell the biographer the details narrated in Book IV, chapters 7 and 8, regarding the virtues of the monks Speciosus and Gregory, destined by St. Benedict for the new monasteries of Terracina and Capua.

Nor must it be forgotten that the papal biographer was, above all, well informed about facts relating to Nursia, because he maintained a regular spiritual correspondence with several ecclesiastics and monks of that city. Among those worthy of special mention is a certain Abbot Stephen, who died in Rome about 590; he personally told Gregory of the life and death of the pastor of Nursia, whose story is narrated in the *Dialogues*.[13]

Besides these testimonies, specifically cited, reference may be made to others to which the biographer alludes in passing:

1. The miracle worked at Enfide, about five miles from Subiaco,

12 *Dial.*, Bk. III, chap. 16.
13 *Dial.*, Bk. IV, chap. 9.

becomes common knowledge, and the miraculous sieve remains suspended over the entrance of the church till the invasion of the Lombards.[14]

2. News of the miracles wrought by the Patriarch spreads beyond the confines of the diocese of Tivoli and reaches even to the capital. Then the nobility of Rome begins to flock to St. Benedict at Subiaco, and several parents offer him their sons: Equitius presents Maur, and Tertullus offers Placid (chap. 3).

It is not too far-fetched to suppose that among these *"Romanae Urbis nobiles et religiosi"* who go to Subiaco, there were also some relatives of Gregory, perhaps his parents Gordian and Sylvia together with his aunts Tarsilla and Emiliana. This tradition of Subiaco, it is true, is based on an apocryphal or interpolated document of the local archives; but behind the legend may well be hidden a nucleus of historical truth.

Then we note that St. Gregory shows such an exact topographical knowledge of the places and the disposition of the various parts of the buildings he describes, particularly at Monte Cassino, that we are led to surmise that in his early youth he visited and carefully studied the locality.

3. The papal subdeacon Florence, who later resorted to flight in order to escape being made bishop of Naples,[15] according to the testimony of Gregory was a grandson of the infamous priest Florence of Subiaco. The biographer makes mention of the fact, as if to confirm the grandfather's unfortunate behavior, which was then on everyone's tongue in the Lateran.

4. Also with regard to Bishop Sabinus of Canosa, bound by the tie of intimate friendship to St. Benedict, Gregory says that he learned of his deeds from certain monks: *"religiosi viri Apuliae provinciae partibus cogniti."* These men, in turn, assured him that their story was based on common knowledge: *"hoc quod apud multorum notitiam longe lateque precrebuit."* [16]

The same observation holds true of Bishop Constance of Aquino,

---

14 *"A cunctis est agnita . . . hoc ipsum capisterium eius loci in ingressu ecclesiae suspenderent . . . quod annis multis illic ante omnium oculos fuit. Et usque ad haec Longobardorum tempora super fores ecclesiae pependit"* (*Dial.*, Bk. II, chap. 1).

15 *Epist.*, Bk. III, no. 15.

16 *Dial.*, Bk. III, chap. 5.

in whose territory Monte Cassino was situated. In Gregory's entire story no other bishop of that part of *Latium adiectum* is mentioned. As a source of information concerning this prelate's saintly life, St. Gregory says: "many testify" and "religious and truthful men who were present . . . on the day of his death." [17] Among those monks, *"religiosi veracesque viri,"* who witnessed the death of the good bishop, were there not perhaps some monks of Monte Cassino, who a few years later had to flee to Rome as a result of the devastation by the Lombards? They would be precisely the *"multi testantur"* to whom Gregory refers.

About Germanus of Capua, whose soul St. Benedict saw going to heaven,[18] Gregory gives some more particulars in Book IV of the *Dialogues.* He mentions this as a source of information: "While I was still a youth and a layman, I heard these things from my elders, who were well informed." [19] Precisely in the year 540, when Germanus died at Capua, St. Gregory was born in Rome. Hence we have in this case contemporary, or almost contemporary, witnesses.

Regarding the exactness of Gregory's story of St. Benedict we could not wish for more. But we are not to believe that the biographer drew everything—names and events—from the storehouse of his memory. When he set out to write, Constantine, Valentinian, Simplicius, and others were already dead for several years. He must have had at his disposition notes and other written matter, so that the witnesses readily fall into two categories: principal sources and secondary sources.

An ancient Roman tradition points to the library of Pope Agapitus I on the Caelian Hill as the spot where the *Dialogues* of Gregory were composed. If this view, dating from the eighth century, is correct, then we must conclude that the first draft of the biography of St. Benedict goes back to the time when St. Gregory still ruled the monastery of St. Andrew on the *Clivus Scauri.*[20]

---

[17] *Ibid.,* chap. 8.
[18] *Dial.,* Bk. II, chap. 25.
[19] *Dial.,* Bk. IV, chap. 40.
[20] We must not forget this case of a *domus patricia,* almost contiguous to the imperial palace and the *Septizonium* of Septimius Severus, which was transformed into a monastic establishment. In the ninth century John the Deacon in his life of St. Gregory records that a considerable portion of the building was still standing. The monastery *ad Clivum*

Following this hypothesis, the work of Gregory, planned and written on the Caelian Hill, scarcely half a mile from the Lateran monastery, where the monastic family of Cassino found shelter, was directed to a well-informed group, on which the imposing figure of the Patriarch of monks had made sufficient impression for it to be able to check the historical exactness of the papal biographer. Hence no serious objection can be brought against Book II of the *Dialogues*.

The thirty-three couplets of the poet Mark in honor of St. Benedict constitute for us another precious historical source. Some have attempted to ascribe the work to the eighth century, that is, to the period of the re-establishment of Monte Cassino under Gregory II, but without success, because the poet shows himself to us as a contemporary of the Patriarch. Instead of recounting the miracles, which exercised such a fascination on St. Gregory, he enthusiastically describes the georgics, that is to say, the great work of agricultural improvement undertaken on the rocky summit of Monte Cassino. Faced with a wonder-worker who even recalled the dead to life, only a poet's soul of Mark's stamp could paint him for us in a secondary aspect of his mission; he stresses particulars relating to agriculture which almost all subsequent Benedictine historians have chosen to disregard.

The *Versus in laudem S. Benedicti* reproduced by Paul the Deacon are too brief to allow of criticism. Mark composed his verses a decade or two before St. Gregory wrote, and hence he is entirely independent of the Second Book of the *Dialogues*. It is not permissible to say that already at that time legend had gilded the historical figure of St. Benedict, though one must grant Mark a bit of poetic license, as when he says that the groves about Subiaco wept with disheveled leaves. Contemporary Latin poets almost all manifest a similar taste for strange figures.

But, *de facto,* Mark has preserved for us some details about St. Benedict that are new. So, for example, the order the Patriarch received from heaven to depart from Subiaco; the angels and the three ravens that accompanied him to Monte Cassino; the hermit ordered by God to leave Monte Cassino, in view of St. Benedict's imminent arrival: "Make place, another friend is coming."

Scauri, whence proceeded so many bishops, abbots, and missioners, almost immediately became one of the strongholds of monasticism in Rome.

Mark alone tells us of the Lenten seclusion of the saint, while out-side the deputation from Subiaco vociferously demands his return to their mountains. Instead of speaking of the shrine of Apollo, he tells us of the temple of Jupiter and the different altars that formerly crowned the acropolis of Cassino.

Likewise it is the poet of Cassino who describes the vast agricultural improvements undertaken by the Patriarch: St. Benedict builds a road along the back of the mountain, causes a spring to gush forth to irrigate the gardens planted by him where before had been only a stony woods. Here is a new aspect of the saint, one which only the poet Mark speaks of.

Naturally, at the present time it is impossible for us to check this brief poetic production. But at all events it was directed to a con-temporary world, when legend did not yet have time to alter the his-torical figure. Let us, then, take the poem as we find it, and let us make use of it with those precautions that poetic compositions always call for.

A Cassinese text of the eighth or the ninth century, which has been several times edited and commented upon, gives some information about the various parts of the monastery at Monte Cassino where the miracles described by St. Gregory are supposed to have occurred. As a study of the setting of the story, it is most interesting. The author bases his statements on a local tradition which goes back to the time of Abbot Petronax, that is, to the re-establishment of the community at Cassino through the efforts of Pope Gregory II. We shall return to it later.

The autograph copy of the Rule, deposited and preserved in the papal archives till the time of Pope Zachary, the original weight of the bread-ration given to each monk, the sacks in which was contained the flour miraculously found at the gate of the monastery, thanks to the common tradition of Cassino, assure us of the truth of the cor-responding chapters in St. Gregory's narrative.

Even the bit of doggerel composed, *invita Minerva*, by Abbot Sim-plicius and prefaced to his edition of the Rule (between 555 and 560) represent for us precious bits of the ancient tradition about St. Bene-dict.

After making this inventory of the sources for the story of the

Patriarch of monks, I may be permitted to pass rapidly in review other local traditions concerning him and his work. Thus, for example, at Nursia, while from the ninth century on the house where St. Benedict was born has been pointed out, today the inhabitants also believe they can indicate the exact spot where the Patriarch first saw the light of day.

The inhabitants of Roiate, which is not far distant from Subiaco, in their turn assert that the saint on his frequent trips to Rome—a valuable detail omitted by Gregory, but credible for evident historical reasons—used to pass through their village.

One time, among others, when Benedict was not allowed to enter for fear of a pestilence that was raging, he was forced to spend the night outside the village and had to sleep on the bare ground. But as if his body, heated by the flame of the Holy Spirit, had become incandescent, the rock, become soft as wax, yielded beneath the weight of the saint, and to the present day it retains the imprint of his side. It is furthermore said at Roiate—to complete the prodigy— that every year on his feast day the stone sweats. The liquid is devotedly gathered up by the inhabitants, who have erected on the spot a chapel dedicated to the Patriarch.

Near the cave of St. Benedict at Subiaco, the monks even now show an old rosebush, on whose leaves a trace of rust depicts a kind of small serpent. Tradition asserts that this is the thornbush into which St. Benedict one day threw himself in order to vanquish a violent carnal temptation.

Also at Monte Cassino tradition maintains that it has preserved some bits of history. There is, for example, the stone on the mountainside with the imprint of a knee; St. Benedict is said to have prayed there as soon as he perceived on the summit of the mountain the smoking altars of Venus and the round roofs of the temples of Apollo and Jupiter.

According to local tradition, a large marble column with a cross in the center, which at one time may well have served as the support of the altar in the ancient church of St. Martin, is nothing less than the *lapis* on which—according to St. Gregory—the devil sat to prevent the monks from moving it. To tell the truth, this block does not seem to fit into the account of Gregory, who speaks of a "great stone, that they intended to use for their building," that is, of material for construction. Nevertheless it is quite possible that this block, which before the destruction of Monte Cassino could be seen near the stairway leading to the church, really goes back to the sixth century and that it was used in the construction of the church of St. Martin.

Until some years ago, the pilgrim to Monte Cassino could see near the porter's lodge an inscription in local stone, used as simple building material in an ancient wall. The inscription spoke of a temple of Jupiter; recently perhaps its marble base has been uncovered.

Columns of porphyry, capitals, bases of serpentine may be observed in several spots about Monte Cassino. Local tradition calls them the altar of Apollo, the base of the statue of some god or other, and so on. It is necessary to exercise a degree of caution with regard to these beautiful marbles, which are certainly ancient. We know that in the second half of the eleventh century Abbot Desiderius made a collection of ancient marbles in Rome to build his churches on Monte Cassino. These stone remains, then, may have come from Rome and have nothing at all to do either with the temple of Apollo or with St. Benedict.

On the other hand, a very authentic monument was formerly near the ancient gate of the monastery. As St. Gregory relates, it was there the Patriarch knelt in prayer and then extended himself over the corpse of a dead child, who at his touch was restored to life. Since that time fourteen centuries have passed. In the meantime Monte Cassino has been struck by dozens of cyclones and storms, and also bad reconstructions. Lombards, Saracens, French, Spaniards, sans-culottes, followers of Garibaldi, Germans and Anglo-Saxons, have passed and repassed and fought for possession of that fortress.

In the eleventh century Abbot Desiderius razed the sacred monuments constructed by St. Benedict and Petronax. Where the first buildings had been built of simple stone and bricks, Desiderius raised up a marvelous monastery glittering with marbles and mosaics.

Again in the sixteenth century Bramante and his successors several times changed the medieval aspect of the celebrated pile to give it the classical lines of the Renaissance or of the Italian baroque. Nevertheless, despite such devastations, no one has ever dared to chisel away that rough rock which even today lies at the doorway of the original monastery. On that rock St. Benedict knelt when he restored the dead boy to life, and all have respected it. Let us hope that it will be found unharmed beneath the ruins.

As historical sources for the life of St. Benedict we have, then, material which, if not very ample, is not too slender either, particularly when we consider that we are dealing with a personage that lived fourteen centuries ago. Several other extremely important figures of St. Benedict's times—popes, ecclesiastical writers, for example, Cassiodorus, Dionysius Exiguus, Eugippus, Pope Vigilius, Dacius of Milan —have no more abundant biographical sources.

To make up for its lack of quantity, we possess historical material of excellent quality. The four principal witnesses may be compared to four solid columns. They can very well support the weight of the famous literary monument which Gregory erected to the glory of the holy legislator. I shall likewise make use of these sources in the following pages, which will present simply a paraphrase of the biography contained in the *fioretti* of St. Benedict, fitted into the contemporary scene.[21]

[21] Several attempts to write the life of St. Benedict have been made in the past. An *Avviso Marescotti*, dated July 18, 1704, reports as follows: "His Holiness [Clement XI], greatly desiring that an account of the life and origin of St. Benedict, founder of the Benedictine Order, be published, has commissioned the bishop of Wales to devote himself to a diligent study of the matter; wherefore the aforesaid prelate, who since the miserable revolution in England, has resided in this Court, has gone to the birthplace of St. Benedict, in order to gather the necessary information, so that it may be published" (Pastor, *History of the Popes*, XXXIII, 505).

CHAPTER II

The Historical Setting

WHETHER he wishes it or not, everyone is born a child of his time. Not even the great historical personages can be studied outside the environment which saw them grow, which formed them, and in which they carried on their activity.

In a certain sense St. Benedict belongs to the beginning of the Middle Ages, at whose entrance he stood. But one cannot call him medieval, just as St. Gregory the Great is not a medieval man. Their education and their spirit reflect the traditional Roman culture. From this standpoint, Augustine, Leo I, Benedict, and Gregory may be regarded as the last Romans. After them came the rule of the Lombards, with Popes Gregory II, Zachary, and Martin I. The Middle Ages had begun.

When St. Benedict was born in 470 or thereabouts,[1] in the city of Nursia, the Western Empire was about to pass out of the picture, thanks to the efforts of Odoacer, who, in his turn on March 5, 493,

[1] St. Gregory gives few chronological notes regarding the life of St. Benedict. Starting with the date of his last interview with the bishop of Canosa, in December, 546, then taking the traditional date for the founding of Monte Cassino in the spring of 529; bearing in mind, too, that when he became abbot of Vicovaro his reputation had already spread through the entire region and that he was then at least thirty years old, we arrive at the chronological table that follows. Naturally, the figures are only approximate. To found the twelve monasteries, the saint may have employed many more than twenty-four years. Every two years a monastery! That seems a bit strong.

The reform of Vicovaro occupied some time before the monks proceeded to their attempt to poison him. Prudence dictated that the Abbot should begin his reform slowly, after a period of preparation. Hence Benedict's stay there most likely lasted several years. The same holds true of his studies in Rome. We have then:

470?—Birth of St. Benedict at Nursia.

had to open the gates of Ravenna to the soldiers of Theodoric, who ordered him killed. Then came a government which was half Roman and half Goth and which, while observing the traditional bureaucratic forms of the imperial republic, was in reality a dictatorship by a barbarian of great ability, who was trying to Romanize himself.

It seems that the contemporaries hardly noticed the change. In the minds of the Italians of the fifth century the *basileus* of Byzantium represented little more than a symbol. In Theodoric they saw his legitimate representative. Rome had become accustomed to the absence of its *augusti*, who, instead of residing on the Palatine, where they used to function as *Pontifices Maximi* of the nearby temple of Vesta, preferred to spend their time in Nicomedia, in Antioch, in Byzantium, or in Milan. In these places they were at least free from the old aristocracy of the senators, who served no other purpose than to set up bureaucratic obstacles to the dictatorship of the *augustus*.

The 468 letters of the *Variarum* of Cassiodorus, among other documents, serve to picture what the government of Italy was like at the time; they likewise describe the part the author played in the rule of the peninsula under the Gothic King. The papal schism during the first years of Pope Symmacus is symptomatic and shows us to what a state of decadence the Christian religion had fallen in Rome.

After the death of Anastasius II in November, 498, the electors of the new pope were divided into two factions. The Romans chose Symmacus in the Lateran; but since his election was displeasing to the Byzantine party, a small number of the people and of the clergy, led by the senators Festus and Probinus, gathered in St. Mary Major and acclaimed Lawrence as the pontiff.

For about three years Rome was the theater of the most savage events, such as, unfortunately, religious fanaticism usually inspires. The schismatics, stronger than their numbers warranted, owing to the

485?-490—Literary studies in Rome.
490?—Flight from Rome, sojourn at Enfide, three-years' retreat, apostolate among the shepherds, spread of his reputation.
500?—Abbacy of Vicovaro, abdication and return to the cave.
505?-529—Foundation of the twelve monasteries at Subiaco.
Spring 529—Arrival at Cassino.
October 540—Vision of the death of Germanus of Capua.
542—Visit of Totila to St. Benedict.
December 546—Siege of Rome, interview of St. Benedict with Sabinus of Canosa.
March 547—Death of the holy Patriarch.

protection of the chief senator, staged regular manhunts in their attacks upon the followers of Symmacus. Many Catholics, among them ecclesiastics and nuns, were slain in the streets. Others were robbed and beaten. The basilica of St. Paul even fell into the hands of the adherents of Lawrence, who then caused his own portrait to be painted in the series of popes.

After a time, in order to put a stop to this religious struggle which was in the way of turning into a civil war, the King cited both contenders to the court at Ravenna. Here Symmacus, who was elected first and who also had received a greater number of votes, won out over his adversary. When he returned to Rome, in the first heat of popular enthusiasm, he celebrated a synod at which seventy-two bishops were present; on this occasion he magnanimously gave his competitor the distant see of Nocera in the Campania. But shortly afterward it appeared advantageous to the Byzantine party to reopen the contest just lately settled and again to throw on the table the whole question of the legitimacy of Symmacus' pontificate.

The Pope, opposed in this manner, resigned himself to the prospect of another trip to Ravenna to justify himself before Theodoric. But, while he was awaiting the audience with the King at Rimini, his adversaries succeeded in amassing such grave accusations against him that the Pope, seeing the situation turn against him, without waiting for the reply of Theodoric, returned to Rome in order to escape capture and imprisonment.

The King of the Goths, an Arian, allowed himself to be influenced by the false accusations presented by the senators to the extent that he regarded the pontifical throne as vacant. Hence he sent a royal visitor to Rome in the person of Peter, bishop of Altino, and ordered him to convoke a synod in order to judge Symmacus. Certainly, a successor of St. Peter could not descend lower than that in the eyes of the government.

And it did not help Symmacus to resign himself to appear before the assembly of bishops as an accused man. On September 1, 501, while on his way from St. Peter's to the Lateran to assist at the second session of the synod, his cortege was attacked by an armed band. With great difficulty the Pope succeeded in regaining the sanctuary of St. Peter's, and he chose not to leave it again.

Fortunately a reaction on the part of the more level-headed element set in. Even among the members of the synod some rose to the defense of Symmacus and admonished the bishops of the false position into which they were placing themselves by setting themselves up as judges of the supreme pastor of the Church. Influenced particularly by two Milanese, Ennodius and Lawrence, a group of seventy-six bishops gathered in the Vatican basilica on October 23, 501, exonerated Symmacus of all guilt, and proclaimed the famous theological canon: "The first see indeed judges the others, but itself can be judged by none."

The schism could be regarded as over. But that did not end the struggles and the street fighting in Rome. The antipope Lawrence still held control of a goodly number of churches, and not a few of the patricians sided with him. Pope Symmacus could, however, peaceably take up his residence in the Vatican. As a votive monument of gratitude to the martyr Pancratius, in the neighborhood of whose cemetery he had dwelt on the Vatican, the Pope erected a new sepulchral basilica on the Via Aurelia. It is quite possible that the oratory dedicated to St. Pancratius in the Lateran also owes its origin to him.

In May, 500, a great public event for a time attracted the entire attention of the people of Rome and for the moment made them forget the papal strife. King Theodoric entered the city in the manner of an ancient conqueror. In the eyes of the Romans he was still the incarnation of the legitimate imperialist principle, inasmuch as he presented himself as the representative of the *augustus*, the restorer of order and justice, the protector of the Empire and its traditional institutions.

The Senate and the clergy, with the Pope at their head, went out to meet him. The King, though an Arian, paid his respects at the tomb of St. Peter, as a Constantine or a Theodosius might have done; then he went to the forum, like a Marcus Aurelius or a Trajan. Near the Curia, in the center of the forum, at a spot called *ad palmas*, he harangued the people like another Octavian, exalting the glory of the *Sacra Urbs* and declaring that his only goal was to restore its ancient splendors. Even today, amid the ruins of the old structures, frequently bricks are found bearing the round seal of Theodoric with the motto: *Bono Romae.*

Some have supposed that Benedict was also in the crowd of noisy students who applauded the King of the Goths in the forum. The hypothesis cannot be absolutely excluded, because we do not know how many years the youth spent at his studies in Rome. The papal biographer says nothing about it and the impressions it created; but we may argue from what the historian of another saint, Fulgentius, bishop of Ruspa, who was in Rome during those memorable days, relates concerning the matter.

Africanus writes that when Fulgentius had heard the discourse of Theodoric, when he had observed the pomp of the *patres conscripti,* the joy and the plaudits of a free people, he lifted his thoughts to heaven and exclaimed: "How splendid must the heavenly Jerusalem be, if imperial Rome is so beautiful!" The imperial soul shows itself even here, in the words of an African biographer.

In the first place, the sovereign of the Goths restored the residence of the *augusti* on the Palatine. Then he distributed money and grain to the impoverished people, and principally through his prime minister Cassiodorus he strongly urged the conquerors to mix with the conquered and to assimilate their civilization.

Like St. Fulgentius, so Benedict during his Roman student days imbibed the imperialist spirit and aspirations. But he lifted himself high above the seven hills and, in the face of a world in the throes of senile decrepitude, he invited his disciple in the Rule to lay on the bright and shining armor of obedience "to fight under Christ, the true King of eternal glory."

As a matter of fact, the very purpose of monastic life is to merit the grace to contemplate, not the splendor of the appearance of Theodoric *ad palmas* in the Forum of Rome, but the palms of Jesus Christ in the forum of the heavenly kingdom: *"ut mereamur eum qui nos vocavit in regnum suum videre."* This idea of the kingdom was deeply rooted in the mind of the monastic legislator, because he speaks of it repeatedly in the Rule: *"in cuius regni tabernaculo. . . . Ut regni eius mereamur esse consortes"* (*Rule,* Prologue).

CHAPTER III

The Impressions of Early Youth

I HAVE said that most likely St. Benedict was born about 470. The older historians commonly give the year 480 as the date, but this must almost certainly be anticipated, because in 529, when the saint went to Cassino, he had been for a time at Vicovaro and had spent at least twenty-five years making his monastic foundations in the valley of the Anio and on the slopes of Monte Taleo.

Let us suppose that he was about thirty years of age at the beginning of the sixth century, when he was elected abbot of Vicovaro; then he must have been born about 470. St. Gregory gives Nursia as his birthplace: *"ex provincia Nursiae ortus";* not because that "ancient city of Nursia," as St. Gregory calls it, was the seat of one of the great provinces of Italy, but in the sense that Nursia at that time represented a modest provincial center not without interest.[1]

As is well known, the peninsula in those days was divided into eight provinces, and Nursia belonged to the province of Etruria and Umbria, the ancient Fourth Region. Referring to the prehistoric origins of this Sabine Nursia, Virgil alludes to its rugged climate among the Apennines and states that it was the birthplace of Ufens, the leader of the troops against Aeneas: *"Quos frigida misit Nursia . . ."* [2]

Better founded, on the other hand, is the tradition that Vespasia Polla, the mother of Vespasian, was a native of Nursia, as well as Q. Sertorius. The coldness of its winter season seems, nevertheless,

---

[1] *Dial.,* Bk. IV, chap. 10.
[2] *Aeneid,* Bk. VIII.

to have found some compensation in the ardent religious spirit of its inhabitants; already in the fifth century the episcopal see of Nursia boasted of its ancient and glorious traditions.

According to the Acts of St. Felician of the *Forum Flaminii,* which go back to about the sixth century, Nursia owes the Christian faith to that saint. He is supposed to have ordained as its first pastor a certain priest Pisentius, and the ordination allegedly took place *"in basilica quae appellatur argentea."* Even to the present day the cathedral of Nursia, successor to an old Roman edifice, bears the title of *Sancta Maria Argentea.*

About 495 (?) a certain Stephen was bishop of Nursia.[3] It can easily be that Benedict and Scholastica, according to custom, were baptized and confirmed by him: *"Quos Stephanus sacerdos lavit et unxit."* It is noteworthy that in the sixth century Nursia had such an important Jewish colony that mention of it is made even in the Acts of St. Simplician.

During the Lombard invasion Nursia also felt its effects. Thus it happened that at the time of St. Gregory it was part of the neighboring diocese of Spoleto.[4] The same Pontiff speaks in his writings of the spiritual friendship he cultivated with certain members of the clergy of Nursia, for example, with the priest Santolus, who used to spend several days with him each year in Rome. Also the monastic life could boast of some glorious champions among the Nursians. The two holy monks Eutychius and Florence, whose virtues and miracles Gregory extols, were contemporaries of Benedict.

Not far from the town was a monastery. Its abbot had died, and Eutychius was appointed as his successor and "ruled the monastery for many years." That the oratory and the hermitage where he had dwelt before might not be deserted, he sent thither his disciple Florence, who in his turn chose as companion and servant—a bear. This preference for a beast instead of a man makes one think. But the people of Nursia related marvelous things about the tame bear, which led the little flock of the solitary to pasture and then brought them back.

Now, so many centuries later, we have difficulty picturing to our-

---

[3] Cf. *Dictionn. d'archéologie chrétienne,* Vol. XII; "Nursia," col. 1814.
[4] *Epist.,* Bk. XIII, no. 36, *ad Chrystanthum Spolet. Episc.*

selves the wooded surroundings where these scenes were enacted, where the bears of the Apennines could come undisturbed into the public squares of the larger towns. The tradition, however, maintained itself for a long time, and many can remember seeing the dancing bear in the streets.

Beside the old temple of *Fortuna Argentea,* later dedicated to the Blessed Virgin, another church of Nursia bore the name of St. Lawrence.[5] This was perhaps the larger church and was rather ample and artistic. After the Lombards had burned it when they occupied the town, the holy priest Santolus undertook its reconstruction at his own expense. For the purpose he employed "many artificers and numerous workmen to assist them," and the work was long drawn out. These good people worked with a will, and the saint, who supplied their victuals, had to have recourse even to miracles to provide bread when flour became scarce.

From Gregory's writings one gathers the impression that Nursia, despite the numerous Jews who resided there, was permeated by Christian piety and spiritual life. Quite naturally the Nursians exalted the miracles of St. Eutychius. Toward the end of the sixth century, whenever a long drought threatened the crops, the good folk used to go in procession along the ways and through the fields carrying the tunic of the holy wonder-worker as the protection of Nursia. Invariably, attests Gregory, there followed a shower of rain to moisten the dry earth and to reawaken in the peasants the hope of a bountiful harvest.

When the stranger visits Nursia today, he finds under a portico on the right side of the church of St. Benedict a stone bench, upon which are disposed nine local ancient measures for grain. In the fifth century such measures and weights were customarily kept near the churches. St. Benedict may perhaps have seen them there and even used them.

When later he speaks in the Rule of the weight of the daily ration of bread and of the measure of wine, his sharply juridical mentality immediately lets us recognize this former son of Nursia, who from

[5] At the present time the cathedral of Nursia has the title of Sancta Maria Argentea. This title was transferred to it when the ancient edifice of Sancta Maria Argentea was razed in 1554 to make room for a fortress, called Castellina del Vignola, which was erected on its site.

his infancy was accustomed to see the nine measures for grain in the shadow of St. Lawrence's. Six miles from Nursia was the monastery of Cample, whose holy abbot Spes, despite the blindness with which he was afflicted for forty years, was a mighty propagator of the monastic life in all that region. Quite naturally the monasteries of the vicinity recognized him as their highest superior.[6]

We have now arrived at the time of St. Benedict, and it is well for us to bear in mind the impressions which the future Patriarch of monks received in his place of origin in order to understand him better. As a matter of fact, St. Gregory the Great, after portraying Spes as a powerful organizer of the monastic life in Umbria, also describes his holy death in the oratory in a manner very like that of St. Benedict.

When Abbot Spes had completed a visitation of all the monasteries under his rule, he returned to his place near Nursia fifteen days before his death. He gathered the monks in the church and gave them a final address. Then, after he had received the body and blood of the Lord, amid the singing of psalms, he gave up to God his blessed soul, which ascended visibly to heaven in the form of a white dove.[7] Later we shall see how Benedict at Monte Cassino will imitate Abbot Spes of Nursia also in the circumstances of his own death.

Not only among the monks, but also among the priests of Nursia who had the care of souls there were not wanting true saints. Gregory the Great, who pays an affectionate testimony to the virtue of his friend Santolus, writes also of another pastor of the place who, after forty years in the priesthood, when he came to die, was comforted by a visit of the apostles Peter and Paul.[8]

It seems, however, that by reason of the Lombard invasion the excellent ecclesiastical discipline of the clergy of Nursia suffered a decline. Gregory intervened at the right moment by giving particular orders to the defender Optatus and to the bishop of Spoleto.[9] We do not know whether St. Benedict, after his departure from Nursia in early youth, ever returned thither. But it certainly is not too much to suppose that his fellow citizens, monks and priests, continued their

6 *Dial.*, Bk. IV, chap. 10.
7 *Dial.*, Bk. IV, chaps. 9, 10.
8 *Ibid.*, chap. 11.
9 *Epist.*, Bk. XIII, no. 36.

relations with him, especially after his fame had spread throughout central Italy.

For us it would be interesting to know what influence these holy examples and the monastic traditions of his birthplace exercised on the soul of the future Patriarch of monks. Unfortunately, of this we are entirely ignorant. We can only assert that from his earliest youth he was well acquainted with monasticism and that in all probability the saintly monks of Nursia made a deep impression on him.

At Subiaco and at Monte Cassino St. Benedict could not forget Eutychius, Florence, Abbot Spes, and the other ecclesiastics attached to his own church of St. Lawrence or to that of Sancta Maria Argentea, if at that time the ancient temple of the Fortuna had already been transformed into a Christian church.[10]

[10] I doubt it very much. In St. Gregory's writings, the principal church of Nursia, the one to which all the attention of the citizens is directed, is that of St. Lawrence. Perhaps only later a Christian church was made out of the temple of *Fortuna Argentea*. Here is a chronological problem that ought to make us careful and that tends to move us to set the date of the Acts of St. Felician at least a century later.

CHAPTER IV

Saint Benedict's Family

A LATE tradition assigns to the parents of St. Benedict the names of Eutropius and Abundantia and makes them out to be descendants of a branch of the family of the Anicii. It is useless to dilate on such entirely unsupported figments of the imagination. For the same reason little importance is to be attached to what Adrevaldus writes in the ninth century about the ruins of the ancestral palace of St. Benedict at Nursia: "The nobility of his birth is attested to by the ruins of his family's palace, situated near the walls of Nursia. So rich and so extensive was this structure that it outshone the palaces of the most powerful kings." [1]

[1] Adrevaldus, *De miraculis S. Bened.*, chap. 1. Notwithstanding this reference of Adrevaldus to the house of St. Benedict's parents at Nursia, we have no documents about the foundation of the *Ecclesia S. Benedicti*, which even to this day preserves his memory. Local historians ascribe it to the sixth century, but the present edifice, rebuilt in 1385, was modified also several times after that date. There is question of a basilica with an apse, with a beautiful thirteenth century façade, and a delicate Gothic entrance. On the lower floor is an attractive crypt of three naves, which perhaps represents the remains of the primitive structure. Recent excavations in this sanctuary have partially brought to light some walls of the imposing structure of which Adrevaldus speaks.

The superintendent of the antiquities of the Marches and of Umbria wrote under date of March 25, 1946:

"From among the remains of the *domus Anicia*, the ancestral home of the saint . . . we have succeeded in laying bare a large room with walls of *opus reticulatum* corresponding to the primitive oratory of the sixth century, later transformed in part into the present crypt and connected with other vaults by means of heavy walls, which apparently continue on the other side of the present church [of St. Benedict]. Hence we are dealing not with the common dwelling of poor people, but with an aristocratic *domus*, which indirectly casts its light on the intellectual and spiritual picture of the great Italian monk."

From the documents at hand and from the evidence of the excavations, we do not

Gregory the Great quite simply says that the saint descended from *"liberiori genere,"* [2] namely, that his parents, who belonged to the old provincial nobility and were rich landowners of the region, could afford to send their son to Rome to pursue his studies. This happened between the years 480 and 485. I do not believe that this sojourn at the capital was entirely spontaneous. Members of the nobility in the sixth century found themselves constrained to enter upon public careers, and hence they had to undertake the necessary preparatory studies.

In this connection St. Ambrose tells us that he as well as his brother Satyrus, after completing their studies in Rome, sought public positions, in order not to appear as cowards. *"Honores . . . quos ideo adepti sumus . . . ne vilis dissimulatio videretur."* [3]

The provincial nobility in particular sent its sons to Rome for higher studies. As a matter of fact, there was a special office where every month a double list of the non-Roman students was drawn up. One of these contained the names of those still studying; the other mentioned the graduates, who might be sent for service to Africa or the provinces.[4] St. Gregory speaks of *liberalibus litterarum studiis,* which St. Benedict pursued in Rome.[5] This makes it clear that at Nursia he had already learned the elements of grammar, that he had frequented a school directed by a *grammaticus.* There remained for him the advanced literary course, which he pursued in Rome under the guidance of a *rhetor* appointed by the government. St. Gregory

---

appear justified in attaching the name of *domus Anicia* to these Roman walls, and much less are we justified in connecting them with St. Benedict. There is simply question of an important building of the imperial era, whose purpose escapes us. How the historian Adrevaldus got knowledge of the imposing ruins of Roman buildings at Nursia we do not know.

[2] It may be well to cite some examples to clarify the phrase. In Plautus *genere bono natus* or *nati sumus generibus* signifies descent from notable parentage, while the *vulgus* cannot boast of a true *genus. Liberius* specifies *genus,* and the Latin phrase *libere educatus* means "nobly reared." Hence there is question of a provincial nobility notable by reason of income and number of servants. Of these the *nutrix* or nurse *sola secuta est* the little master when he, *relicta domo rebusque parentis,* fled into the solitude. The rest remained in the service of the illustrious house in Nursia and in Rome.

[3] *De excess. Satir.,* Bk. I, no. 25.

[4] *Cod. Theodos.,* XIV, 9, 1.

[5] A century earlier, the parents of St. Jerome, living in distant Dalmatia, felt the need of sending their son to Rome for his literary studies under the tutelage of the celebrated Aelius Donatus. According to a law of Valentinian, these provincial youths could remain in Rome till their twentieth year (*Cod. Theodos.,* XIV, XI, 1).

adds that the faithful nurse of Benedict was appointed to accompany him to the capital.

When the saint broke off his studies to flee into solitude ("*relicta domo rebusque patris*") not only did he say farewell to the codices of Maro and of Plautus, but freely renounced his patrimony.

The *liberius genus* to which the biographer assigns the Patriarch of monks, rather than designating a degree of nobility, as the *clarissimum genus* did for the *patres conscripti,* simply signified a provincial aristocracy respectable by tradition and wealth. Such may have been that of the descendants of Vespasian, whose monuments, about six miles from Nursia, Suetonius describes, or that of the families of Sefius Oluvianus Romulus and Cinnamus who were high officials in Nursia in 452 A.U.C. A Roman epigraph in the municipal museum of Nursia preserves their memory.

The name *Benedictus* is not new in Christian nomenclature; it was not uncommon even among the Jews. Originally it was an adjective attributable to all the faithful, according to the word of Christ: "*Venite benedicti Patris mei.*" [6] In this sense we find inscribed over one of the entrances of the old basilica of St. Paul the words: "*Ingredere, benedicte Dei.*" [7]

In an inscription in the cemetery of Pretextatus we read:

FLORENTI

BENEDICTE

with the symbols of Noah in the ark and the anchor.

With Tertullian, *benedictus* already appears as a title of respect given to the pope: "*Sub episcopatu Eleutherii benedicti*"; [8] "*Bonus pastor et benedictus papa concionaris.*" [9]

[6] Matt. 25:34.

[7] Writing of the rhetorician Endelechius, St. Paulinus of Nola says: "*Alius libellus ex his est, quos ad benedictum, idest Christianum virum, amicum Endelechium scripsisse videor*" (*Epist.* 28). Hence it appears that *benedictus* was the proper title of or a synonym for a Christian.

[8] *De praescript.,* chap. 30; *PL,* II, 42.

[9] *De pudicitia,* chap. 23; *PL,* II, 1103.

In an inscription published by Fabretti, we see the same play on words that St. Gregory employs: "*gratia Benedictus et nomine*" (*Dialog.,* Bk. II, chap. 1):

ANIMA SANCTA CATA NOMEN BENEDICTA

Worthy of mention is a Jewish inscription, now in the Lateran Museum:

BENEDICTAE MARIAE

MATRI ET NUTRICI

In the cemetery of Pamphylus occurs the following acclamation:

SANCTI BONI
BENEDICTI BOS
ATIVITATE QVIRACV

(*Martyres sancti, boni, benedicti, vos adiuvate Quiriacum*).

In St. Benedict's own time, among others his name was borne by a pope between the years 574 and 578 and a saintly monk martyred by the Lombards in the Campania in 542.[10]

In the catacombs of Callixtus, and precisely in the crypt of St. Cecilia, we find the *graffiti* of various priests who functioned there: *Benedictus Presbt; Sergius Presbt; Adeodata mater eius; Iohannes Mercurius Presbt; Felix Presbt. scrin(iarius S.R.E.).* Mercurius was the private name of John I (533–35), in whose time St. Benedict began the constructions at Monte Cassino. But the *graffiti* in the catacombs of Callixtus may be of a later date.

St. Benedict had a sister, Scholastica by name, who followed his footsteps on the road of evangelical perfection. The name *Scholasticus* or *Scholastica* was not unusual in the sixth century. We find a girl of seven with the name of Scholastica at Lyons.[11] In his letters St. Gregory mentions a certain Scholasticus, defender of the Roman Church at Catania.[12] Another Scholasticus was *iudex Campaniae*.[13]

VERE BENEDICTAE
EN EIRENE

Hence also among the Jews the biblical name of *Benedictus* (Hebr. *Baruch*) was in use (cf. *Dictionn. d'archéologie chrétienne*, VII, 2503).

[10] *Dial.*, Bk. III, chap. 18.

[11] Cf. *Dictionn. d'archéologie chrétienne*, Vol. X, Part I, col. 123.

[12] *Epist.*, Bk. VIII, no. 23.

[13] *Epist.*, Bk. III, no. 33. In the cemetery of St. Felicitas occurs this inscription from the year 403:

... O SCOLASTICO QVI VIXIT
... III DEP IIII KAL FEB IN PACE
... INUS ISCOLASTICUS SORORIS
VG TEODOSIO ET RUMORIDO CONSS

The sister of St. Benedict was received among the consecrated virgins at an early age: "*omnipotenti Domino ab ipso infantiae tempore dedicata.*" Such was the custom in some places, despite the fact that various conciliar decrees already required a more advanced age. We possess, for instance, a decree of the emperors Leo I and Majoranus, dated at Ravenna in 458, which requires that the subject be at least forty years of age for such a consecration.

Already before that, the Council of Saragossa (380) had enacted similar legislation; but these canonical prohibitions did not in all instances prevent virgins from being con-

Concerning Irene, the sister of Pope Damasus at Rome, the brother states in her epitaph that she was consecrated with the veil of virginity before attaining her twentieth year: *"Bis denos hiemes necdum compleverat aetas."*

Similarly Fuscina, the sister of Bishop Avitus of Vienne (d. 517–18), was consecrated to God from her infancy. When ten years old, she had put on the white garb of a virgin, and under the tutelage of her pious mother was prepared for the prudent ruling of other virgins. She was acquainted with the entire Holy Writ. Her brother dedicated to her the poem entitled, *De consolatoria laude castitatis. Ad Fuscinam sororem Deo virginem sacratam.*[14]

In like manner, about 567, St. Radegunda had her adopted daughter, while still quite young, made abbess of her monastery of the Holy Cross at Poitiers.[15]

Scholastica, then, was "dedicated to the Lord" from her early childhood, precisely in contravention of the imperial constitution quoted above: "Whoever shall cause his daughter to receive the veil of virginity before the age set by law shall forfeit the third part of his goods." [16] We do not know exactly where this *dedicatio* or rather *velatio virginis* took place, whether at Nursia or in Rome, though according to rule the rite was reserved to the proper bishop.

This circumstance of Scholastica's consecration to God at the initiative of her parents gives us some idea of the kind of family to which the two great patrons of the Benedictine Order belonged. It seems that from his mother's milk and from his childhood environment St. Benedict derived that gentle character of supernatural paternity which characterizes his Rule.

---

secrated to God while still minors. St. Jerome mentions the twenty-year-old virgin Blasilla who burdened herself with penances (*Epist.*, 19, 20). In St. Simplician in Milan the following inscription occurs:

HIC IACET DEUTERIA
CUM CAPETE VELATO QUE
FUIT IN CORPORE ANNIS
PLUS MINUS XXI ET MENSE
UNO POST CONSULATU BASSI
III IDUS OCTOB.

Without doubt the words *"capete velato"* refer to the veil of virginal consecration.
14 Cf. N. Moricca, *Stor. della Letterat. Latina Crist.*, Vol. III, Part I, pp. 141–51.
15 Cf. N. Moricca, *op. cit.*, p. 231.
16 *Cod. Theodos.*, XIV, tit. 16.

When, toward the end of his life, he wrote in the chapter concerning the abbot, "Let him show now the stern countenance of a master, now the loving affection of a father," it is quite possible he recalled to mind the dignified *patria potestas* of his own father, from whom he had learned such lessons of government. We are well aware how the Roman aristocracy regarded this authoritative dignity of the father in the absolute government of his house.

CHAPTER V

Roman Studies

———

However strong may have been the attraction of a family environment so pregnant with supernatural energy as was that of Nursia, Roman tradition, as I have intimated, subjected the youths to a strenuous education. The better families were more or less obliged by custom to have their sons well trained, in Rome if at all possible.

I am not in a position to say whether the parents of St. Benedict were enthusiastic about sending him to Rome for his studies. Besides the proverbial escapades and the licentiousness of the Roman students, the city offered such a pleasant life that from the *Variarum* of Cassiodorus one gets the impression that whoever had an opportunity to go there, did so most willingly. Further, sending boys thither for their studies was equivalent to turning them over to the government before their time, to consigning them to the hated offices of the curia.

A rapid paging through the letters of Cassiodorus brings out some interesting incidents. There is, for example, a letter of King Theodoric to Festus: "Let not permission to leave be granted to those destined for the curià, but let them rather make progress in their studies." [1]

A certain Philagrius of Syracuse had accompanied his nephews to Rome to enter them in the public schools and afterward found himself forbidden to leave the city. He had to ask the special permission of Theodoric. Another unfortunate native of Syracuse, Valerian by

———

[1] Bk. I, no. 39.

name, had brought his sons to Rome for their studies. The King of the Goths refused the father permission to depart from the city.[2]

Hence after the age of childhood,[3] the parents of Benedict decided, or perhaps were obliged, to send him to Rome that he might devote himself *liberalibus litterarum studiis*. To prevent his becoming contaminated by the corruption of the schools, they had his pious nurse, a sort of foster mother, accompany him. A late tradition has given her the name of Cyrilla.

In the later Middle Ages it was believed that the Roman residence of the young Benedict was in the Trastevere, not far from the *titulus Caeciliae*, where till this day stands the church of St. Benedict in Piscinula. Abbot Constantine Gaetani in the seventeenth century did his best to have the tradition accepted, but with little success. The oldest records of the church do not go back farther than the tenth century; at that time Abbot Leo of Monte Cassino rented it to a certain Adelarius.[4]

Judging by St. Gregory's manner of expression, one gathers that the parents of Benedict remained at home to look after their affairs.

From the writings of various Fathers of the Church, we know what were the *liberalia litterarum studia;* undoubtedly they included the trivium and the quadrivium.

Great importance was attached to the ability to speak well, since that was supposed to be the key to public offices. Referring to the Roman schools particularly, Theodoric writes: "Let not Rome be displeasing to anyone, since in fact it is foreign to no one. She is the fruitful mother of eloquence; she the spacious temple of all the virtues." [5] Naturally Cassiodorus had to speak thus, because none of the provincial students cared to remain in Rome any longer.

At that time Benedict must have been about fourteen years old, perhaps somewhat older. The *liberalia studia* followed upon those of the *magister grammaticus* and were more or less equivalent to our university courses. The youth must already have laid aside the *toga praetexta* and assumed the man's toga of the Roman citizen. St.

[2] Bk. IV, no. 6.
[3] An inscription at Lyons speaks of a boy of scarcely ten years: IN STUDIIS ROMAE DEFUNCTUS (cf. *Dictionn. d'archéologie chrétienne*, X, Part I, col. 123).
[4] Leon. Ostiens., *Chron.*, chap. 51.
[5] Bk. I, no. 39.

Gregory calls St. Benedict *puer* even after his flight to Enfide; today we would call him simply a young university student.

In fact, Gregory in other circumstances gives the appellation of *puer* to young men of eighteen years: "We forbid boys to be received into the monasteries before their eighteenth year." [6] In another letter to Columbus, bishop of Numidia, the same Pontiff prescribes "that boys be not admitted to sacred orders." [7] In all these cases he is speaking of young men, not of boys. St. Jerome likewise calls all boys "infants": "Let us not marvel that a barbarous tongue has its own peculiarities; even at Rome nowadays all boys are called infants." [8]

The schools where *liberalia litterarum studia* were pursued were public; Christians and pagans frequented them together. At that time a clear-cut distinction between classical and Christian culture was not yet possible. The ancient Greek and Roman authors formed the basis of literary instruction. St Jerome himself, while teaching grammar in his monastery at Bethlehem, expounded Virgil, Plautus, and the ancient Latin poets to the boys. "In the monastery at Bethlehem, not many years ago, he [St. Jerome] taught grammar and explained his Virgil as well as the comic, lyric, and historical authors to the youths who had been entrusted to him so that they might learn the fear of God." [9] This is precisely the program which St. Augustine [10] calls the *liberales litteras,* the same which Julian the Apostate, in his zeal to withdraw the youth from the influence of Christianity, forbade Christians to teach in the public schools.

At that time instruction was a privilege of the highest classes of society; yet it was not such an absolute monopoly that members of the provincial aristocracy and the rural middle class could not aspire to it. Small African cities, such as Tagaste and Medaura, had their schools, and they were attended not only by the sons of the *viri clarissimi,* but also by those of the provincial middle class, as Alipius, Augustine, and so on.

St. Augustine gives us a clear picture of the way these schools were conducted and the discipline there in vogue when he remarks on

6 *Epist.,* Bk. I, no. 2.
7 Bk. III, no. 48.
8 *Quaest. in Gen.,* XXI, 14.
9 Rufinus, *Contr. Hieronym.,* II, 8.
10 *De civ. Dei,* XXVIII, 55.

the unruliness of his pupils in Africa. The modest son of Monica, teacher of rhetoric in an unimportant school, though still himself a Manichean, was so sickened by what he experienced that finally he abandoned Africa for Rome, with hopes of finding something better on the banks of the Tiber. Unfortunately he was so disillusioned there that shortly after he continued on to Milan, where again he was thoroughly disgusted by the licentious behavior of the students.

Concerning the literary courses then pursued in Rome, we have a treatise of Ennodius of Pavia, entitled *Paraenesis* or *Concinnatio didascalica Ambrosio et Beato,* written between 505 and 511. Two noble youths, Ambrose and Beatus, studied in Rome and asked the deacon Ennodius for some directions with regard to their studies. The author replies with a lengthy composition, in which, beginning with some rules of diet for the preservation of chastity, he recommends to the two students the modesty of the blushing cheek, the purity that sustains the Cross, the faith that draws believers. These three virtues must be accompanied by a love of literature.

At the door—the nurse, as it were, of the other sciences—stands grammar, which prepares and fits out the young for future battles. When the students have completed their course in grammar, th₁ trumpets of rhetoric call them to the field of eloquence, which, as ₐ cuirass is strengthened with mail, supplies them with weapons for the defense of causes.

Eloquence occupies the first place immediately after the Divinity [11] because a powerful speaker can make black white, can make an innocent man out of a criminal, can do anything. Rhetoric, personified, thus states her endowments: "Since you belong to me, have no fear, even if you have committed a crime; with the help of my art, we shall wash away the stains of life. If, by the judgment of the court, someone is declared whiter than snow, we shall oblige all to say that he is the child of darkness. To be guilty or innocent depends on our word alone. By a word we bring the will into subjection."

Toward the end of the treatise, Ennodius counsels his two young friends to seek in Rome the treasures of eloquence from the senators Festus and Symmacus, who are acquainted with all knowledge, whose houses glitter with the rarest virtues. Furthermore, the poet urges

[11] *Post apicem Divinitatis.*

them to become acquainted with Probinus and with the patrician Cetegus, who, though still young, possesses the prudence of an old man. They are also to frequent the houses of Boethius, Agapitus, Probus, as well as that of the noble matrons Stephanie and Barbara.

This same Ennodius gave his nephew Partenius, who was going to Rome, a letter of recommendation to Pope Symmacus and to his friends Faustus and Luminosus. The youth used to send his uncle his rhetorical compositions. One time Ennodius sent back this criticism: "The tenor of your little discourse, though it did not strike me particularly by the splendor of its eloquence, nevertheless manifests a certain taste of Romanism. The style has a degree of harmony; but it has need to become more sonorous through the aid of much reading." [12]

The writings of Ennodius furnish sufficient material to reconstruct the cultural setting during the years immediately following St. Benedict's sojourn in Rome.

In a few well-chosen words St. Gregory describes the scholastic state of the time when he writes that St. Benedict, after scarcely beginning his studies, "when he perceived that many of the students were rushing headlong into ruin, withdrew his foot which he had set, as it were, upon the threshold of the world; lest, if he attained a full knowledge of it, he too might plunge into the abyss." Apparently the nadir had pretty well been reached. This description should be compared with those which have been left us by Gregory of Nazianzen about student life in Athens (Orat., 43, 15–19), by St. Augustine and St. Jerome about the happenings in Carthage and in Rome. The students were imbued with the same spirit as the populace, and this in the decline of imperial paganism had fallen to a very low moral level.

In the fifth century, during a time of great need, the government, while expelling from Rome all the unemployed, was obliged to retain not less than 3,000 dancers, who were regarded as indispensable.[13]

I shall not speak of the theaters, concerning which St. Augustine writes: "And these are the more tolerable plays, namely, the comedies

---

[12] Cf. N. Moricca, Stor. della Letterat. Latina Crist., III, 1241 f., 1253 f.
[13] Ammian. Marcell., XIV, vi, 18.

and tragedies . . . containing indeed much that is shameful but at least not filled, as so many others, with obscene words. These also in the studies which are called good and liberal, youths are forced by their elders to read and learn." [14] This should not cause wonder. There were indeed Christians, and in the cities there may have been many; but basically Roman civilization, art, and literature had remained pagan, and it was only natural that the spirit of the society should be reflected in the mores of the individuals. As far as the Roman clergy of his day were concerned, St. Jerome draws a rather interesting though depressing picture. [15]

The friction that developed in the papal elections of Damasus, of Siricius, of Boniface I and of Symmacus are thus explained by a pagan historian, Ammianus Marcellinus. After relating how, during the quarrels preceding the election of Pope Damasus, 136 corpses were left on the floor of the basilica of St. Mary Major, the author observes: "Considering the splendor of the capital, I do not wonder that a prize of such value should inflame cupidity. . . . The candidate who succeeds in obtaining the post is certain to enrich himself with the offerings of the matrons, to drive in a coach through the streets of Rome, carefully and elegantly garbed; the sumptuousness of the imperial table does not rival the numerous delicacies prepared for the Roman Pontiffs." It is indeed true that this historian is a pagan, but Christian writers confirm what he says.

Popes and holy men also pronounced some strong indictments against certain pontiffs and bishops. Thus St. Basil accuses Damasus of pride; and St. Paulinus of Nola, referring to Siricius, deplores the *"urbici papae superba discretio"* (*Ep.* 13).

Upon the death of Felix III, who had enjoyed the favor of Odoacer, the African Pelagius I became pope; he occupied the chair of Peter from 492 to 496, during the sojourn of St. Benedict in Rome. The *Liber pontificalis* assures us that the Pope by his charity saved Rome from famine, while by a letter directed to the senator Andromacus he

[14] *De civ. Dei*, II, 8.

[15] "Sunt alii (de mei ordinis hominibus loquor) qui ideo presbyteratum et diaconatum ambiunt ut mulieres licentius videant. Omnis hinc cura de vestibus, si bene oleant, si pes laxa pelle non falleat. Crines calamistri vestigio rotantur, digiti de annulis radiant, et ne plantas humidior via aspergat, vix imprimunt summa vestigia. . . . Quidam in hoc omne studium posuerunt, ut matronarum nomina, domos moresque cognoscant" (*Ad Eustoch., Epist.* XXII).

attempted to have outlawed the obscene procession of the pagans, who during the month of February celebrated the Lupercalia.

After him Anastasius II governed for two years (496–98); he was a good man in his way, much more conciliatory than the African Pope. But precisely because of his character, a strong party of the clergy rose against him, and they made him out, more or less, as a heretic. Dante approved of their accusation and as a result put Anastasius into hell.

These conditions in Rome—the famine, the obscene Lupercalian celebrations, the pontifical schism, and so on—must have produced such disgust among the good that it is little wonder the pious young Benedict, to escape from this hell, about the year 490 determined to flee from Rome in order to seek a port of safety in the solitude of monastic life. St. Gregory appears to throw all the blame on the corrupt life of the thoughtless students and the ultra-liberal scholastic programs then in vogue: "When he perceived that many of the students were rushing headlong into ruin, he withdrew his foot which he had set, as it were, upon the threshold of the world, lest, if he attained a full knowledge of it, he too might plunge into the abyss." [16]

In conclusion the ex-consul says: It is necessary to flee from Rome in order not to lose the kingdom of Christ. That is precisely the conclusion, too, at which the young Benedict arrived.

[16] Both reasons are true; they must be put into the historical setting of Rome. They are thus described by an ex-consul, Paulinus of Nola:

> Te nunc sollicitat variis malesuada figuris
> Heu! validos etiam vertere Roma potens.
> Hoc tamen et repetens iterum iterumque monebo
> Ut fugias durae lubrica militiae.
> Norunt eunuchos et magna Palatia passi
> Et quisquis Romam, sponte miser, patitur,
> Quanto sudoris praetio damnoque decoris
> Constet ibi clamidis, hic honor officii!
> Proh dolor! hos propter remoraris in Urbe, Licenti,
> Et Regnum Christi spernis ut hiis placeas.
> Hos vocitas dominos, curva et cervice salutas
> Quos ligni servos conspicis et lapidis.
>   (Carmen ad Licentium)

CHAPTER VI

Literary Progress

THE studies, then, were interrupted: "*Recessit igitur scienter nescius et sapienter indoctus,*" in the words of the biographer. Care must be taken not to separate too much *nescius* and *indoctus* from *sapienter,* otherwise we shall hardly be able to explain what Gregory says regarding the deep knowledge of the saint and his crystalline and melodic prose rhythm: "While the man of God was famous for the many miracles he wrought, he was no less distinguished for his wisdom in matters pertaining to religious life. He wrote a Rule for monks, a book commendable both for its good sense and attractive style." [1]

Traces of the literary culture of the Patriarch of monks can be discerned in the Rule, whose principal chapters are composed according to the exact rules of the prose rhythm then observed by the better writers. A certain metrical arrangement of clauses and other stylistic elements already formed a part of grammar, but it was especially taught in rhetoric. Cicero remarks that this oratorical rhythm, balanced and harmonious, demanded much scholastic exercise and long practice. [2]

A recent historian, who has made a careful study of the prose rhythm in the Rule of St. Benedict, comes to this conclusion: "In writing his text, he was in a position habitually to compose his periods in accordance with the *numerus* taught by the grammarians . . . ; they presuppose and manifest a notable scholastic preparation." [3]

[1] *Dial.,* Bk. II, chap. 36.
[2] *Exercitatione et consuetudine adhibita.*
[3] Cf. Anselmo Lentini, *Il ritmo prosaico nella Regola di S. Benedetto,* Monte Cassino, 1942, p. 142.

Besides the allusions to Holy Writ and the Fathers and the passages derived from those sources, we find in the Rule references also to classical authors: Curtius, Sallust, Terence, Virgil, Statius, Horace, Juvenal, Livy, and Ovid.

It cannot be proved that St. Benedict knew Greek, because he may have known, in Latin versions, the Greek sources to which he refers. We should note that this frequent recourse to scriptural and patristic sources on the part of the saint, his keeping up to date on literary productions, his knowledge and use of the versions of his contemporary, Dionysius Exiguus, immediately point out the former university student, the man of study who wishes to keep abreast of current thought.

Hence we are not to exaggerate the significance of his breaking off his studies to flee to the desert: *"scienter nescius et sapienter indoctus."* A casual examination of the sources of the *Regula monasteriorum* will serve rather to give added force to the judgment of St. Gregory, that the author, besides being a saint, was also a learned man who spoke and wrote according to the best rules of the masters of eloquence: *"inter tot miracula quibus in mundo claruit, doctrinae verbo non mediocriter fulsit."* [4] Accordingly the sojourn in Rome must have extended over a period of several years.

[4] *Dial.,* Bk. II, chap. 36.

CHAPTER VII

Flight to Enfide

WHEN St. Benedict informed his pious nurse of "his serious intention" to leave the slough of the city in order to save his soul in solitude, he was, as the biographer says, still a *"religiosus et pius puer."*
By this expression St. Gregory wishes to convey the idea that he had
not yet reached the years of full virility; hence that he was still a young
man.

The relations of his old nurse with Benedict took in more than
the economic character of a housekeeper. Apparently she was one of
those pious women from the mountains, full of faith and generosity.
The young master regarded her as a second mother, and she showed
him truly maternal affection. *"Nutrix quae hunc arctius amabat, sola
secuta est."* St. Gregory stresses the *sola;* hence this is a sign that the
familia of Benedict in Rome included also other persons, relatives or
slaves assigned to the various duties of the house.

Such affection for Cyrilla was perfectly in accord with Roman tradition. Who does not recall the nurse of Aeneas, Caieta by name, im-
mortalized in Virgil's *Aeneid?* She also accompanied her former
charge in his flight from Troy and in his many wanderings, until death
caught up with her not far from Cassino, on the gulf of Gaeta. Aeneas
buried her there, and the place was named after her.[1]

While Gregory was writing of the faithful Cyrilla, he may have been
thinking of his own nurse, concerning whom he says to the patrician

-----

[1]   *Tu quoque litoribus nostris, Aeneia nutrix,*
           Aeternum moriens nomen, Caieta, dedisti.

43

lady, Rusticana: *"Nutricem meam, quam mihi per litteras com-mendasti, omnino diligo."* [2] If Cyrilla alone of all his house followed him, it is possible that she was also the only one who knew his secret because she alone could understand its sublime nature.

It is pleasing to recall with Tosti,[3] how the future Patriarch of the monks of the West, accompanied by his trusted nurse, who carried the basket of provisions, thinking perhaps of the heroic life of the monks of his native Nursia—leaves Rome by the Porta Tiburtina and, after passing close by the basilica of St. Lawrence, takes the road for Tivoli. Why did he go that way? Did he desire to stop at the church of the patron saint of Nursia, in order to place himself under his protection? We do not know. We do know that by short stages the two pilgrims reached the little town of Enfide, where they sought shelter from the pastor.

Enfide, better known nowadays as Affile, lies about fifty miles from Rome, close to the mountains of Arcinazzo, some two thousand feet above the sea. The distance from Affile to Subiaco is about five miles.[4]

It is hard to understand the plan of the two travelers and to surmise whither they intended to go. Perhaps they arrived at Affile in such a sad condition that the good people of the town had pity on them and constrained them to remain there for a while. St. Gregory adds that this prudent violence was inspired by true Christian charity.[5]

It is agreed that they were lodged in the hospice attached to the church of St. Peter and that the goodhearted citizens saw to their maintenance, so as not to burden the poor pastor unduly. The fact

[2] *Epist.*, Bk. IV, no. 46.

[3] *Vita di S. Benedetto*, Monte Cassino, 1892.

[4] Historians supply the following information about Enfide. Originally it was inhabited by the Equi, and later it became a not unimportant colony of Rome. In the seventeenth century there still existed a Roman triumphal arch of good proportions (cf. Pietro de Angelis, *Affile*, Rome, 1935).

At various times marble fragments, inscriptions, pipes and walls of *opus reticulatum* have been uncovered in the vicinity of Affile. In the place called Bagni there are still to be seen walls of great squared stones, like to those called cyclopean. The present church is dedicated to the martyr Felicitas. In the outside wall have been inserted various Roman inscriptions, among them one of a certain Lucius of Affile, a priest of Pan.

The church of St. Peter, mentioned by St. Gregory, is near the cemetery. It possesses no notable architectural features, but it has several frescoes of the fifteenth century, among them one showing the episode of the miracle of St. Benedict which took place in that very church. It is said that until the present day devotion to St. Benedict is deep-rooted among the inhabitants of Affile.

[5] *"Multisque honestioribus viris pro charitate se illic detinentibus."*

that in former times a xenodochium was joined to bishops' residences, to monasteries, and to the principal churches, is well known to archaeologists.[6] But that also in a small town like Enfide Christian hospitality should have been so honored makes us moderns wonder. Perhaps in present-day Affile one would not find such generosity, and the authorities might discover a number of reasons for not receiving and maintaining two unknown wayfarers in the town. Fortunately a different practice prevailed, and Benedict and Cyrilla took up lodgings near the church of St. Peter and there deposited their few belongings. The intention was to remain there, under the guidance of the good pastor: *"Cum in beati Petri ecclesia demorarentur."*

This story is neither a romance nor a piece of fiction. Hence we cannot divine the plan of St. Benedict, or what kind of understanding he had reached with the priest. Did he perhaps, as someone has supposed, intend to continue his intellectual formation with the help of the pastor? Did he perhaps agree to help the pastor, particularly with the instruction of the children of the village, as was then customary?[7] I do not venture to offer a solution. It seems certain at any rate that the sojourn in Enfide was rather long, if the good Cyrilla had to see even to the provisioning of grain.

Even today it is customary in the towns of the Sabine and Latian regions for every family to have its little oven and to bake bread for its own use. Strangers and the poor purchase their bread from the baker. The rest bake once or twice a week. If for some unforeseen reason a family runs out of bread, it borrows a few loaves from a neighboring family and pays them back at the next baking. One time, among others, Cyrilla had to clean the grain before bringing it to the mill to be ground. As luck would have it, the sieve of terracotta, carelessly left on the table while no one was in the house, fell on the floor and broke in half. No doubt, it was the cat!

---

[6] A trace of this Christian usage is found in an ancient prayer, which even today the bishop recites in the dedication of new churches: *"Ut semper hic letitia quietis, gratia hospitalitatis, reverentia religionis, copiaque sit salutis."*

[7] In the Council of Vaison (507), held under the presidency of Caesarius of Arles, it was ordained: *"Ut omnes presbyteri qui sunt in paroeciis constituti, secundum consuetudinem quam per totam Italiam salubriter teneri cognovimus, iuniores lectores, quantoscumque sine uxore habuerint, secum in domo sua recipiant, quos ut boni patres spiritualiter instruant in psalmis, lectionibus divinis et in lege Domini, ut sibi dignos successores provideant."*

When Cyrilla returned, we can imagine the consternation of the pious woman, especially since the sieve was not hers; she had borrowed it from a neighbor. Thereupon she began to cry, as women are accustomed to do; but the tears of Benedict's foster mother so moved the good youth—*"religiosus et pius puer"*—that, without saying anything, he took the fragments, went to his room, and prayed. Cyrilla bemoaned the damage; Benedict, on the other hand, from that moment began to shed tears of filial tenderness in the embrace of his soul with God.

When he finally rose from prayer, he found the sieve whole and entire on the table, as if it never had been broken. He had performed the same prodigy as Bishop Donatus and Nonnosus on Monte Soracte, whose deeds Gregory describes later in the *Dialogues*. Full of joy he immediately called Cyrilla, gave her back the sieve, comforted her, and reminded her that God helps those who put their trust in Him. Cyrilla may indeed have been a holy woman, but she was talkative, too. In all probability Benedict enjoined silence upon her regarding the incident, lest their neighbors might not lend them anything in the future.

But what could he expect? The miracle was such a great event that to command the woman to keep its secret locked in her heart would have exposed her to the danger of bursting. Immediately she ran to tell the pastor of it; perhaps she also confided it to the lector of the parish and the chaplain; and so it went from mouth to mouth, and by evening the story had made the rounds of the town. Everyone wished to see the sieve, to hear the account again. Then, since the prodigy had occurred right there, in the house attached to St. Peter's, they decided to hang the vessel over the door of the church, to serve as a memorial of the happening: *"quod annis multis illic ante omnium oculos fuit."* [8]

The inhabitants of Affile kept the sieve there for about three-quarters of a century. Mothers used to point it out to their children and tell them of the pious youth Benedict, who from an early age had

---

[8] Similarly at Milan a crystal chalice which had accidentally been broken and then made whole through the intercession of the martyr St. Lawrence was suspended in the church near the altar of the saint in memory of the miracle: *"Pontifex loci, suspenso super altare calice, et tunc agens [ann. 445–449] et in posterum per singulos annos devotissime festa [S. Laurentii] instituit celebrari"* (Gregor. Turon., *De gloria martyrum*).

given such proof of extraordinary sanctity. Later, however, the Lombards reached Enfide and in their bestial fury did not spare even the church of St. Peter—and the *capisterium* also was destroyed. But by that time history, which by reason of Gregory's work would insert the account in its annals, had firmly taken hold of the prodigy. To the mute witness hung on the façade of the church was added the literary monument of Gregory, and this the centuries will not succeed in destroying.

But Cyrilla, with her talk, had made a decided *faux pas* and compromised her young master. Thenceforth the inhabitants of Enfide regarded him as a little saint; they all recommended themselves to his prayers, so that he might procure from God a shower of miracles. Gone was the peace of that hospitable retreat near the church of St. Peter; gone, too, the austerity of a life unknown to the world, but precious in the sight of God.

The young Benedict grasped the danger of his new position as wonder-worker in the eyes of the simple, uncultured folk of the village. In order not to adapt himself to it in any manner whatever, he took one of those generous resolutions which even saints are scarcely capable of. Secretly he left Cyrilla and the village, which had been so good to him, and went in search of the Cross wherever God would have him find it. To say simply that he left Enfide is putting it too mildly; the biographer speaks of flight.[9]

[9] *"Dum fugiens pergeret."*

CHAPTER VIII

At Subiaco

THE road, after about five miles, finally brought him into the neighborhood of the lake of Claudius, which mirrored a large complex of buildings in ruins, all that remained of the place which once had been the pleasure palace of Nero. But now the villa was deserted. Where formerly had been flower gardens, framed by paths and decorated with statues, now snakes, lizards, and wild animals lived undisturbed; weeds and thornbushes covered the mass of ruins with a thick green carpet.

The state no longer had the means for the upkeep of public buildings, and consequently they went to pieces. In the *Variarum* occurs frequent mention of these abandoned monuments that could no longer be maintained. Occasionally someone offered to remodel them at his own expense, and thus make them serve at least some purpose.

So Nero's palace was disintegrating. At night the mournful cry of owls was heard there, while the Anio roared at the bottom of the steep valley. Emperor Claudius had built two solid dams to collect the water of the river in an artificial lake, whence the villa received its name of *Sublacum*. Pliny records that this project occupied 30,000 workmen for about ten years and that it cost the treasury half a million sestertia. But it was money well spent, because there was question of channeling the waters of the Anio and of bringing them to Rome by means of large aqueducts, the imposing and melancholy remains of which are still seen in the Roman campagna.

In 539, when St. Benedict had been at Monte Cassino already ten

years, Witigis, king of the Goths, cut the aqueducts in order to deprive Rome of water. Later, Pope Hadrian I restored them. After
that the lake remained intact till 1305, when a heavy flood broke the
dams, and the river returned to its natural course.

It is difficult to understand how so sumptuous a villa, the property
of the government, could have been closed and allowed to go to ruin.[1]
True it is, after the death of Nero, in hatred of the tyrant, his *Domus
aurea* at the foot of the Palatine was destroyed and buried, and baths
were constructed over it. Nothing of a like character seems to have
befallen the residence at *Sublacum,* which in all likelihood was put
into the hands of retired caretakers, who lived there till the invasion
of the Goths.

We must, then, take into account the incursion of Theodoric into
Italy; on that occasion, as happens so often in time of war, many
edifices were destroyed by the soldiery. Besides, one must not lose
sight of the critical conditions under which the new government was
laboring. For want of money and material, Rome was forced since
the fourth century to demolish more ancient buildings in order to
construct new ones according to need. A classical example is the arch
of Constantine in Rome; when erecting it, the Senate simply had the
ancient arch of Trajan pulled down and used its classical bas-reliefs
in the new construction.

At the present time Roman ruins are common in the vicinity of
Subiaco, from the Anio to the summit of the small hill on which the
city is situated. Are they all parts of one palace? This is hard to say,
though Giovannoni regards the hypothesis as probable. Excavations
carried on at various times in the hilly region toward the monastery
of St. Scholastica have uncovered some vast remains, walls lined with
marble to a height of about eight feet and painted by the encaustic
method. Varicolored floors of marble have been found and two very
beautiful fragments of sculpture: the Ephebus of Subiaco and the
head of Arianna, both at present in the Terme museum in Rome.

These excavations show that a little way above the so-called bridge
of St. Maur, where the Anio makes a sharp turn, Claudius and Nero

---

[1] The cowardly King Theodatus (534–536) was accused of having dissipated and badly
administered the royal patrimony of Tuscia: *"Accusant Theodatum ex mera libidine
cum in alios quosvis, tum in Domus Regiae fundos, quos Patrimonium vocant, in-
volantem"* (Procop., *Bell. Goth.,* I, IV). This happened in St. Benedict's time.

constructed a causeway and a bridge with rather low arches. On the other side of the bridge, on the left bank of the river, there was a nymphaeum, of which considerable remains can still be seen. On the right side of the causeway, near the place called St. Clement's, rose a vast building; many remnants in *opus reticulatum* have survived.

Ascending about 300 feet on the right bank of the lake, below the present monastery of St. Scholastica, there rose another group of buildings, probably joined to the first by a level path or a series of porticoes along the water's edge.

It seems indisputable that the imperial residence was made up of the entire complex of buildings distributed here and there on the hillside and down to the shore of the lake. Apparently the construction was most sumptuous, at least if we are to judge from the fragments of alabaster flooring, of red and green porphyry used to veneer the walls, of serpentine, *giallo antico, cipollino,* and other very rare stone.

In the cloister of St. Scholastica are preserved parts of a grandiose architrave, sections of columns of *cipollino* over thirty inches in diameter—hence they were more than twenty feet high—bases of columns, marble capitals of various sizes: sad remains of decoration, which in St. Benedict's time, no doubt at least in part, preserved its original splendor.

It cannot be said that the district around the villa of Nero was entirely uninhabited. As a matter of fact, not far away was a village of poor peasants, to whose church of St. Lawrence on the other side of the lake was attached a pastor by the name of Florence.

Monastic life was not absolutely unknown either in the diocese of Tivoli or on the Simbruini mountains, at whose base the Anio flowed. Not far from Subiaco, but on the rocky mountain, rose the monastery of Abbot Adeodatus. In the direction of Tivoli lay the monastery of Vicovaro, and on the hills of Palestrina was that of St. Peter. In St. Gregory's time Bishop Floridus of Tivoli had come from the monastic ranks; he had had as his master another bishop, also a former monk, Herculanus of Perugia.[2] In these mountains monastic life must have been of rather long standing, if at Vicovaro, in the monastery of the martyrs Cosmas and Damian, the regular observance had declined as from senile decrepitude.

[2] *Dial.,* Bk. III, chap. 13.

An ancient tradition of Subiaco still indicates in the chapel of the Holy Cross the spot that marked the first meeting of the youth Benedict with the monk Romanus, who invested him with the monastic garb. In this place the biographer is entirely too conservative in his words. He says simply that this Romanus saw the young man wandering about among the cliffs and asked him whither he was going. When St. Benedict had expressed his desire, Romanus promised to keep the secret and gave the youth the religious habit. This lacuna can without any doubt be filled by recourse to canon law.

The hermit Palemon also gave the monastic vesture to St. Pachomius; but he did it only after thoroughly trying the novice and after, as it were, impregnating the habit with holiness and blessing by an entire night of prayer.

Assuredly Romanus did not act otherwise. According to the ancient discipline described by Cassian, he first tried the vocation of the novice, by means of conferences instructed him on the duties and dangers of the eremitical life, and finally with the accustomed rites conferred on him the habit of *sancta conversatio,* as the monastic garb was then called. All these things required time and were not done in the middle of the road.[3]

[3] The prayers which accompany the monastic profession even at the present day go back to a pre-Benedictine period; they appear already in an Ambrosian manuscript of the *Liber diurnus.* It is remarkable that they in no way were inspired by St. Benedict; while indeed treating of the renunciation of the world, they manifest an entirely independent ideology. If we are to judge by the contents of these prayers, it seems that the year of novitiate prescribed by St. Benedict does not yet exist, but that the subject passes immediately from the world to the monastic habit and religious profession.

In Rome the parochial churches used to be called *tituli;* thus the candidate who flees from the world to seek safety in the monastic state *"confugit sub titulo Christi,"* where he finds the door opened to him (*"gratiae tuae ianuas aperiri"*) and where *"felici muro vallatus, mundum se gaudeat evasisse."* It is true that the idea here is akin to the idea of St. Benedict, who calls his monastery *"domus Dei,"* but it is not identical.

Neither is there identity in the other concept which the Patriarch develops in the Prologue to the Rule, where he comments on the divine invitation: "Come, my children, listen to me; I will teach you the fear of the Lord." In the *Ordo* to which I refer, the supernatural invitation is thus expressed: "Thou hast deigned to call sinners, saying, 'Come to me, all ye that labor, and I will refresh you.'"

Rather curious is the prayer of the abbot who confers the *habitus religionis,* when he asks God that his own unworthiness for such an act should not hinder the novice from receiving its entire spiritual fruit: "Let not the son bear the iniquity of his father . . . let it be no obstacle that he receives the habit of religion from us who are so unworthy." The negative aspect of monastic life is stressed: *"Oratio renuntiantium saeculo,"* and the claustral observance is referred to as *"iter disciplinae regularis."* No mention of profession according to the text of a special rule is mentioned.

Let not the canonists break in here to tell us of novitiate, admission to vows, profession, and so on. These legal formalities came later. According to the custom then in vogue, if one received and put on the monastic garb, it was understood that he also professed the essential vows. Among the ancients it was truly the habit that made the monk.

Nevertheless, if the holy man Romanus had not received some intimation from heaven regarding his meeting with the young novice, it seems quite unlikely that he would immediately, without further ado, definitely bind an unknown candidate irrevocably to the monastic state and invest him with the sacred garb. That would have been contrary both to canon law and still more to monastic usage. There must have been some kind of novitiate.

As a matter of fact, St. Gregory insinuates that regular conferences or interviews began between the two, as between master and disciple. "He . . . gave him aid . . . and served him as far as lay in his power." Hence it seems that the future Patriarch of monks opened his soul to the venerable religious, and he on his part promised absolute secrecy. We must not forget that he had fled from Enfide, only a few miles distant from Subiaco. There lies the motive for the secrecy ("*et secretum tenuit*").

The young saint, far from home and relatives, desired to imitate the prodigies of the virtue of that monastic life which from childhood he had admired at Nursia. But for the moment, more than the monastic life, intimate intercourse with God in solitude was his immediate aim, following the example of the holy monk Eutychius, whose garment the inhabitants of Nursia carried in procession in order to obtain divine favors. Meanwhile Romanus, after trying the spirit that led his young disciple, judged that the time had come to give him the

---

The four long prayers do not take a single thought or phrase from the *Regula monasteriorum*. The entire rite gives the impression of having been composed even before the time of St. Benedict, at a time when any monk by the name of Romanus could invest others with the monastic habit. Custom permitted a tried monk to give the religious garb to a novice.

In the ancient legend of St. Euphrosyne, whose death the Greek Metaphrastus puts toward the end of the fifth century, hence about St. Benedict's time, we find an identical investiture with the monastic habit by a simple monk: "*Exurgens senior, facta oratione, abscidit comam capitis eius [Euphrosinae], induitque eam tunicam schematis, et orans pro ea dixit: Deus, qui liberavit omnes sanctos suos, ipse custodiat te ab omni malo. Et haec dicens senior, discessit ab ea.*" The ceremony took place in Euphrosyne's own house, in the absence of her father (cf. *Acta SS., Febr.*, II, 538).

monastic habit and, as a sign of his definitive consecration to God, the tonsure. In the East there are not wanting examples of hermits giving the sacred garb to others, as Elias handed his wonder-working mantle to Eliseus and thus invested him with his own prophetic mission. But in the Italy of the sixth century, canonical discipline already reserved this function to priests and to abbots, who were not permitted to invest a novice unless he had been sufficiently tried.

For this reason Gregory the Great censured a certain abbot, by the name of Barbatianus, because he had not observed this law: "Rashly he tonsured a layman before he had been tried." [4] Another time the Pontiff was called upon to decide on the action of a certain nun, Pomponiana by name, who without due authorization, had conferred the religious garb on girls and made them nuns.

While not denying the illegality of such an investiture, Gregory nevertheless judged that the girls in question were not to be disturbed.[5] Hence it is clear that not every investiture with the religious habit was regarded as canonical. During the first three centuries, since true monasteries did not yet exist, the religious state was represented by the ascetic who wore the philosopher's mantle and by the sacred virgins who lived with their families.

In order to favor such vocations, the Church did not set many obstacles by way of novitiates, scrutinies, admissions, temporary or triennial professions. Under the guidance of the bishop, whoever wished to do so could consecrate himself perfectly to God by assuming the exterior insignia. The Church then took the state under her protection and, once someone had assumed the habit and the monastic state, she demanded the perpetual observance of the annexed obligations and vows.

In Sardinia a certain Gavinia was abbess of a monastery of virgins for many years, although she had never received the monastic habit. Until the day of her death, she wore the garb that used to identify the priestesses, that is, the wives of priests in ancient times. What was to be thought of the case? St. Gregory replies that the fact that she did not receive the habit was supplied by her consecration as abbess.[6]

---

[4] Bk. X, no. 24.
[5] Bk. XIV, no. 2: "*sed in ea qua sunt conversatione . . . permaneant.*"
[6] Bk. IX, no. 7: "*Postquam solemni more abbatissa ab episcopo ordinata est.*"

In accord with the norms of canon law then in force, the monk Romanus, who we must suppose was at least a priest, conferred the sacred habit on the future Patriarch of monks and dedicated him to the monastic state.[7] At that time the tonsure already formed part of the sacred rite.

Canon 42 of the Council of Trullo makes a clear distinction between true monks in the canonical sense and the hermits who were such by their own choice. To be truly a monk, a man had to receive the monastic habit and the tonsure, and the so-called hermits readily complied with these two conditions.[8]

In memory of the rite carried out by St. Romanus, the monks of Subiaco still have the custom of conducting the postulants somewhat outside the monastery of St. Scholastica, to the oratory of the Holy Cross, in order to invest them with the holy habit in the place where Romanus, according to tradition, invested St. Benedict.[9]

---

[7] *"Eique sanctae conversationis habitum tradidit."*

[8] *"Eos qui dicuntur heremitae, qui quidem nigris vestibus induti, et capite comati, urbis obeunt . . . statuimus si elegerint quidem, tonsis comis, reliquorum monachorum amictum suscipere, eos in monasterio constitui et inter fratres referri"* (Mansi, XI, 935 f.).

[9] The juridical condition of these anchorite monks is illustrated by the proceedings of a Roman council held by St. Gregory in 601. Abbot Probus presents a petition in which he explains that, after he became a widower in advanced age, he desired to dedicate his last days to the service of God in the eremitical state. Hence he had become a religious; however, he decided to live not in a monastery, but in a private retreat: *"Quoniam dum ante hos annos, ex laico, ad religiosum migrassem officium, disposueram in cellula mea super me solitarius habitare."*

As far as the juridical status is concerned, the case is exactly parallel to that of St. Benedict in the Sacro Speco, where the saint *"ex laico ad religiosum migravit officium."* Like St. Benedict, too, Probus could not for long enjoy this blessed solitude. One morning when he went to make his obeisance to the Pope in consistory, the latter profited by the occasion to free himself from a difficulty. Precisely at that time the abbatial office in the Roman monastery of SS. Andrew and Lucy *in Renatis* was vacant, and the Pope did not find it an easy task to fill the position. Now when the hermit Probus chanced to enter the consistory, both Gregory the Great and his advisers agreed that no one was better qualified to be abbot than he. And so, *nolens volens*, they proclaimed him abbot without even giving him an opportunity of returning home to settle his family affairs. Probus left behind him a son, who afterward demanded of his father his portion of the inheritance. Contemporary legislation forbade a man, once he had entered a monastery, to dispose of the goods he possessed either by right of inheritance or by donation.

But the law also wisely ruled that all dispositions with regard to the patrimony were to be made after free and mature deliberation, before entrance into the monastery. This condition precisely was wanting in the case of Probus; and Gregory together with his advisers, finding his petition justified, gave him permission to transfer his goods to his son, an action which he could not carry out before by reason of his sudden promotion to the abbatial office.

From the chapel of the Holy Cross to the Sacro Speco toward the base of Monte Taleo is about fifteen minutes' walk. Romanus led his young novice thither. Benedict wished to dedicate himself to the eremitical life. Very well. Precisely in this spot the breaking away of the mountain opened various caves of calcareous rock bedewed by a continuous infiltration of water; these could well serve him as a hermitage.

Since, however, there was no path from Romanus' monastery on that side of the mountain, because the cliff rose vertically like a wall above the chosen cave, the provisioning of the anchorite by the master was made all the easier. At scheduled times he let down with a rope a small basket containing the meager remains of his own meal.

St. Benedict's cave at Subiaco became an object of veneration from the time of his death. His biographer already regards it as a kind of sanctuary and he recounts the miraculous healing of an epileptic who spent the night there and came forth cured in the morning. By the ninth century it had been converted into an oratory dedicated to Pope St. Sylvester; Pope Leo IV, after the piratical attacks of the Saracens, sent sacred vestments there as a gift.[10]

Here the Lateran chronicler causes a bit of confusion. There are two sanctuaries and three altars: the altar of the Sacro Speco was dedicated to St. Benedict; in the upper church, on the other hand, was the altar of St. Sylvester. In the monastery of the Anargyri was the altar of St. Scholastica. Hence three altar cloths and eight veils to surround the altars of the monastic churches.[11]

Just as Abbot Probus, so also St. Benedict could without difficulty be made abbot of Vicovaro, since contemporary legislation recognized the religious character of hermits dwelling in their cells. We do not know whether or how the Patriarch disposed of his patrimony. The law could not take into account internal dispositions of the soul. Apart from a formal renunciation by a legal act, at the death of the parents the property went to the necessary heirs, as we know from many instances of most saintly persons in Christian antiquity.

Gregory the Great himself inherited from his parents very extensive possessions, which he later used to found monasteries in Sicily and in Rome.

10 *"Obtulit in monasterio S. Silvestri sanctique Benedicti, et sanctae Scholasticae quod nuncupatur Sublacum, vestes de fundato III et vela similiter de fundato VIII."* Lib. pontif., ed. Duchesne, II, 117.

11 The *Chronicon Sublacense* enlarges on the information contained in the *Liber pontificalis* and asserts that Leo IV came to Subiaco to consecrate two distinct altars: *"et dedicavit in Specu altare unum in honore S. Benedicti et S. Scholasticae, et alterum in honore S. Silvestri papae."*

While the lower monastery today is called St. Scholastica, its original church was

From what we can gather out of the meager sources of antiquity, at a time which cannot be determined more exactly, above and close to the cave inhabited by St. Benedict an oratory dedicated to St. Sylvester was erected. After the Saracens had despoiled the sanctuary, restorations were carried out under Leo IV, and the Pope sent some liturgical furnishings thither. Since the passageway from the oratory of St. Sylvester to the Speco, which was more or less the crypt of the church, was open to the sky, when Abbot Humbert rebuilt St. Sylvester's more artistically and spaciously, he joined the lower crypt to the upper church by means of a descending corridor. This passageway, however, proved too narrow for the growing importance of the sanctuary; wherefore Abbot John V had the stairway built which still exists.[12]

In the Speco or crypt scarcely any remains of the pictorial decoration carried out under Leo IV survive. On the rock to the right of the altar is depicted *Maria Regina* on the throne with the Infant; to right and left are two saints. The one on the left has his name over the nimbus that surrounds his head: LUS—*Sanctus Laurentius*. The one on the right is anonymous, but from the dalmatic he wears we gather he is a deacon, namely, St. Stephen.

The two figures are youthful and beardless. St. Lawrence holds the grate, the instrument of his martyrdom. St. Stephen wears a richly ornamented dalmatic, and on the left shoulder appears the top of the diaconal stole which he wears under the dalmatic. The presence of St. Lawrence here is accounted for by the fact that the parish at Subiaco was dedicated to him.

The oratory was an object of veneration from the early Middle Ages because St. Benedict dwelt there three years and there began his apostolate. The basilica of Cassino before its unfortunate destruction was beautiful in its splendor; but the Speco of Subiaco has a beauty all its own: it is the true Benedictine Bethlehem.

---

dedicated to the martyrs Cosmas and Damian; the primitive little church of the hermitage of Sacro Speco was dedicated to Pope St. Sylvester. The *Chronicon Sublacense* is explicit: Leo IV *"aedificavit Specum in honore S. Silvestri, atque Scholasticae quae appellatur Sublacum."* And if this does not suffice, we also have some information regarding Abbot John V (beginning of the twelfth century): *"Fecit in Specu cryptas et gradus ab exitu ecclesiae S. Silvestri usque ante S. Benedicti ianuam, quae nimis parva erat"* (p. 17, 2). Before him, Abbot Humbert (1051–61) *"fecit in Specu Ecclesiam pulcherrimam et firmam; cooperta crypta"* (p. 9, 5).

[12] *"Et gradus ab exitu ecclesiae S. Silvestri usque ante S. Benedicti ianuam, quae nimis parva erat."*

CHAPTER IX

The Anchorite of Subiaco

THE seclusion of Benedict in the cave of Monte Taleo extended, as I have said, over a period of three years. During this time, Romanus —or, rather, as Zachary calls him, ὁ τιμιώτατος Ρωμανός—"*in quantum licuit ministravit:* served him to the best of his ability." Hence there is question not only of letting down that little basket with a bit of bread, but the master continued to care for his disciple in other ways, helping him also spiritually: "*et adiutorium impendit.*" Gregory's phrase here is rather inclusive and completes the preceding one.

It is dangerous to conjecture concerning the studies and labors of the anchorite during this period. The apostle Paul in the Arabian desert, Ignatius Loyola in the grotto of Manresa, and others made their novitiate under the immediate direction of the Holy Spirit. So it was with St. Benedict.[1]

Apart from Romanus, he forgot the world, as the world had forgotten him; and, illumined by the rays of the divine eye that looked on him from on high, he awaited his transformation into the image of Christ. St. Gregory gives us a precise description of this spiritual state when he writes of him: "*solus in superni Inspectoris oculis habitavit secum.*" Later on, in the Rule, the Patriarch will put his

---

[1] When as a student in Rome Benedict, on feast days, following the example of St. Jerome, went out on the Via Appia to visit the tombs of the martyrs in the Catacombs of Callixtus, he must frequently have read on the tomb of Hippolytus the inscription composed by Pope Damasus, in which his monastic life is described as the "*prima Fides . . . caelestibus armis* QUEM MONACHI RITV TENVIT SPELVNCA LATENTEM." At Subiaco St. Benedict did not hesitate to imitate him, and in the Rule he will also speak of "*obaedientiae praeclara arma.*"

disciples on guard, lest they hazard the dangerous life of the hermit without first having exercised themselves for many years in the ascetical life of the community. The common norm is certainly this: first one battles the devil in the ranks of one's battalion; only later may one go out to the single combat of the desert.

But with the future Father of monks, God somewhat modified this program and had Benedict go through the spiritual trials of the eremitical life even before he knew cenobitic life by experience.

One may assert with St. Thomas,[2] that the exception confirms the rule. When, under the direction of Romanus, St. Benedict entered the cave at Subiaco, he was no longer a tyro in the ascetical life—this youth who already at Enfide had attained so high a degree of union with God that his simple prayer brought forth tears and produced wonders. St. Gregory alludes to the exalted state of perfection which the young saint had reached by that time.[3]

The good Romanus took care of the material needs of life. His monastery of St. Blase was situated on a sort of plateau on the other side of the steep rock. The air distance could not have been great; but since no path led to the bottom of the cliff, he would have had to make a long detour, ascending from the valley of the Anio, before he could have reached the cave of his disciple.

Necessity is the mother of invention, and Romanus soon surmounted the difficulty. Escaping the watchful eye of Abbot Adeodatus, on certain predetermined days, when the charitable monk was not able to visit the cave, he let down from the top of the cliff the little basket of bread by means of a rope. In order to notify the holy hermit, he used to attach a little bell; at its sound Benedict would go to get the bread, and the basket would be pulled up, perhaps with a written list of his needs for Romanus. The oratory of St. Blase still exists, but it was removed somewhat from its original site by Abbot John V of Subiaco; he likewise had it consecrated by the bishop of Tivoli in 1114.

Hence the present position does not fit St. Gregory's description. As a matter of fact, Romanus had but a few steps to go to reach the

---

[2] *Summa theol.,* IIa IIae, q. 189, a. 1, ad 2.

[3] St. Gregory writes: *"Benedictus puer conversationis gratiam a quanta perfectione coepisset."*

edge of the precipice; thence with a rope or cord (a good fifty yards long) he was able to let down the bread to St. Benedict who dwelt below. In no other way could he have escaped notice. If the nature of the place is taken into consideration, the reason for the little bell mentioned by St. Gregory is better understood. Romanus could not lower the basket directly in front of the Sacro Speco because of the overhanging rock and the steep fall below it. Hence, that St. Benedict might grasp the rope, it was necessary to let it down a bit to the left, where at the foot of the rock wall there is a slight niche; but the saint could not see it from the cave. Hence the little bell.

In 1772 the small church of SS. Blase and Romanus was rebuilt according to the plans of Quarenghi and at the expense of Martin Gerbert, abbot of St. Blase in the Black Forest. An inscription fixed into the inside wall of the church calls attention to the fact.

Let us not imagine that Romanus could put very much into this basket of Christian charity for his disciple. St. Gregory tells us that it contained the bare remains of the poor cenobite's fast, that is, what he could steal from his own hunger, hiding it carefully from the watchful eye of Abbot Adeodatus. Tosti has supposed that together with the crusts of bread, Romanus occasionally put into the little basket also some biblical codex: the Psalter, the Gospels, the Letters of St. Paul. Possibly; but there exists no basis for this archaeological reconstruction of the three years passed by St. Benedict in the greatest solitude.

Perhaps we are not to stop at this scene of the basket. As a matter of fact, St. Gregory informs us that Romanus helped his disciple and served him to the best of his ability. He visited him when he could: *"diebus certis, Benedicto panem ferebat."* And there were intimate spiritual colloquies, perhaps a loan of books, and almost certainly Eucharistic Communion. It was a difficult task for the aged Romanus, and God took account of it by disposing that the Benedictine family should honor his memory as that of a father.[4] The biographer also recognizes the hard labor the good old man performed by these periodic visits to St. Benedict.

The question has been raised whether during this seclusion the

[4] *"Cum vero iam Deus . . . Romanum vellet a labore quiescere"* (chap. 1).

holy hermit received the sacraments. Many hermits, concerning whom Cassian and St. Jerome tell us, living in the desert and far from any church, could not assist regularly at Mass, but reserved the Holy Eucharist in their cells and administered Communion to themselves. St. Basil assures us that this was a common practice in the East.[5] St. Theodore the Studite mentions that this ancient custom lasted till his time.[6]

Some hold that Romanus was a priest. Given this hypothesis, it would be easier to explain, in accordance with the canonical discipline then in force, how he by his own authority could confer the monastic habit on his novice, and thus admit him to the profession of vows.

According to the canon law of that time, the right to confer the veil of the consecration of virgins was reserved to the bishop, who could impose it only on certain determined solemnities in the course of the year. The consecration of monks, on the other hand, under Gregory I seems to have been regulated by both civil and canonical law in such a way as to allow the solemn rite only during the celebration of Mass, in the presence of a notary and witnesses. Gregory, who simply states that Romanus "supplied him with a religious habit," did not give the phrase a meaning different from that current at the time.

If the hypothesis of Romanus' priesthood is sound, then also the question of the reception of the sacraments is readily explained. As a matter of fact, when Romanus becomes sick or can no longer communicate regularly with St. Benedict, the latter completely loses the precise idea of time, and does not even know exactly on what day Easter falls in a particular year. Fortunately, the Lord provides with

---

[5] *"Omnes enim in solitudinibus monachi, ubi non est sacerdos, Communionem domi servantes, suis ipsorum manibus sumunt"* (*Epist. ad Caesariam*).

In the life of St. Luke the Younger, about the year 900, is described the rite whereby the anchorites gave Communion to themselves. *"Primo igitur ac praecipue quidem sacerdotem adesse decet. Quod si ille necessaria omnino ratione desit, imponendum sacrae mensae, sive altari, praesanctificatorum vasculum siquidem oratorium sit; sin autem cellula, scanno mundissimo. Tum explicato linteolo, propones in eo Sacras Particulas, accensoque thimiamate, Typicorum psalmos, aut hymnum Trisaghium cum Fidei symbolo decantabis; trinaque genuflexione adorans, manus quidem contrahes, ore autem praetiosum Christi ac Dei nostri Corpus sumes, dicendo Amen.*

"Loco autem Sacri Laticis, vini poculum bibes" (*Acta SS., Febr.*, II, 92).

[6] *"Una mihi consolatio superest, quam et tibi exponam necesse est, mi Pater! Quod nempe didicerim ex lectione et usu Orientalium oportere eos qui vitam in secessu agunt, singulis diebus, siquidem fieri possit, participare divinam Communionem. Hunc morem servavi"* (S. Theodori Studit., *Ad Platonem abbatem montis Olympi*).

a miracle, and precisely on Easter Day sends to the Speco another priest with a new basket containing the Easter gifts.[1]

The episode of St. Benedict's fast on the paschal solemnity is not clear. Was Romanus already dead? St. Gregory seems to intimate as much; [8] and this is all the more true, since, in order to provide food for the saint, God no longer sends Romanus or one of his colleagues, but causes a pastor of the territory to come from a long way off to bring victuals to him. This may be regarded as a sign that not even heaven put very much trust in the monastery of Abbot Adeodatus, who thenceforth disappears from the story completely.

[1]
> *In specu in quo militat*
> *Dei Miles se cruciat;*
> *Rex mundi cui militat*
> *Hunc sacerdote visitat.*

Gregory's account of the relations between the monk Romanus and the young anchorite Benedict is too sketchy to allow of much reconstruction. Romanus belonged to a monastery situated on a mountain at Subiaco under the discipline of Abbot Adeodatus. Having encountered St. Benedict on the heights and having discovered his desire to lead a life in solitude, *"et secretum tenuit, et adiutorium impendit, eique sanctae conversationis habitum tradidit, et in quantum licuit, ministravit."*

These four things evidently were not simultaneous, particularly the service, which lasted for about three years. The *"secretum tenuit"* can be understood, because the town of Affile was not far distant. But why did Romanus also keep the matter secret as far as Abbot Adeodatus was concerned, so that, in order to do a service periodically for his protégé, *"pie eiusdem patris sui furabatur horas"*? This question cannot be answered unless we are to suppose that Romanus did not put much trust in the superior of his own monastery

St. Gregory says expressly that the assistance rendered by Romanus to the young anchorite did not consist solely in letting down periodically the little basket of food, but that it included various other kinds of help. He also makes a distinction between the spiritual consolation and the material help: *"adiutorium impendit et . . . ministravit,"* three times stressing this voluntary service: *"modis congruentibus ministrare non desiit."*

[8] See note 4 *supra.*

CHAPTER X

Pasch of Charity

MATTERS would have gone almost too well had not the devil put in his hand. Jealous as ever, even of the miserable refection of Benedict and the great charity of Romanus, Satan wished to cause some annoyance. One day he threw a rock at the little bell and broke it. Romanus immediately understood who had done him this evil turn and then had disappeared so completely. But, not to give in to the devil, he continued his charitable assistance as best he could. It was, as I have said, great charity. Nevertheless, leaving the cloister stealthily in order to go several times a week in all kinds of weather to let down the basket could not continue. This labor of Romanus and the seclusion of the disciple had already lasted three years, when God finally said: "It is enough."

In one of the many villages scattered throughout the mountains lived a good priest, whom medieval tradition has simply called the pastor of Monte Porcaro. This name occurs frequently in the documents in the archives of Subiaco, and designates a *castrum* rebuilt by Abbot John V at the beginning of the twelfth century. On that occasion the abbot transported a colony of workers to Monte Porcaro.[1] No documents of antiquity identify more exactly the pastor referred to by St. Gregory. The pontifical biographer simply says that his parish was rather distant: *"longius manenti."*

The first rays of light were appearing in the east on the morning of Easter Sunday. Some think it was the year 497; others put it about 520.

[1] *Chron. Sublac.*, pp. 14, 27.

The latter date is absolutely to be discarded. Romanus, whether he had already entered into his eternal rest—*"cum . . . Deus Romanum vellet a labore quiescere"*—or for some other reason, unknown to us, could no longer retain frequent contacts with his fervent disciple. Now it happened that St. Benedict in his cave continued to suffer hunger, as if Lent were still going on, while his spirit was so taken away from things of earth that he did not even notice that Easter had arrived.[2] Then the Lord took a hand.

The good pastor of Monte Porcaro, according to the rite then in use, had passed the greater part of the night of Holy Saturday in church with his parishioners celebrating the liturgical vigil, singing selections from the Scriptures and litanies; perhaps he also administered baptism to the catechumens. When dawn seemed at hand he ascended to the altar to celebrate the Mass of Easter and to intone the alleluia. After the Communion he finally turned to the faithful and gave them permission to depart: *Ite, missa est.*

All returned to their homes, and since they all, including the children, had passed the preceding day fasting (as was then the custom on Holy Saturday), everyone hastened to prepare a rather bountiful Easter meal. Similarly the poor pastor returned home. But there was no Perpetua in his house, and therefore, despite the fatigue of the labors in church, he had to light his own fire and prepare a bite to eat. After the long Lenten fast he also, quite naturally, desired to celebrate somewhat on this day—*"delicias paras,"* says the biographer.

He must have been a holy man. While he fed the fire and brought the utensils to the tripod, he was occupied with spiritual affairs. Quite naturally his thoughts dwelt on the risen Lord who had appeared to Peter and the other disciples. Among his pots and pans in that poor smoky kitchen of a country rectory, the Lord appeared also to him and said: "What, you stand here preparing dainty dishes, while over in the mountains one of my servants is almost dying of hunger!"

The pastor, just as he was, girded with an apron, fell on his knees

---

[2] For the ancients the date of the Lenten fast and the feast of Easter easily caused difficulties and led to consultation among the bishops. Things arrived at such a pass that in the nineteenth year of the reign of Justinian (546), he postponed Lent for a week and ordered the butchers to sell meat (Migne, *Patrol. graeca*, XCVII, 699). Precisely in order to obviate these inconveniences, Dionysius Exiguus about 525 wrote two letters *De ratione Paschae*, on the manner of calculating the date of Easter.

before the risen Lord. I do not know if he intoned, as he had already done in church: "*Surrexit Dominus vere*—The Lord has truly risen and has appeared to me." In any event, the good priest, as soon as he heard that there was a work of charity to be performed, not considering his fatigue, the feast of Easter, want of sleep, and the pangs of hunger, took a basket, put into it all the good things he had prepared for himself, and departed. No one in the village was aware of it, because outside the day had scarcely dawned and the faithful were all in their houses to take their meal and then to retire.[3]

So the good pastor went on his way in the direction indicated and walked all that morning, climbing mountains, descending to valleys, and even examining some caves. Finally, as God had willed, he found the young anchorite in the Speco when the sun was already high in the azure springtime sky of Easter Sunday.

At first sight of a strange face after so long a time, Benedict did not manifest surprise. The anchorite readily assumed the aspect of the Roman student of yore, self-assured and well-bred, in accordance with the social condition of his family. He greeted the priest, asked his blessing, inquired who he was and requested to know what good fortune had brought him thither. The priest returned the greeting, told him that he was the pastor of a neighboring parish, knelt down with the youth, so that prayer might first sanctify this visit of Christian charity. This was also the practice of the Fathers of the Desert and, as Rufinus observes, it was an excellent precaution against the delusions of the devil.[4]

After a common prayer, they rose and sat down. Then began a conversation which recalls that of St. Anthony when in the depths of a cave he discovered Paul the Hermit. The priest asked of this youth the reason for his extraordinary manner of life. Benedict began to speak of the things of God. And thus, while the one was more or less in ecstasy and the other continued to ply him with questions, time passed, and still the basket with food stood on the floor untouched.

But after a while, the prudent pastor interrupted this colloquy.

---

[3] Also in Rome in the early Middle Ages on the Sunday following the night of Ember Saturday there was no stational Mass: *Dominica vacat.*

[4] "*Forma huiusmodi inter monachos observatur, ut si quis ad eos veniat . . . ante omnia oratio fiat . . . quia si fuerit aliqua transformatio daemonis, continue, oratione facta, diffugiet*" (*Histor. Monachor. in Aegypto*, I).

"Rise," he said to the young man, "it is time for us to take food to-gether, for today is Easter and there is no fast."

"In very truth," the anchorite replied pleasantly, "today is indeed Easter for me, because God has brought me the favor of your visit."

He thought of everything, except that this was the day of the Lord's resurrection.[5] But when the priest insisted that this day was really Easter, and that the Lord had sent him on purpose so that they might feast together, St. Benedict, whose three years of solitary life had not robbed him of his innate courtesy, kindly thanked his host and broke his fast with him.

By that time evening was approaching. The good priest bethought himself of the parishioners who were awaiting him in the church for the office of Easter evening. Hence, after the meal he gave thanks to God, bade farewell to Benedict—Pope Zachary relates that he embraced him—and returned to his parish deeply edified.

When the faithful saw him arrive out of breath from his hasty journey, it was only natural that they were curious to know the reason for his strange absence from the parish on Easter Day. Quite true, the Mass of the Resurrection had already been celebrated during the night, but on such a solemn feast one certainly does not go away from one's own church.[6]

Hence, in order that the inhabitants of Monte Porcaro might not think evil of him, the good pastor felt himself obliged to tell them what had happened to him, how, after he had seen the Lord that morning, he had discovered some miles away the Wonder-worker of Enfide, a true saint, no smaller in spiritual stature than the famous anchorites concerning whom St. Jerome and Cassian had written.

[5] If St. Benedict in the Speco did not know it was Easter, we may recall that at that time the computation of Easter was not such a simple thing as it appears to us with our calendars. In the letter of Pope Vigilius to Bishop Profuturus of Braga (536), the coming Easter is announced as follows: *"Pascha vero futurum nos, si Deus voluerit, X. Kalendarum Maiarum celebraturos esse cognoscite."*

If not even the bishops knew the exact date of the paschal equinox, we need scarcely be surprised at St. Benedict's ignorance.

[6] The Council of Orleans in 538 decreed that on feast days, when the parish priests left their churches to celebrate with their bishops, the Pontifical Mass had to begin at nine o'clock, so that the priests might return to their parishes for the evening office: *"Ut tertia hora Missarum celebratio inchoetur, quo facilius inter horas competentes, ipso officio expedito, sacerdotes possint ad vespertina officia, idest vespertino tempore, convenire. Quia sacerdotem vespertinis officiis ab Ecclesia talibus praeterea diebus, nec decet deesse, nec convenit"* (can. 14).

Now the secret was out. For St. Benedict the life hidden in God had come to an end, and his new mission, thus described by the biographer, begins: "God wished . . . to show forth the life of the servant Benedict as a pattern for men, that, being set as a light on a candlestick, he might shine unto all that dwell in the house of God."

The mission of Romanus had also come to an end. Henceforth it will be the devout visitors to Benedict who will provide for his material needs.

By this time the novice had been completely formed. As a matter of fact, when Pope Zachary refers to the dialogue between St. Benedict and the holy pastor, whenever the latter speaks to the saint, though he was a priest and the other a mere boy, he puts on his lips the respectful title of "Father." For this Oriental Pope, St. Benedict could be compared to the "Holy Fathers" of the Egyptian desert.

CHAPTER XI

Franciscan Roses on Benedict's Thornbush

LOCAL tradition has given to St. Benedict's retreat at Subiaco the name of "Cave of the Shepherds," because precisely there, among the shepherds, the Patriarch began his social apostolate.

Gregory the Great relates that, shortly after the visit of the pastor of Monte Porcaro, certain shepherds drove their goats to pasture on the slopes close to the Speco. Among the green of the flowering bushes at the mouth of the cave, they espied something moving about and thought they recognized the skin of an animal; immediately they concluded that some ferocious beast was hidden there. They decided to find out what it was. Imagine their surprise when upon entering they found instead the young saint covered with the monastic cowl of goatskin, breathing penitence and devotion. Far from being a wild animal, it was a saint.

Just as was the case with the pastor of Monte Porcaro, so an intimate spiritual relationship immediately sprang up between St. Benedict and the shepherds. These poor people, by always consorting with their animals, had themselves become brutalized. It seems that the pastor of St. Lawrence had been somewhat wanting in his work.

The conversations with the saint helped to convert them: *"a bestiali mente conversi sunt."* These first shepherds then acted as propagandists among their companions. Thus it came about that on those slopes, where before not even goats had been seen, a daily procession of people to and from the Sacro Speco now commenced. No longer were there isolated visits; the biographer says that many from all the towns of the vicinity hastened to Subiaco. What must have been the joy of the inhabitants of Enfide at finding their little saint again! No doubt the good pastor of Monte Porcaro many times led groups of his parishioners to the cave.

St. Benedict refreshed all with the spiritual bread of evangelical instruction; on their part his visitors gave him in exchange that bit of food which was necessary to keep him alive. This solicitude, mentioned by Gregory, almost certainly first came into the mind of the pastor of Monte Porcaro, a spiritual man, but also of sound practical sense. Did not God Himself send him the first time with the Easter dinner? Nothing can equal the simple beauty of Gregory's words in describing this new phase of St. Benedict's work: "While they offered him food for his body, they received in return from his lips the food of life."

The school of the Lord's service was now established. At Subiaco, as once at Bethlehem, the first pupils were simple shepherds. This is a simple historical fact, which, as it were, presaged the future. How many apostles and pastors of souls would go forth from the school of St. Benedict!

If so many people now approached the anchorite of Subiaco as on pilgrimage, also the devil wished to have the satisfaction of visiting him. St. Gregory notes that on a certain day Benedict happened to be alone, an evident indication that the hours of quiet, with so many people coming to him, were now rather few.

Outside the warmth of the advanced spring season, the blue sky, the trees in bloom invited him to enjoy his youth. An impertinent blackbird flew from a bush and entered the cave; frightened, as if it could not find the way out, it began to wheel about the anchorite, to strike his head, to brush against his cheeks with such persistence that, had he wished, he could easily have caught it.

The saint, however, immediately perceived who had sent the blackbird. He made the sign of the cross, and at once the terrified bird flew away. But in the members of the young saint an unwonted movement of the passions made itself felt, and he had to fight strenuously to overcome it. As had happened to St. Jerome in his cave at Caleide, when, though his members were already dried up by mortification, the memory of the singing and dancing girls of the Roman Circus Maximus returned, so a vivid recollection of a young girl whom he had formerly known in Rome assailed St. Benedict, and there was some danger that his very vocation to the eremitical life might go by the board.

With great simplicity St. Gregory goes about describing the fire which the devil caused to flare up in that emaciated breast. Benedict almost felt himself forced out of the Speco, to tread again the road back to the bright lights of imperial Rome. But God never permits a temptation without at the same time assuring the grace of victory. So it was also in this case. While the devil fostered in the breast of Benedict the fire of lust, the Holy Spirit began to cast into his heart burning coals of divine love, which, since these were the stronger, overcame the other. St. Benedict, with a resolve both generous and unforeseen, decided to conquer the attraction of passion by pain. From heaven the angels with great admiration must have watched this bloody struggle for Christian chastity. As St. Anthony after his temptation in the Thebaid, so St. Benedict now could also ask: "Lord, where were You when I was struggling with Satan?" And God could easily have replied, as He did to Anthony: "I was in you and supported you by My grace."

Throwing off his cowl and shirt, entirely nude, the pious youth cast himself into the thorny bushes that grew luxuriantly near the cave and rolled back and forth on that extremely uncomfortable bed.

This exercise lasted for a considerable time ("*ibique diu volutatus*") and did not cease until his entire body had been bruised and lacerated by thorns and thistles.

In any case, this kind of ascetical surgery proved eminently successful. And on His side God also rewarded him, because from that time forth, as the Patriarch later confided to his disciples, he never more experienced movements of the flesh. "*Ignem exstinguit ignibus*," the Middle Ages sang in his honor. The burning of the bloody wounds had extinguished the fire of lust.

The biographer's statement that the Patriarch himself later related the story of his struggle and victory to his most intimate disciples is most interesting. In the first place it indicates the immediate source of Gregory's narrative. Then, the confidential communication made by the Patriarch himself to his disciples of the rare gift granted to him by the Lord as a reward for his strenuous battle against his passions, makes us understand better the affectionate and fatherly way St. Benedict used to reveal himself to his most intimate followers. By his own spiritual experience he taught them how to overcome carnal movements.

We shall see later how this love of the saint for holy purity gave his body such a fragrance, that a contemporary writer asserts his very tunic produced a more paradisiacal odor than all the perfumes of Araby.

The Franciscan historians relate that about the year 1223, when St. Francis passed through Subiaco on his way to the Neapolitan territory, he engrafted some rose branches on the thorny bush in which St. Benedict had rolled himself. The gentility of this act is indeed worthy of the great saint, whose portrait was painted near by, in the chapel of St. Gregory, in memory of his visit.

Here the Patriarch of the Friars Minor is portrayed as not yet advanced in age, barefooted, a hood on his head, wearing a knotted cord, while in his hand he holds a scroll with the Gospel greeting: "*Pax huic domui.*" And his name is also given: *Frater Franciscus.* This picture is regarded as anterior to the canonization of St. Francis, which took place on July 16, 1228. But the arguments adduced are rather weak, since the painter of the Roman school could justify the absence of the title *Sanctus,* by referring simply to 1223, the year in which the Poverello visited Subiaco.[1]

This rosebush, which is named after SS. Benedict and Francis, still blooms. On each leaf one may see the outline of a small serpent caused by a parasite, and it is said to be a reminder of that other serpent which at one time tempted St. Benedict in that spot. It seems to be simply a caprice of nature; but since for centuries that rust-colored serpent has appeared on the leaves of the rosebush, it begets in me a feeling of fear, because it calls to mind the dread serpent which fourteen centuries ago slid over these thorns spewing its venom upon them.

[1] He did the same thing with regard to Gregory IX, representing him in the act of consecrating an altar, performed by him in the Sacro Speco when he was still cardinal of Ostia.

The sons of St. Benedict have shown themselves duly grateful to the Poverello for his poetic gesture. Apart from the gift of the Portiuncula of St. Mary of the Angels in the plain below Assisi, the earliest registers of the Franciscans are full of bulls and documents referring to the donations of ancient Benedictine monasteries to the sons of St. Francis during that first golden century.

Another circumstance likewise must not be forgotten. From the very beginning, Cardinal John of St. Paul's had covered the Franciscans with his protecting purple. When in the papal consistory his colleagues wished to show Pope Innocent III that the new rule of the Poverello was not feasible, the former monk of St. Paul's rose to the defense of the new institute. "Take care," he said, "what you are doing. By condemning this man and this rule, does it not seem that you are condemning the Gospel and declaring it also impossible?" And they agreed with him. These were Benedictine roses grafted on the thorns of St. Francis at Rome.

CHAPTER XII

St. Benedict at Vicovaro

MEANWHILE the years of adolescence had passed, and the faithful, who knew nothing of St. Benedict except his divine wisdom united to great holiness, continued to stream to Subiaco in ever increasing numbers. He must have been about thirty years old at this time, and Gregory with his deacon grasps the occasion to offer some pertinent considerations on the maturity of age that is demanded for the government of souls.

If Cyrilla still remained at Enfide, perhaps she also enjoyed making the journey of five miles which separated her from the Sacro Speco in order to see again him whom she loved as her own son. But if Cyrilla no longer was there, the good inhabitants of Enfide remained, and no one could forbid them to visit their former guest from time to time. Many people of the villages approached the anchorite in order to hear him preach. In his varied audiences some persons, inspired by his words and example, resolved to abandon the world forthwith and to consecrate themselves to the service of God as monks.

About this time the abbot of the monastery of Vicovaro died, and there was question of finding a successor. The extensive building of the ancient monastery situated on the left bank of the Anio about thirty miles from Rome still exists under the name of St. Cosimatus. It was transformed several times and finally converted into a Franciscan convent. No special interest attaches to it except the primitive refectory hollowed out of the mountainside with the central table hewn out of the living rock. Mabillon and Montfaucon visited it in the seventeenth century and described its condition in their *Iter Italicum.*

The edifice is set on the summit of a rock (about 1,000 feet high), whose steep sides make the climb difficult. At the foot of the hill, on the one side, a torrent roars, while the Anio runs on the other side. It gives the impression of being an eagle's nest and a hideout of assassins.

Unfortunately, about the year 500, this monastery did not spread abroad the good odor of virtue. The long episcopate of Candidus of Tivoli, which extended from 465 into the early part of the sixth century, sufficiently explains the relaxation of monastic discipline at Vicovaro. The aged and ailing bishop left things to take their course so long as the sickness did not degenerate into a canker. The new bishop, Catelus or Generosus, wished indeed to remedy affairs, but he came too late.

The monks themselves agreed that a reform was called for. But each one was convinced that it ought rather be applied to the others than to himself. To re-establish their reputation with the people, they decided to elect as abbot the saintly anchorite of Subiaco, whose virtue and wisdom was on everyone's tongue.

One day St. Benedict remarked a group of monks ascending to the cave from the valley of the Anio. After they had introduced themselves, they declared they were a delegation of the community of Vicovaro, come to ask him to be their abbot. There was something strange about the choice. Apart from the comparative youth of the elect, there was something worse, namely, that he was aware by reputation of the kind of monks the sackcloth cowls covered. Hence he immediately replied with a refusal. But when the delegation insisted on knowing at least his reasons, he explained to them quite clearly and in detail that his ideals did not at all accord with their loose manner of living, which was known to all. He would not be agreeable to them; let them remain good friends, but at a distance.

The monks of Vicovaro, however, in order not to return home without results and thus be a laughingstock among the folk, continued to insist, promising miracles of holiness. St. Benedict, still young and inexperienced in the trickeries of old foxes, who indeed may change their skins but not their wiles, finally allowed himself to be persuaded by their honeyed words.

We must also hold that the authority of the bishop of Tivoli [1] was invoked to ratify the choice and to confer the blessing together with the insignia of office on the new abbot. At the time of St. Gregory this practice had entered into the juridical custom of the Church. "When, therefore, Our letters have been received, let our brother-bishop Victor be invited. And he shall celebrate Mass there and ordain the aforesaid Domitius abbot." [2] On the newly-elected were conferred the insignia of his hierarchical position, the pastoral staff and the prelatial shoes, as the *Penitentiary* of Theodore of Canterbury informs us.[3]

So, after St. Benedict had recommended to God his first visitors from among the shepherds and the inhabitants of the neighborhood, he took his cowl and staff, and in company with the monks of Vicovaro he went to govern that monastery.

Needless to say, hardly had he assumed the reins of government, when the monks became aware of his firm hand. Before, with the abbot dead, each one had gone his own way; but now, with the new abbot, they had to toe the mark in accord with the norms of the rule; otherwise there was penance, excommunication, imprisonment. At that time both canonical and civil legislation granted great power to abbots and bishops to maintain discipline in the monasteries. From the very beginning there was disillusionment at Vicovaro. "What? Is this the saint whose name is on everyone's lips? Where is his Christian charity? Where is the discretion that should mark the government of every good superior? Is this the man in whom the bishop placed so much confidence?" There followed murmurings, and these finally degenerated into open revolt against this simpleton of an abbot, who took it upon himself to lay down laws for them, who were already veterans in the monastic life.

In the cloister and in the vicinity of the monastery small knots of monks often gathered. What were they doing? It can easily be imag-

[1] In the series of the bishops of Tivoli, we find a Candidus, who occupied the see from 465 to 502. After him Gams mentions Catelus, but with a question mark; the name may also be Candidus. Hence we do not know the name of the bishop who promoted St. Benedict to the abbatial throne of Vicovaro (cf. F. Lanzoni, *Le diocesi d'Italia*, I, 138 f.).
[2] Bk. XI, no. 48.
[3] "*Pedules cum baculo*" (Mabillon, *op. cit.*, I, 231).

ined. They were murmuring against the young abbot. The older foxes upbraided the younger: "Now you have him; see what you can do with him. We told you, did we not, that we ought to settle our own affairs and that we ought never to choose as abbot one who, besides not belonging to our monastery, is too young and entirely inexperienced in the monastic life."

St. Benedict heard this angry buzzing of the wasps, but he let them be. As far as he was concerned, he went his way, turning neither to right nor left, and when necessary he was not sparing in punishments, feeling himself supported by the jurisprudence then in force.[4] Seeing that they could look for no support from the bishop, the disaffected monks reached a point of exasperation where even the prospect of a crime no longer caused any horror. With this unfortunate abbot at their head, there simply was no hope. Hence they decided to get rid of him by poison. Who would know it? A splendid funeral, a lugubrious announcement of his death sent to the bishop of Tivoli, and then a new and a more provident election of a successor. To use violence to kill him; that might be dangerous. But to poison him was a simple affair.

Even till this day the people of the mountains know how to produce liquors of *Cent'Erbe*, stomach preparations and other elixirs, using the juice of herbs and of flowers of those high regions.

Without recalling the example of a friend of St. Benedict, Sabinus of Canosa, whose own archdeacon served him poisoned wine at table, we may observe that history offers many parallels. Ten centuries after the Patriarch, at Milan other religious, the Humiliati, will repeat the act of their predecessors of Vicovaro; to rid themselves of St. Charles, the archbishop and reformer of the Order, they will pay a deacon to shoot him.

The coup prepared by the monks of Vicovaro was more astutely laid. The foxes in this case were more experienced. At that time the Oriental art of distilling poisons from herbs was widespread among the slaves and the lower class of society, and such it remained throughout the Middle Ages. They could unfeather a hen without its letting out a sound; that is to say, they could send some poor devil to the next world without his even suspecting the cause of his illness. It was

---

[4] Greg., *Epist.*, Bk. X, nos. 22 f.

agreed among the monks to mix the death-dealing poison into St. Benedict's cup of wine.

Now the plot was laid. While the monks, seated at table with the Abbot, appeared to listen to the spiritual reading with great recollection, the keeper of the cellar appeared on the threshold with the tray on which were the glass *heminae* full of wine for the community. One was apportioned to each monk. On that day, restrained by a remaining bit of the sense of shame, the monk stopped a short distance from the Abbot, while according to custom he asked the blessing over the glasses: "*Jube, domne, benedicere.*"

St. Gregory makes special mention of the fact that the poisoned vessel was kept at some distance.[5] Benedict lifted his hand to give the blessing; but, *mirabile dictu,* as if the sacred words were so many stones thrown against the glass, it broke into bits, spilling the poison over the very hands and clothes of the one who had prepared it. Nothing more was needed to make the Abbot understand that the cup certainly had contained a fatal potion from the moment it could not resist the blessed sign of life.

He rose immediately from the table,[6] and ordered all to assemble in the chapter room. When they were all together, St. Benedict, calm and quiet, as if that attempt on his life did not concern him, accused them all of murder: "God forgive you, my brothers; what did you wish to do to me? Did I not tell you at the very beginning that my ways would not agree with yours? Go, get yourselves an abbot according to your taste, because from this moment on I have finished with you."

The monks, confused and fearful, calling to mind also the juridical effects of their attempted crime, slunk away, and St. Benedict, in order not to remain an instant longer among these outlaws who were capable of anything, lifted his eyes to God who had taken care of him, and then took the road to Tivoli to give back to the bishop the staff which had been handed him so shortly before. After giving an account of his mission, the saint received the blessing of the bishop and returned to his former place of retirement at Subiaco.

The memory of Vicovaro never passed from his mind. We find some

---

[5] "*Vas quod longius tenebatur.*"
[6] "*Illico surrexit et vultu placido, mente tranquilla.*"

veiled references to it in the Rule, particularly when he writes that the fool has need of stripes and punishment, because he will not be corrected with words (chap. 2). Here Gregory the Great introduces a juridical observation into the text, which, however, he places on the lips of his interlocutor, Peter the Deacon. Was it licit for St. Benedict to abandon the flock of which he had been appointed the legitimate abbot? The axiom says: *"Semel abbas, semper abbas."* The Pontiff replies by observing that the pastoral obligation remains as long as, even in the midst of the disaffected, one simple poor soul wishes to profit by it.

If, however, the efforts of the pastor prove totally useless and are repulsed universally, rather than waste his time it behooves him to pass on to a less sterile field. As a matter of fact, concludes the biographer, Benedict resuscitated many more souls spiritually elsewhere than he could have tamed with all the sanctions of the rule at Vicovaro.

But the chapter of the *Regula monasteriorum* that most clearly reflects the irregular condition of a monastery like that of St. Cosimatus at Vicovaro is the sixty-fourth: *"De ordinando abbate."* There the Patriarch envisages the case where an entire community of degenerate monks would choose an abbot willing to connive at their vices. In such a case, the saint rules, let the Christians of the vicinity inform the bishop of the place or bring the matter to the regional chapter of all the abbots, and thus prevent the design of the evil men from prevailing. But the one who has the authority to act or to put in his veto is always the bishop of the place.[7] So, too, it must have happened in the case of Vicovaro.

---

[7] *"In notitia episcopi ad cuius diocesim pertinet locus ipse."*

CHAPTER XIII

Beginnings of the Benedictine Institute

THE months of the stay at Vicovaro proved difficult for the inexperienced anchorite of Subiaco. The experiment had been unsuccessful, and now the saint felt the need of burying himself anew in the solitude to rid himself by a spiritual bath of all the filth in which he was constrained to walk during his sojourn there. Hence he returned to his beloved cave and again sought the company of God. This is St. Gregory's expression: *"Ad locum dilectae solitudinis rediit,"* just as centuries later Abbot Gerson would say in the *Imitation of Christ: "Cella continuata dulcescit."*

But very little occasion was granted him to re-enter into the divine light and to enjoy tranquillity; because very soon the crowds returned, and finally his disciples became so numerous that, in order not to have them all together, he sent them out like swarms from a beehive, until there were twelve monasteries nestling among the rocks of the mountains. The biographer, whose intention is to write simply for edification, without taking into account historical and juridical exigencies, is content to delineate in a few brief words the birth of one of the most powerful institutions in the Catholic Church, Benedictine monachism. We, however, cannot be satisfied with so little, and we must pause to offer at least a comment on St. Gregory's words.

This second sojourn of Benedict the anchorite in the Speco was evidently rather prolonged, if in the meantime he worked all the miracles that produced a continuous affluence of the faithful to

Subiaco: "While in the solitude he was growing in virtue and becoming known for his miracles" (chap. 3).

Some came, asked a blessing, a counsel, a word of encouragement, and then departed. But many others desired to remain near the wonder-worker. Thus finally the problem arose of organizing all these aspirants to the religious life.

Before long more than 150 monks desirous of serving God were gathered about St. Benedict. The set-up of this first group of cenobites recalls to mind Anthony, Pachomius, and Theodore the archcenobites whose disciples in Egypt and Palestine began to build their huts around those of their masters. From the organization of such contiguous cells or huts the Oriental *laurae* and monasteries arose. St. Gregory assures us that from the very beginning there were many novices: "A great number of men left the world and hastened to become his disciples."

As a consequence the saint's reputation soon spread throughout the Simbruini region, and naturally the ecclesiastical authorities had to interest themselves. As long as St. Benedict remained an unknown anchorite, he could pass unnoticed by the ecclesiastical hierarchy. But by now he has been an abbot almost at the door of the episcopal palace of Tivoli; he has many disciples; already he is organizing monasteries. There is need of several oratories with priests attached to them. Hence the time has come to interpose the episcopal authority in order to give a canonical status to the new institute.

In this connection we may not forget a canon of the Council of Chalcedon: "It is decreed that no one may ever build or constitute a monastery or an oratory without permission of the local bishop." [1]

Thanks to the epistolaries of Gelasius I and St. Gregory, we know how monastic foundations were made in those centuries. In the metropolitan province of the pope, not even diocesan bishops could proceed to the erection of a religious house, for either male or female religious, without the special permission of the Roman Pontiff. In like manner he authorized his suffragans to consecrate monastic chapels; it was he who approved abbatial elections and caused investiture to be granted to the persons so elected and nominated in the Lateran. Documents XXVI and XXVII of the *Liber diurnus* preserve the relevant papal

[1] *PL*, LVI, 539.

formularies: "Of Dedicating an Oratory within a Monastery" and "Of Depositing Relics within a Monastery."

In the metropolitan province of the Roman Pontiff simple bishops could in no way presume to exercise such rights. The abbot had to have recourse directly to the pope, who then by a special decree would order the bishop to go to the new oratory and proceed to its consecration.[2]

We do not know on whom the territory of Subiaco depended ecclesiastically, whether on the episcopal see of Tivoli or on that of Trebbia Augusta at the mouth of the Anio. It is certain that there were already parishes in the vicinity; because, apart from the good pastors of Enfide and Monte Porcaro, St. Gregory tells us of the priest Florence, the pastor of the church of St. Lawrence, situated close to the monastery of Subiaco, but on the other side of the lake.

This sanctuary of St. Lawrence—not only the oldest, but also the *ecclesia matrix* of Subiaco—is situated on the highest point of the left bank of the Anio, opposite the present-day city of Subiaco. I say "present-day city" advisedly, because the ancient city of Subiaco was situated on the plateau which extends to the south of St. Lawrence. Today all that remains is a simple chapel, remodeled in the twelfth century, but showing traces of an earlier period. The church is said to have been erected by the patrician Narses and to have been dedicated August 3, 369. The document is spurious or interpolated; but in the tenth century it was regarded as genuine.

Toward the beginning of the twelfth century the right of baptizing was still reserved exclusively to the church of St. Lawrence, notwithstanding the fact that for several centuries already Subiaco had moved a good half-mile away to the right bank of the river. In the same century the processional of the Rogation Days ordained that the *litania maior* of April 25 be made at St. Lawrence's. It seems well established, therefore, that Florence, "the priest of the neighboring church," was precisely the pastor of St. Lawrence.

Since, according to St. Gregory, the postulants who came to place themselves under the spiritual discipline of the holy Patriarch were numerous, he was obliged, after a time, to give some thought to their

---

[2] "Quatenus ad praedictum locum . . . accedas, veneranda solemnia dedicationis impendens."

housing. Instead of gathering the monks into one vast monastery in imitation of Pachomius, Benedict, who was still under the influence of the example of St. Anthony, chose a middle course: he divided the monks into various deaneries and assigned each group to a monastery with an abbot at its head.

Tradition allowed two abbots to rule the same monastery simultaneously. In the life of St. Fulgentius mention is made of the monastery of Iuncense in Africa, "where two outstanding priests exercised the office of abbot." [3] This practice was suppressed by canon 12 of the Council of Chalons in 644: "That there be not two abbots in the same monastery." [4]

These first twelve monasteries, perched on the mountains or set up in the deserted halls of Nero's palace, recalled quite exactly the habitations of the cenobites described by Cassian and St. Jerome in Egypt and Palestine. It seems that at Subiaco the monastic concepts of St. Basil found less favor with St. Benedict. The tradition of Subiaco claims to know at least the name and the location of these twelve monasteries; of some of them very few traces remain at the present day. Mirtius, when collecting the local traditions and the various documents of the archives, drew up the following list: [5]

   1. SS. Cosmas and Damian, St. Scholastica;

   2. The Holy Angel *post lacum,* near the present-day city of Subiaco;

   3. St. Mary Primorana, now Blessed Lawrence Loricatus;

   4. St. Jerome, one of the three on the mountain;

   5. St. Donatus;

   6. St. John the Baptist, on the mountain;

[3] Mabillon, *Annales O.S.B.,* I, 37.

[4] *Op. cit.,* p. 538.

[5] In the early Christian ages titles of churches were mostly derived from the relics of the saint preserved in the altars. In this way the sanctuary took the place of the primitive *"cella memoriae"* of the martyr. As far as the traditional titularies of the twelve oratories erected by St. Benedict are concerned, we must perhaps exclude St. Jerome, whose liturgical cult is of a considerably later period. The chapels of SS. Cosmas and Damian, of St. Clement, and of the Holy Angel correspond to ancient Roman churches of the same names. The relics of the archangel were represented at that time by the altar cloth of the celebrated basilica of St. Michael on the Via Salaria, whose feast was celebrated on September 29. St. Victorinus is the celebrated regional martyr of Amiternum. The cult of St. Blase, however, appears to have begun in Italy somewhat later.

7. St. Clement, on the left bank of the lake;
8. St. Blase, above the Sacro Speco;
9. St. Michael, below the Sacro Speco;
10. St. Victorinus, at the foot of Monte Porcaro;
11. Eternal Life, near Jenne, farther down;
12. St. Andrew of Rocca di Botte, in the valley of the Turano.

Each monastery had its own chapel [6] consecrated, in all probability, by the bishop of Tivoli, and each one was governed by a superior with the title of abbot. St. Benedict, as happened at Tabenna under St. Pachomius, reserved to himself the supreme government of this kind of monastic congregation; at the same time, residing at St. Clement's, he supervised the immediate training of his novices. This last particular is significant.

We have not sufficient data at hand to pronounce on the tradition of Subiaco, which even today claims to be able to indicate the name and place of each of the twelve monasteries. St. Gregory simply asserts that they were situated "round about" ("circumquaque") and that three of them stood on the mountain ("tria sursum in montibus erant"). In fact they correspond to the three monasteries of St. Mary, St. John, and St. Jerome. If their names indeed go back to St. Benedict's time, then great significance must be attached to them. St Jerome was the great promoter of the monastic life in Rome and later in Palestine. St. John the Baptist in the desert about the Jordan represents one of the great precursors of the monastic life; later on St. Benedict dedicated a chapel to him at Monte Cassino. The Blessed Virgin Mary necessarily called forth a special devotion in this son of Nursia, who always remembered the small but beautiful Sancta Maria Argentea.

This flowering out of monasteries and oratories must quite naturally have required the confirmation of Rome. We know, indeed, that about that time Gelasius I reminded the bishops of Lucania that they

[6] The consecration of these monastic oratories necessarily required the intervention of the bishop, and possibly also the authorization of the pope. We possess a letter of Gregory the Great to the subdeacon Peter regarding the consecration of the oratory of St. Mary in the monastery of Abbot Marinianus. Since the monastery is poverty-stricken, the Pope desires to contribute to the celebration, so that the poor may also enjoy it. Hence he orders his agent to furnish the following supplies for the day: in auro solidos decem, vini amphoras XXX, agnos CC, olei dorcas II, berbices XII, gallinas C (Epist., Bk. I, no. 56).

should not dare to dedicate chapels without receiving from the Holy See a decree authorizing them to do so.[1]

The Patriarch resided with his young monks within the abandoned halls of Nero's villa, which rose near the lake. Perhaps he chose this spot because it was most centrally located and most suitable for the youths. As a matter of fact, among the candidates to the monastic life were some boys and young men, as, for example, Maur and Placid, whom the parents themselves accompanied from Rome to offer to St. Benedict at Subiaco. While the Greek government seemed intent only on sending the unfortunate Italians to the devil, these good Roman patricians wanted at least that their children be freed from the inferno of the Capital and consequently brought them into the wilderness of the Simbruini, so that the saint might teach them belles-lettres and educate them to the service of a better and more permanent Sovereign. Was there also a hidden idea to withdraw them thus from the obligations of government positions? It must be understood that the Lateran favored Benedict's undertaking.

The frequenting of Subiaco on the part of the Roman nobility more or less coincides with another episode that created a great stir in the city. In the summer of 513, under a grave accusation of political crime, Bishop St. Caesarius of Arles was obliged to appear before Theodoric at Ravenna. His excellent defense of himself and especially his eminent virtues so succeeded in impressing the court that Theodoric, as if to make amends for the hardships of this undesired journey, took him back into his favor and gave him a large silver tray as a souvenir.

On the following day Caesarius had this precious tray sold in the Forum and with the proceeds redeemed a certain number of prisoners. That was his way. When news of these events reached Rome, Pope Symmacus also manifested a desire to see Caesarius, who then had to undertake a pilgrimage to the Eternal City.

Late in the fall of 513 the saintly metropolitan of Arles entered Rome, preceded by his reputation as an apostolic man and a propagator of monastic life. His biographer attests that during his sojourn in the city he exercised a profound influence on the Roman nobility:

[1] *"Basilicas noviter institutas, non petitis ex more raeceptionibus, dedicare non audeant"* (Gelas. I, *Epist. ad Episc. Lucaniae*, no. 6).

"After this, upon his arrival in Rome, he was first presented to Pope Symmacus and then to the senators. All gave thanks to God and to the King. . . . Having seen the apostolic man . . . they strove to outdo one another in loving and respecting him."

Symmacus in particular desired to give a manifest sign of his admiration; he approved the monastic foundations of Caesarius, granted him the use of the pallium, and allowed his deacons to wear the dalmatic which the Roman deacons wore.[8]

Certainly it is not going too far to suppose that among the admirers of St. Caesarius during the winter of 513–514 were precisely those same "nobles of the city of Rome" who had established relations with St. Benedict at Subiaco. This supposition helps to explain the great influence which the monastic rule of the metropolitan of Arles exercised on the immortal code of the Patriarch of Cassino.

Among the members of the Roman nobility who showed the greatest interest in monachism must be mentioned Rusticana, Proba, and Galla, the daughters of the Consul Symmacus. Rusticana married Severin Boethius; the virgin Proba carried on a correspondence with Abbot Eugippius of Lucullanum, with Dionysius Exiguus, with the deacons Paschasius and Ferrandus, and with St. Fulgentius of Ruspa. Almost the only name missing from the list is that of the Abbot of Cassino. Further, the excerpts from the works of St. Augustine gathered by Eugippius are dedicated precisely to the virgin Proba. We shall return to them later.

Galla, after her husband died, founded a monastery for women near St. Peter's, and there she died a holy death. Procopius relates that when Totila occupied Rome in 546, Rusticana, the widow of Boethius, was brought to him under the accusation of having destroyed the statue of Theodoric in revenge for the death of her husband. Totila, under the influence of the prophecy of St. Benedict, manifested a generous spirit toward her.

It is beyond dispute that at Subiaco Benedict was organizing something entirely new in Italian monachism, something that preceded by at least nine centuries the powerfully centralized organizations of present-day religious orders and congregations: a number of abbots

---

[8] *Acta sanctorum*, August, VI, 71.

dependent upon a common superior general, with a common school for the formation of the novices. Let us become acquainted at least with one or the other of these youths.

We know that Placid [9] came from a noble family, because his father Tertullus is designated as a "patrician." Such a name, rather than indicating a title of office, may simply point to nobility of parentage or royal privilege. In the *Variarum* of Cassiodorus occur various formularies of the chancery for the conferring of such honors.[10] First comes a panegyric on the one to be honored, on the dignity of the patrician, and then with pedantic eloquence the insignia and garb are described.

I wish to observe, incidentally, that it must have taken a good dose of courage on the part of the patrician Tertullus to withdraw his little son Placid from the service of the Gothic state to offer him to Christ instead. It may be mentioned that on one occasion the court of Ravenna sent a document, drawn up by Cassiodorus himself, no less, to a certain nobleman of Rome, *"illustri Magnitudini tuae,"* granting him permission to leave the Capital for not longer than four months.[11] So low had civil liberties fallen.

Certain historians of the past have spilled much ink trying to discover or to establish some connection between Tertullus and the Anicii, and then a blood relationship which supposedly existed between St. Benedict and the parents of the boy Placid. They have done the same thing with regard to the family of Eutychius, whose origins they attempted to trace to the Gens Iulia. Unfortunately the documents on which such castles of nobility are built inspire little confidence; consequently I shall not consider them at all in this place.

[9] St. Gregory calls him *"monachus,"* though at the same time he states that "he was as yet a mere child."

To understand the canonical condition of these boy-monks, we must keep in mind a canon of the Council of Trullo: "He who wishes to enter upon the monastic life must be at least ten years of age; this matter is left to the investigation of the superior" (Mansi, XI, 935). A canon of the Second Council of Toledo in 539 sets down that children who had been offered or tonsured in the episcopal schools, were free at the age of eighteen to choose between the monastic life and marriage (Mabillon, *op. cit.*, I, 75). As is clear from Gregory's narrative, Placid had not yet been tonsured.

[10] *"Patricius"* was the senatorial title given to Odoacer as the head of the government and was distinguished from the military title of *"imperator"* (cf. Cassiod., *Var.* I, Ep. 3).

[11] *Var.*, Bk. III, no. 21.

We know nothing of St. Maur except that, having received the education that corresponded to his age and his social position, he was soon in a position to render the master substantial assistance in the school established at St. Clement's. Seeing him endowed with such eminent qualities above his companions, St. Benedict chose him as his helper or second in command. Only very extraordinary gifts could justify such a choice on the part of the master.

St. Gregory applies the most attractive titles to the young man.[12] Unfortunately, Odo's Acts of St. Maur are not worthy of credence, since in that strange document all verifiable data are false. Ruinart's apologia of them [13] is an able effort, but not convincing, because not all the documents he cites are genuine. It seems certain that in the ninth century St. Maur's mission to France was generally admitted by the authors; but to get back to the sixth century constitutes a leap into the dark.

One author observes that when St. Benedict departed from Subiaco, he left St. Maur behind to succeed him in the government of the monasteries. But St. Gregory, in enumerating the sources of his biographical information, although he speaks of the immediate successors of the Patriarch at Monte Cassino and even of the aged Honoratus of Subiaco, never again mentions St. Maur.

An ancient Cassinese tradition, which perhaps is independent of the Acts of St. Maur, speaks of a lame man cured by the saint: "At the foot of the tower outside the gate St. Maur healed a lame man." Unless St. Maur died before his master, it certainly seems strange that, after the demise of the Patriarch, he would not assume the position which he had occupied from his early years.[14] But apparently the hypothesis of the pre-decease of St. Maur must be excluded, because St. Gregory alluded to the bright youthful hopes that were realized.

The tradition regarding St. Maur's mission to France, even under

12 *Bonae spei soboles, Magistri adiutor, Dei famulus*, etc.; and Pope Zachary translates: τῆς καλῆς ἐλπίδος τὰ τέκνα; συμεργὸς τοῦ διδασκάλου; τῷ δούλῳ τοῦ Θεοῦ; τουτῶν θεομιμητῶν ταπεινολογίαν, and so on. By reading between the lines one feels that the two popes refer to a story of St. Maur that was commonly known, which confirmed the brilliant expectation of his years of adolescence. Sad to say, their veiled allusions are not supported by any authentic document.

13 Cf. *Acta SS. O.S.B.*, 1, 582 f.

14 "*Magistri sui coepit adiutor existere.*"

the auspices of the Holy See, would very well account for his absence from the later story of St. Benedict, and would better explain the rapid diffusion of the *Regula monasteriorum* in France in the first two decades of the seventh century. Gregory of Tours never mentions St. Maur; but it is also true that he does not make the slightest reference to the Rule of St. Benedict, which certainly was spreading like wildfire in France during those years.

The medieval chroniclers of Subiaco occupied themselves with a juridical question, and by means of apocryphal documents tried to prove that the most ancient part of the patrimony of the abbey came to St. Benedict by way of donation from St. Gregory's family. These documents, as I have said, are spurious; nevertheless there must be some foundation in truth. Otherwise we have difficulty in explaining how the saint was able to obtain possession so easily of a considerable portion of Nero's villa.

According to the prevailing laws, this building, probably government property, abandoned by the state and falling into ruins, had to be ceded by King Theodoric for religious purposes.[15] Formularies for similar donations occur several times in the Epistolary of Cassiodorus.

Interested perhaps in the grant were the bishop of Tivoli and the same representatives of the Roman nobility whom Gregory mentions in connection with St. Benedict: "At that time several noble and pious men from Rome also came to visit him in the solitude and entrusted their sons to him and to almighty God for the purpose of receiving a religious education." That he might establish a kind of seminary for these young candidates for the monastic life, it was necessary for the holy Patriarch to move from the cave he had hitherto inhabited to a more commodious structure. Nothing could better serve his purpose than the deserted villa of Nero that was spread out below his cave. Such schools were becoming more common, not only in connection with cathedrals, but also in monasteries. At the beginning of the

---

[15] The story of Hadrian's villa at Tivoli runs quite parallel to that of Nero's at Subiaco. Ten years, 125 to 135, were required to construct it. Under Constantine the villa was partially despoiled of its wonderful sculptures, which were transported to Constantinople. During the barbarian invasions it was sacked several times, and finally was buried under its own ruins.

seventh century, in the monastery of Emerita, under Abbot Renovatus, lived "a group of boys, who under the discipline of teachers devoted themselves to the study of letters." [16]

St. Gregory is extremely concise. But we are more exigent and should like to know at least under whose pressure or influence Benedict made the change from the eremitical to the cenobitic life, notwithstanding his unfortunate experience at Vicovaro. It is easily understood that this change must have been requested by the authorities, either religious, as the bishop of Tivoli, or purely political, as those members of the Roman patriciate who entrusted the education of their sons to him. His reputation had reached even to Rome, to the governing class.[17]

Also Hormisdas, who succeeded Symmacus on the throne of St. Peter, seemed convinced that it was necessary to codify the diffuse monastic legislation for the purpose of subjecting the monasteries to one and the same discipline under the government of the metropolitan, the bishop, or even the Roman Pontiff. Caesarius of Arles had already succeeded in prescribing a single rule for all the monasteries of his metropolitan province. He had likewise written a rule for women, and the Pope had approved these endeavors. The papal document expresses the pleasure of Hormisdas for the work carried out by Caesarius and for the glory which he conferred on his episcopal city, already so noteworthy for its many ecclesiastics and numerous monasteries.[18]

Unfortunately, almost contemporary with the misadventure of Vicovaro, a deputation of Scythian monks arrived at Rome, led by a certain Leontius, who petitioned Hormisdas to approve a peculiar theological thesis of theirs: "One of the Trinity was crucified."

Since the Pope did not show much interest in the equivocal Byzantine abstrusity which would be directed against the Nestorians, the Oriental monks felt offended, plastered challenges on the walls of

---

[16] Mabillon, op. cit., I, 64.

[17] Among the members of the Roman patriciate who were devoted to a life of religion and piety and who had also given a warm reception to St. Caesarius, must be mentioned, besides Tertullus and Equitius, also that Theodore to whom Fulgentius of Ruspa sent his letter, "De conversione a saeculo." Theodore had been consul in 505 (Letter V; Patr. lat., LXV, 348–352).

It may also be recalled that St. Caesarius miraculously healed the patrician Liberius, who had been wounded by the Goths. This Liberius in his turn became the founder of the monastery of St. Sebastian at Alatri, of which Servandus was made abbot.

[18] PL, LXVIII, 1285.

the city in order to stir up the people against Hormisdas, and directly accused him of heresy.

These poor enthusiasts, after remaining for more than a year, finally left Rome. But Hormisdas had received such an unfavorable impression that he wrote to Possessor, an African bishop: "There are monks who come to us, not indeed to learn, but to discuss. . . . They are monks only because they wear the habit; they are not at all acquainted with the basic virtues of the monk, humility and obedience." When St. Benedict in his Rule writes of monks whose "tonsure marks them as liars before God" and declares that he wishes to construct the cenobitic edifice on the foundations of humility and obedience, we seem almost to hear an echo of Pope Hormisdas' words.

The judgment of Hormisdas and Benedict on this type of monachism seems to have become common and almost official in the Eternal City. We have an instance of it in the so-called Leonine Sacramentary, which contains several liturgical compositions directed against the false monks. "They think that no one sees them . . . with honeyed words they deceive the credulous . . . ; in order to give a show of learning they run through the volumes of the Scriptures, which, however, condemn their works." [19]

"May the Lord grant us the light to distinguish the true from the false brethren." The latter "cause annoyance by their begging" and they create for themselves a liturgy according to their own likes. They profess rigorism and condemn the Christian liberty of Catholics; they foster relations with widowed and married matrons to abuse their generosity; they care little for personal cleanliness and are filthy; they sell bones of the dead baptized by them as saints and martyrs of the East.[20]

Such an attitude against monachism in general persisted for a long time in the official circles of the Papal Curia; and we find traces of it even after the time of Gregory the Great. Thus it is easily explained why the popes of this period felt the ever-increasing need of disciplining monastic life in the West on the basis of a common rule promulgated by the supreme authority of the Apostolic See. This situation must be well kept in mind in order to understand the signif-

[19] *PL*, LV, 65.
[20] *Ibid.*, 74 f.

icance of the new monastery of St. Pancratius erected about this time near the sacristy of the Lateran basilica, which Valentinian governed for many years as abbot.

Similarly in Gaul the conviction was growing that to prevent the decadence of monastic life, it was expedient that the Holy See prescribe a common rule. In this sense spoke the Fathers gathered in the sanctuary of St. Maurice at Agaunum about the year 520 to organize this new foundation of King St. Sigismund. They discussed the question: "To whom and to what rule ought the monks to be subject? And they said: 'It seems best to us that they show gratitude to the king; but for their direction and doctrine they shall look to the Apostolic See.'" [21] A report of this council must have been sent to Pope Hormisdas. We shall see later what attitude Rome took toward this undertaking.

The request of the monks of Agaunum has a curious parallel in the Acts of St. Maur, which relate the saint's visit to the monastery of St. Maurice. The story is generally rejected by historians, who, however, are unable to discover its source or origin.

Meanwhile in Italy the relations between the Goths and the Romans grew worse. True, St. Benedict at Subiaco received Goths among his novices; but it must be kept in mind that since 523 a latent war was going on between King Theodoric and the basileus of the East. The King of the Goths began to carry out reprisals against Emperor Justin in Italy. At Verona, for instance, he destroyed the chapel of St. Stephen; furthermore, he promulgated a law forbidding Romans to carry arms; he tried the consul Albinus; he executed Severin Boethius and Symmacus, chiefs of the Senate, because they had dared to defend innocent victims. To top it all, in 525 he ordered Pope John I to Ravenna and forced him to go to Constantinople to plead the cause of the Arian Goths, in order that their confiscated churches might be returned to them.

Accompanying the Pope were several bishops, among them Ecclesius of Ravenna and Sabinus of Canosa. Since the legation did not produce the expected results, Theodoric had John I, upon his return to Ravenna, thrown into prison, where he suffered want and hunger. After a time the Pope fell a victim to the maltreatment, and later his

[21] *Gall. Christ.,* IV, 12.

corpse was brought to the Vatican. The Romans manifested a high degree of bravery when they wrote on his tomb in St. Peter's that the high priest of Christ had fallen with honor.

There was talk of a general persecution against all Catholics; on a determined day all their churches were to be seized. But precisely the opposite came to pass, for on the very day appointed Theodoric died (August 30, 526).

Owing to Cassiodorus' authority in the court of Ravenna, Felix IV, a saintly man, great-uncle of Gregory the Great, member of a family in which Christian virtue added great splendor to the ancient nobility of the house, became successor to the deceased Pontiff. The choice was excellent. The senatorial party offered no objection to this selection of the government, and thus good relations were re-established.

What the condition of the Church was under the Goths is clear from a decree of King Athalaric, which deplores the fact that frequently the lay power disturbs the liberty of ecclesiastical tribunals. Another ordinance of the Roman Senate of about 531 is also significant; by this document members of the assembly were forbidden to spend money for the purpose of instigating intrigues in the election of the Roman Pontiff.

When later Felix IV appointed his own successor, he declared in the relevant document that he was induced to take this step because of the great expense the Roman Church would otherwise have to bear. On such occasions it would have to satisfy especially the cupidity of the courts of Ravenna and Byzantium, in order thus to gain the adherence of the powerful and of the common people. In the light of such facts we can more easily judge the conduct of the monks of Vicovaro, and even of the priest Florence.

As if the Gothic war were not enough, the monks also did their bit to cause trouble to the pope and to the bishops. After the Scythian monks, it was now the turn of the Acemites of Constantinople, who espoused their cause by defending Trinitarian errors. They were dubbed Acemites or Insomniacs, because neither by day nor by night was the choir of their church quiet. As at Agaunum at the tomb of St. Maurice, so in their monastery on the Bosphorus groups of cenobites in unbroken succession kept up the psalmody.

This, however, did not prevent these servants of God outside the choir from being as hardheaded as granite, willing to yield neither to theological arguments nor to the authority of the bishops. Finally John II condemned them in a synod held in 534.

Fortunately the noise of this whirlpool of theological and political arguments and strife did not reach the quiet valley of the Anio, where in the meanwhile St. Benedict was concerned about developing his own institute. No doubt, the social conditions of the time contributed to the increase of vocations. Many, sick of the world and disgusted with the evil turn of political affairs, stole away from the city and took the road to the cloister.

The juridical condition of the monastic congregation of Subiaco is so novel and exceptional that it calls for some study in the light of both the civil and the ecclesiastical law of the time. Novella 133 of Justinian already speaks of abbots general, who were obliged annually to visit the monasteries subject to them. In the copious material furnished by Gregory, we find a single example of this new juridical figure. Besides St. Benedict, there is that of Abbot Equitius, "of the province of Valeria," who in that same region was the superior of many monasteries, not only of monks, but also of nuns.

St. Gregory supplies this twofold reason for his position: his outstanding sanctity and his obedience to the Roman Pontiff.[22] This second circumstance is particularly significant. Despite the fact that the saint dwells in the region of the Abruzzi and carries on his activity there, he depends directly on the Roman Pontiff and not on various local ordinaries. Consequently the competent tribunal for him is not that of the diocesan bishops but of the Roman Curia.

After the Lombard invasion of Italy, St. Gregory was occasionally forced to confide the government of a second and even a third monastery to the same abbot.[23] These unions, however, were always regarded as something exceptional and made by express pontifical mandate, never by private authority. If, then, St. Benedict at Subiaco was able to retain the supreme government of twelve monasteries, each one presided over by its own abbot, one must admit that, in accord with the authority of local bishops, as also in the case of Equitius, a special decree was required on the part of the Roman Pontiff.

[22] *Dial.*, Bk. I, chap. 4.
[23] Cf. *Epist.*, Bk. X, no. 61; Bk. XII, no. 72; Bk. XIII, no. 2.

Contrary to the common law, the authority of this kind of abbot general over his monasteries was complete; at the end, before his departure for Casinum, Benedict reorganized all his communities, changed their superiors, increased the number of cenobites, and gave orders with regard to disciplinary matters in his absence. No one raised the slightest objection. This privileged juridical situation of St. Benedict at Subiaco cannot be explained in Italy except by recourse to a special mandate of the Roman Pontiff. On the contrary supposition, certainly some would have made opposition; if no others, then at least the priest Florence, the bishop of Tivoli, and even the interested communities.

Treatment of juridical questions did not at all enter into Gregory's purpose, but perhaps there is an allusion to this situation when, after describing the organization of the various monasteries, he tells of the visits of the members of the Roman patriciate to Subiaco, who persuade St. Benedict to open a school for their sons at St. Clement's. In a word, the undertaking of St. Benedict in the valley of the Anio was so new that it cannot be explained except by supposing the intervention of the bishop of Tivoli and of papal Rome and by recourse to the contemporary law of Justinian.

CHAPTER XIV

The Restless Monk

_____

In one of the monasteries established at Subiaco was a monk so rest-less that when his brethren, after the psalmody, prostrated themselves to pray and to meditate on what they had said to God in the Office, he would always find a pretext to leave the choir and thus to disturb their devotion. Abbot Pompeian had frequently reproved him for his con-duct. Finally, not knowing what else to do, he brought the monk to the Patriarch, who gave him the scolding he deserved. For one or two days after his return to the monastery, the monk seemed to be cured, but on the third day he returned to his old tricks. When the matter was again referred to St. Benedict, he said: "I shall come and personally reprimand him."

Local tradition, backed by a fourteenth-century picture of the Sacro Speco, asserts that the scene I am about to describe took place in the monastery of St. Michael *post lacum*, in the direction of the present-day city of Subiaco.[1] The distance, therefore, from St. Clem-ent's was not very great; and this circumstance helps to explain the goings and comings of Abbot Pompeian, of the restless monk, and finally of St. Benedict and St. Maur.

So the Patriarch, accompanied by St. Maur, went thither; at the time of the Divine Office he entered the choir of the monastery in order to recite the psalms with the others. At the end of the psalmody,

[1] The *Liber diurnus* (no. 25) preserves the papal formulary for giving the order to transmit relics (*brandea*) of the archangel Michael for the dedication of a new oratory in his honor. Such relics or veils were taken from the altar of the archangel in the Roman sanctuary on the Via Salaria.

when the cenobites had already prostrated for their prayer, St. Benedict, pointing to the restless monk who was getting ready to leave the church, asked Maur and Pompeian: "Do you not see who is dragging out the poor man?" They replied in the negative, and the saint added: "Let us pray that you also may see." They persisted in prayer for two days, while the monk each time repeated his act. At the beginning of the third day, Maur finally was privileged to see: he observed a little black devil with horns who grasped the unfortunate monk by the habit and drew him out of the church. Abbot Pompeian, poor man, still saw nothing. But St. Benedict, who was particularly interested in the formation of St. Maur, waited till the fourth day, then left the choir and went to meet the monk.

With some individuals words are of no avail, as the Patriarch himself writes in the Rule.[2] In this case he decided to knock some sense into the wanderer with the abbatial staff he had carried to choir.

At this, as if the devil had received the strokes instead of the monk, the tempter fled and made a resolution not to have any further encounters with St. Benedict, who used such telling arguments with him. "Curse the Pandects and the discipline of the Canons," grumbled Satan.

Commentators on the Rule rightly observe that our monks from the very beginning, besides the liturgical prayer of the choir, also practiced private prayer. St. Gregory has a faint allusion to it when he mentions in the cell of St. Benedict at Monte Cassino the presence of a "mat on which he was accustomed to pray." [3]

Of this intimate and personal prayer, grafted on the Divine Office, the present-day Roman liturgy preserves an insignificant mention. On some penitential days, after the scriptural reading, the deacon invites the faithful to kneel and to pray in silence: *"Flectamus genua."* After a little while he gives the signal to rise, *"Levate";* and the priest chants the concluding collect. This custom of adding private prayer to the Office was practiced also by the monks of Egypt, and Cassian mentions it frequently in his monastic writings.

St. Benedict in the Rule expressly calls attention to this form of prayer; but for the sake of the weak, he desires that it be brief and

[2] *"Stultus verbis non corrigitur"* (chap. 2).
[3] *Dial.,* Bk. II, chap. 11.

that at a sign from the superior all rise: "In community, however, let prayer be short, and when the superior gives the signal let all rise together" (chap. 20).

In this place we must not overlook the title *Dei famulus* ("servant of God") which St. Gregory attributes to St. Maur and by which he always indicates the reputation of a saint. St. Zachary does the same thing and calls him Μαύρῳ τῷ δούλῳ τοῦ Θεοῦ. These are the first references to the sanctity and the cult of St. Maur.

Before closing this chapter, I should like to remark an archaeological detail. St. Benedict, after leaving the choir, struck the restless monk with the rod he had in his hand. We must not think that he used a stick to lean upon, since he was not yet advanced in age. The ceremonial of Theodore explains the significance of the rod when it describes for us the Roman custom of consigning *baculum et pedules* ("the staff and the buskins") to abbots at the time of their blessing. Hence St. Benedict brought with him to choir the staff which was the insigne of his abbatial office.

Today, indeed, no abbot would go about with the pastoral staff in his hand. But in the sixth century, when both civil and canon law meticulously regulated the whole of life, it was necessary to abide by this etiquette also at Subiaco: so, for St. Benedict, distinct footgear and a rod in the hand.

CHAPTER XV

The Miraculous Spring

O<small>N</small> one occasion the monks of the three monasteries situated on the mountain (St. Mary's, St. John's, and St. Jerome's) held a kind of protest meeting. They began by complaining that it was too difficult for them daily to go down to the lake to fetch water. The path on the rocky slope of the mountain, besides being long, was also dangerous, particularly in inclement weather and during the winter freezes. Why live up there with the eagles, when they could dwell much more comfortably in the valley watered by the river? Did the monks of St. Clement's perhaps enjoy some special privilege? They decided to go in a body to the holy Patriarch and to ask him to make a change in his general plan of the holy mountain. These three monasteries, taken all together, were so small that to pull them down and rebuild them elsewhere would not cost much effort.

I have already said that at Subiaco St. Benedict showed a preference for the spirituality of St. Jerome, Cassian, and the Egyptian fathers; in their eyes, according to Macarius the Egyptian, a sign of relaxation of the monastic discipline was manifested precisely by the transfer of a monastery from the sandy desert to the pleasant banks of a river.

The holy Patriarch immediately detected the hand of the tempter. Hence, after he had kindly let the monks have their say, he sent them away with words of encouragement, assuring them that he would immediately give thought to the matter. Thus, for the moment, he calmed their anxiety. Later on, in the Rule, he reminds the cellarer that when he has to deny something, his "no" be not harsh, but that the refusal be "spiced" at least by a good word. "Let him give a good word in reply" (chap. 31).

On the following night, taking with him the boy Placid, Benedict by the light of the moon gained the rocky summit and reached the level space on which the monastery of St. John *ad aquas* was built.

From the Sacro Speco by way of the little monastery of St. Mary, now called Blessed John Loricatus, a climb of a good hour is required to reach the spot. Of the ancient monastery little remains except a chapel with a narrow window, dating from the twelfth century, and a few mosaic fragments of the kind called Cosmato work. Abbot John V of Subiaco restored this monastery, put a small group of monks into it, and endowed it modestly with some lands for its support (1065–1117). This information is contained in a part of the *Chronicon Sublacense* that perhaps goes back to the twelfth century.

Arrived near the monastery, the holy Patriarch knelt down under the starry sky and prayed for a long time. Meanwhile the little boy Placid also joined his hands and tried to imitate the devotion of the master. Finally the prayer ended. The saint, aided by the boy, placed three stones one upon the other, as if to indicate the exact spot of their prayer, and as the moon was sinking they descended the hill to St. Clement's.

In the early morning another deputation of monks came to inquire what decision he had reached with regard to the water. They were nervous and excited. Already they had resigned themselves to the task of transferring their habitations to the lake, when instead the saint sent them back up the mountain with these instructions: "Return to your places, brethren, and there on the level where you will find three rocks placed one upon the other, dig a little hole. Almighty God can make you find water even on the mountaintop."

In those heroic times, a living faith served as a check upon the nerves. They went and found as he had told them. About the rocks the ground was already moist, by reason of a vein of water that sought an opening to the surface. The monks dug, and so copious a supply of water gushed forth, that a small stream was formed that ran down the mountainside. The water is still there, and the spring is held in great veneration by the inhabitants of Subiaco. Further, it is the only water in that immediate vicinity.

How many times did St. Benedict, while visiting the catacombs of the martyrs in Rome as a youth, see in the chapels, on the arcosolia and on the sarcophagi the scene of Moses producing water from the rock! This biblical miracle was known to all in Christian antiquity. Hence we can easily understand the promptness of St. Benedict's reply to the monks: "Almighty God can cause a spring to flow even on the summit of that mountain." The early Christians of the catacombs occasionally substituted in place of the figure of Moses striking the rock, that of St. Peter who with the sanctifying waters of baptism regenerated in grace the first believers of Rome.

A gifted artist might conceive a similar representation with regard to St. Benedict. The Patriarch of Western monachism causes the waters to flow from the rock of the mountain at Subiaco, so that, with the pure water of his wisdom, he might slake the thirst of the whole world. We shall see later how the great saint repeats the same miraculous deed at Monte Cassino; how, at the touch of his rod, "the dry earth revealed wonderful waters," in the words of Mark the Poet.

CHAPTER XVI

The Benedictine Program: "Pray and Work"

CASSIODORUS perceived the situation clearly. The Roman Empire no longer had the power to resist the onslaughts of the young barbaric nations, which, just as they were avid for booty, so they also thirsted for religion and civilization. Hence, when he was the prime minister at the court of Theodoric and his immediate successors at Ravenna, Cassiodorus dedicated all his genius and his position to the realization of his cherished dream: the fusion of the two races and the Latinizing of the Goths, particularly by means of the Catholic faith.

But the day came when the old statesman lost heart in the face of the difficulties; after resigning his office, he retired to his possessions in Calabria, where he built a monastery and became a monk. We shall see later, when we analyze a portion of Cassiodorus' *De anima,* what part St. Benedict played in this determination.

The statesman indeed passed out of the picture, but the design of Providence did not fail, nor was it forgotten after his death. St. Gregory took it up, and his successors carried it on with happy results, till the day when Leo III, in the midst of a gathering of Italian and Frankish bishops and abbots, consecrated the beginnings of the ninth century with the imperial coronation of Charlemagne. Precisely from the fusion of the Latins with the Lombards, who had become Catholic, the Italian race arose.

As St. Benedict chronologically stands between Cassiodorus and

Gregory, so also, from the few remarks of the biographer we see that he likewise shared their hopes and ideals with regard to the conversion of the Goths. From the *fioretti* I choose the following pleasing narrative.

One day a Goth, who wished to be clothed in the monastic habit, knocked at the gates of the monastery. We are acquainted with several choice intellects among the Goths, particularly in the court of Theodoric.[1] On this occasion, however, the Goth, besides belonging to a barbaric tribe, was also *"pauper spiritu,"* a man of little intelligence. (This is still the biographer speaking.) Yet the saint "most gladly received him: *libentissime suscepit."* This *"libentissime"* is Gregory's term, and it portrays a whole program of ecclesiastical policy.

The abbot, then, joyously took in the Goth. Since sending him to one of the twelve monasteries might cause some disturbance, he retained him at St. Clement's. While the Goths were devastating and burning the country through which they passed, the saint, as if to make amends, supplied the new Goth monk with a pruning knife or brush hook, so that during the hours when the others were in school, he might at least clear the ground on the bank of the lake, where a garden for the students was to be planted. He seemed incapable of doing anything else.

To work for a living must have been a new experience for the Goth, accustomed as he was to draw his sustenance from the booty of war. But since the vocation to the monastic life was really present, he adapted himself to it and set himself to work with a will. It just happened that his head was not made for books, as on the contrary that of St. Maur was.

Lustily he swung the blade to right and left, cutting off the brush, digging out the stones, rooting out the weeds and thorns, so that it seemed he intended to level the entire area at one blow. But while he was delivering himself of these powerful strokes, the curved blade, slipping from the old handle, suddenly sailed off into the lake, and the Goth was left with only the handle in his hand. For a worker like him, this was a nasty trick the devil had played.

[1] St. John Chrysostom received Goths into his clergy, ordaining some of them priests, deacons, and lectors. He himself preached to the Goths through an interpreter (Theodoret. V, XXX; Socrat. VI, 6).

The novice, a good religious and observant of the Rule, ran immediately to the monk Maur and, all wrought up by this ridiculous trick of the devil, and mixing some of his quasi-Germanic dialect with his Latin, accused himself as best he could of this involuntary fault. We today would rather call it an accident or, at the most, an act of carelessness. But Gregory uses the strong terminology of his time and calls it a *"reatus."* As a matter of fact, those first working monks frequently considered the instruments of their labor on the same plane as the sacred vessels of the altar, since, because they belonged to the monastery, they also pertained to the worship and the service of God.

If today the fields of Italy are well cultivated and constitute one of the principal sources of national wealth, gratitude is due to the sons of St. Benedict. Whereas the ancient Romans looked upon labor as a punishment for slaves, and the barbarians disdained it as an occupation not suited to warlike peoples, St. Benedict elevated work to the dignity of religion and consecrated the ranks of his disciples to it.

Maur, quite young at the time, imposed a suitable penance on the Goth and then went to inform the holy Abbot of the happening. Calm and serene as always, Benedict rose to go to the place of work. The Goth was still there, confused, the handle in his hand, searching among the weeds and thorns, because he could hardly convince himself that the iron had gone into the lake. Then the saint, saying nothing, took that handle from the Goth's hand and immersed it in the lake. Marvel of marvels! As if the wood had become a magnet, the blade came up from the bottom, floated on the water and fixed itself anew on the handle.

"Take it and work," said St. Benedict, giving over the instrument to the poor Goth, "and do not be sad any more: *Ecce labora et noli contristari."*

In the life of the Prophet Eliseus an identical scene, in similar circumstances, is described. The iron returned to the surface of the lake and joined the handle which Eliseus immersed in the water. This similarity between the prodigies performed by St. Benedict and the marvels wrought by the patriarchs and prophets of the Old Testament prompted St. Gregory to say that the legislator of Cassino shared in the holiness of all these "great spirits": *"Omnium Iustorum spiritu plenus fuit.*" The observation is exact, and the Church has even made it a part of the liturgy. We must add, however, that Benedict had his soul orientated toward these gigantic figures of saints and that he emulated their faith.

In more recent times it has been customary to express the Benedictine program in this motto: "*Ora et labora;* Pray and work." Perhaps it owes its origin to the story told by Gregory of the miracle wrought in behalf of the poor Goth. But to be entirely complete and exact, it ought to include another most important element, expressly mentioned by the biographer: "Go back to work and be not sad." Prayer and work are very commendable, but those in prison and those condemned to forced labor also perform it. St. Benedict associates with it a supernatural sense of generous spontaneity, of joyous liberty, which alone preserves for men their dignity as sons of God. For this reason the saint lays down in his Rule: "That no one be troubled or saddened in the house of God" (chap. 31).

Let us pause a moment. Where are we? If the miracle was wrought close to the lake, then we are certainly close to the monastery of St. Clement, which was set up by the saint within the walls of Nero's palace, lapped by the waters of the Anio. Ruins of this monastery are still visible. Between two Roman walls of *opus reticulatum* and spaces filled with brick may still be seen what appears to be an apse of rough masonry. Giovannoni attributes it to the sixth century. There we see the first Benedictine school and novitiate, personally directed by the holy Patriarch.

A small monastic family continued to dwell in St. Clement's till the earthquake of 1227. Even after that date, devotion to this place, formerly consecrated by the presence of SS. Benedict, Maur, and Placid, persevered. In 1474 a citizen of Subiaco petitioned the Curia of Sixtus IV for an indulgence of one hundred days in favor of those who would help toward the reconstruction of the destroyed oratory and would piously visit it on the feasts of St. Benedict, St. Scholastica, and St. Sebastian.[2]

If the dedication of the chapel to St. Clement is original, then the choice of this saint is not without significance. In the sixth century the cult of St. Clement was rare, and in Rome we find only his an-

---

[2] Cherub. Mirzio, *Chronicon Sublac.,* pp. 49 f.

cient home on the Caelian Hill converted into a *titulus* in his honor.

For a native of Norcia, however, St. Clement was not merely any kind of saint. An ancient legend, which gained considerable currency in the sixth century, made him a relative of the consul Flavius Clemens, and hence of Vespasian. It was also known that the saint suffered martyrdom in Chersonesus by being drowned in the sea. Perhaps here we have the reason why the holy Patriarch dedicated the chapel and the monastery where he dwelt near the lake to St. Clement. Who knows? The inhabitants of Norcia, at least those who, like St. Benedict, could pride themselves on a descent from "distinguished parentage," used also to glory in a distant relationship with Vespasian, with the mother of Vespasian, and with Pope St. Clement.

CHAPTER XVII

Maur Walks upon the Waters

To work miracles is wonderful. But we are here principally concerned with knowing the products of the *"Dominici schola servitii,"* ("the school of the Lord's service") opened by St. Benedict at Subiaco. Without a doubt the manual of that school is the Rule. But did the students draw any profit from the austere lessons of the master? Gregory the Great at once satisfies our legitimate question. In a special chapter, redolent of poetic spirituality, he describes for us simultaneously the wisdom of the teacher and the marvelous obedience of the first disciples.

The biographer gives special importance to the virtue of monastic obedience, because in the Rule the treatment of obedience represents not only the foundation of monastic discipline, but is a summary of the entire spiritual doctrine of the Patriarch of Cassino as well.

That is the way posterity has understood the matter. Even to our own day the story of St. Maur has a popular appeal, especially because he walked dry-shod over the waters of Claudius' lake. When the stranger and the pilgrim go to Subiaco nowadays, the guide, soon after leaving the city, will point out a bridge over the Anio. If you ask its name, he will reply: "That is the bridge of St. Maur, because near this spot the saint walked on the water with dry feet."

But let us return to Gregory's account. Be it well understood, we are still in the monastery of St. Clement. One day while St. Benedict was intent on prayer in his cell, one of his young monks, Placid, went to fetch water at the lake. He leaned too far out with his vessel, lost his balance, and the current, which ran strong there, carried off the child; he tried to do what he could, without any hope of help from his companions, who were far from the spot.

But the spirit of the Abbot was watchful over the house. Without being informed by anyone, Benedict, in the light of God, perceived the danger threatening the child. "Brother Maur, Brother Maur, hurry," he cried. Maur, who was near at hand, ran up at the unusual summons, and the saint added: "Go quickly, because the boy Placid has fallen into the water and is being carried off by the current."

St. Maur waited for nothing more. He receives the blessing of the Abbot, goes out, and, concerned only with the thought of carrying out the order of fraternal charity, on the wings of obedience hurries to the lake, walks on the water as if it were dry land, to the spot where he still sees the head and the arms of the unfortunate Placid, who thrashed about and cried for help. Maur, still lost in God, did not seem to notice where he was; he grasped Placid by the hair which the youth still wore long, lifted him and drew him behind himself to the shore. Only then the obedient disciple, gazing back at the raging waters, became conscious of the miracle that had happened and turned to Benedict to give the merit to him. Not at all marveling at the prodigy, the Patriarch, well knowing the robust virtue of his wonder-working disciple, tried to persuade St. Maur that it was through obedience that he had wrought this miracle. But the other, out of humility, dissented.

In this edifying dispute between the two saints, the third party, the boy saved by the miracle, acted as arbiter; he declared that, while battling desperately in the waters, he suddenly seemed to descry the cowl of his Abbot above him; and he believed that it was Benedict who drew him from the waves and brought him unharmed to the shore.

A singular school, this of St. Clement, where the master gives an order to his pupil to work unusual prodigies, as some other teacher might assign to his pupils a composition on the *Aeneid* of Virgil! And all this in an atmosphere so supernatural and at the same time so humanly attractive that, while Maur through obedience passes over the waters of the lake with dry feet, the Abbot perseveres in prayer, asking safety for both of his disciples. I admire the master, but I must also confess that the first pupils were worthy of him.

Here the exegetes of Gregory's text find the place to introduce an elegant question regarding the juridical status of the children who were then offered to the service of God in a monastery by the authority of their parents. These oblates, as St. Benedict later explains in the Rule (chap. 59), according to the ancient law were regarded as true monks. The defect of age in the selection of their state of life was supplied by the authority of the paterfamilias, who could very well order the choice of his own child, as St. Paul observes writing to the Corinthians. "The monk is made either by the father's dedication or by his own profession; . . . hence we forbid them to return to the world." Thus the Fourth Council of Toledo (can. 49).

Similarly the Council of Trullo had to consider these children who were offered: "If one is to undertake the monk's obligations, let him be at least ten years of age; we shall leave this matter to the investigation of the superior." [1] There is extant on the same subject a Visigothic law, forbidding those to return to the world who "had received the habit of religion by the pious offering of their parents." [2]

Hence Gregory writes of "the child Placid, who was a monk under the direction of the man of God"; but at the same time he informs us that he still wore long hair. Therefore it seems that the monastic tonsure was deferred till a more mature age, when perhaps the oblate himself ratified the offering of his parents and received the monastic garb.

The rite of these oblations of children at God's altar in order to consecrate them definitely to the monastic life in virtue of the *patria potestas* is fully described in the *Regula monasteriorum* (chap. 59).

During the Holy Sacrifice, the parents, in the presence of witnesses and by a public act, made a formal request of the abbot (*petitio*). After the Scripture readings, at the time of the Offertory, together with the family's oblation of the child, the document itself and the hand of the boy were wrapped in the altar cloth, and thus he was understood to be presented and offered to God.

The rite of wrapping the hand of the child in the altar cloth signified the concept of acceptance on the part of the Divinity; the altar cloth symbolized the very garment of Christ. Furthermore, in ancient

[1] Conc. Trull., II, can. 40; Mansi, XI, 935.
[2] *Lex Visigoth.*, III, V, 3; *Mon. Germ. Leg.*, S.I., Vol. I, p. 16.

times the objects offered to God or to an exalted member of the hierarchy were precisely wrapped in a cloth.

This custom of receiving into monasteries even small boys in order to educate them for the service of God gave rise to the various kinds of monastic schools. St. Benedict laid the first foundation at Subiaco. If he desired to reserve to himself in a special building at St. Clement's the training of the young recruits, it was doubtless because he had to teach literature and impart biblical knowledge to Maur, Placid, and their companions from the better families of Rome. This is precisely what St. Jerome did in the monastery at Bethlehem; this also was done, according to St. Caesarius, by all the pastors of Italy.

That this hypothesis has some foundation in fact appears from the injunction of the Patriarch that the hours of the night between the end of the vigils and the beginning of the Office at dawn be dedicated to the study of Scripture, also as far as the older monks were concerned, who perhaps "need a better knowledge of the Psalter or the lessons" (*Rule,* chap. 8). Can we suppose that St. Benedict would have excused his youths from school?

Pope Zachary evidently understood the thought of the biographer in the same sense when he translates that at St. Clement's St. Benedict ὑπό τε ἑαυτοῦ διδασκαλικὴν παιδαγογίαν ποιμανθῆναι ἔκρινεν (chap. 3). Furthermore, he directly gives the title of διδάσκαλος to the Patriarch, in accord with St. Gregory, who in this same circumstance calls him "*Magister*" and describes him as "very capable of educating" his young candidates. Hence there is question here of a true monastic school, such as could exist at that time.

Unfortunately, as St. Benedict himself confesses in his Rule (chap. 59), these young vocations, educated by him for God and in letters, sometimes brought him bitter delusions. Boys of good expectations, who, after a long formation in the cloister and after offering their vows at the altar, at the first notice of an inheritance left them by an uncle, a grandfather, or some other relative, had let the news go to their heads and ended by throwing their cowl into the bushes. Such sad occurrences also happened at Subiaco and Monte Cassino.

These disappointments always remained as thorns in the heart of the holy legislator. It was not so much the treason against him, as rather the eternal damnation of the apostate which he decried: ". . .

whereby . . . he might be deceived and ruined, as we have learned by experience." This confidence of the wonder-worker, which escaped him while he was writing his Rule, is precious; it is such a rare demonstration in his solemn and authoritarian style. We do not know the particular cases to which he alludes. In any case, he also had his Judases.

Later the biographer several times portrays the wonder-worker at Monte Cassino with a book in his hand, while he guards the gate of the Roman fortress and at the same time attends to his studies. This love for books, which is manifested by the numerous biblical, patristic, and classical references in the Rule, was certainly not a thing reserved to the last years of the master.

If Roman patricians went to Subiaco to present their sons to Benedict so that he might rear them in the service of God, these parents were very much concerned that these youths "of good expectations" should not grow up uncouth and ignorant, so as to belie the nobility of their origin. Hence this is a sign that the saint, from those early days, instituted for them a "school of the Lord's service" under his own direction. It is only natural that the university student of yesterday should, as the first thing, organize a school with its own system and program.

St. Gregory clearly insinuates this when, after telling how the man of God distributed his monks among twelve monasteries, he informs us of a separate and special common school for these young men, "whom he deemed it expedient to teach in person."[3] Here there is question of "erudition," that is, of student instruction, as the Latins understood the term,[4] in a suitable locale, not merely of spiritual direction, which could equally well be imparted in a community of monks.

In that golden age of Benedictine fervor, only special scholastic exigencies can explain St. Benedict's decision to keep all the boys together at St. Clement's, in order to take personal charge of their education. Thus also St. Gregory understood the situation; although he speaks of twelve monasteries at Subiaco, he excludes from that

---

[3] *Dial.*, Bk. II, chap. 3.

[4] The Latin dictionaries under *"erudio"* give these examples: *"Erudire puerum omnibus artibus,"* Liv.; *"Laboribus erudiunt iuventutem,"* Cic.; *"Erudire aliquem artibus,"* Ovid. It is used in a scholastic sense.

number the house or "cell" of St. Clement, which was in fact a common monastic school, capable of accommodating more than twelve persons.

This subtle distinction of the biographer must be given its due importance. The former anchorite now resigns himself to dwell outside the twelve monasteries in order to devote himself to the teaching of the youths committed to his charge, particularly by members of Rome's upper class.[5] Here we have a new aspect of St. Benedict in which it is easy to recognize the former Roman university student. The Roman period was decisive for the future life of the saint.

In connection with St. Benedict's teaching, the Beuronese school has represented him at Monte Cassino in the role of architect, explaining to his disciples the plan of his monastery. The idea is new, but it has a foundation in the narrative of St. Gregory who, after describing the great work of adaptation of the fortress of Casinum as a monastery for monks—an undertaking impossible without a competent architect—puts these words into the mouth of St. Benedict: "This entire monastery which I have built and all that I have provided for the brethren has been delivered up to the barbarians" (chap. 17).

Here the word *"construxi"* is certainly to be understood in the sense of "planning"; since also for the new monastery of Terracina St. Benedict reserved to himself the work of drawing up the plan of the building, indicating very particularly the parts which were to compose it. Hence the work of an architect, whose directions had to be followed under penalty of spoiling the material and of compromising the stability of the edifice. Every man to his profession!

Sidonius Apollinaris, in the epitaph of the priest and monk Claudian (d. 473), gives us a good idea of what may have constituted the learning of a monk devoted to study. This was not an isolated case. If St. Benedict, well versed in the seven liberal arts, was not another Claudian, the fact nevertheless remains that at his time studies were being encouraged in various monasteries. The attention of the public was being directed to them. From what we know of St. Benedict's academic learning, his eloquence, his rhythmic prose, the school

---

[5] These schools for children consecrated to the service of God by their parents existed also at the Lateran. The epitaph of St. Martin I attests to the fact.

opened by him at Subiaco, the temptation arises to attribute to him the eulogy of the other priest and monk, Claudian.[6]

[6] Concerning the Lateran school, where Pope Martin I was educated as a child, we read in his funeral eulogy:

> *"Haec te nascentem suscepit Ecclesia Mater.*
> *Uberibus Fidei nutriens devota beatum.*
> *Parvulus utque loqui coepisti dulcia verba,*
> *Mox Scripturarum pius, indole factus.*
> *Haec tibi lectori innocuus fuit aurea vita.*
> *Diaconus hinc factus iuvenis meritoque fidelis."*

CHAPTER XVIII

One Raven; or Rather, Two

THE sacred fire of divine love that burned first in Benedict's heart enflamed his disciples and then spread out over the whole vast territory;
the monastery of Subiaco had become a sanctuary and a place of pilgrimage whither the crowds flocked daily. As usual, St. Gregory informs us concerning the progress of the Benedictine apostolate.
"When the love of Jesus Christ had enflamed all the surrounding
territory far and wide, many abandoned the world to take up the
sweet yoke of the Redeemer" (chap. 8).

"His reputation spread in the places round about. From that time
forth he began to be visited by many who, when they offered him
bodily food, from his lips received into their hearts food of eternal
life" (chap. 1).

Among these pilgrims some desired only a blessing for the sick or
consolation in their sorrow. On the other hand, some came to put
the burden of their woes at the feet of the Patriarch and declared that
they did not wish to leave, but that they desired to dedicate themselves to the service of Jesus Christ. Many of them did not come empty-
handed. Since they knew that the monks did not subsist on air and
that they would receive there that warm and courteous hospitality for
which the saints are famous, a goodly number brought gifts. At sight
of this generosity, the pastor of the place, Florence by name, grew
envious: *"vicinae ecclesiae* [1] *presbyter, Florentius nomine."*

----

[1] In contradistinction to *basilica, oratorium,* etc., in olden times *ecclesia* always signified either the cathedral or the parish church in the country districts. In any case, if
the priest Florence does not claim any right over the monastery of St. Benedict—indeed

It seems that in those days there was no other parish church than that of St. Lawrence on the high cliff on the left bank of the Anio, opposite the present city of Subiaco. St. Gregory's words cannot be brought as an objection to this localization when he says: *"Cum praedictus presbyter stans in solario Benedictum discessisse cognosceret"* (chap. 8), in the sense that the pastor from the balcony of his house actually witnessed the departure of St. Benedict. The historian does not say that he saw him with his own eyes, but that he knew he was going.

Certainly at the present time from St. Lawrence's neither the monastery nor the bridge nor the road which leads to Ciociaria can be seen. But until the time of Gregory XVI the road to Alatri passed several hundred yards to the south of St. Lawrence's and was easily visible from the church. A late tradition would place the site of the priest Florence's house among the ruins of Nero's nymphaeum, just about opposite St. Clement's on the other side of the lake. But this story does not go back farther than the thirteenth century.

Differences between religious and the local ecclesiastical authorities are not new. Not even Benedict at Subiaco could escape this unpleasantness. The biographer tells us that the villain in this piece was the pastor of the neighboring parish. His disedifying story was well known in the Lateran; it was so freely discussed that it did not even offend the grandson of the same name, a subdeacon in the papal palace.

Before receiving orders the priest Florence was married and had had a son, who perhaps lived in the parish house with his father. The discipline of the age did not forbid the *presbytera,* or wife, to live a life of perfect chastity in the same house as the pastor, to look after the education of the boy. Rather, the presence of the good woman in the house was beneficial, because, if nothing else, it served to keep the priest from falling into the abyss of vice. Unfortunately, when the *presbytera* died, some girls of the neighborhood began to frequent the house. Disparaging remarks were made openly about the merry widower who "did not desire to lead a praiseworthy life," as St.

---

it is he who deserts the Patriarch rather than the other way around—this is without doubt an indication that the twelve monasteries had been withdrawn from the jurisdiction of the pastor.

Gregory says. Jealousy and envy are the keys to the crimes which we are about to relate.

But first a bit of chronology. When Florence died, about 529, his son must have already reached the age of adolescence, if we keep in mind the sacred condition of his parents. Later he married, and when a son was born, he called him Florence, in honor of the unfortunate pastor. His birth must be placed about the middle of the sixth century, because in 592 the grandson of the priest of Subiaco was already a subdeacon, was administrator of the papal patrimony of the Campania, and as a matter of fact was elected to the episcopate of Naples. Hence he must already have reached mature age.

This choice pleased St. Gregory, who thought thus finally to put an end to the vacancy of the see of Naples. But Florence, terrified by the dangerous conditions of the city, refused the honor and fled to Rome to beg the Pope not to confirm the election. Gregory, despite himself, then had to notify the Neapolitans to proceed to another election.[2]

Let us return to the story of the grandfather of Florence. At the beginning he imitated the others, that is, sought the company of Benedict and showed an interest in him. Subsequently he became jealous of the growing concourse of people to the little church of St. Clement and finally attempted to run competition by initiating an unusual movement in his parish in order to draw people thither and to gain popularity for himself.[3]

Little by little his visits to the Patriarch grew more rare, till finally he no longer desired to set foot in the monastery. *"Desertor fiebat,"* says St. Gregory. But ordinarily a deserter does not stop there. Continuous criticism of the saint, advice to the faithful to stay away from Benedict, reproofs and threats against the pilgrims . . . *"Eiusdem*

---

[2] *Epist. deb.,* III, no. 15.

[3] St. Gregory describes the crowds that flocked to the saint in order to receive advice with regard to eternal salvation, not to receive the sacraments. Juridical tradition forbade the faithful from assisting at the divine mysteries in chapels of monasteries, so that they would be obliged to go to their own cathedral or parish church. Significant is the account given in the life of St. John, founder and abbot of the monastery at Tonnère toward the end of the fifth century. A certain pious layman by the name of Agrestius one Sunday morning went to the monastery to assist at Mass and receive Holy Communion from the hand of the abbot. Abbot John, on the contrary, ordered him out of the place: *"Ne sanctorum Patrum praecepta et regularem censuram transgredi videamur"* (Mabillon, *op. cit.,* I, 42).

conversationi derogare; quosque etiam posset ab illius visitatione compescere." This *compescere* immediately reveals a man of violence, one who does not stay clear even of crime.

Since, however, the people were attracted not by the places, but by the sanctity of the man who dwelt there, the pastor began to do everything in his power to prevent the people who were flocking to the monastery of St. Clement from leaving the parish church empty. What! Should St. Lawrence, a martyr so famous for his miracles, take umbrage at some old pope, a Nursian by birth, who, besides, was so sparing with miracles?

Florence himself was not above acquiring a reputation as an apostle. But the folk, who considered deeds and not beautiful words, compared the angelic life of Benedict with that of the merry priest and discovered a hundred reasons for preferring the one to the other. The parish church was progressively less frequented.[4] Finally the pastor lost his self-control. Nothing worse can be imagined than what happens when passion gets the upper hand over a religious soul and masquerades under the deceitful appearance of a holy zeal, of the good of souls, of rights of one's own church, and the like. The Gospel also speaks of those who kill their neighbor for the greater glory of God! That is precisely the role the priest Florence wished to play. But he was a sly old fox and did not wish to oppose the monastery openly. On the contrary, he called himself its friend; he even made a show of praising the saint, but then by his venomous insinuations he stabbed him in the back.

One day—perhaps it was Easter or the feast of St. Lawrence—he sent Benedict a eulogia, according to custom; that is, one of those blessed breads, which were offered at the altar and which bishops and priests used to give, as sign of special friendship, to those who deserved well of the Church. This practice is well known to liturgists. At Rome and in the different dioceses of Italy the bishops every Sunday, as an earnest of ecclesiastical unity, sent the Blessed Eucharist to the city

[4] The worst was that the treasury of the church also became emptier, since, as the *Liber diurnus* informs us (no. 26), the offerings made in monastic oratories became the property of the community: *"Ut si quid pro diversorum devotione commoditatis accesserit, cum monachis in eodem loco deservientibus debeat proficere quidquid offere contigerit."*

parishes, and as a sign of affection sent to their friends or colleagues part of the bread that had been offered by the faithful at the altar.

St. Paulinus sent a loaf of bread as a eulogia to his friend Severus with these words: "We have sent you a loaf of the Campania as a eulogia" (*Ep.* 1). When sending another to St. Augustine, he makes this request: "We ask that you bless the loaf which we have sent you as a sign of unity" (*Ep.* 41).

In Book IV of the *Dialogues* St. Gregory tells the story of a certain pastor of Civitavecchia, who for his health's sake was forced to go to a bathing establishment where there was sulphurous water. Was it perhaps Vicarello? The bath attendant was so courteous and helpful that the priest one day brought him as a gift "two loaves, begging him kindly to accept what was offered him in the spirit of charity." But the other, who was a soul from purgatory, refused to touch the blessed bread: "That bread is holy; I may not eat it." [5]

When the messenger of the priest Florence arrived at the monastery with the eulogia of the holy patron of the parish, the young monks most likely winked maliciously at one another. No doubt also St. Benedict, who knew his Virgil, must have recalled the verse: "*Timeo Danaos et dona ferentes.*" What could the gift signify?

Nevertheless he showed all courtesy to the messenger and instructed him to thank the priest. When he had received the loaf into his holy hands, he immediately felt that the devil was hidden in it, namely, that the priest Florence had poisoned it. His heart filled with a deep sorrow, not so much on account of the serious danger to which he was exposed by the presence of the unfortunate man, but more especially on account of the soul of the priest, who obstinately persisted in walking the road to hell. [6]

The visitor to Subiaco or Monte Cassino always sees the ravens which are kept in the cloister and which stir the curiosity of strangers. The story of those ravens is very old and goes back to the time of St. Benedict himself. Gregory relates that at Subiaco a raven used to fly in from the neighboring woods to the little square in front of St. Clement's in order to receive some food from Benedict. This was an innocent diversion also for the Patriarch's disciples when they took a

[5] *Dial.*, Bk. IV, chap. 55.
[6] "*Venerabilis autem Pater . . . illi magis quam sibi doluit.*"

breath of fresh air and a bit of sun after the noonday meal. The raven had gradually become tame and no longer was afraid of the youthful group.

The saints at times regain some of that dominion over creation which God had given to Adam in the earthly Paradise. Nature, water, storms, birds, and fish obey St. Benedict, St. Francis, St. Anthony, while, on the other hand, Gemma Galgani will have her guardian angel act as letter carrier to the monastery of her spiritual director, Father Germanus.

At Nursia the holy monk Florence had tamed a bear that kept him company in his hermitage, a fact with which St. Benedict was acquainted. Indeed the saints extend their charity to all creatures. While St. Francis of Assisi sings the praises of Brother Sun, St. Francis of Paula calls forth from the heated oven a beloved lamb which the masons had killed and set to roast.

So on this day, at St. Clement's, the raven appeared for his food at the usual hour. When the bird had settled at the saint's feet, he threw him the poisoned loaf, so that he might carry it far off out of harm's way. Here St. Gregory tries his hand at a bit of word-painting; he describes the raven as circling the loaf and cawing, as if trying to indicate that he wished to carry out the order of the Abbot, but that the poisoned bread nauseated him. But St. Benedict persisted and repeated his order: "Take it, take it. Do not be afraid. Carry it away." His disciples stood about to see what would happen.

The animal hesitated for a while, *"diu demoratus."* First he looked at the Abbot, then at the young monks, who cheerfully urged him on. Finally he grasped the loaf, flew away and disappeared from view. Three hours later he returned, and cawed more than usual in order to make himself heard outside the accustomed hour, while the monks were singing None; it almost seemed as if he were demanding overtime pay for those hours of extra work. Naturally he was satisfied and received his food from the hand of the Patriarch.[7] With what evangelical simplicity life went on at St. Clement's!

The horrible crime of a priest who employs a blessed loaf to despatch one of his colleagues to the next world is something so monstrous that it calls to mind the kiss with which Judas betrayed his Lord. But

---

7 *"De manu hominis Dei annonam quam consueverat accepit."*

so it is. When the salt of the earth loses its savor, nothing can restore it.

Florence does not stop there. Since the attempt to kill the master failed, he still hoped to poison the souls of his disciples. The monks who resided in the reconstructed rooms of that part of Nero's villa that was reflected in the lake were the younger ones; they had greater need of a more careful literary and ascetical formation. Maur had come to Subiaco already possessed of a certain degree of education and, now no longer a boy, assisted the master in this task.[8] Since the community was small, the help which Maur gave must have had reference to the various classes in the school rather than to the government of the house.

The pastor knew this, and on a hot summer's day he sent seven shameless wenches who, after they had crossed the bridge and entered into the garden of St. Clement's planted along the bank of the lake, danced about for a long time half naked, as was then the practice in the theaters.[9]

From the windows of the monastery Benedict observed the scandalous spectacle and grasped the Satanic malice back of it. To spite him, the priest tried to undermine the untried virtue of his youthful disciples. What to do? Exactly what Jonas did when he realized that the entire ship threatened to be swallowed up by the raging sea. For this reason he said to the pilot: "If this tempest has come on my account, throw me into the sea, so that your danger may cease."

These thoughts ran through St. Benedict's mind, and for the welfare of his young students [10] he decided to withdraw from the envy of the priest Florence by a strategic retreat. This was precisely the advice which in similar circumstances Abbot Poemen used to give, as stated in the *Dicta seniorum,* from which St. Benedict expressly cites in the Rule.

When did these events occur? The papal biographer, as usual, does not bother about chronology. This defect is somewhat supplied by the historians of Cassino, who place the foundation of that monastery in

[8] *"Maurus iunior, cum bonis polleret moribus, Magistri adiutor coepit existere."*
[9] The *Codex Theodosianus* contains copious legislation with regard to these ballerine. They were true public women, hired by the state for the entertainment of the mob: *"Mimas diversis adnotationibus liberatas, ad proprium officium revocari decernimus, ut voluptatibus populi ac festis diebus solitus ornatus deesse non possit"* (Cod. Theod., XV, VII, an. 413).
[10] *"Lapsumque adhuc tenerioribus discipulis pertimescens."*

the year 529. By that time St. Benedict had passed his prime and was approaching sixty. He spent a good thirty years at Subiaco, laying the bases of his monastic institution. Possibly the first draft of the Rule, that which perhaps Maur, according to the well-known legend, took with him to Gaul, was made while the Patriarch resided at Subiaco. We shall give the reasons for this view later.

Mark the Poet, a contemporary, throws a charitable veil over the story of the priest Florence, and instead brings forth a different reason for St. Benedict's departure from Subiaco which he insists on relating. About this time God Himself had informed the man of God that now his mission at Subiaco was completed and that he must begin a new apostolate in a place He would show him in His good time.[11]

The persecution of Florence was simply the external occasion which hastened the departure, but the true reason was another. So true is this that, when the saint was informed of the sudden death of his adversary, while only a few miles from Subiaco, he no longer desired to go back to his monasteries which he had left broken-hearted, but continued his way to the place whither God was leading him.

Mark the Poet reveals the secret of that resoluteness. The saint abandoned the woods of Monte Taleo because he was *monitus* from heaven. God took him away from there, as once, a long time before, He had ordered Abraham to leave his fatherland, Ur of the Chaldees, to go to a new land which He would show him. So also it happened with St. Benedict. The Lord indeed gave him the command to leave on a new mission, but without indicating either the place or the kind of work which would be assigned to him.

God desired that the holy man, abandoning the first congregation at Subiaco and the beloved places where he had spent his youth, should cast himself trustfully into the arms of divine Providence. In the same way the angel ordered St. Joseph to flee to Egypt with the holy family: "Go thither and remain until I shall tell you."

[11]   *"Ad quem te ex alto monitus cum monte venires,*
          Per deserta tibi dux, via Christus erat."
("When you, admonished from on high, from the mountains of Subiaco betook yourself to Cassino, passing through the deserted territory of Latium, Christ acted as your guide and your way.")

CHAPTER XIX

The Missionary Vocation

IF one is acquainted with the jurisprudence of former ages, so cold, so meticulous, so authoritarian, it seems altogether inconceivable that St. Benedict, in a territory of the diocese of Tivoli, where there were already regularly constituted monasteries and parishes, should have been able, of his own accord, to take over an important building belonging to the state, erect oratories, construct twelve monasteries with a central government and a common house of studies, appoint at least a dozen abbots, without any intervention on the part of the authorities either ecclesiastical or civil.

St. Gregory, in his concern to relate only the miracles, does not bother with the juridical aspects of all these foundations, which he presumes are known to his readers. But we cannot omit consideration of them. Unfortunately we must here admit a lacuna in the historical sources which we are not in a position to supply. Juridical relations between St. Benedict, Tivoli, Rome, and Ravenna, even if they cannot be shown, are nevertheless postulated by the law. Any other view is out of the question. If members of the aristocratic circles of Rome came to the Patriarch to entrust the education of their sons to him, we would be foolhardy to presume that the Gothic government, the Papal Curia and that of the bishop of Tivoli showed no interest in the grandiose work undertaken by Benedict at Subiaco.

After the abbacy of Vicovaro, situated almost at the gates of Tivoli, it is not possible that the bishop left St. Benedict out of his sight and disregarded his institution, so novel and so daring. Then who else but the bishop of Tivoli could have consecrated the oratories of the first twelve monasteries at Subiaco? Everything must have been ordered according to the civil and canonical laws in force at the time.

The *Liber diurnus Romanorum Pontificum* preserves some formulas that were used when the pope granted local bishops permission to transfer relics to monasteries, to consecrate oratories, to ordain priests or deacons to the sacred ministry. These formulas of the chancery supplement Book Two of the *Dialogues* and point out what must have been the relations of St. Benedict with the civil and ecclesiastical authorities.

Through the intermediary of the bishop of Tivoli or some other powerful friend, long negotiations must have been carried on between Benedict, the court of Theodoric at Ravenna, and the Holy See before the holy Patriarch was assured first the use and possession of Nero's deserted villa of *Sublacum* and then, about 529, also of the ancient *fanum* of the fortress of Casinum. In another place I have related the possible historical reasons which decided this new direction of St. Benedict's life.

In the *Codex Theodosianus* (Bk. XIV, Tit. X, 20, an. 415) we find a constitution which grants the Christian Church the right to demand from the state possession of the pagan temples which were closed and hence useless.[1] To execute the transfer, however, the ecclesiastical authorities had to present a petition to the state, as was done in Rome by Pope Felix IV for the temple of Roma and by Pope Boniface for the Pantheon. We do not know of any other changes of this kind in the Eternal City.

If, then, St. Benedict, when he arrived at Monte Cassino, immediately began the evangelization of the pagans who inhabited the mountain villages, and then set about transforming into churches their ancient temples on the mountain top, thus running the risk of stirring up the ire of the idolaters, he had, in order not to run foul of the authorities of the *castrum*, without doubt to produce in his favor a twofold grant, one papal and the other civil.

The biographer tells us that under Theodoric also the monks of other monasteries were accustomed to undertake journeys to Ravenna

---

[1] "*Ea loca, quae sacris error veterum deputavit . . . quae multiplicibus constitutis ad venerabilem Ecclesiam voluimus pertinere, Christiana sibi merito religio vindicabit.*"

in order to settle their affairs in the royal court.[2] St. Gregory the Great in a letter to Bishop Marinianus of Ravenna, in favor of the monastery of SS. John and Paul *in Classe*, expressly declares: "As often as an abbot desires to come to the Roman Pontiff in the interests of his monastery . . . he shall be free to do so." [3]

Soul of the court and universal benefactor of Italy at that time was Cassiodorus. He realized that the future of Europe rested with the vigorous peoples of the North. He understood, too, that for the conversion of the barbarian hordes, the efforts of the small number of the clergy would not be sufficient. Who would preserve in the libraries the treasures of the ancient classical and Christian civilization? Who would profit by them, conning the parchments, as Horace says, day and night, in order to transmit the fruits of that ancient wisdom to new generations? Who would open schools in distant lands? Who would preach the faith?

To carry out this generous and stupendous undertaking, the Roman Pontiff would need to have at his disposition workers and missioners who were organized and trained. Now, in the eyes of Cassiodorus, there was but one class of persons who could prepare themselves for the task: the monks. We know from Cassiodorus that with this in view he had suggested to Pope Agapitus I the founding in Rome of a school of higher theological studies. Attached to this institute was to be a large library, similar to those which formerly existed in the most celebrated Christian schools of Asia Minor, Syria, and Armenia.[4]

This generous plan did not materialize, because of the political condition of Italy; but perhaps Rome dropped it because for its own reasons it did not wish to curry the favor of the prime minister of the Goths. For us it is interesting to note that both Pope Agapitus and Cassiodorus independently set up in Rome two libraries which in some way have become historical. The library of Agapitus on the *Clivus Scauri*, near the paternal house of St. Gregory, is commemorated by an inscription which has come down to us in the ancient collections.

[2] *Dial.*, Bk. I, chap. 11.
[3] Bk. VIII, no. 15.
[4] "*Cum studia saecularum litterarum magno . . . desiderio fervere cognoscerem . . . gravissimo sum, fateor, dolore permotus, quod Scripturis divinis magistri publici deessent, cum mundani auctores celeberrima procul dubio traditione pollerent. Nisus sum ergo cum beatissimo Agapito papa Urbis Romae, ut . . . collatis expensis in Urbe Romana professos doctores scholae potius acciperent Christianae.*"

It assures us that in those chambers, decorated with sacred images and with mosaics, St. Gregory made the first draft of the four books of his *Dialogues*.

After all these centuries we are not in a position to raise any serious objections to this ancient and monumental testimony. Cassiodorus himself refers to his own library: *"Quem [librum] in bibliotheca Romae nos habuisse atque legisse retinemus, qui si forte gentili incursione sublatus est, habetis hic Gaudentium Mutiani latinum"* (*Inst.*, Bk. II, 5).

How and why the project of Cassiodorus failed is less clear, just as it is difficult to conceive the real reason why the aging statesman, now in the sixties, one day laid aside the insignia of his office and retired to his estate at Syllacium in Calabria. On a mountain lapped by the waves of the sea and bathed in the blue of the sky, the former minister of Theodoric initiated at Vivarium that monastic school of higher studies which he had longed for in vain in Rome. The fact stands that Cassiodorus at Vivarium, with a largeness of view and a maturity of experience surprising in a belated vocation, began that special form of the monastic life entirely dedicated to prayer and study which, previously written into his Rule by St. Benedict, inaugurated a new era of Christian civilization.

The guiding principle of the program of medieval monachism was contained in the motto, *Ora et labora*, which was common both to St. Benedict and to Cassiodorus. We must consider the ideas that dominated those chosen and far-seeing men, who, despite the catastrophe that befell the Empire at the hands of the barbarians, foresaw for the Church a new era of Christian reconstruction; thence the Benedictine ideal of training workmen for God, "the school of the Lord's service."

In other writings I have developed researches and comparisons, in order to show how the text of the Benedictine Rule in many ways imitates preceding monastic rules written by the bishop of Hippo, by Eugippius of Lucullanum, and by the metropolitan of Arles, and corresponds to the special program of the episcopacy of the time to bring about unity of discipline and government in the monasteries of men by imposing the same code on all.

The *Regula monasteriorum* of St. Benedict, as is clear from the very title, is directed and refers rather to the government of the entire class of cenobites than to the single monks. Hence the author exercises a universal authority which does not propose or counsel, but directly imposes on bishops, abbots, and monks the obligation of the Holy Rule, reforming abuses and stamping as temerarious those who would dare to question its authority. Such an attitude not even Caesarius, metropolitan of Gaul, hazarded, but he felt the need of leaning on the papal authority of Hormisdas (*Patrol. lat.*, LXVII, 1285).

To think that St. Benedict almost at the gates of Rome—as a matter of fact, John IV calls him a "Roman" abbot—was able by his own authority to promulgate a common rule for all the monasteries, even if only of the various Italian provinces, simply does not make sense. At that time the monasteries depended upon the several bishops and were not self-governing. The only supreme authority in whose name the whole of monasticism, *"coenobitarum genus,"* could be reformed was that of the Holy See. Even though documents backing up this assertion are not at hand, the very nature of the juridical situation points to the fact; no other explanation is possible.

Did not Pope Hormisdas commission Dionysius Exiguus to compile a canonical compendium of the Greek authors? The relevant papal document is wanting, but Dionysius himself assures us of the fact in the preface to the work. Abbot Eugippius at Lucullanum, besides disseminating the theological thought of St. Augustine, also desired to introduce at Naples the monastic rule of the bishop of Hippo, retouching it and adapting it to the conditions of Italy. But, despite the excellence of the work, which St. Benedict later followed to a large degree, the Augustinian code at that time did not meet with much success because it represented the personal work of Eugippius and did not bear the Holy See's seal of approval.

But why—as has been objected—does not St. Gregory say anything of these relations of St. Benedict with Rome? Because, I reply, the Pope is not writing a biography, which he could well suppose was known to his readers, but simply relates some miracles. For this reason he prescinds from the juridical and historical conditions under which were founded Subiaco, Monte Cassino, Terracina, and other monasteries. It sufficed for him to inform us that Benedict, besides performing miracles, is also the author of a monastic Rule. Why, he thought to himself, does not everyone know that a universal Rule, in order to be truly such, must be promulgated by the Holy See?

History tells us that when St. Benedict died about 547, without having put the finishing touches to his work, the Rule lay in the library of Monte Casino for a good ten years, until the throne of Peter was filled in the person of Pelagius I. At the time of St. Benedict's death, Pope Vigilius was a prisoner at Constantinople, and Pelagius, still a deacon, was paying in prison for his obstinate fidelity to the famous Three Chapters.

When things began to take a turn for the better for the Holy See, and Pelagius saw his authority well established in Rome, then finally Simplicius, the third abbot of Monte Cassino, thought the moment opportune to bring forth the sacred deposit of the Rule in order to put it at the disposition of all.[5]

But precisely when did St. Benedict receive from the Holy See the assignment to evangelize the pagans dwelling in the various towns around Casinum and, at the same time, to draw up the new *Regula monasteriorum?* Were these two missions perhaps combined on purpose? That is precisely what St. Ambrose did when he sent to Vigilius, bishop of Trent, three monk-clerics of his monastery at Milan, to evangelize the pagans of Val di Non. Grafting the missionary life on the monastic vocation was already in the minds of the great sixth-century representatives of monachism.

I stated before that possibly the first draft of Benedict's monastic code dates from the time when he was at Subiaco. Otherwise we can hardly understand the definitive organization of those monasteries by the Patriarch prior to his departure from that place. Yet the biographer assures us that the reorganization was a radical one.

Benedict began by substituting simple priors in place of the abbots, choosing for this office of lesser importance men who in his absence would be capable of governing their monasteries in dependence on a common abbot. He made a different distribution among the personnel of the various communities, perhaps decreasing their number, but reinforcing the families, and above all laying down orders and

[5] *Simplicius famulus Christique minister*
Magistri latens opus propagavit in omnes.

norms, lest the constitutional unity of his congregation in the identity of its discipline and spirit should be broken up.

To succeed to St. Benedict's office at Subiaco, in preference to any of the old abbots, was chosen the man who from his early years had been the Patriarch's right hand in the school of St. Clement and was considered the heir to his spirit, St. Maur. Zachary calls him: ὁ τοῦ ἁγίου Πατρὸς φοιτής. Later we find Honoratus occupying the abbatial throne at Subiaco, but always as the only abbot of the various monasteries.

Hence it is possible that when Gregory the Great says that the Patriarch, before his definitive departure from Subiaco, "*oratoria cuncta ordinavit,*" he means to refer to a true economic organization, imposing a stable law which all should follow as the common rule of life. At least that is the usual meaning of the word "*ordinavit,*" as when Livy writes: "*ordinare milites,*" and Cicero: "*ordinare rem publicam.*" Similarly the word "*ordo,*" in the sense of a rule, has passed from classical to ecclesiastical usage. Thus we have the famous *Ordines Romani.*

To the primitive Pachomian concept of simple deaneries or squadrons of a dozen monks with their own corporal or superior, as things were arranged at Subiaco, succeeded the concept of the monastic citadel, well disposed, organized and ample, containing all necessary buildings, so that the cenobitical life might be carried on in a normal manner.

According to the chronology of the abbey of Cassino, as we have said, its foundation is to be put in the year 529. It is possible that about this time the Patriarch was also elevated to the priesthood; and it is precisely by virtue of this quality that he could be charged by the Holy See to carry out the work of a missioner in the Campania. As a matter of fact, it is indisputable that in the twelve *oratoria* attached to the monasteries Mass was celebrated and the sacraments administered to the members of the communities.[6]

Now, in Gregory's account no other priests or deacons appear.

---

[6] In a contemporaneous novella of Justinian (no. 132) it is prescribed that in every monastery five or six of the more advanced monks be ordained priests. Probably the law was not observed in Italy, but none the less it manifests the spirit of the jurisprudence of the time. Also the *Regula monasteriorum* presupposes that the abbot has the dignity of the priesthood.

Everywhere and always it is only St. Benedict who appoints and removes superiors, who preaches to monks and laymen, who is daily visited by pilgrims, who is in a particular manner attacked by the pastor of St. Lawrence, jealous of the Patriarch's apostolate in all the surrounding territory.[7]

Here there is question of works of zeal exercised far and wide outside the monastery. Hence the reason for the jealousy of the pastor of St. Lawrence. Now, supposing that his promotion to the priesthood was the result of his new position as legislator and father of twelve monasteries, it is easier to understand the envy of the priest Florence —the "deserter," as St. Gregory stamps him—against a colleague in the priesthood of Christ.

A deserter from what? The epithet is rather strong, and in the mind of Gregory it must have had its precise juridical meaning. Evidently a deserter from the elevated spiritual direction which Benedict exercised over the surrounding territory. Whether that pre-eminence of St. Benedict was simply moral or also hierarchical, the biographer does not say. Instead he affirms that Florence, by departing from the saint, *"desertor fiebat*—he became a deserter."

If the abbot of the monasteries at Subiaco had remained a simple layman, without any pre-eminence over the priest Florence, the latter certainly would not have merited the accusation of "deserter" merely because he discontinued his visits. If nevertheless Gregory calls him that, it is a sign that the secession of the pastor constituted for him a kind of treason.

We should note particularly the biographer's statement that Benedict's beneficent activity embraced the entire region. In view of the fact that it was not restricted to the parish of St. Lawrence, but went beyond its limits, what does the "deserter" pastor do? He does not dare to oppose the saint openly; he does not complain to the bishop about an invasion of his parochial rights, but resorts to sinister practices.

He begins by trying to compete with Benedict's works of zeal, perhaps he even criticizes them: *"Sancti viri studiis coepit aemulari."* Then he proceeds to defame the Abbot, and attempts, at times even

---

[7] *"Cum iam loca eadem in amorem Domini . . . longum lateque fervescerent . . . Florentius sancti viri studiis coepit aemulari."*

by violence, to prevent the faithful from visiting him. But St. Gregory observes that in this attempt he did not always succeed. He would like to enjoy the same reputation as the wonder-worker.[8] Finally he makes a desperate attempt to kill him by sending him the eulogia of blessed bread, as used to be done by Paulinus of Nola, Augustine of Hippo, and other priests of those times.[9]

The envy of the "deserter" priest makes plausible the hypothesis that at that time St. Benedict had been ordained priest for the benefit of his monasteries and the numerous penitents who daily flocked to him.[10]

[8] *"Quia conversationis illius appetebat habere laudem, sed habere laudabilem vitam nolebat"* (*Dial.*, Bk. II, chap. 8).

[9] Pope Gelasius I in a letter of the year 493 to the bishops of Piceno envisages a case similar to that of the girls sent by the priest Florence: *"Qui insuper leges dedit . . . ut servi Dei cum puellis sacris congregatione dedecorissime miscerentur? . . . Adhuc maius scelus accrescit, ut sub conspectu et praesentia sacerdotum . . . contra apostolicam disciplinam, non solum monachos, sed etiam ministros Ecclesiae cum foeminis ad peregrinos migrantes remeare rursus . . . ?"* And the Pope concludes by commanding: *"Discreta suis habitationibus virorum atque foeminarum, sicut sanctum propositum decet, exerceatur circumspecta devotio."*

[10] The *Liber diurnus* presupposes that every monastery has its own priests for the service of the community. In Formula 26, to the order given to a bishop to consecrate the oratory of a monastery, is added the injunction that he go there when he is called: *"Cum postulaverit, ingravanter accedat, veneranda solemnia dedicationis impendens, quoties necesse fuerit, a presbyteris ecclesiae in suprascripto loco deservientibus celebrentur Sacrificia veneranda Missarum."*

CHAPTER XX

Departure from Subiaco

THE persecution on the part of the disgraceful pastor and a series of other reasons, some of which are unknown to us,[1] around the year 529 brought about in St. Benedict the determination to migrate from Subiaco to Monte Cassino.

Mark the Poet does not speak at all of the deserter priest, but assigns a divine command as the reason for the departure of St. Benedict from Subiaco. *"Sed iussus veniens, heremoque vocatus ad alta."* The motives brought forth by the two historians can be harmonized. The saint is about to begin a new life which, without substantially differing from that which he led as anchorite and abbot at Subiaco, will complete the figure of the Patriarch with the aureola of the apostolate among the idolaters. To justify this change of place and vocation, according to the testimony of Mark the Poet, God directly intervenes.

We are in the last years of the pontificate of Felix IV (d. 530), an ancestor of Gregory the Great. He came from Samnium, and could look upon himself as a protégé of Cassiodorus. He showed himself most affable to Caesarius of Arles; in Rome he established the basilica of the martyrs Cosmas and Damian on the Via Sacra. This church—

---

[1] Possibly we may attribute one of these reasons to St. Benedict's assiduous reading of the *Dicta Seniorum*, which he expressly cites in the Rule: *"Licet legamus: vinum omnino monachorum non esse"* (chap. 60).—The passage from which he quotes is this: *"Dixit abbas Poemen: noli habitare in loco in quo cernis nonnullos tibi invidere: alioquin non facies progressum. Narraverunt . . . de aliquo monacho quod vinum non biberet. Et dixit: vinum omnino ad monachos non pertinet"* (*Act. SS., Aug.*, VI, p. 34). Hence in departing from Subiaco, St. Benedict acted according to the advice of Abbot Poemen.

still standing in the Roman Forum, near the arch of Titus—is the end result of the transformation of two classical buildings of antiquity for the purpose of Christian worship by grant of the court of Ravenna. The two buildings in question are the circular temple of Romulus, behind which rose the temple or *augusteum* of the Penates or, according to some, Vespasian's library of the Forum of Peace.

The dedication of the new sanctuary must have made a great stir in all of Latium. No doubt bishops, priests, and laity came from all sides, and the monasteries cannot have escaped the interest which the event called forth. The Roman Missal to this day preserves the liturgical formulas first used on that festive occasion. All these circumstances appear meaningful to us. One of the monasteries erected by St. Benedict on the hill overlooking the lake was dedicated to SS. Cosmas and Damian. These contemporaneous dedications to the two Oriental martyrs, both in the old imperial buildings in Rome and in the deserted halls of Nero's villa at Subiaco, can have a distinct significance.

Also later St. Benedict, in order to convert to Christian use the various pagan temples on the summit of Cassino, most assuredly had to obtain—as did Felix IV at Rome—the permission of King Athalaric through the agency of Cassiodorus. I have difficulty in ridding myself of a suspicion. Was there not possibly some relationship between St. Benedict and the family of Gregory I? Some historians are of that opinion.

We must not suppose that the Patriarch's departure from Subiaco was precipitate. Before leaving the place where he had sanctified the beginnings of his monastic congregation and where more than a hundred men by virtue of religious profession, as understood at the time, had acquired the right to have him perpetually as their master and father, the saint devoted considerable thought to the matter. "After reflection, he yielded to the priest's jealousy." Therefore, in agreement with the bishop, he took all the time required to give a stable and definitive organization to that group of monasteries. *"Pertractans,"* evidently with the superiors.

The biographer adds: "He made provision, accordingly, for all the monasteries he had established by appointing priors, each of whom was to govern a certain number of monks." The Pope uses the words *oratoria* and *monasteria* as synonyms. In another work I have already described the juridical conditions of the sixth century, according to which oratories that were attached to monasteries could be consecrated by diocesan bishops only after these had received the authorization of Rome.

The word "*ordinavit*" does not say very much, but it does let us understand that the transfer of power came about in a regular manner, with the intervention of the diocesan authority and perhaps the publication of a *lex collegii* for the entire confederation of cenobites. It is to be noted that the Latin word "*ordinare*" has not the same meaning as the English verb "to order." The classical phrases, "*magistratus in plures annos ordinavit*" (Sueton.), "*ordinare rem publicam*" (Cicero), regularly imply juridical appointment to an office. St. Benedict employed the word "*ordinare*" in that same sense: "*De ordinando abbate*"; "*In ordinatione praepositi.*"

When the historian relates Benedict's departure from Vicovaro, he allows Peter the Deacon to interrupt to ask if an abbot is allowed to forsake his community. This same objection might be raised with regard to St. Benedict's leaving Subiaco. In view of the canon law in force at the time, how was it possible for him to desert the twelve monasteries in order to undertake the conversion of the pagans at Casinum? Regarding the case of the monks at Vicovaro, Gregory indeed admits the perpetuity of the abbot's government, but observes that the monks themselves made Benedict's continued presence among them useless.

Such a circumstance certainly was not present at Subiaco. Hence the solution of this juridical question is to be sought in the intervention of the Apostolic See or the episcopal authority rather than in a divine command. This entire change certainly was not due to the simple initiative of St. Benedict. Ecclesiastical law was opposed to it, and clergy and people would have risen up against it. It would be still harder to understand how the bishop of Tivoli would have permitted the Patriarch of twelve monasteries to depart after a residence of more than thirty years in his jurisdiction.

When everything had been settled, accompanied by a few disciples the saint took his sad departure.[2] He left St. Clement's in such a manner that the people were not aware of it, and even this was intended

[2] "*Paucis secum monachis ablatis, habitationem mutavit loci.*"

as an act of kindness and charity toward the unfortunate pastor.

Several decades later, the monk Mark, describing the scene in his poem, according to the bad taste of the period depicts the mountains, the woods, the lake itself as weeping bitterly at the leave-taking: "*lacerata genas, lacerata capillos!*"

Not even the old raven is satisfied. Perhaps the monks will be bound by the secret, but not he. What to do? He flies to the woods, summons two companions, and together they accompany the little caravan.

> "*Credar ficta loqui, nisi te, ne solus abires,*
> *Tres subito corvi promeruerunt sequi.*"

Mark is a clever poet and makes nature express his sentiments. In all probability the monks wept at St. Benedict's departure; but certainly neither the priest Florence nor the ballerine, who were his accomplices, saw any reason for sadness in the event. Indeed, when the pastor learned the time of departure, he mounted to the balcony of his house that he might witness the retreat of his enemy.

God, it is true, permits evil men to act, but He does not allow them to triumph. The accursed work of the pastor entered into the designs of Providence for the execution of a plan. The priest Florence may indeed have been the cause of the wonder-worker's decision to abandon Subiaco, but he was not allowed to enjoy his victory. God's vengeance struck him on that balcony whence he had intended to watch the caravan of monks who, going toward the plains of Arcinazzo, directed their steps in the direction of the Via Latina. Suddenly the railing of the balcony gave way. . . . Florence fell with it and died on the rocks below.

The priest's house was not far from the monastery of St. Clement. Soon after, the happening was known throughout the *vicus,* and I leave it to each one to imagine what an impression it created. The justice of God! In haste St. Maur sent a messenger after the master to entreat him to return, since his enemy now was dead. The man caught up with the monastic caravan, which had made about five miles and was preparing lodgings for the night. Had Benedict perhaps gone by way of Enfide? The distance from Subiaco would more or less agree.[3]

---

[3] With regard to the tradition about St. Benedict's stops at Roiate every time he went

When he learned the sad news, he was deeply moved. The fact that the hand of God had struck the unfortunate man filled him with terror. But that now his dearly beloved Maur should congratulate him besides, was so contrary to the spirit of the Gospel that this defect in the disciple greatly increased the sorrow of the master.

To return to Subiaco: he could not think of it. God desired him elsewhere, and Benedict well knew it. He could not restrain his tears; he therefore sent back the messenger and imposed a salutary penance on St. Maur, because he had shown delight at the misfortune of the poor "deserter." That is the way saints act.

St. Gregory, in commenting on the event, observes that the holy Patriarch wished to imitate David, whose lamentation at the death of Jonathan and of Saul, his former enemy, is described in the Bible. Perhaps no one in the parish of St. Lawrence wept at the sad death of the pastor. But the Patriarch of monks did weep, and let us hope that at least those tears benefited the deceased.

St. Gregory tells us very precisely that of the parish house of St. Lawrence nothing fell except the *solarium*, that is, the balcony on which Florence was standing. The rest of the house suffered no harm, and thus the son of the priest was safe. Later he went to Rome, married, and in his turn consecrated a son to the service of the Church and the Lateran court. St. Gregory mentions him several times as *"huius noster subdiaconus Florentius."* Possibly, after his refusal of the bishopric of Naples, he may be identified with the priest Florence of St. Lawrence in Damaso mentioned in Book IV, chapter 31, of the *Dialogues*. It seems to have been a trick of fortune that he became pastor of St. Lawrence's in Rome in order thus to remind him of the sad story of his grandfather.

---

to Rome, Mirtius appeals to local memories. In 967 Subiaco possessed some holdings there (cf. V. Federici, *Monasteri di Subiaco, La biblioteca e l'archivio*, doc. 93). The church dedicated to St. Benedict is mentioned in 1342 (*op. cit.*, doc. 1198), and the nuns' convent is mentioned in 1461 (*op. cit.*, doc. 886).

The chapel built over the rock with the supposed imprint of St. Benedict's body, rises on a small hill just outside of Roiate. It has nothing ancient about it. Mirtius mentions various miracles supposed to have occurred in his time by the use of the "manna of St. Benedict," the liquid collected from the calcareous rock. Egidi (*I Monasteri di Subiaco, Notizie storiche*, p. 51) lists a number of writings treating of these imprints of St. Benedict in the stone at Roiate.

CHAPTER XXI

Guidance of the Angels

A NUMBER of writers have attempted to describe the itinerary of St. Benedict on his way from Subiaco to Cassino. The first is Mark the Poet; he is also the most authoritative, because he was a contemporary. The man of God departed without knowing exactly the goal of his journey. On the way he was escorted by three ravens, and at every fork in the road two angels under the guise of wayfaring youths pointed out the direction he was to take.

Of the priest Florence never a word. The saint leaves Subiaco by the order of God. Twice the poet insists on this divine revelation. St. Gregory on the other hand says nothing either of the itinerary or the angels or the ravens, but states that the Patriarch was accompanied by a number of disciples.

The trip is long, and several villages of *Latium adiectum* are met with; the group lodges near the churches and visits the tombs of the martyrs that are there. At Fondi it was St. Magnus, at Anagni St. Secundina, at Alatri St. Quintianus, at Sora St. Julian. Finally, after several days they reached the vicinity of Aquino.

Tosti relates that after St. Benedict had descended to the fields of Arcinazzo (elevation about 2,500 feet), he went by way of Torre, where he fixed his staff into the ground; afterward it grew and became a flowering bush. Later, in that locality was founded a convent of Benedictine nuns, where the tree produced flowers of Christian virginity which never fade.

From Torre the Patriarch went to Guercino (elevation 1,875 feet), where, until the eighteenth century, a church bearing his name served as a monument of his passing. Thence the saint proceeded along the River Cosa and entered the territory of Alatri. This old city of the Hernicians supplied St. Benedict with some idea of the topography and the religious conditions he was to meet on the heights of Cassino. Until the present time the city is surrounded by an extensive polygonal wall dating back to the sixth century before Christ, the most complete of its kind in existence. The acropolis still exists intact with its ring of Hernician wall, its five gates with enormous monolithic arches. The Porta Civita and the Porta Minore are well preserved.

At Alatri he was the guest of the deacon and Abbot Servandus, in whose monastery of St. Sebastian, until recent times, a small bell was shown, which St. Benedict is said to have given to repay the hospitality he received. In former times three other churches sought to claim the honor of having sheltered the saint at Alatri: St. Benedict alle Piaggie, St. Benedict at the Gate, and St. Benedict on Monte Pizzuto.

From Alatri the route lay over Veroli, where other Benedictine sanctuaries and monasteries arose; thence the Patriarch descended down the valley of the Liri, until finally he reached the Via Latina. This itinerary appears to be a very likely one, but unfortunately it is based on evidence both late and not very trustworthy. The only halt that has any documentary backing is that with the deacon Servandus.

We know from St. Gregory that the monastery of St. Sebastian at Alatri had been founded half a century earlier through the efforts of the patrician Liberius, whom Cassiodorus praises in the *Variarum*.[1] Liberius had passed with honor from the service of Odoacer to that of Theodoric, and had been found so deserving by the Gothic government that after his death the King promoted his son Venantius to the position of *comes domesticus*.

Besides, from the life of St. Caesarius of Arles we know, though not precisely under what circumstances, that Liberius was wounded by the Goths and that he was miraculously cured by the wonder-worker

[1] Bk. II, no. 16.

of Arles. The wife of Liberius, in that account, is given the name of Agrestia.[2]

St. Gregory places this monastery of Liberius "in the Campania," [3] "about forty miles distant from Rome." The present monastic building goes back to the eleventh and twelfth centuries, and it stands on the saddle of a spur of Monte Pizzuto, which extends toward the west. It is a good hour's walk from Veroli. The place is praised for the mildness of its climate and for the vast panorama that it commands. At the "abbey," as the building is still called, despite the fact that the monks abandoned it centuries ago, is shown the cell which St. Benedict is said to have occupied during his stay at Alatri.

St. Gregory tells us that about the year 540 the monastery of St. Sebastian was governed by the deacon Servandus, a man of great learning and of a holy life. Even today his memory is preserved in a medieval inscription on the altar.[4]

The inscription in Leonine verse is engraved on the small pilasters of the alter. Nothing else in the church has any true artistic value. Of the times of the patrician Liberius not a vestige remains. After Servandus' death the monastery unfortunately had no worthy rulers. St. Gregory was obliged to remove Abbot Secundinus for his crimes; in his place he appointed a certain Theodosius, who in his turn was obliged to have recourse to the Pontiff on account of the unruliness of his monks. Vicovaro is not an isolated case.

From the acropolis of Alatri, gazing about him, St. Benedict could have seen Monte Pizzuto, the plains of Arcinazzo, Guercino, Veroli, and, behind Veroli, Monte Cairo, on the other side of which rises Monte Cassino. Who knows; perhaps the two angels who acted as his guides may have shown him from afar the sanctuary of Apollo on Monte Cairo and, close to it, the temple of Apollo of Cassino, which he would convert into a Christian church.

After this brief stage to Alatri, let us continue our way to Aquino and Casinum. In the meantime a commotion arose among the people

---

[2] *Acta sanctorum*, August, VI, 77.

[3] *Dial.*, Bk. II, chap. 35; *Epist.*, Bk. IX, no. 24; *Dial.*, Bk. III, chap. 8.

[4]   HOC OPUS ALTARIS SPLENDET DE MARMORE FACTUM
       MONACHUS ECCLESIAE THOMAS QUOD FECERAT APTUM
       COLLOCET HUNC DOMINUS POST MORTEM SEDE SUPERNA
       MARTYRIS ET SANCTI SERVANDI PRECE BENIGNA

of Subiaco. They demanded the return of their wonder-worker, and could not understand how he had yielded to the malignity of the priest Florence. But the evil in the whole of Italy was far more deep-rooted than the people generally could imagine.

If, at Subiaco, almost under the very eyes of the bishop of Tivoli, the perfidy of a priest, a deserter from canonical discipline, was able to compromise the future of that primitive congregation of twelve monasteries, it is necessary to keep in mind that in those days of wars and religious struggles, it was not easy for the bishop to have recourse to the supreme religious authorities against the pretensions of an ecclesiastic.

At the time of St. Gregory it would have sufficed simply to recur to Rome to prevent any repetition of the invasion of the ballerine on the shores of Nero's lake. But, during the first half of the sixth century, the very government of Ravenna had so little respect for the Roman Pontiffs that Theodoric made them travel from Rome to Ravenna and even to Constantinople at his behest; if then they were not compliant enough, he had them thrown into prison, there to suffer the greatest privations.

Pope Felix IV was elected by will of the King. In his turn, on August 30, 526, Theodoric himself died, the glory of the first years of his reign eclipsed by the cruelties of his senile decrepitude. This general disturbance so impressed Pope Felix IV that, feeling a presentiment of death, in order to forestall any possible electoral intrigues on the part of the Goths, he appointed as his successor the archdeacon Boniface and gave him the pallium in anticipation. The choice was agreeable to the government of Byzantium.

As could be foreseen, upon the death of the Pontiff on September 22, 530, followed a kind of schism and civil war. The clergy, assembled in the Lateran, as a sign of protest against the arbitrary act of the deceased, chose Dioscurus as pope, had him consecrated immediately, and acclaimed him pope in the basilica Julia in the Trastevere.

By good fortune Dioscurus died on November 12 following, and his former adherents had the good sense to transfer their allegiance to Boniface II. Thus the schism was snuffed out at its birth. Among the first acts promulgated by the new pope was a constitution forbidding any offering or acceptance of money in connection with a papal election.

When Boniface II died on October 17, 532, he was succeeded at the beginning of the following year by John II, who occupied the throne of Peter for scarcely a year and a half. The spirit then animating the Church at Rome appears from an edict of King Athalaric, which he ordered the prefect of the city, Salvantius by name, to have engraved in stone and affixed to the façade of St. Peter's. In this decree it was laid down that, for the purpose of eliminating abuses which occurred in the papal elections, when even the goods and furnishings of the Church were sold to buy votes, the confirmation of the election had to be sought from the sovereign. In the eventuality of a dispute among various candidates, the controversy was to be settled by the Arian king, but for the proceedings not more than three thousand soldi were to be spent.

On May 8, 535, through the influence of the Byzantines, Agapitus II, a former partisan of Dioscurus, obtained the succession. With him the senatorial group began to raise its head, and the star of the Goths went into decline. King Theodatus in a moment of rage threatened to exterminate the Senate, but was brought around by Cassiodorus' milder counsel and induced to treat with the *patres conscripti* in order that his troops might be quartered at least outside of Rome.

CHAPTER XXII

Toward Cassino

TAKING advantage of the governmental troubles in Italy, the pagans of Casinum reverted to their worship of Jupiter, Apollo, and Venus in the face of all the ancient imperial laws proscribing paganism. In the year 341 Constantius had ordered the abolition of all the idolatrous sacrifices, and the following year only the temples situated in the vicinity of Rome were excepted from the general destruction.[1] About 346 a new decree was issued, threatening death to anyone violating the law which ordained the closing of all the temples.[2] Later, in 391, a fine is imposed on judges who should dare to enter a pagan temple. But still in 399 special reference is made to pagan temples of outstanding artistic value; these might be preserved, but only for that reason.

Notwithstanding all the Roman jurisprudence, however, the persistent vitality of paganism, particularly in rural areas and among the lower classes, is proved by too great a number of testimonies to permit us to doubt its continued existence. Precisely in St. Benedict's time, during the Gothic wars, Procopius mentions a consultation of the Sibylline Books, whence it was declared that during the month of July Rome would have nothing to fear from the Goths. But when facts gave the lie to the forecast, the pagans pointed out that the old Sibyl had indeed promised safety to Rome during the month of July, but had not specified the year.[3]

[1] *Cod. Theodos.*, XVI, X, 2.
[2] *Ibid.*
[3] *Bell. Goth.*, I, 24.

Since the Catholics in Italy were accustomed to enjoy this protection of the law against the exercise of idolatrous worship, we can picture their consternation when, about 525, King Theodoric, as a reprisal against the Byzantine emperor who had ordered the closing of all Arian churches, countered by demanding that Catholic churches be closed. We may hold, however, that the decree represented nothing more than a threat against the emperor. On the other hand, all the ancient constitutions with regard to the closing of the pagan temples remained on the books. The popes insisted on their enforcement. In this sense already Anastasius II had written to Theodoric.[4]

In these circumstances it should not cause wonder if the twofold authority, ecclesiastical and civil, considering the long and obstinate resistance of the dwellers of Casinum to the closing of their ancient temples and to the cessation of their idolatrous sacrifices, about the year 529 mutually agreed to confide the difficult mission to an apostle well versed in the ways of rural and mountain folk, St. Benedict.

The experience of almost two centuries had shown that, to vanquish paganism, more was necessary than the simple publication of imperial decrees. The people, particularly in the rural areas, resisted fanatically, even though Christianity had permeated the whole of civil and political life. Family customs as well as public and municipal feasts were based on mythology; hence to break with the ancient paganism was to run the danger of easily estranging the populace.[5]

Thus one can understand how at Casinum, not very distant from two celebrated episcopal sees, even in the year of the Lord 529 the pagans were able to carry out their rites undisturbed. Who would ever have had the hardiness to attack Apollo in his temple on the hill, braving the religious ire of the pagans? We discover a similar case in Gaul. The monk Paternus with his colleague Scabilius settled near Scicy "to purge the temple where till that time the inhabitants

[4] *"Theodorico regi. Certum est magnificentiam vestram leges Romanorum principum, quas in negotiis hominum custodiendas esse praecepit, multo magis circa reverentiam beati Petri Apostoli pro suae felicitatis augmento velle servari"* (Gelas. PP. Epist.; Thiel, Epp. RR. PP., p. 489).

[5] St. Maximus of Turin in two sermons (101, 102), *De idolis auferendis de propriis possessionibus,* bears witness that the idols which had been expelled from the cities by imperial edicts found refuge in the country districts, where sacrifices were still offered to Jupiter, Diana, and Bacchus. He describes how a priest of Diana, wearing a wig, his arms and breast bare, with the fury of one possessed brandished a knife to divide the flesh of the victims.

used to practice the execrable rites of their superstition." The two monks had to overcome fierce opposition from the pagans. Later Bishop Leontianus of Constance ordained Paternus a deacon and subsequently priest. This was about 530.[6]

The authorities had arrived at the conclusion that paganism could be vanquished only through the efforts of the monks. St. Martin and St. Ambrose had given splendid examples of success in this field in Gaul and in northern Italy. In the Orient as early as the fourth century the Antiocheans had imposed silence on the oracle of Daphne by transporting to the infamous spot the body of the martyr Babila and building a church there in her honor.

We must keep in mind, above all, that Casinum at that time was a *castrum,* that is, a fortress, a military post of prime importance, the door, as it were, between Campania Felix and Latium. It was, however, a special fortress, because at the same time it served as a protection for an ancient temple of the Samnites and in a way symbolized the paganism of the entire region. It was certainly a happy solution that Cassiodorus discovered, namely, to repeat at Casinum what Justinian I had done when he captured Carthage from the Vandals. The Emperor founded near Mendracijm a fortress-monastery, that is, a *castrum-coenobium,* and fortified it with walls and impregnable towers.[7] Hence, in circumstances which we do not know perfectly, but which we must fit into the twofold legislation of the sixth century, the mission to evangelize the pagan oasis which was Casinum in the middle of Campania Felix, or better, of Latium adiectum, was confided to St. Benedict.[8]

6 Mabillon, *op. cit.,* I, 73 f.

7 Procop., *De. aedific.,* VI, V; Ben., III, 339.

8 The condition of the pagans in the various villages about Casinum was without any legal sanction. This fact explains how they were not in a position to oppose any juridical resistance to the apostolic undertakings of St. Benedict as long as he limited himself to preaching the Gospel to them. But as far as gaining possession of their temples was concerned, obtaining ownership of them, and converting them into Christian churches, a governmental grant was absolutely required, and here without a doubt Cassiodorus enters into the picture.

Apparently the events took place in the following manner: First the Patriarch, after receiving a heavenly admonition, departs from Subiaco under the guidance of divine Providence and is directed by two angels. Arrived at Casinum, he takes up lodgings there, and the Lord, perhaps through the bishop of Aquino, reveals His designs to him. The necessary steps are taken at the court of Ravenna, which, to purge the summit of Casinum of the last vestige of idolatry, consents to its transformation into a monastic sanctuary.

I have already said that the mission to Cassino to preach to and convert the pagans, to transform into churches their ancient temples on the summit, implies that St. Benedict had already been ordained a priest. According to the prevailing canonical discipline, it could not have been otherwise; for the preaching of the word of God was so much under the episcopal authority that it was not granted easily even to priests, much less to simple monks, to whom it had been expressly forbidden by Leo I: "Monks shall not be given permission to preach, and they shall be absolutely forbidden to arrogate to themselves what is reserved to priests." [9] St. Leo insists strongly on this prohibition. Concerning it he writes to Bishop Theodoretus of Ciro: "Besides the priests of the Lord, no one shall dare to preach, whether monk or layman, no matter how learned he may be." [10]

We possess, besides, an ordinance of Pope Celestine I by which even priests are forbidden to preach, because of the fear that some of them, without sufficient preparation, might advance non-orthodox ideas, particularly with regard to divine grace.[11] Such was the then rigorous discipline of the Roman Church. Only later, when rural parishes were established, was permission given to the simple priests attached to these parishes to announce the word of God. As far as Gaul is concerned, the second canon of the Council of Vaison (November, 529) extended to priests the ministry of preaching which hitherto they had been forbidden to exercise.

In St. Benedict's time the old rule was still adhered to at Rome. For this reason there was issued against the monk Equitius, who went about Latium and the Abruzzi preaching the Scriptures, an order of arrest that he be brought to Rome and subjected to a trial. "Who is

---

Thence derived a twofold advantage. With the sacred precincts of the hill converted into a monastery, the Byzantine soldiery could not regain possession of that strategic spot for an eventual action against the Goths. On the part of Theodoric, the grant of the hill to St. Benedict for religious purposes represents a neat and clever solution of an embarrassing situation. As a matter of fact, in 589, when Duke Zoto of Beneventum had to withdraw to the other side of the Liri River, he hastened to get possession of Monte Cassino. According to St. Gregory, the capture of the heights took place at night without warning. It seems, however, that the Lombard duke had no intention of harming the monks. Indeed they were allowed to depart, taking their most precious treasures with them. Hence Zoto was interested only in the spot as such, and he did not care to take prisoners or booty.

[9] *Epist.*, 193; *PL*, LXVI, 1040.
[10] *Loc. cit.*, 1054.
[11] *Decret.* 21; *PL*, L, 528.

this rustic, who presumes to arrogate to himself the right of preaching and, unlearned as he is, to usurp the office of our lord the Pope?" [12] This same remark had been made to the holy monk by a compatriot of St. Benedict, a certain Felix, a noble of Nursia and father of Castorius, a notarius of the Roman Church. Marveling that Equitius "did not seem to have received orders and yet went from place to place preaching," one day he asked: "You who have not been ordained and have not received any commission from the Roman Pontiff, under whose jurisdiction you live, how do you dare to preach?"

In the *Regula pastoralis* St. Gregory the Great manifests the same mentality. The office of preaching is so proper to the pastor, to the bishop, to the priest, that Gregory devotes the entire third book to an explanation of its obligations and conditions.[13] Hence the words of the same holy doctor, when he states that at Cassino Benedict eradicates idolatry, converts the pagan temples into Christian oratories, and, by preaching ceaselessly, calls the inhabitants to the faith, are to be understood in the light of the ancient Christian monuments and the canon law of the period. We shall see the biographer later describing the holy Patriarch in the exercise of his sacerdotal functions, numbering him among those who *"locum sancti regiminis fide et moribus tenent,"* that is, among the priests. The attestation of the Pope is explicit.

Similarly in the Rule, St. Benedict presupposes that the abbot normally is a priest. This was already a custom which later became universal.

Occasionally in the documents of the early Middle Ages these monk-missioners are simply styled bishops, that is, authorized preachers. Thus it was that St. Richarius, St. Furseus, and St. Gregory of Utrecht were given the title of *episcopi* though they were simple priests. Even in the late Middle Ages St. Francis calls St. Anthony his bishop, in the sense of being the preacher of his Friars Minor.

[12] *Dial.*, Bk. I, chap. 4.
[13] Pope Vigilius in 549, in a letter directed to two Roman deacons, Rusticus and Sebastian, after their defection, among other accusations reproaches them for having continued to preach without the previous permission of the bishop (*PL*, LXIX, 43). The Roman discipline on this point was extremely strict, precisely during the years of St. Benedict's apostolate at Casinum.

CHAPTER XXIII

Monte Cassino

THE grandiose monastery of Monte Cassino rose on the summit of an isolated mountain which lifts its head over the green valley of the Liri. Casinum from ancient times was regarded as a strategic point; it was successively occupied by the Etruscans, and finally, about 272 before Christ, by the Romans, who established there a *castrum*, that is, a fortified place. Of the former greatness of Casinum few appreciable ruins remain. Particular mention must be made of the famous amphitheater, erected at the expense of the eccentric matron Hummidia Quadratilla, the same woman whose square burial cell was transformed into a Christian oratory about the year 1000. It still exists.

When Benedict arrived at the Roman town of Casinum,[1] he found

---

[1] For the history of Cassino, I refer to the work of Gian Filippo Carrettoni: *Casinum*, Istit. di Studi Romani, 1940, sect. 1, Vol. I. It must be kept in mind that these pages were written before the destruction of Monte Cassino in the late war.

St. Gregory regularly calls Casinum a *castrum*, a term equivalent to *oppidum*, signifying a fortified town, with particular reference to its strategic position in the valley of the Liri.

It is possible that the religious center represented by the *fanum Apollinis* on the summit was more ancient than the primitive village of Casco or Casinum of the Samnites. Archaeologists distinguish a twofold fortification of Casinum. On the heights, about the acropolis, was a double circle of cyclopean walls for the protection of the temples and the fortress that had been built there. From the walls of the acropolis, at the southeast corner, another set of walls set off and descended down the back of the mountain; built in the form of a rectangle, they also included the *oppidum*, situated lower down on the hill on a spot drier and more salubrious than the site of the medieval village of St. Germanus, which later developed into the modern city of Cassino. When the Empire fell, that is, when the *oppidum* became the *castrum* Casinum, the need was felt of repairing the old walls; on the north side they were brought in somewhat closer, and towers were added to the polygonal defenses.

it half destroyed. This destruction was the work of the Goths who had been there thirty-five years previously. St. Gregory speaks particularly of a "foolish group of rustics," possibly because the ancient bourgeoisie of the Hummidii, of the Rubri, and of the descendants of Varro had disappeared in the convulsions of the time. The mountain continued to be inhabited by peasants.

But to bear witness to the former nobility of Casinum, about 530 there still remained the amphitheater,[2] the temple, the aqueducts, the baths, the tombs along the Via Latina, and the remains of Varro's villa, of which considerable ruins can be seen to this day. Christianity must have been known in Casinum for a long time, if an old tradition, naming St. Peter as the apostle of the region, can be believed. The temple erected by Hummidia Quadratilla near the amphitheater of Cassino was perhaps converted into a Christian church about the sixth century, because we can find no trace of any church in the territory, though a bishop and his clergy resided at Casinum.

According to the ancient historians, in the eighth century this temple, after considerable restorations ordered by Scauneperga, the wife of Gisulph, was dedicated to the Prince of the Apostles: S. Petrus in Civitate.[3] But it is likely that this dedication is much older and that it reflects the tradition of the region, according to which St. Peter

---

The strategic importance of the fortress and its system of fortifications, which made of the *oppidum* and the acropolis the only bulwark for the defense of the plains of the Liri, make it quite untenable that St. Benedict and his community should have been able, on their own initiative, without opposition from the governmental authorities and from the priestly college of Apollo, to take possession of these fortified heights.

[2] In 1727 near the amphitheater of Cassino was found the following inscription:

VMMIDIA. C. F
QVADRATILLA
AMPHITHEATRVM. ET
TEMPLVM. CASANATIBVS
SVA. PECVNIA. FECIT

It dates from the second half of the first century after Christ. The amphitheater is well known. The *templum* is identified with the church of St. Peter, which, according to Leo of Ostia, in the eighth century Scauneperga, the wife of Duke Gisulph, is said to have erected in the "*templum idolorum.*" It stood near the mausoleum of the Hummidii and was destroyed in 1621 "by order of the abbot." To think that St. Benedict had preached there. Cf. Carettoni, *op. cit.*, pp. 92 f.

[3] Cassinese documents of the eighth century indicate two churches dedicated to St. Peter. One served as the parish church of the city of Cassino; the other on the top of the mountain flanked the basilica of St. John the Baptist.

founded the episcopal sees of Casinum and Atina. Very rightly this building represents the primitive cathedral of Cassino.[4]

Under Abbot John II, toward the end of the eleventh century, also the mausoleum of Hummidia Quadratilla was converted into an oratory and dedicated to St. Nicholas of Bari. Leo of Ostia gives the following information: "Near St. Peter's he constructed a basilica in honor of St. Nicholas in an ancient crypt which had been built with immense stone and beautiful work by the pagans in honor of their gods" (Bk. II, 25). Today St. Nicholas has yielded the honors to the Most Holy Cross.

The historians of Casinum say that the *oppidum* remained well populated until the period of the decadence, when the barbarians arrived. Mention must be made of the incursions of the Goths (410), of the Vandals (435), of the Eruli (476), and finally of its partial destruction through the efforts of Theodoric (493–94). But perhaps the damage was not considerable, since in 478 Casinum was still an episcopal see and the *oppidum* was transformed into a *castrum*, that is, a fortified place.

The topographical description of the *castrum* made by Gregory the Great is evidently the work of one well acquainted with the fortress. The village, or *castrum*, on the side of the mountain is built in a kind of pocket which widens near the Via Latina, not far from the Liri. Dante marvelously translates St. Gregory: "*Quel monte a cui Cassino è sulla costa.*"

The mountain rises to a height of 1,680 feet; but the biographer describes the summit as lost in the clouds, because it is gained by a steep ascent about three miles long. The ancient mule path winding up the southeast flank of the mountain and leading to the monastery is of pre-Roman origin and is the same road that St. Benedict used fourteen centuries ago when he made his first entrance into the acropolis. It calls for strong legs and requires about an hour's walk. On the summit of the mountain, in the midst of the green groves

---

[4] The *Liber diurnus* (no. 38: "*Basilica quae post incendio reparatur*") preserves the text of a papal bull by which Bishop N. is authorized to dedicate "*basilicam quam in castro N. dilectio tua post incendium asserit praeparatum, et in honore beati N. habitatores loci illius desiderant consecrari.*" The Pontiff sends the relics to be put into the new altars. The document requested by the bishop of Aquino to repair and reconsecrate the church of St. Peter in the *castrum Casinum* must have been of the same tenor.

sacred to Apollo, were lined up under the beautiful domed sky, usually of a deep blue, the ancient temples on whose altars, well into the sixth century, the incense and the victims still smoked. As a protection for the temples, from the times of the Samnites, a double circle of walls had been constructed.[5] When about the fourth century the Romans felt the necessity of putting the heights in a state of defense as a protection for the *castrum*, they closed off the extreme point of the fortress with a short stretch of wall strengthened with towers; perhaps for the purpose they employed a part of the ancient circle.[6] At that time pagans must have been few in Italy. But this obstinate persistence in idolatrous worship, especially in the rural regions, is found, besides that at Casinum,[7] in St. Gregory's own time at Cagliari [8] and even at Terracina.

Let us not forget that, while he was spending the years of his early adolescence in Rome, St. Benedict's sense of modesty was several times offended by the celebration of the pagan solemnities of February 15 in honor of the god Februus. At the time a powerful senatorial party was promoting the worship of the Dioscuri, Castor and Pollux, and desired that sacrifice be offered to them at Ostia. Pope Gelasius opposed this sort of thing by the spoken and the written word, but without much effect.

No doubt the young Benedict often met in the streets of Rome the *cultores* of Februus, who, their nakedness scarcely covered by the skins of sheep and wolves, went in procession to the grotto of Pan, patron of the flocks against the wolves. If such scenes occurred in the open city toward the end of the fifth century, it is little to be marveled at that thirty years later St. Benedict found the altars still smoking on the acropolis of Cassino. St. Gregory speaks distinctly of the temple or

[5] The walls of Casinum, running out from the circle about the acropolis at its gates, thence to descend along the side of the mountain, nevertheless constitute one system of military fortifications; in documents of the twelfth century they are still called "*mura dominici*" or "*dompnici*." Is this a souvenir of the governmental character of the heights? Cf. Carettoni, *op. cit.*, p. 66.

[6] Cf. Carettoni, *op. cit.*, p. 59.

[7] It is strange that among the copious archaeological remains of Casinum, nothing of early Christian origin is found. The suspicion arises that the episcopal see was established there very early by reason of the special difficulties encountered in evangelizing that place. Casinum for a long time remained a kind of stronghold of the ancient superstition.

[8] *Epist.*, Bk. X, no. 26.

fanum of Apollo and then of the altar of the same god, which stood several hundred feet higher up, on the very crest of the mountain.[9]

Certain archaeological findings of recent date have convinced one student that also this *fanum* was protected by a small building with terra-cotta decorations. Recently all the prehistoric material uncovered at Monte Cassino was gathered into a museum. Besides decorative pieces of terra-cotta, decorations of a naos, there were found also, as votive offerings, Etrusco-Italian bronzes and bronzes of various other periods.

Mark the Poet mentions a temple of Jupiter, forgotten by St. Gregory, and adds that formerly the acropolis was a kind of pantheon, where all the gods of Olympus could enjoy the perfume of incense.[10]

[9] The *oraculum* of Apollo on the rocky summit of the mountain was so narrow that the Samnites built the naos somewhat lower down, where there was a larger level space. In the successive enlargements of the basilica of Cassino, both Abbot Gisulph and Abbot Desiderius abstained from leveling off the crown of the mountain, which thus remained about eight steps higher than the nave of the church.

Desiderius discovered the original tomb of the Patriarch at a depth of three cubits (about four and a half feet) under the floor and covered it with a marble cenotaph: *"In transversum basilicae, idest a septentrione in meridiem."* This point is noteworthy because it does not correspond to the orientation of the original tomb, in which the corpse was placed facing the east. Also to be noted is the depth of the tomb: three cubits. If to this depth be added three more cubits for the two stories of the double tomb, we have a trench about nine feet deep carved out of the rock of the mountain. This suggests the hypothesis that the very first origin of this subterranean hollow must be sought in the augural rite of the priests of Apollo, who gave their replies or oracles from this opening.

For several reasons Abbot Desiderius abstained from opening the tomb of the founder. He sought the advice of his *seniores*, and it was decided neither to change its location nor to open it: *"Ne illum aliquatenus mutare praesumeret . . . eundem tumulum eodem quo situs fuerat loco, praetiosis lapidibus cooperuit, ac desuper arcam de pario marmore in transversum basilicae, idest a septentrione in meridiem quinque per longum cubitis opere nimis pulchro construxit."* Hence there was some thought of moving the venerable tomb elsewhere.

What Abbot Desiderius did not dare to do was nevertheless carried out in 1683 when the high altar of the basilica over the original tomb of the founder was "moved back three palms and one palm toward the Gospel side" by the architect Cosimo Fanzaga, in order to center it under the cupola.

[10]
> *Templa ruinosis hic olim struxerat aris*
> *Queis dabat obsceno sacra cruenta Iovi.*
> *Hunc plebs stulta locum quondam vocitaverat Arcem*
> *Marmoreisque sacrum fecerat esse Diis.*
> *Quod tunc si vero signasset nomine quisquam*
> *Tartareum potuit iure vocare Chaos.*
> *Ad quem caecatis errantes mentibus ibant*
> *Improbo mortifero reddere vota Iovi.*

The existence of a temple of Jupiter, distinct from the naos of Apollo, is freely admitted by several more recent historians. (Cf. Carettoni, *op. cit.*, pp. 61 f.) Further, the hypothesis has been projected that to it belonged the wall of squared stones found in 1930 beneath

It seems that the dedicatory inscription of this temple of Jupiter was discovered at Monte Cassino during the work carried out in 1880.[11]

It should be kept in mind, however, that since the third century the Oriental cult of Mithras had succeeded in uniting Jupiter and Apollo in the one divinity of the sun god. Hence there would be question of but a single temple dedicated to Jupiter Helios, that is, Apollo. The *porticus* mentioned in the inscription joined the *templum* to the *fanum*, and disappeared only in the eleventh century, when the work of reconstructing the monastery under Abbot Desiderius was being carried out.

An ancient local tradition declares that on a small eminence below the acropolis grew a *lucus*, or grove sacred to Venus. This spot is today called Monte Venere. As a matter of fact, an ancient Cassinese inscription makes mention of a sanctuary of Venus, with a priestess attached to it and with its devotees.[12]

St. Gregory does not specify further, but merely states that around these very ancient temples groves had grown up, in which the peasants of the region tenaciously preserved the traditional order of feasts and sacrifices described in the calendar of the *castrum Casinense*.[13]

Before the Patriarch's arrival at Monte Cassino, to which episcopal see did that territory belong? Some have tried to find extremely ancient origins for an episcopal see of Cassino, whose incumbent al-

---

the archives of Cassino. Alinari observes that this construction "has all the characteristics of the platforms of temples, since it was made of large squared stones, regularly connected." Near by have been found some antique vessels, which Alinari considers certainly of Roman origin.

[11] It reads: M. OCTAVIUS. M. F. CALVINUS
Q LATERINUS. Q. F. Q.
AEDEM IOVIS A SOLO ET PORTICUM
CUM AEDIFICIIS EX C. C. P. P. FACIEND
CURAVERUNT.

[12] Cf. Carettoni, *op. cit.*, pp. 30 f.

[13] Carettoni cites various inscriptions that record at Casinum a temple or a sanctuary of Venus, which speak of a priestess of the goddess and of a devotee who, after seeing the goddess in a dream, restored her sanctuary (*op. cit.*, pp. 30 f.).

The citation from Tertullian regarding the worship which the ancient Cassinese paid the god Delventinus is isolated (*Apolog.* XXIV; 8th ed., Walzung, Paris, 1929). It is possible that later this god of purification (*deluo, lavo*) was confused with Apollo and Jupiter-Mithras. In a dedication to a Cassinese personage by the name of L. Lucius Iberus, his function is described thus: "*sacerdos sacrorum Savadiorum.*" The *Sacra Savadia* consisted of a feast in honor of Dionysus-Savatius, a Thracian divinity, likewise identified with Jupiter (Carettoni, *op. cit.*, p. 31).

legedly was that St. Severus to whom Abbot Theobald dedicated a chapel on the holy mount in the eleventh century. He was present at the council held in Rome under Pope Felix III in 487; in the preceding council of 465, celebrated by Pope Hilary in St. Mary Major, a certain Caprasius had signed as bishop of Cassino.

It is possible that after the incursion of Theodoric and after the death of Bishop Severus, the church of Cassino was so depleted in persons and means as to render a new election useless. This circumstance does not imply, however, that the *castrum* remained abandoned and without a pastor, since we know from the Epistolary of St. Gregory that such widowed sees were entrusted to some neighboring bishop.

For this reason it seems that the *castrum* did not in its entirety relapse into idolatry, particularly since, according to St. Gregory, the pagans were not found in the cities, but among the peasants of the mountains. He likewise speaks of a certain church to which were attached at least a priest and a deacon; further, he mentions some consecrated virgins. Finally from the poet Mark we know of a hermit who dwelt on the mountain undisturbed, suffering no harm at the hands of the idolaters.

The presence of a deacon would indicate an episcopal, or at least an important, city, where the *diaconus episcopi* carried out administrative functions.

In 499, the bishop of Aquino was Asterius; he was present at the Roman synods of 499, 501, 502, 503, and 504, when the conflict between Pope Symmacus and the antipope Lawrence was raging. Later, between the years 527 and 573, we find Constance, a man of holy life and endowed with the gift of prophecy, bishop of Aquino. But from what St. Gregory tells us, the diocese of Aquino must have been reduced to a miserable condition since, after the death of Constance, a successor was chosen in the person of an aged laundry-man by the name of Andrew, after whom came a certain Jovinus, an old muleteer. Apparently there was no better choice. When Jovinus died, no further canonical election was possible, since there were wanting both candidates and electors.

From the Epistolary of Gregory we learn that in many dioceses there was at that time only a bishop with a few clerics. When the bishop passed away, no one remained to baptize or to administer the sacraments to the dying.

In a word, in the series of documents regarding the life of St. Benedict, we find gaps that it is difficult to fill. The question is this: Did the Roman Pontiff or Constance, the local bishop, confide to St. Benedict the mission of converting the pagans? The answer is not easy, but without any doubt there must have been such a mission and such an appointment. It cannot have been otherwise.

This is not an isolated case. In the Epistolary of St. Gregory we find a repetition of almost stereotyped letters by which was entrusted to a certain bishop also the spiritual care of a neighboring diocese where, by reason of the wars, no one could be appointed bishop. In such a case, the Pope grants to the bishop in question the right to ordain a certain number of priests or deacons to take charge of various parishes in the vacant diocese. This was precisely the situation in the widowed diocese of Casinum.

It will be worth while to cite at least one of the formulas of Gregory's chancery: "Gregory to Bishop Balbinus of Rosella. We have learned that the diocese of Populonia no longer has a pastor, and that consequently no one remains to absolve the dying and to baptize the infants. To remedy the situation, by virtue of these presents, you will go as Apostolic Visitor to that widowed cathedral church and there ordain a priest and two deacons. In the parishes of the diocese you will ordain three more priests. See that they be worthy." [14]

Let us change the name on the document and instead direct it to Bishop Constance of Aquino, instructing him to take over the rule of the abandoned flock of Casinum. He shall ordain a priest and several deacons for the service of the ancient cathedral, and for the few parishes of the diocese he may ordain a priest or two. As a matter of fact, from Book II of the *Dialogues* we gather that in the *ecclesia* of Casinum deacons served during the Mass (chap. 23), and the neighboring *vici* of the mountains were taken care of by St. Benedict with his monks (chap. 19).

Sometimes the Pope appointed a neighboring bishop as Apostolic Visitor, but if he came across a good priest, he named him directly to some parish, simply informing his delegate of the fact. Here is one

[14] Bk. I, no. 15.

example of a formula among many: "To Importunus, bishop of Atellanus. Since We have learned that in your diocese the church of St. Mary in Campisone is vacant, know that we have appointed as its pastor the bearer of this letter, the priest Dominic." [15]

When there was question of undertaking a missionary campaign among the pagans, Rome attached such importance to it as to demand that the bishop should personally dedicate himself to this work or at least that the priest should receive authorization either from his bishop or directly from the Apostolic See. We shall cite a few examples.

Bishop Eutychius of Tindaro in Sicily informs Gregory that he is devoting himself to the conversion of the pagans in his diocese, but that the civil authorities are causing him some difficulty, because they protect the pagans. The Pope replies that he has already taken steps with the praetor of Sicily, requesting his aid in the undertaking. And he adds: "You will indeed be leading a life worthy of a bishop if by your deeds and by your words you bring back dissenters to the unity of the Church." [16]

Another time St. Gregory entrusted the conversion of the pagan Barbaricini in Sardinia to Bishop Felix and the monk Cyriacus. At the same time he exhorted the civil authorities to lend their assistance to the two missioners.[17] Again the Pope writes: "If I shall find a single pagan in any bishop's territory in Sardinia, I shall proceed vigorously against that bishop." [18]

More instructive is the story of the forty monk-missioners sent by him from Rome for the conversion of the Angles. In his letters the Pope complains that hitherto the Frankish episcopate had not shown sufficient interest in their conversion. To make up for this deficiency, he himself entrusts this work to a group of Roman monks, with Augustine at their head, at the same time requesting the civil and ecclesiastical authorities of Gaul to show them every consideration. Since, however, the Roman missioners are not proficient in the language of the Angles, Gregory orders Augustine to take with him from Gaul several priests, who are to act as interpreters.[19]

[15] Bk. II, no. 16.
[16] Bk. III, no. 62.
[17] Bk. IV, nos. 22-25.
[18] Bk. IV, no. 26.
[19] Bk. IV, nos. 51 f.

When Augustine departed from the Caelian Hill, he was a simple prior, but also a priest. During the journey the Pope made him abbot, in order that he might act with greater authority and decorum (no. 51). Only later, after the first successes among the Gauls, did Gregory order him to be consecrated a bishop by the metropolitan of Arles.[20]

It must be kept in mind that this missionary work among the pagans was regularly consigned by the Roman Pontiff under the generic name of "preaching": *"placuit ut . . . monasterii mei monachum in praedicationem transmittere, Deo adiutore, debuissem,"* [21] just as Gregory will use this term to describe the missionary activity of St. Benedict: *". . . commorantem circumquaque multitudinem praedicatione continua ad fidem vocabat."* [22]

Later on Rome so strictly reserves to itself the right of sending missionary bishops to the pagan peoples of the West, that Pope Sergius expressly calls the monk Willibrord to Rome in order to consecrate him apostle of the Frisians. Subsequently Pope Gregory II does the same with his disciple Wilfrid and with the Cassinese monk Willibald. In those times, in order to work for the conversion of the pagans, regularly an express delegation either of the bishop or the Roman Pontiff was required.

It was the custom of the Church not to allow anyone to harvest in another's field.[23] Hence each missioner retained the spiritual care of his own neophytes. If, then, as we shall see, St. Benedict will keep in his own hands the direction of the villages he brought to the faith, he will be doing so because he was their apostle and the father of their souls. In this sense Gregory writes to Augustine in England: *"Per alienam messem transiens, falcem mittere non debet. . . . Falcem ergo iudicii mittere non potes in eam segetem quae alteri videtur esse commissa."* [24]

Naturally, the episcopal rights of Bishop Constance will be respected. It will be his affair to consecrate the new oratories erected by St. Benedict on the acropolis of Cassino, just as the baptism and confirmation of the converted pagans pertains to him. Similarly to him

---

[20] Bk. VIII, no. 30.
[21] Bk. VIII, no. 30.
[22] *Dial.*, Bk. II, chap. 8.
[23] Bk. IX, no. 64.
[24] Bk. XI, no. 64.

will be reserved the ordination of priests and deacons, even in the hypothesis that the new monastic foundation at Casinum should have received from the Roman Pontiff a privilege of exemption from the episcopal authority as far as the internal affairs of the monastery were concerned. Indeed the *Regula monasteriorum* restricts episcopal intervention in the monastery to a few extraordinary and particularized cases.[25]

[25] In the Council of Carthage held in 535, mention is made of monasteries exempt from the jurisdiction of the diocesan bishop and subject directly either to the primate of Carthage or the pope of Rome. As a result the priests of the exempt monastery were ordained, not by the diocesan bishop, but by him under whose jurisdiction the monastery had passed. "*Quin etiam Adrumetinos monachos, praetermisso eiusdem civitatis episcopo, de transmarinis partibus, hoc est de Italia, presbyteros sibi semper ordinari curasse.*" Furthermore, in the Canon of the Mass the priests so ordained simply commemorated their ordaining bishop, not the bishop of the place. Cf. Mabillon, *Annales O.S.B.*, I, 39: "*Inter Sacrificia vero, ordinatores suos tantummodo . . . recitent. Hoc enim convenit paci.*"

CHAPTER XXIV

The Chained Hermit

A TRADITION transmitted by the poet Mark relates that, before St. Benedict came to Casinum, a hermit lived there in a cave. Historians have identified him with the anchorite Martin of Monte Marsico, whose miracles St. Gregory recounts. He was a man of a holy and austere life; not even the pagans dared to disturb him.[1] Shortly before the arrival of the Patriarch from Subiaco, the Lord gave him to understand that his mission was about over. He was to leave the field open to a new apostle, who would organize on that mountain the definitive form of the monastic life.[2]

Tradition adds that Martin, obedient to the divine instructions, left the territory of Cassino and settled on Monte Marsico where, narrates St. Gregory, surrounded by a group of disciples and regarded as a saint by the crowds that flocked to him, he spent many years in a narrow cave without ever leaving it. At the beginning of this voluntary seclusion the good Martin, in order to show his disciples that he had no intention of migrating again, got a chain, attached one end of it to his ankle, and fastened the other firmly in the rock. Thus

[1] According to a Cassinese tradition, the so-called "cave of the hermit" was behind the monastery, toward the northwest, in the direction of Monte Cairo. We know neither the origin nor the authenticity of this tradition. The hermit probably lived on the mountain, not far from the acropolis, and his remaining there might have embarrassed St. Benedict, who came to carry out a new and different program. The hermit, closed up in his cave, chose to leave the idolaters in peace and contented himself with giving them a good example and praying for them. St. Benedict, on the other hand, no longer remains in a grotto; he himself goes from village to village, calling the peasants to the faith.

[2]   *Hic olim viventi iusto praedixerat uni:*
     Hiis tu parce locis, alter amicus adest.

he resembled a watchdog, unable to go one step beyond the length of his chain.[3]

Later on, when St. Benedict learned of this action on the part of Martin, he sent two monks from Monte Cassino with this message: "If you are a servant of God, do not bind yourself with an iron chain, but by the love of Christ." This is precisely the maxim which better than any other expresses the spirit of the holy Patriarch and which he inculcated again and again in the Rule: "Let them prefer nothing to the love of Christ." The two monks laboriously climbed Monte Marsico, presented themselves to the solitary in his cave, and delivered their message. He listened, then without saying a word he broke the chain and thus regained the liberty of the sons of God. But from that day forth he observed a still stricter enclosure; notwithstanding the crowds that came to him, he never took another step. The iron chain remained fastened to the wall with a screw. Still later, when a considerable number of disciples settled about the cave, he had its entrance walled up, and communicated with others through a small window.

One day the monks came to him complaining that the rope which they used to draw water from the well easily became frayed and regularly broke. While the wars were raging, it was difficult to get a new one. So they asked him for the use of his chain. The holy man had merely to remove the screw, and he gave it to them, all rusty, just as it was. The fact remains that this piece of chain, attached to the rope, gave excellent service for many years, and the bucket no longer fell into the well.

St. Gregory, who relates these details,[4] says that he learned them from Pope Pelagius and from many other witnesses. This indicates that at the Lateran the monastic movement, which had established itself in central Italy through the efforts of St. Benedict and other contemporary saints, was being followed with considerable interest.

[3] This form of penance was well known in monastic antiquity; those who practiced it were called "*ferrocincti,*" that is, "chained." Even before St. Benedict's time, St. Jerome had spoken harsh words against these chained monks: "*Sed ne tantum videar disputare de foeminis, viros quoque fuge quos videris catenatos, quibus foeminei contra Apostolum crines, hircorum barba, nigrum pallium, et nudi in patientia frigoris pedes. Haec omnia argumenta sunt diaboli*" (*Epist. XXII ad Eustoch.,* no. 28; *PL,* XXII, 413).

[4] Bk. III, chap. 16.

The classical inscriptions of Casinum are almost entirely mute concerning the ancient Samnite sanctuary on the mountain, but St. Gregory furnishes us with some important data. The temple of Apollo containing the *idolum* of the god rose on a level space of the mountain. From this sanctuary a covered passageway led to the summit, where the *vetustissimum fanum* stood, represented by a small building with the "altar of the same Apollo." Perhaps near by was the hollow whence the priests gave their oracular replies.

All about, to the right and left of the passageway, was the sacred grove, *"in cultus daemonum luci succreverant,"* not to be touched or penetrated by the profane. The sacrificial worship in this ancient sanctuary was still in full activity in 529, when St. Benedict arrived at Casinum.

The fragment of the Acts of the Arvales recently discovered in the subsoil of the Vatican basilica may throw some light on these Cassinese rites. At Rome, on the Via Campana, the sanctuary of the goddess Dia embraced, as at Casinum, a whole complex of structures. The hill was covered with a sacred woods, which hid from the profane both the altar of the divinity erected at the summit of the hill and the small sanctuary that stood somewhat lower, where burned the tripod of the goddess. Near by was the columned portico, where the sacrificial banquets of the priests were held.

"May 29, during the consulate of the same. . . . In the grove of the goddess Dia, Master M. Valerius Junianus sacrificed two expiatory pigs for the purification of the woods and for the works to be performed, and near the tripod of the goddess Dia he sacrificed a white cow in her honor. Then the priests sat down in the portico and banqueted on the sacrificial meats; after putting on their praetextae and the crowns made of ears of wheat, they went out and ascended to the grove of the goddess Dia, and there Master M. Valerius Junianus and Sextus Cecilius, the chief flamen, sacrificed some fat lambs, after which all offered incense and wine. Then, having laid aside their crowns and anointed the statues, they chose Sextus Cecilius the master for one year, from the forthcoming Saturnalia till the succeeding ones, and L. Claudius Modestus the flamen for a year. They set there a table and banqueted, M. Valerius Junianus being master. After the meal, M. Valerius Junianus, veiled and wearing a crown of roses, rose up, went to the starting line, and gave the signal to the chariots and the riders."

The college of the *Fratres Arvales* consisted of twelve priests devoted to the worship of Ceres, under the presidency of a *magister* and a *flamen*, who remained in office for a year between the celebration of two Saturnalia.

The entire ceremonial functioning of the Arvales was restricted to the three-day period of the Ambarvalia in the month of May. The ceremonies of the second day of this triduum began with the sacrifice of two expiatory pigs for the purification of the sacred wood and of the *religiosae arbores*, which otherwise could not be entered without sacrilege. The *luci* of the Apollo of Cassino enjoyed the same religious significance. There followed a sacrifice at the *foculum deae Diae*, namely, at the tripod that burned near the tetrastyle, where also the sacrificial table was laid. The official garb was the short praetexta, with a crown of wheat ears, woven together with ribbons.

After the banquet, at which only the priests participated, they were obliged to enter the inviolable grove in order to gain the summit of the hill on which stood the altar of the goddess with statues of the other gods. There also they offered a sacrifice of fat lambs among clouds of incense and libations of wine. The rite concluded with the anointing of the statue of Ceres and the other divinities who kept her company in that shady *lucus*. Thereafter the priests laid aside their ritual crowns, chose officers for the ensuing year, and gave the signal for the races to begin.

The table at which they ate had to be covered with an ornate purple cloth. At these rites assisted four youths belonging to senatorial families, both of whose parents were living. While the rest ate, they were charged to carry to the altar of the divinity on the summit of the hill the sacrifice of wine and incense that the priests offered during the banquet.

From other fragments of the Acts of the Arvales we know that the song in honor of the goddess was executed in her sanctuary before the election of officers for the following year took place. The text of the hymn: "*Enos Lases iuvate . . .*" was scarcely intelligible to the *Fratres Arvales:* "*Sacerdotes libellis acceptis, carmen tripodaverunt in verba haec.*" In these concise minutes of the meetings of the *Fratres*

Arvales we discover a parallel to the classical archaeology of Cassino.

As at Rome on the Via Campana, so likewise on Monte Cassino the temple of Apollo stood outside the *lucus,* but the altar of the god rose on the summit of the mountain, covered and protected by the deep shade of the sacred wood. No doubt also at Casinum annual expiatory rites were celebrated on account of the necessary violation of the sacred grove. In fact, Gregory tells us that crowds of devotees penetrated into the grove in order to reach the *fanum;* but a special passageway had been constructed so that they would not set foot on the ground reserved to Apollo. So at Rome on the Via Portuense the *vulgus* was kept off at a distance from the *ara* of Dia. For this reason the tripod and the tetrastyle of the priests stood at the foot of the hill, and the *lucus* surrounded and covered the top.

When St. Benedict had converted the pagan Cassinese to the faith of Christ, "he broke the idol, threw down the altar, burned the trees in the groves; the temple of Apollo he converted into an oratory in honor of blessed Martin, and where the altar of the false god had stood, he built an oratory in honor of St. John the Baptist." Most likely the statue of the god was in the lower temple, while the *ara* of the *fanum* of the acropolis, in the midst of the grove, was protected by a simple structure open in the front. The biographer's precise language is to be noted.

The old statue was smashed to pieces; the altar on the other hand was overturned. Since it was not possible to root out or successively to saw all the trees of the *lucus* for lumber (as Tosti would have it), St. Benedict, following the biblical example of Gideon, fired the entire grove, which was considered equivalent to execration. Without such a radical remedy, the pagans would not have yielded, and some day the worship of the sacred trees might have been resumed.

As may easily be seen, St. Benedict could carry out such acts only because he was protected by legal dispositions and by the police force. Any other solution is untenable.

CHAPTER XXV

War on the Devil

GREGORY THE GREAT, mystical doctor that he was, compares the mission of St. Benedict among the pagans with the Patriarch's greater and much more difficult ascent of the mount of Christian perfection. At Subiaco his struggle was merely against the ministers of Satan; on Cassino, where he will overturn the altars of the devil, he will face personal encounter with Lucifer, who will appear in visible form in order to strike terror into him and his disciples.

Theologians say that when a soul is raised to the vision of the world of good spirits, angels and saints, at the same time, in order to humble it and to counterbalance the effect, God permits also the sensible apparition of the evil spirits. That is precisely what happened to the Patriarch of monks. He went to Cassino to wage war on the devil; the devil accepted the challenge and did not retreat. "The holy man, by migrating to other regions, indeed changed abode, but not his adversary. For from that time he faced battles more severe, because he had to fight personally against the very master of all evil." [1]

St. Benedict's combats to some extent recall those which St. Athanasius describes in the life of St. Anthony. The Patriarch of Cassino treats of this particular state of a mystical soul, when in the Rule he describes the exercises and struggles of the life of the anchorites, who, during the long years passed in the common monastic discipline, "have learned by the help of many brethren how to fight against the devil" (chap. 1). In any case, he is speaking of the mystical struggles not of be-

[1] *Dial.,* Bk. II, chap. 8.

ginners, but of those well trained and already almost perfect ascetics.

Of the events that followed upon St. Benedict's first entrance on his new field of labor we know nothing. It must have been the beginning of Lent. The saint, to imitate Christ, who, before beginning His missionary apostolate among the peoples of Galilee, retired into the desert for forty days, desired to do the same.[2]

This Lenten seclusion, then rather commonly practiced by monks, took place either in the cave of the hermit Martin or in Casinum itself, before St. Benedict attacked the stronghold of the devil on the acropolis. It was precisely here that, toward the end of the Lent of 529, the delegation of the abandoned people about Subiaco met St. Benedict and tried to induce him to return to their territory.[3]

A liturgical note in this connection is likewise of interest to us, namely, that the man of God waited until the solemn night of the Easter vigil before leaving his retreat, in order that he might participate in the feast of the Resurrection with the rest of the people.

There is question here not of a hermitage, but of a church, attended by clergy, where the liturgical vigil of Easter was celebrated, perhaps in what used to be the temple built by Hummidia Quadratilla. *"Noctis pia festa sacrae."* St. Benedict dismissed the disconsolate delegation from Subiaco, and on the very night of Easter began his new missionary apostolate at Casinum.

The choice of this date is rather significant. As at Easter, Christ arose triumphantly from the grave, so to the sound of the Alleluia St. Benedict comes forth from his Lenten retirement and appears

[2] These Lenten retirements, still practiced in the East, were common also in the West in ancient times among the holiest and most austere monks. St. Radegunda in her monastery of the Holy Cross at Poitiers remained enclosed in her cell during the whole of Lent. This practice led Venantius Fortunatus to say:

> *Longior hic mensis, quam celer annus erit.*
> *Et licet hic lateas brevibus fugitiva diebus.*

And when on the paschal solemnity the queen finally came forth from her seclusion, the poet sang:

> *Abstuleras tecum, revocas mea gaudia tecum,*
> *Paschalemque faciebis celebrare diem.*
> (Mabillon, *Annales O.S.B.*, I, 126)

[3]
> *Hic quoque clausum populi, te teste, requirunt*
> *Extactas noctis cum pia festa sacrae;*
> *Qui velut orbati raucis tibi flere querelis*
> *Instant, convictu quod caruere tuo.*

The poet assures us that he received this information from St. Benedict's own lips: *"te teste."*

among these people to announce to them the resurrection of the world in Christ the Savior.

Toward the end of this same sixth century, when the colony of monks sent by Gregory will set foot on the soil of England, they will, according to Bede's narrative, go forth in procession, carrying before them a silver cross and exhibiting an image of the Redeemer, singing the antiphon: *"Deprecantes te, Domine, in omni misericordia tua, ut auferatur furor tuus et ira tua a civitate ista et de domo sancta tua, quoniam peccavimus. Alleluia."* The rite followed by St. Benedict in his ascent to the acropolis of Casinum cannot have been different.

We have no means of knowing at whose initiative and under what conditions the government of Ravenna made a grant of the entire acropolis of Cassino for religious purposes. It must have been a long procedure, difficult and laborious, particularly when the military importance of the place and the tenacious attachment of the pagans to the oracle of Apollo are considered. They might easily have repulsed the apostle if his zeal did not have the backing of the law and of powerful protectors.

I have already spoken of the grant made by the Gothic king to Pope Felix IV, whereby he was permitted to transform the *Heroön* of Romulus in the forum into a Christian church. Even a century later, when Pope Boniface IV desired to transform the Pantheon of Agrippa into the Church of St. Mary of the Martyrs, he had to obtain the special authorization of Emperor Phocas.

It is very probable that during the fifth century something analogous took place at Casinum. When the rather small population had become entirely Christian, the temple of Hummidia Quadratilla, through the efforts of one of the bishops that survived the great barbarian invasions which had laid waste the *oppidum,* was changed into a church dedicated to the apostle Paul. In fact, at Cassino we find no trace of any other church, at least for those first centuries of the Middle Ages.

The collection of the *Variarum* of Cassiodorus is particularly instructive with regard to the passage of government property into private hands. At Rome there are some old *horrea,* half fallen together, which the government cannot repair because of lack of money. Paulinus, a patrician, requests that they be granted to him. Theodoric consents because the new structure—that is the motive mentioned in the decree—will without doubt contribute to the beauty of the capital (Bk. III, no. 29).

The deacon Elpidius of Spoleto—we are getting close to Nursia—asks for the grant of an old building and a piece of land contiguous to the baths, in order to put up a new building. The request is granted without hesitation.[4] Someone else requests that the king give him an edifice belonging to the state. Cassiodorus replies, granting him the structure *vetustate consumpta*, reserving to the state precious antiquities that may be discovered there.[5]

In the light of the public law of the times and of these documents we must likewise consider the grant of the acropolis and the *lucus sacer* of Cassino made to St. Benedict.

[4] Bk. IV, no. 24.
[5] *"Proprietario iure concedimus, praeter aes, aut plumbum, vel marmora, si tamen ibi fuerint latere comperta"* (Bk. VII, no. 44).

CHAPTER XXVI

On the Heights of Casinum

An ancient tradition of Monte Cassino maintains that, hardly had St. Benedict seen the walls and the towers as he approached the acropolis, when he knelt down in prayer. Even today, near that slight depression above which rises the hill called Monte Venere, the stranger is shown a rock in which appears a hollow which looks like the impress of a knee. There the Patriarch, seeing the altar of Satan, is said to have had recourse to prayer, and the rock, like soft wax, yielded to the weight of the saint, preserving the impression of his knee.

Although St. Gregory does not say so expressly, it is evident that the conversion of these villages to the faith and the transformation of their temples into churches required, besides the grant of the authorities, an apostolate of several years, accompanied by grave dangers and fatiguing labors. For a better understanding of this undertaking, it would be necessary to read the lives of St. Martin and of St. Boniface in order to see how tenaciously the pagans of Gaul and Germany remained attached to their ancient places of worship.[1]

[1] If, on the arrival of St. Benedict, the peasants about Casinum not only worshiped Apollo in his *"vetustissimum fanum,"* but on various altars in the neighboring woods *"sacrificiis sacrilegis insudabant,"* it is a sign that some ancient sacerdotal college of the *oppidum* still remained, despite the devastation of the country caused by Theodoric. Taking into account the juridical conditions of the time, it was necessary that the public authorities should intervene to root out the last vestiges of idolatry, to prevent any reaction or insurrection on the part of the peasants. Possibly the royal authority of Ravenna requested the intervention of the religious power to confide the position, so important strategically, to a monastic community, and thus prevent its falling into enemy hands, in case of an invasion, to the detriment of the Gothic state.

Toward the end of the fourth century, the three monks sent by St. Ambrose to undertake missionary work in the territory of Trent were killed.

Abbot Attala, a disciple of St. Columbanus, sent to Tortona the monk Meroveus, who, when he saw on the banks of the river Staffore a pagan *fanum* together with a sacred grove, without further ado set about demolishing it. In a rage the pagans almost beat him to death and were on the point of throwing him into the river (*Mon. Germ. Meroving.*, IV, 149).

In 754 St. Boniface and about thirty other monks, after many years of missionary toil in Germany, were slain by the infidels precisely because the holy bishop had destroyed their temples and the great trees sacred to their gods.

On Monte Cassino the same danger, in all likelihood, threatened St. Benedict and his companions. Little by little, by reason of the zeal of the new missioner, who, according to his biographer, "instructed a great number of the people round about and converted them to the faith," the villages dispersed among the mountains were successfully gained to Christ. But daily preaching and many miracles were called for. So deep-rooted was paganism in the rural areas!

Gregory's phrase: *"praedicatione continua ad fidem vocabat,"* has a juridical and liturgical significance that may easily escape us moderns. As the saint so well explains in his *Regula pastoralis, "praedicationis officium"* in olden times comprised the entire missionary work of a bishop, since then it was principally the bishops who preached. "Some laudably desire the preaching office [missionary work], while others must be forced to undertake it" (Bk. I, chap. 8). He is speaking of the episcopal state.

Thus also the missionary campaign of Augustine in England is simply called "preaching." [2] The missionary monks indeed number forty, but the office of preaching is reserved solely to Augustine, as a candidate for the episcopacy.

This preaching regularly took place during the liturgical action after the Gospel of the Mass or during the celebration of the Divine

---

[2] *"Placuit ut monasterii mei monachum in praedicationem transmittere, Deo adiutore, debuissem"* (Bk. VIII, no. 30).

Office. Among the ancients it normally was based on some scriptural passage which was read to the people during the ceremony.

It is unfortunate that Gregory, because of the purpose of his book, fails to give us the story of the evangelization of Casinum, at least condensing it into a single phrase. Had he done so, he would without doubt have revealed a side of St. Benedict of which we are today entirely ignorant. We would see him preaching and catechising the pagans and neophytes; we would witness his struggles with the infidels; we would know the perils to which he exposed himself, the great difficulties these hard-headed mountain folk frequently put in the way of their conversion, and then finally, we would see him, accompanied by the authorities and carrying a decree of the Gothic king in his hand, undertake the assault on the ancient temples and the burning of the sacred groves.

All this, as is clear, cannot have been done in a few weeks and not without putting his life in danger. To be convinced of this, one need only ask present-day missioners in pagan regions.

The burning of the woods displeases Tosti; he prefers the reading of the manuscripts that have: *"lucus succidit"* ("he cut down the groves"). The beams went into the construction of Monte Cassino! I do not wish to quarrel with the celebrated author, but the reading *"lucosque succendit"* is supported by the Greek version of St. Zachary: καὶ τὰ ἄλσε ἐνεπύρησεν. St. Benedict, by overturning the altars and setting fire to the infamous groves evidently wished to imitate the gesture of Gideon (Judg. 4:28). In war, buildings are bombarded and burned; there is no time to pull them down piecemeal.

Besides speaking of the *castrum Casinum* and the people living in various hamlets on the mountain, St. Gregory relates this particular: "Not far from the monastery . . . was a village in which a great number of people were converted from the worship of idols to belief in God by Benedict's preaching." It is difficult to identify this *vicus*, since there were several on the mountain. An inscription found near the medieval monastery of Albaneta seems to indicate that the vicinity was formerly inhabited. The distance fits, since it is *"non longe a monasterio,"* about a half-hour's walk. Another inhabited place must have been situated at the foot of the western slope, about the church of St. Scholastica. A stone inscription discovered in the sixteenth century makes mention of a *pagus Lapillanus*, but we do not know where it was.³

In the *vicus* mentioned by St. Gregory,⁴ which Pope Zachary in his turn describes as an *emporion*, that is, a market place, there lived also some virgins consecrated to God, who were the special object of the Patriarch's care. Other nuns, on the other hand, dwelt in their own house not far from the *castrum Casinum*.

From Monte Cassino St. Benedict maintained the spiritual direction of this *emporion*, and frequently, when he did not go there himself, he sent one of the monks to give conferences both to the nuns and to the neophytes. "Benedict frequently sent thither some of the monks to instruct them." The word *"crebro"* ("frequently") is to be noted. Hence it was he who had the pastoral charge of this populous village.⁵

Since now the old altars of Apollo, the sacred groves, and the hole of the oracle had become useless, St. Benedict gave some thought to their transformation. As a residence for himself and his disciples he chose the Roman castle on the acropolis, which was fortified and which with its walls and towers was all the more suitable in those times of war and perhaps of danger on the part of the infuriated pagans. Naturally some remodeling had to be done, and it seems that the plans for the changes were drawn up by the Patriarch himself: "While on a

³ Cf. G. F. Carettoni, *op. cit.,* pp. 44 f.
⁴ In paraphrasing and commenting on the text of St. Gregory one must proceed cautiously. The biographer speaks in the first place of the *castrum Casinum*, which was a *colonia* or fortified tower; in 487 it still had its Bishop Severus. The faith must have been preached here for several centuries, if there existed an episcopal see and an organized clergy and if the city could boast of martyrs mentioned in St. Jerome's Martyrology (Cf. Carettoni, *op. cit.,* p. 3).

Quite different, on the other hand, was the condition the various *pagi* which surrounded the *oppidum*, especially those situated on the higher ground behind Monte Cassino toward Monte Cairo. St. Gregory very definitely attributes idolatrous practices, not to the inhabitants of Cassino, but to the *"stulto rusticorum populo,"* who consequently dwelt *ruri,* that is to say, in the *pagi*. He even determines more exactly where these idolatrous peasants lived. After describing the condition of the sacred acropolis, he adds: *"Circumquaque etiam in cultu daemonum luci succreverant, in quibus adhuc eodem tempore, infidelium insana multitudo sacrificiis sacrilegis insudabat"* (*Dial.,* Bk. II, chap. 8). Hence the sacrifices of the peasants were offered not only in the temples, but also in the sacred groves.

⁵ Attention must be called to St. Gregory's precise language. *Praedicatio* is a priestly duty performed during the Mass, and the Pope attributes it to the holy Patriarch. On the other hand Benedict frequently assigns his monks *"exhortandis animabus,"* those, namely, who perhaps had no sacred orders.

certain day the brethren were at work building the monastery"
(chap. 9).

Near the old gate of the second or inside ring of the acropolis rose
the watchtower; opposite it was fitted out the monastic dormitory,
giving on a balcony or podium, which the documents speak of as late
as the eleventh century. The saint chose the tower for his own dwelling; it served at the same time as an excellent point of vantage. From
it the Abbot not only had a magnificent panorama of the entire valley
of the Liri as far as Aquino, or even to Gaeta; but it was particularly
easy for him to see who descended the mountain, who entered or left
by the gate of the monastery. This tower had two stories, with an
inside stairway. Several windows lighted the two small cells, in one
of which he studied and prayed, while the other served as sleeping
quarters.

The exact location of the dwelling of the Patriarch on Monte Cassino is to be sought near the original gate of the monastery, some remains of which are still to be seen not far from the present chapel of St.
Joseph. According to Dom Morin, the most recent archaeological findings at Monte Cassino place the tower in that spot. The remains of
the tower show forth evident Roman characteristics. Perhaps it was of
Etruscan or Samnite origin, until such time as the primitive sanctuary
of Apollo was defended by a circle of walls.

From this tower walls of large stones, of the same kind as those of
the external circle, still run out. But the place has undergone many
changes so that now it is not always easy to recognize the original parts.
Opposite the tower extended the large dormitory of the monks with
its balcony to supply light and air.[6]

Following the old mule path, one came to the small naos or temple
of Apollo, which St. Benedict transformed into an oratory dedicated
to St. Martin of Tours. The choice of this patron for the first church
of Cassino is significant. St. Martin was the great propagator of the
monastic life in Italy and Gaul. Further, he was noted as an apostle
of the Christian faith among the infidels, whose temples, sacred groves
and trees he destroyed, to replace them with churches, baptistries,
and monasteries.

---

[6] "Ante eamdem vero turrim, largius erat habitaculum, in quo utriusque discipuli
quiescebant."

It is known that Pope Symmacus dedicated a church to St. Martin in Rome, perhaps at a time when Benedict was still engaged in his studies. Possibly St. Caesarius brought to Rome the relics of the saint which the Pontiff placed in the altar of the new church. The Bishop of Arles had dedicated to St. John and to St. Martin the two altars of the church of his convent of nuns. At Casinum St. Benedict followed his example.

This transformation of two pagan edifices for the purpose of Christian worship involved some legal difficulties which the saint had to overcome. In ancient times the Christian mentality abhorred these transformations. Of this we discover an echo in canon 33 of the Council of Epaon: "We refrain from using for sacred purposes the churches of the heretics, which we hold in such detestation that we believe they cannot be purged of their pollution."

As a matter of fact, in Rome instances of such transformations are rare: the basilica of SS. Cosmas and Damian on the Via Sacra, the Pantheon, the basilica of Junius Bassus, and the church of St. Agatha of the Goths: no others. At St. Gregory's time the case was still so uncommon that the Pope, making an exception in favor of the Angles recently converted to the faith and by tradition tenaciously attached to their temples, felt the need of justifying such a grant, in order to convince St. Augustine, the apostle, himself.

For this reason the Pontiff writes to Abbot Mellitus, sent by him to help the missioners: "When Almighty God shall have brought you to our brother Augustine, tell him what I have decided regarding the Angles, namely, that the temples of the idols of that people be not pulled down, but that the idols which are in the temples be destroyed. Let water be blessed and let the temples be sprinkled with it; let altars be erected and relics placed therein. For if the temples are well built, it is fitting that they be converted from the worship of idols to the service of the true God. When the people see that their shrines are not destroyed, they may give up the errors of their ways and, recognizing and adoring the true God, they may more readily come together in the places to which they have been accustomed." [7]

About seventy years before Gregory's time, St. Benedict on Casinum had followed the same policy. But we cannot believe that he did this

[7] Bk. XI, no. 76.

on his own authority, when St. Gregory himself felt the need of justifying this concession to the Angles in a long letter which could well be quoted in full.

As in England, so on Monte Cassino it was regarded as a wise move on the part of the authorities not to annoy the pagans unduly by destroying their *"vetustissimum fanum."* It was therefore destined to the new worship, so that the converted neophytes might go there anew: *"ad loca quae consuevit familiarius concurrat."*

The missionary work of St. Benedict at Casinum had a decisive influence on the apostolic activity of his spiritual progeny. In 494 the general conditions of Italy and the paucity of priests induced Pope Gelasius I to open the doors of the sanctuary to monks, and in their favor he reduced the period of preparation for the priesthood to one year.[8]

When, after 575, Gregory the Great exchanged the insignia of his civil office for the monk's cowl, he wished to repeat on a grand scale what St. Benedict had done in the limited territory of Casinum, and immediately made preparations to go to the English missions. Pope Benedict I, at the insistence of the Romans, refused to let him depart, but the Benedictine ideal of the monk-missionary never passed from his mind. In 596, scarcely five years after he ascended the papal throne, a favorable occasion for carrying out his plan presented itself, and he immediately took advantage of it. To England he sent Augustine with forty other monks of his monastery of St. Andrew on the Caelian with the twofold injunction to preach the gospel to the pagans and to introduce the observance of the monastic Rule of St. Benedict.

These zealous monks went about their work with a will, and so well did it prosper that on Christmas Day, 597 Augustine was able to baptize ten thousand pagans in the waters of the Thames. Not long after, the apostle consulted the Pope about the kind of life the missioners were to lead. Gregory replied that they must continue to live the monastic life according to the norms of the Rule. The biographer of St. Benedict had before his eyes the example of the Patriarch, who had grafted the missionary vocation on the venerable trunk of the monastic life.

About twenty years later the question again arose, and in a Roman

[8] *Epist. ad episc. Bruttiorum,* no. 3.

council, celebrated under Boniface IV, it was discussed whether or not monks ought to fill the functions of priests. The decision was in favor of the monks, and the fathers stressed the examples of St. Martin of Tours, St. Gregory, and St. Benedict, who by their deeds and writings had authorized this new orientation of monastic life in the West. We do not possess the authentic acts of the council referred to, but the facts and the resolutions are beyond discussion.

The oratory of St. Martin, where St. Benedict celebrated the choral offices during his lifetime and where he desired to breathe forth his soul to God, stood near the Roman tower, in front of the oratory and refectory of the primitive community. This location may be regarded as safe, because all the ancient sources agree on the point.[9]

This original gate of the fortress of Cassino was rediscovered in 1880 about thirty feet behind that erected by Abbot Desiderius, which in its turn was fortified with a tower. It is in this spot that local tradition places the stone on which once upon a time the Patriarch prayed when he restored to life the corpse of the boy lying on the threshold of the monastery.

In the Vatican Latin MS 1202 we find a miniature executed about 1072, showing Abbot Desiderius in the act of offering to St. Benedict, together with some new liturgical codices, also the two basilicas of St. John and of St. Martin which were rebuilt by him. In this picture there is first of all the tower of two stories where the Patriarch lived. Next to it rises the small basilica of St. Martin, with a long covered passage connecting it to the ancient oracle of Apollo on the summit of the mountain.

This passageway, which served no special purpose for the primitive community, is most likely of Samnite origin, and is perhaps the one mentioned in the inscription cited above: AEDEM IOVIS A SOLO ET PORTICUM CUM AEDIFICIIS. . . . Such a portico or covered way, crossing the sacred grove, marked the limit beyond which it was sacrilegious to set foot. This portico is mentioned both by the anony-

[9] About the eighth or ninth century, the anonymous commentator on the miracles of St. Benedict writes:

In turre iuxta sanctum Martinum
Ad pede de turre, extra portam
In poio qui est in dormitorio ante porte de turre
In fronte ipso dormitorio et de sancto Martino
Da foris porta a pede de turre.

mous Cassinese: *"In pede de rabe que vadit a sanctu Iane,"* and by Leo of Ostia: *"(Apollinaris abbas) sepultus est prope ecclesiam sancti Benedicti, iuxta gradus porticus, quae tunc pergebatur ad ecclesiam sancti Martini."* [10]

In the miniature of the MS in question, the portico with its roof of green tiles curves about the old naos of Apollo and extends to the gate of the fortress. After Desiderius' work of reconstruction no more mention of it is made; in all probability it was sacrificed for the new refectory and dormitory to the southwest of the fortress. It suffices for the purpose to cast a glance over the topographical plan made by Antonio and Giovanni Battista da Sangallo between the years 1507 and 1512.

Originally the basilica of St. Martin was so small that at the time of the first reconstruction of Monte Cassino under Abbot Petronax it had to be lengthened by about twenty-five feet by the addition of a presbytery closed off by a semicircular apse. Later on Abbot Desiderius rebuilt it along somewhat ampler lines; but even then it measured barely sixty-five feet in length by some fifty in width. The mosaic in the apse with an aperture in the middle must have appeared rather puny, if the historian Leo says: *"Secus ipsam quoque ecclesiam, curvato pariete, brevem quidem, sed perpulcram domum ad eiusdem ecclesiae ministerium construxit."* He refers to the small sacristy behind the semicircular apse. The church was divided into three parts by two rows of nine columns; the nave was thirty-six feet high, the two side aisles were only twenty-four.

The enlarging of the basilica of St. Martin near the ancient gate of the fortress induced Abbot Desiderius to move out the towered entrance of the abbey by about thirty feet; thus the new edifice remained as it was before, within the limits of the abbey.[11]

Leo likewise speaks of another church of St. Stephen *"iuxta portam monasterii de foris sita,"* which the Cassinese calendars mention from the eighth century on. This historian accurately describes its location: it was situated outside the gate of the monastery, lest the reader confuse it with St. Martin's, which was also near the gate, but *"intra monasterii ambitum."*

[10] *Chron.* Bk. I, 17, 20.

[11] Leo Host., *Chron.*, Bk. III, 33: *"Ecclesiam beati Martini, quae sola fere iam intra monasterii ambitum de veteribus aedificiis remanserat."*

Following the example of St. Benedict, who had dwelt "*in turre iuxta sanctum Martinum,*" Desiderius, notwithstanding that the traditional residence of the abbots was the palace of Abbot Richarius beside the basilica of St. John, had a cell built for himself: "*Iuxta eamdem vero basilicam, mansiunculam in qua ipse maneret construens, trabibus oppositis, tegulis desuper operuit.*" Hence it was a considerable work: he raised a beamed ceiling over the loggia of the tower and covered it with tiles. But despite all these structural changes, the Roman tower, consecrated by the residence of St. Benedict, stood untouched near St. Martin's.

Peter the Deacon speaks of it anew in chapter 30 of Book IV of the *Chronicon Cassinense,* where he relates that at night angelic choirs were heard in that place. This is at the beginning of the twelfth century.[12]

Abbot Otto, to whose attention the matter was brought, decided to change the ancient tower of St. Benedict into an oratory: "*Iam dictam turrem cum largo habitaculo in oraculum Domini Salvatoris . . . et Eius Genetricis Virginis Mariae dedicari constituit.*" One author asserts that the Cassinese chroniclers put this dedication in the year 1143; [13] others, on the contrary, maintain that Otto's plan was never carried out.

At Monte Cassino the oratory of Otto was easily identified with the basilica of one nave discovered in 1880 near Desiderius' gate to the abbey. This *oraculum* rested in part on the first story of the tower and of the cell of Desiderius, and was distant from the neighboring basilica of St. Martin, which stood on somewhat higher ground.

An attempt has been made to identify the remains of the little church discovered in 1880 with the basilica of St. Stephen *extra portam.* But this solution does not hold, because the church of the protomartyr erected for the use of guests was situated outside the enclosure of Desiderius and near the large guesthouse which the same abbot had built.

Thus it came about—as may be seen in the Processional of Monte Cassino (MS 199)—that when the procession of monks from the church

12 "*Dum Iohannes cognomento Affidatus in mansiuncula quae turri patris Benedicti conlateralis est . . . audivit dulcisonum officium ante nocturnalem synaxim in beati Patris aedecula ab angelis celebrari.*"
13 Cf. Gattol, *Accessiones,* II, 829.

of St. Mary at Albaneta returned to the abbey, they arrived first at the gate of the outside circle of the fortress, built of great stones. Then, continuing to ascend, the cortege left to the right the chapel of St. Agatha in order to pay its respects to St. Stephen and St. Martin respectively without and within the great gate erected by Abbot Desiderius. Always they went upward. The choir of monks, after ascending the grand stairway of Desiderius to the atrium or *paradysus*, to the right and left of the façade of the church found the two chapels of St. Michael and St. Peter.[14]

The basilica of St. Martin disappeared after the earthquake of September 9, 1349, which destroyed almost the entire abbey. Also the tower of St. Benedict, in the course of the centuries and by the successive reconstructions, underwent so many and such considerable changes that nowadays there remain but small portions, built of small stones irregularly set, which would indicate a Roman construction of late date.[15]

[14] *"Revertentes cum psalmis et antiphonis tempori congruentibus, cum ingressi fuerint portam veterem* [that is, the first circle of walls of the Samnite fortress] *cantent: Vidi civitatem . . . ; et cum appropinquaverint ad ecclesiam sanctae Agathae* [halfway between the first gate and the second of the second circle of the fortress] *dicant antiphonam ipsius. Deinde, cum portam maiorem intraverint* [namely, the towered gate of Desiderius between the basilicas of St. Stephen *foris portam* and of St. Martin] *dicant antiphonam s. Stephani et s. Martini. Post haec dicatur antiphona s. Angeli et s. Petri, et sic ingredient ecclesiam maiorem."*

[15] Cf. Carettoni, *op. cit.,* p. 59.

CHAPTER XXVII

New Structures on Monte Cassino

THE oratory of St. Martin was the place where St. Benedict intended to breathe forth his soul to God; even though several times enlarged and restored, it survived until the eleventh century. At that time Abbot Desiderius had it pulled down in order to replace it with a more sumptuous church. Unfortunately there were no archaeologists among the advisers of Abbot Desiderius.

The frequent earthquakes and the building activities of the abbots of Monte Cassino during the fifteenth and sixteenth centuries in their turn showed little regard for Desiderius' church, which certainly should have been looked upon as one of the most sacred treasures of the archabbey. In the sixteenth century, St. Martin's was completely razed to satisfy the plans of Bramante, who decided to level all the medieval structures in order to make a majestic court surrounded by a classical cloister. Aesthetics prevailed over Christian sentiment.

About the year 1880, in the excavations carried on near the tower constructed by Abbot Desiderius were discovered the remains of a basilica with an apse, which at the time some wished to identify as that of the Holy Savior erected by Abbot Otto near the tower of St. Benedict. Later these remains were interpreted as the ruins of St. Martin's or again as belonging to the small church of St. Stephen *extra portam;* finally, however, other excavations at the foot of the stairway leading to the cathedral revealed the remains of the true St. Martin's in the corner of the cloister near the entrance.

We are already acquainted with the attitude and the legislation of the ancient Church regarding the transformations of old pagan temples. The Bishop of Aquino, fortified without doubt with a rescript of Theodoric and a *praeceptum* of the Pope, ascended to Monte Cassino in company with his clergy to celebrate the dedication. First the church was sprinkled with blessed water; then the relics of St. Martin and of martyrs were placed into the new altar, on which the Bishop of Aquino celebrated the first Mass.

Such functions used to bring together, also in the monasteries, a large crowd of the poor; indeed, sometimes St. Gregory himself had to provide means for the sustenance of the pious visitors. On one occasion he wrote to the subdeacon Peter: "We desire that for the dedication you contribute for distribution among the poor ten golden solidi, thirty amphorae of wine, two hundred lambs, two tuns of oil, twelve sheep, one hundred chickens." [1] The occasion was the dedication of the oratory of a monastery. [2]

It may be that every year on November 11 and on the anniversary of the dedication St. Constance visited Monte Cassino to celebrate Mass there. At least St. Gregory mentions a practice of that kind: "On the feast day of the patron or on the anniversary of the dedication of the aforesaid monastery, the bishop shall go thither to celebrate Mass." [3]

About a hundred yards from the temple of Apollo, on the very crest of the mountain, stood the altar of the god, protected by a small edifice with decorations of Greek inspiration; from a cavity below the replies of the oracle were perhaps given. Some fragments of the terracotta ornamentation have recently been gathered *in situ*, not far from the apse of the modern basilica of Cassino. We can hardly suppose that these fragments were carried thither from the naos of the temple of Apollo, which stood somewhat lower.

The biographer, in speaking of the *vetustissimum fanum* of the

---

[1] Bk. I, no. 61.

[2] The distribution of comestibles to the people on the occasion of dedications goes back to classical antiquity. An inscription in the museum of Algiers of the year 197 records the distribution of the customary *sportulae.*

QUE DEDICATE VIIII KAL
IANUARIAS T SEXTIO. LATERANO C.C. . . . O
RUFINO COS. A. P. CLVIII OB CUIUS DEDICATIO
NEM SPORTULAE DATAE SUNT

[3] Bk. VII, no. 12.

Samnites, distinguishes two places: first, the *templum Apollinis*, and then the *ara eiusdem Apollinis* surrounded by various *luci*, that is, sacred groves. In this place, separated from the buildings, St. Benedict prepared his tomb *sub diu*, surrounded by the cemetery of the community. The chapel in the grove was named after St. John the Baptist, who had dwelt in the wilds. It is worthy of note that St. Caesarius dedicated a nuns' convent to St. John the Baptist, with a chapel in honor of St. Martin. Similarly on the Vatican, Pope Symmacus erected the oratories of SS. Martin and John.

From the primitive monastery which rose in the shadow of St. Martin and the Roman tower, the ancient portico rose by steps to the summit of the mountain. The papal biographer says simply: "Where the altar of Apollo had stood, he erected the oratory of St. John." For the sake of clarity, he adds this topographical note: "The oratory of St. John the Baptist stands on the very summit of the mountain." And a third time he refers to this oratory in the *Dialogues* when he speaks of the burial of St. Benedict: "He was buried in the oratory of St. John the Baptist, which he erected (*construxit*) after overturning the altar of Apollo."

The word *construxit* has a definite meaning in St. Gregory's mind. When he says of the chapel of St. Martin, which we know was not rebuilt but only adapted, *"In ipso templo Apollinis oraculum beati Martini . . . construxit,"* he means to convey the idea that the saint's work was limited to erecting an altar, while the naos remained intact. On the other hand, in the case of the chapel of the Precursor, since on the mountain's top there was only the altar of Apollo, protected perhaps by a roof, the merit of building belongs entirely to St. Benedict (*construxit*). This preciseness on Gregory's part is worthy of note. The Greek version of Pope Zachary adds nothing new. He likewise distinguishes the naos of Apollo from the *bomos* and the *agalma* of the god.

From the various Cassinese documents published by Dom Morin, we learn that in the eighth century two separate altars were in the apse of the church of St. John. The principal one in the center of the semicircle was dedicated to the Baptist; the other, only a few yards distant, stood over the original tomb of St. Benedict.

St. Gregory attributes to the Patriarch in general all the building

operations, of the monastery as well as of the Cassinese churches, always using the word *construxit:* *"omne hoc monasterium quod
construxi,"* etc. Later when St. Benedict appeared in a dream to the
abbot and prior of the monastery of Terracina with a plan of a new
monastery to be built, he indicated distinctly: "I shall show you where
you are to build the oratory, the monastic refectory, the guesthouse,
and other necessary structures." There can be no doubt that such
architectural skill or perhaps the simple experience in the builder's
art after the thirteen monasteries built or remodeled at Sublacum
found an ample field of application at Casinum.

The Patriarch of monks attributes a particular importance to the
ground plan of his monasteries. Perhaps for this reason medieval tradition preserved its outline very jealously, so that effectively the
grand complex of ancient monastic architecture, of which so many
magnificent examples still remain in Europe, in the last analysis goes
back to St. Benedict and to the Roman art which he must have studied
in his youth in the schools of Rome. Regarding this point he himself
writes: "The monastery, in as far as possible, ought to be so constructed
that within it be found all that is necessary: a well, a mill, a garden
and various shops" (chap. 66).

I consider it worth-while to introduce some observations on the general plan of the Benedictine monastery as it can be deduced from
the text of the Rule and the words of St. Gregory cited above. For
the monastery at Terracina, St. Benedict appears to the abbot and the
prior with the plan in his hand and shows them how to construct the
oratory, the refectory, and the guesthouse, as well as the other parts of
the monastic building.

In the text of the Rule, on the other hand, are mentioned rather the
traditional dependencies of the Roman villa, that is to say, the external parts of the monastery, as far as they ought also to be within the
enclosure. Thus, the well, the mill, the gardens, the storehouses, and
the shops for the various arts and crafts.

Noteworthy is the stress placed on the guesthouse in those centuries,
even in the case of a new and small foundation, as was that, for example, of Terracina. The history of the Lombard era amply justifies
this provision, which was a kind of presage. In fact, in the Italian
monasteries of the early Middle Ages, this *susceptio hospitum* de-

veloped to such an extent that finally it became almost a social institution confided to the Benedictines and in time gave rise to the homes
for the aged and the infirm and even to the military orders of hospitalers, as happened in the eleventh century in Jerusalem.

The faithful of the time endowed the monasteries with extensive
landed patrimonies. This they did because they knew that the income
from these lands, well cultivated and administered, was used to succor
the pilgrims and the poor. The general history of these monastic charitable institutions in Italy has still to be written. From the little I know,
I believe it would be a revelation to the modern world. Besides the
monks, throughout the centuries many generations of Italians have
lived on the ancient patrimony of St. Benedict. In other countries the
same story undoubtedly could be repeated.

Since we are speaking of the primitive monastery of Cassino, a
question arises in my mind. At Subiaco the candidates came in such
numbers to receive the monastic habit that St. Benedict had to erect
twelve monasteries, we suppose one every two years. How did things
go at Monte Cassino? The historians speak of but one monastery
there, which even in the eighth century was called that of the fortress. Later, under Abbot Petronax, another dedicated to the Savior
was built at the foot of the mountain.

How large was the original community of Cassino? Was it small, or
did it embrace a large number of monks, divided into deaneries, as
they are mentioned in the *Regula monasteriorum?* Unfortunately we
have no documents to furnish an answer. Simply taking Gregory's
text, although we find there *praepositi* chosen by St. Benedict for
Subiaco and Terracina, no mention is ever made of deans or deaneries
in the Pachomian sense. And still in the Rule the saint shows a manifest preference for that form of monastic organization. We know from
Paul the Deacon that the original basilica of St. Martin used by the
community was so small that at the time of the restoration under
Petronax it had immediately to be enlarged.

From these indications we conclude that the original Cassinese
community must have been small. A single chamber served as a
dormitory for all: "Before the tower was an extensive building in
which the brethren were sleeping." [4] Note the topographical exact-

4 Bk. II, chap. 35.

ness of the biographer. Similarly the place where the food was kept was in proportion. In the *cellarium* was a single *dolium*, that is, a great-bellied clay vessel, still used in that region. It is ordinarily covered with a wooden lid, such as St. Gregory describes (Bk. II, chap. 24). The *dolium* can hold twenty-five gallons at the most, certainly not much for a large community.

That the number of monks at table was not large is confirmed by the biographer when he relates that the disobedient cellarer on a certain day intended to use as the seasoning for the soup the bit of oil that remained in the bottle.[5]

It is true, however, that on another occasion heaven sent a gift of two hundred sacks of flour. But that was a very munificent boon of divine Providence, intended to supply the needs not only of the monks, but also of the guests and the many poor who daily knocked at the door of the monastery.

But we may ask: If the primitive community of Cassino at the time of St. Benedict appears small in number, whither did the saint send the many candidates who undoubtedly came to him? [6] Unfortunately I cannot give an answer to that question, and I recognize that there are many details in the life of St. Benedict that we cannot find out with certainty. Quite likely Rome, Subiaco, Terracina, and Capua do not represent the only offshoots of Cassino in St. Benedict's time. Speaking about the Patriarch's death, St. Gregory tells us of some disciples *"longe manentibus,"* to whom the Abbot manifested the prearranged sign that would indicate his passage into eternity.[7] Evidently, as long as St. Benedict lived, he retained in his own hands the government of all the monasteries founded by him. Such was the juridical custom of the age.

[5] *Ibid.,* chap. 28.

[6] In the early Middle Ages, only a small part of the community dwelt on Monte Cassino; the rest resided at the foot of the mountain, near the church of St. Peter. This arrangement may go back to St. Benedict himself, who is said to have confided to the monk Theoprobus the government of the part of the religious family residing in the town.

[7] *Ibid.,* chap. 37.

CHAPTER XXVIII

The Devil as Saboteur

In St. Gregory's biography of St. Benedict a number of chapters refer to the first years of the monastic life at Cassino, when the Patriarch and his companions were occupied with adapting the old fortress to new uses. The labors must have been considerable, because toward the end of his life the Abbot expressed himself in a manner which would imply that he had constructed everything: "This entire monastery which I have built and all that I have prepared for the brethren . . ." (chap. 17). Various incidents which happened during the work, in St. Gregory's words, offer a foretaste of the Franciscan *Fioretti*.

One day the monks were engaged in the construction of a new wing of the building (chap. 9). As may be seen even at the present time, they used the material of the old buildings and had no hesitation in employing even those inscriptions which today are the delight of the archaeologists.

Thus it happened that they found in the ground a large marble slab which appeared suitable for insertion into the wall. But the stone proved too heavy. They exerted themselves to the utmost to move it. One, two, three. . . . But to no purpose. It seemed to have sunk roots which spread themselves in the earth. Suddenly someone remarked: "Perhaps the devil is sitting on the stone." The phenomenon was brought to the attention of St. Benedict, who then went to the spot to watch the workers, saw the stone, and made the sign of the cross over it. At this blessing the devil departed, and the monks were able to remove the stone with ease.

At Monte Cassino the guides used to point out this famous "devil's block." But there is question of a large slab of white marble, marked with a cross, which used to serve as the support of a sixth-century altar. The great block which the biographer mentions was in the ground and easily gave rise to the suspicion that it might serve as the cover of some hole or hiding place. Every ancient temple could have its underground chambers. A doubt arose in St. Benedict's mind. When the stone had been removed, he ordered an excavation to be made on the spot. In fact, an ancient bronze statue was uncovered, *"aereum illuc idolum,"* hidden there for some unknown reason. The biographer notes that the hole was deep.

It is useless to conjecture about the statue. Whence had it come? Was it of Samnite, Greek, or Roman origin? What relation did it have to the other Greco-Roman statuettes discovered at various times on Monte Cassino? Was the large slab covering the hole supposed to hide, or did it rather wish to indicate, as in the case of the *lapis niger* of the Roman Forum, the precise spot where a profaned idol had stood? Had the statue been hidden a short time before to prevent its falling into the hands of the Christians, in accordance with the imperial edicts? These questions cannot be answered.

Since the place of the archaeological discovery was close to the kitchen, near the refectory and not far from the church of St. Martin, the statue was, for the time being, transported to the *coquina*, awaiting further disposition.[1] To be exact, St. Gregory does not say "transported," but "thrown into the kitchen." Hence the statue was most likely not very large and could be put in a corner of the kitchen among the sweepings. But after the service of the kitchen was finished and the refectory closed, while no one any longer gave a thought to the statue, suddenly from the windows and the roof of the wing issued forth flames, which little by little engulfed the entire building.

The terrified monks began to cry: "Fire! Fire!" Some hastened to fetch water from the cistern; others with axes tried to isolate the conflagration. At the unwonted noise the Patriarch hurried out to the spot, but the strange thing was that, while others were occupied with

[1] According to law, as we have already seen in the collection of the *Variarum,* the work of art had to be turned over to the state. *"Proprietario iure concedimus, praeter aes, aut plumbum, vel marmora, si tamen ibi fuerint latere comperta"* (Bk. VII, no. 14). We are not told what was done with this ancient Cassinese idol.

the flames, he saw nothing. Or rather, he indeed saw that the kitchen
was not oversupplied with victuals, but that it was neat and clean, as
the Rule prescribed.

The saint forthwith understood that the fire, which had so frightened his disciples and for a short time disturbed the silence of the
community, was altogether the result of a diabolical illusion. After
praying for a short time with his head between his hands, as was his
custom, he made the sign of the cross over the kitchen and requested
that the monks make the sign over their eyes. The diabolical spell
immediately ceased. Often the power of Satan is not real, but only a
kind of phantasmagoria by which he tries to gain control over souls.
The first means of defense is prayer; the second, fearlessness.

CHAPTER XXIX

Protests of the Dethroned God

FROM now on, a contest began between Satan and St. Benedict: while the saint tried to rout out from the place Beelzebub's cohorts, Satan caused him all the trouble possible. One time while the Abbot was engaged in prayer in his cell, Lucifer suddenly appeared in a horrible guise, with bloodshot eyes and a distended mouth, from which issued forth a stream of burning lava.[1] Benedict made the sign of the cross, and the devil fled.

Stranger still were the quarrels between St. Benedict and the devil. Frequently the other monks heard their dialogues. Satan began by calling the Abbot by name: "Benedict, Benedict!" Since he did not reply, the devil, enraged, cried out: "Maledict (that is, accursed), not Benedict! What have you against me? Why do you persecute me?"

The monks trembled when they heard these infernal threats and considered that if war were being waged against the general, the army would be caught in the middle. But the Abbot was not frightened; against Satan he opposed the shield of the cross and repeated: "*Deus, in adiutorium meum intende,*" as St. Anthony had done in the desert. From the saint's combats and victories over Satan came in the Middle Ages that special form of exorcism which is commonly called the cross of St. Benedict. It is an invocation to the Holy Cross inscribed in the form of a cross on a medal,[2] which various popes have enriched

---

[1] "*Corporalis eius sese ingerebat . . . hostis teterrimus et succensus apparebat, qui in eum ore oculisque flammantibus saevire videbatur*" (chap. 8).

[2] The cross is formed from the initials of the following invocation:

with copious indulgences. Now it is found throughout the world, even in far-off Ethiopia. As a matter of fact the Copts there have a great devotion to St. Benedict and even assert that they possess his holy remains.

Crux sancta sit mihi lux:
Numquam daemon sit mihi dux.

Around the edge runs the exorcism:

Vade retro, Satana, numquam suade mihi vana;
Sunt mala quae libas: ipse venena bibas.

Considerably older than this formula is another that goes back to Venantius Fortunatus and was widespread in antiquity:

Crux Domini mecum, Crux est quam semper adoro,
Crux mihi refugium, Crux mihi certa salus.

In the catacombs of St. Lawrence, within the tomb of a famous personage, Pius IX found a golden cross with this inscription: CRUX EST MIHI VITA-MORS INIMICE TIBI.

CHAPTER XXX

The Monk Restored to Life

ANOTHER time a new wing of the building was being raised, and the walls had reached a goodly height: ". . . *quia res ita exigebat, paulo altius aedificarent"* (chap. 11). While the monks were engaged on the scaffolds, some in carrying mortar and bricks, others in building, the Abbot gave himself over to prayer in his cell. Beelzebub appeared to him, as usual, and seeing him thus occupied began by casting insults at him. Then he told him that that morning, in order not to disturb his devotions, he would pay a visit to the monks on the scaffolding instead. Just to show that he also interested himself in the progress of the work! Having said this, he disappeared.

But St. Benedict thought to himself: "Today Satan will pull one of his tricks." For this reason he immediately called one of the monks who acted as porter and sent this message to the workers: "Be careful, brethren, because the devil is coming to you." The messenger had scarcely finished speaking, when behold, the new wall collapsed with a great noise and buried beneath it a poor monk who was assisting the masons. Besides, he was the son of a *curialis*. The *curialis*, being a person of rank and influence, might cause trouble for the monastery.

Imagine the sorrow of the monk's companions at this misfortune. They were at once on the spot of the accident with poles and spades in order to dig out the victim. But, alas! They came too late; because, when they reached him, they found him crushed to death. Hence they placed the corpse on a blanket and noted that the height of the fall as well as the weight of the masonry had even broken the bones (chap. 11).

Without delay they sent someone to announce the sad news to the Abbot, who, without interrupting his prayers, ordered that they bring the corpse to him. They fetched it on the blanket and deposited it in the little room on the ground floor of the tower on the mat where the Abbot was accustomed to prostrate himself in prayer. After dismissing them, the saint, heavy of heart, closed the door and continued his prayer more fervently. Did he perhaps recall Elias who, standing in the cell of the house where he had received hospitality, resuscitated the little son of his host? The fact is that the fruit of this solitary prayer was the same.

Suddenly the dead man rose from the mat and announced that he was cured. St. Benedict spoke words of encouragement to him, gave him his blessing, and sent him back straightway to continue his work, assuring him that no further harm would come to him. He could not concede the victory to the devil. We can imagine the surprise of the monks when they saw reappear on the scaffold the dead man restored to life.

I have said that the young monk belonged to a distinguished family and that his father was one of the *curiales*. These *curiales*, whom Cassiodorus calls "*minor senatus*," [1] constituted a special class in the cities, the officialdom. They were loaded down with honors, but still more with fiscal obligations, which they could not escape, not even by entering a monastery. In St. Gregory's time, the curial dignity was little more than a kind of slavery, so burdensome that, in order to prevent these officials from fleeing in desperation from the cities to become monks, various emperors forbade them to be received in monasteries.

We possess an edict of King Athalaric, received in the *Variarum*, in which the praise of the *curiales* is sung: ". . . *quibus a provida sollicitudine nomen est.*" But in the document the purchase of their immovable property is forbidden; likewise it could not be mortgaged. It had to remain at the disposition of the government and as a guaranty of the *curiales* themselves. Any kind of alienation was simply

[1] *Var.*, Bk. X, chap. 2.

declared invalid.[2] Reading between the lines of this document, one understands better the desperate condition of the bourgeoisie of the provinces; they were not sufficiently their own masters to leave their immovable property to others, and thus save it from the rapacity of the Byzantine government.

A Cassinese document of the eleventh century gives the name of Severus to the monk who was called back to life. *"Et ibi resuscitavit Severum contritum."* Since the text in question leans upon a local tradition which may go back as far as the times of Petronax, I do not find any serious objection to offer against it. It ought not to pass unnoticed that this son of a *curialis* acted as a mason's assistant in the monastery; he worked and prayed like the others, without distinction of class. It was precisely this perfect union of supernatural and natural energies in the spiritual family of St. Benedict that contributed so mightily to the formation of the Europe of the Middle Ages. *"Habitare fratres in unum."*

[2] Bk. II, no. 11.

CHAPTER XXXI

The Devil as Veterinarian

On another day St. Benedict was on his way to mount to the chapel of St. John in order to pray for those buried in the cemetery surrounding the oratory.[1] At the entrance to the passageway he was met by Satan decked out in the garb of a veterinarian (*mulomedicus*),[2] with a three-legged stool, a horn with medicaments, and the tools of the veterinarian's craft.

"Where are you going?" inquired the saint.

"To give your monks a good cathartic," replied Satan, and vanished into thin air.

The man of God did not at all let this hinder him from his prayer, but mounted up to St. John to satisfy his devotion. But as soon as his prayer was finished, he hurried down, because he knew in his heart that Satan was going to play him one of his tricks that day. When he reached the monastery, he discovered a poor monk near the cis-

[1] Regarding the right of monasteries to have their own cemeteries, we possess a letter of St. Gregory I to the bishop of Urbe Vetere.

Abbot Agapitus of the monastery of St. George had recourse to Rome against his bishop, John by name, "*quod in eodem monasterio missas prohibeatis celebrari, sepeliri etiam ibidem mortuos interdicatis*" (*Epist.*, Bk. I, no. 12). The Pontiff orders the prelate to desist "*a tali inhumanitate.*" Worthy of note is what the same Pope tells us in Book IV, chapter 47, of the *Dialogues*, about the cemetery of his monastery of St. Andrew on the Clivus Scauri.

In the so-called Leonine Sacramentary much is made of the fact that the martyrs John and Paul are the only ones who were privileged to rest there on the Caelian, in the heart of the city. A good century later Gregory erects a cemetery in the same locality for his monks as a monastic right which no one ever dared to question.

[2] In the *Codex Theodosianus* we find a long list of professional men, among whom are the following: *mulomedici, barbaricarii, scasores* (Book XIII, Title IV, 2).

tern, which was situated in the center of the court; the monk was writhing and twisting in a curious manner, throwing himself on the ground and croaking like a reptile. His confreres related that a short time before he had gone with a bucket to draw water from the cistern; there the devil had obsessed him and brought him to this sorry condition.

We always see the saint full of dignity and displaying that authority which became his character as lawgiver. As on a former occasion at Subiaco he had thoroughly whipped the devil to free the monk with the wandering tendency, so now he proceeded to use the same tactics at Monte Cassino. While Satan was afflicting his victim and perhaps awaited some complicated conjuration, the saint, without any ceremony or exorcism, simply fetched him a healthy slap, as one would an insolent child.

At this curious means of attack, which, instead of affecting the obsessed monk, seemed to trouble the devil greatly, the latter came to the conclusion that there was little to be gained from such an adversary. Hence he decided to depart from the poor religious and to seek elsewhere, if not better fortune, at least a more diplomatic manner of being expelled. Certainly unusual methods these which the Patriarch employs. Without ever sacrificing any of his dignity, he humiliates Satan with beatings and slaps. The proud devil, while he even dares to dispute with others, as, for example, with St. Martin or St. Bernard, cannot tolerate to be humiliated to the point of being slapped. When he sees himself thus shamed, he takes to sudden flight.

CHAPTER XXXII

The Sharp-tongued Nuns

In the life of St. Benedict two periods may be distinguished: the exclusively monastic one at Subiaco and that of the legislator and apostle at Cassino. It is true that also in the silent cave of Monte Taleo he exercised an apostolate so widespread and above all so efficacious as to stir up the jealousy of the misguided priest Florence. But as far as Subiaco is concerned, St. Gregory is primarily concerned with describing the founder of the twelve monasteries, Benedict's miracles, and his first disciples.

At Cassino, on the other hand, St. Benedict's social mission undergoes a change. He is now about sixty years old, and together with age has reached the summit of evangelical perfection in the fullness of life's experiences and in the sublimity of the priestly state. When he mounts to the fortress of Casinum he is no longer an unknown hermit, whom the monk Romanus secretly takes under his wing. His position as an apostle must by this time have come to the notice of the highest authorities. Besides, at Monte Cassino St. Benedict appears endowed with pastoral jurisdiction over the neighboring villages which had been evangelized by him.

In another place I have already elaborated the arguments concerning St. Benedict's sacerdotal state; hence I shall not repeat them here. Following St. Gregory, we note that at Casinum Benedict not only dedicated himself to preaching; but after he had converted some of the surrounding hamlets, he established there the parochial clergy and reserved to himself the pastoral jurisdiction.

"Not far from the monastery there was a village [1] in which lived not a few persons converted by Benedict's instruction to the true faith from the worship of idols. . . . Thither Benedict frequently sent some of the brethren to instruct them." [2] In this place was likewise a convent of nuns (ἀσκτήριον ἐτύγχανεν . . . σέμνων παρθένων), according to Pope Zachary's translation; and the servant of God used regularly to send monks there to give spiritual conferences. Later on I shall relate an unpleasant incident that occurred on one of these excursions outside the monastery.

In another spot in the vicinity of Casinum two consecrated virgins of noble lineage, according to the ancient discipline, resided in their own house,[3] practicing the Christian virtues—and making others exercise them too. Besides an old nurse, they had a good man, full of piety and zeal, to serve them. But, according to his mistresses, he did nothing satisfactorily; every day the house resounded with scoldings and insults. The old nurse vacillated between the two parties.

The good man bore up with this sort of abuse in silence for a time, but finally, in order not to make a scene before the nuns—so great was his respect for them—he thought of laying the whole matter before the servant of God. They treated him worse than a slave, so much so that sometimes, as he himself confessed, he had to swallow harsh words and was then expected to speak gently to the ladies.

He climbed Monte Cassino and laid the entire affair of the sharp-tongued women before the Abbot. Under the virginal veil of Christian humility, asserted the servant, they preserved all the vain practices of the old Cassinese nobility of pagan times.

The Patriarch listened patiently to the outpouring of the poor man

---

[1] The "vicus non longe ab eius monasterio" was perhaps situated near the spot where the monastery of Albaneta was erected in the Middle Ages, more or less on the summit of the mountain, but on the slope opposite the castrum Casinum, on the side of Monte Cairo. In fact, an ancient inscription was found there (cf. Carettoni, op. cit., 45). Another vicus, considerably more distant, must have been at Villa S. Lucia, to the west of Casinum, where the mule path follows the tracks of a very ancient mountain trail (older perhaps than the Latina), which served to join the various villages spread over the mountainside.

[2] Dial., Bk. II, chap. 19.

[3] Of these cellae of one or two virgins who led an ascetical life in their own houses amid the tumult of the town, St. Leander speaks in a depreciatory manner in his rule for his own sister Florentina: "Fuge quaeso privatam vitam; nec velis imitari eas virgines quae in urbibus per cellulas demorantur" (PL, LXVII, 886). This was precisely the condition that existed at Casinum.

and tried to calm him. He ordered the monk who gave the conferences and who went to the village occasionally to hold catechetical instructions, to inform the nuns without any apologies: "Hold your tongues; unless you correct yourselves, I will excommunicate you." St. Gregory observes that this was not a sentence of excommunication in the canonical form, properly speaking, but only a threat (chap. 23), or, as the law says, a *prima admonitio*.

Ecclesiastical excommunication was one of the gravest penalties which at that time could be inflicted on the faithful; it was a kind of spiritual sword that separated the delinquent from the body of the Catholic Church and forbade him the reception of the Holy Eucharist. In the sixth century ecclesiastical law had already determined the norms according to which bishops and pastors of souls could employ this extreme remedy of canonical justice. I must add, however, that it was a rather dangerous undertaking for the surgeon himself. As a matter of fact not rarely in St. Gregory's letters the proceedings of these promulgators of anathemas are considered, and the sentences are nullified where he finds them not in conformity with the law.

The one who excommunicates from the body and blood of Christ, says Gregory, must be a bishop or at least a priest, a minister of the Eucharist, never an outsider or a simple lay abbot. Still less could a superior of monks excommunicate nuns, who were under the special jurisdiction of the bishop. To prevent bishops and pastors from too readily excommunicating their subjects, the Fifth Council of Orleans in October, 549, promulgated the following canon: "II. No priest is permitted to prohibit a believer from the reception of Communion for slight causes, but only for those faults which the Fathers of the Church sanctioned." [4]

In the Letters of St. Ambrose there is a most interesting case of a virgin of Verona, who was constrained to appeal from her own bishop to the metropolitan of Milan. The saint was greatly provoked that a virgin consecrated by St. Zeno should have to suffer such an affront.

In general, in connection with excommunication we have an instructive letter of St. Gregory to Bishop Chrysantus of Spoleto, in whose territory Nursia was situated. The priest and abbot Valentine

[4] Mansi, IX, 130.

had had recourse to the Pope, complaining that the bishop's priests too readily admitted to Holy Communion those monks whom the abbot had excommunicated. The Pope took up the question and decided that the abbatial excommunication held also outside the monastery and had to be respected by the pastors. If at any time a monk felt that the abbot's sentence was unjust, he could have recourse to the diocesan bishop as to a court of appeal. The jurisdiction of the abbot and priest Valentine was indeed local and personal, but restricted to his own community.

With St. Gregory we must also distinguish the simple excommunication from the anathema in the strict sense. The former signifies a temporary deprivation of Mass and Holy Communion, whereas the anathema separates the culprit definitely from the body of the Catholic Church and consequently also deprives him of Holy Communion.[5]

In both cases, however, there was question of a true canonical sentence with most serious consequences; hence the ecclesiastical judge could pronounce it exclusively on his own subjects. The sentence would not affect the sheep of another shepherd. St. Benedict forbids it expressly in the Rule: "We decree that no one be allowed to excommunicate . . . any of his brethren unless the abbot has given him the authority" (chap. 70). If, then, the Patriarch excommunicated the two religious women residing in their own house near Monte Cassino, it signifies that he exercised over them a special ecclesiastical jurisdiction, so much the more important because there was question of consecrated virgins.

After some time had passed, the two noble virgins—in the Neapolitan area, Tosti assures us, there was never a shortage of nobles—died and, according to custom, were buried in the church.[6] Which church? The biographer does not say. But I have a suspicion that it was that of Casinum, the only one in the vicinity worthy of this name. In former times the *ecclesia* was generally the cathedral; other places of worship

[5] *Epist.,* Bk. VII, no. 31.
[6] The ancient cemetery of the *oppidum* of Cassino was to the west, just outside the walls; its nucleus was the strip of land between the Via Latina and the mausoleum of the Hummidii. About the fifth century there arose the practice of burying the faithful in the churches; the Christians, particularly those in the villages, did this in order to avoid having to bury their dead among the pagans.

were called either basilicas or *oratoria*. In the *ecclesia* in question some vestiges of the former episcopal setup remained: the assistance of the deacon at Mass, the departure of the catechumens and the penitents before the Offertory, and so on. These liturgical particulars necessarily would not hold of a small village church. Most probably, then, the locale is the ancient temple of Hummidia Quadratilla at Casinum.

The one most affected by the sudden death of the two virgins was their faithful nurse. As was her custom when they were still living and assisted at the Sacrifice in the church, the good woman wished to continue to present at the altar also the offering of her deceased mistresses. "Poor things," she said to herself; "they were two saints."

Such was then the manner of offering suffrages for the dead. St. Monica, discoursing with St. Augustine and with her children and grandchildren concerning her approaching end, requested that after her death they should present offerings also for her at the altar of the Lord.

Shortly after the death of the two nuns, the devoted nurse went to Mass with the offerings. But at the moment after the Gospel, when the deacon used to dismiss the catechumens (*"Si quis non communicat, det locum"*) she, the good nurse, noticed that among those who withdrew were, alas, also her former mistresses.

The first time this occurred, she thought it was a dream or the product of her imagination, overexcited by sorrow. But since the event recurred regularly, she recalled the threatening words which the holy Patriarch had directed to these nuns. Without a doubt, she thought within herself, in the world beyond they still feel the weight of the excommunication of the Church on earth.

Full of consternation, the woman, together with some companions, —of the poor male servant, who had had to suffer so much at their hands, no mention is made—climbed Monte Cassino to tell the servant of God what had happened in the church below. They conjured him to restore the Communion to the two poor nuns by readmitting them to a participation in the Church's Sacrifice. The saint was deeply moved. Then, giving to the afflicted nurse one of the breads, crown-shaped or round, which then were used for the Eucharist, he said: "Go and have this offered to the Lord for them, and they shall no longer be excommunicated" (chap. 23).[7] The order was duly carried out. After that the two dead nuns rested in peace in their tomb.[8]

To this account St. Gregory the Great adds a bit of theological comment. Peter the Deacon, marveling at this prodigy, asks the Pope how Benedict, even admitting his eminent sanctity, could give absolution to souls who no longer were part of this world, but had already been judged by God's tribunal. Theologically this is a nice question. No one will deny that the priests of the Church can bind and loose in heaven and on earth. Peter the Deacon expressly grants that Benedict, "a venerable and most holy man," does honor to the priestly state. But here we are concerned not with absolving penitents still alive or assisting the deceased with prayers and the suffrages of the Mass. The case is decidedly different. The question is: How is it possible for a priest, no matter how venerable and holy he may be, "to release souls that already stood before the invisible judgment seat of God?"[9]

After stating the question thus clearly, the Pope solves the problem by appealing to the fullness of the power of the keys given by Christ

---

[7] In Bk. IV, chap. 51, Gregory relates a similar story. In a village of the Sabines was a nun whose chastity indeed was above all suspicion, but whose tongue was as sharp as a needle. In God's time she died and was buried in the parish church. The following night the sacristan had a vision. He saw the deceased nun being brought before the altar for judgment. The sentence was severe. Since she had been half virtuous and half evil-tongued, she was condemned to be sawed in two: one half of her body remained intact, the other half was burned. The next day the sacristan related the affair to his friends and, to show them the exact spot where the deceased had been punished, he brought them to the altar of the church. First with wonder and then with terror they noticed that on the marble of the floor could still be seen traces of the fire of the preceding night.

[8] While the excommunication lasted, the offering could not be accepted. Canon 2 of the first Council of Vaison laid down this rule: "*Pro iis qui poenitentia accepta, in bonae vitae cursu satisfactoria compunctione viventes, sine Communione, inopinato nonnunquam transitu, in agro aut in itineribus praeveniuntur, oblationem recipiendam et eorum funera ac deinceps memoriam ecclesiastico affectu prosequendum*" (*PL*, LIV, 1475). Later we shall see that penance without the Eucharist was not regarded as complete reconciliation *in facie Ecclesiae*.
Here the council of Gallic bishops refers to the discipline followed by St. Benedict. For this kind of deceased penitents, who had passed into eternity before readmission to the Eucharist, an offering was received at Mass, and they were commemorated.

[9] *Dial.*, Bk. II, chap. 23. In Bk. IV, chap. 55, St. Gregory recounts a similar incident. A soul in purgatory appears to a priest of the diocese of Civitavecchia and requests prayers: "*Omnipotenti Deo pro me offer hunc panem (oblationum coronas), ut pro peccatis meis intervenias.*" The priest satisfies the pious desire and after a time is informed that the deceased has received pardon.

to St. Peter and, in general, to all who exercise the care of souls: "Those who now rule the Church in his [St. Peter's] stead, also receive the power of binding and loosing." The Pontiff attributes a special value to these two pastoral virtues, *fides et mores*, just as already before Peter had called Benedict "a venerable and most holy man."

In Book I of the *Regula pastoralis* St. Gregory himself explains what he means by *"locum regiminis,"* which he regularly identifies with the episcopal and priestly dignity. A few examples may suffice:

Chap. 2: *Ne locum regiminis subeant qui vivendo non perficiant quae meditantur.*

Chap. 3: *De pondere regiminis.*

Chap. 4: *Quod plerumque occupatio regiminis soliditatem dissipet mentis.*

Chap. 5: *De his qui in regiminis culmine prodesse exemplo virtutum possunt.*

Hence for Gregory *regimen* or *sacrum regimen* regularly signifies the priesthood. If, therefore, St. Benedict could absolve souls which had already been presented before God's judgment seat, this was possible because he was "a venerable and most holy man," as Peter the Deacon admitted, and because he occupied *"locum sancti regiminis"* in the hierarchy of the Church.[10]

I must add another observation. Every time the Patriarch of monks has occasion to give absolution to the dead, the biographer wishes us to note that he gives the Eucharistic oblation *propria manu* as a sign of reconciliation. For the ancients, indeed, Holy Communion represented not only a sacrament of a strictly personal character; it was the badge of Christian fellowship.

The Eucharist was received from the hand of the pastor, and it was

---

10 In the homily pronounced in the Lateran on the octave of Easter, St. Gregory treats at length of the power of binding and loosing, which he attributes directly to bishops and priests: *"Horum profecto nunc in Ecclesia episcopi locum tenent. Ligandi atque solvendi auctoritatem suscipiunt, qui gradum regiminis sortiuntur. Grandis honor, sed grave pondus . . ."* Then the Pope goes on to discuss how this power is to be exercised by priests: *"Causae ergo pensandae sunt, et tunc ligandi atque solvendi potestas exercenda est."* He observes how the apostles loosed Lazarus from his bonds not while he was dead, but after he had been called back to life by Christ: *"Si enim discipuli Lazarum mortuum solverent, foetorem magis ostenderent quam virtutem ex qua consideratione intuendum est, quod illos nos debemus per pastoralem auctoritatem solvere, quos Auctorem nostrum cognoscimus per suscitantem gratiam vivificare"* (Book II, Homily XXVI). And he concludes: *"Haec de solutionis ordine breviter dixerim, ut sub magno moderamine pastores Ecclesiae vel solvere studeant, vel ligare."*

considered the external sign of Catholic union with him and the other sheep of the flock. Hence they used the expressions: to separate from one's communion; to readmit to one's communion. For this reason St. Benedict by giving with his own hand either the Eucharistic offering or the Eucharist itself, in accordance with the custom then in vogue, performs an action which was required to express readmission to his communion and his favor. It was equivalent to an absolution from excommunication.

It should be noted that such an absolution, as a decree issued by Pope Felix III in 488 reminded the bishops, could be given only by the bishop or priest who exercised true ecclesiastical jurisdiction over the culprit, not by others: *"Omni cautela est providendum, ne quis fratrum coepiscoporum nostrorum aut etiam presbyterorum, in alterius civitatis vel diocesis poenitentem . . . suscipiat."*

I stated above that in former times the virgins were under the special care of their own bishop. The writings of the Fathers of the Church from St. Cyprian to St. Augustine and St. Caesarius indicate what great diligence the bishops manifested in regard to the group of virgins; each one looked upon them as the most precious gems adorning his episcopal miter.

In church the virgins occupied a separate and distinct place. St. Ambrose notes that during the Mass, at the moment when the faithful exchanged the kiss of peace, the matrons competed with one another in gaining the enclosure of the virgins and giving them the embrace.

Different popes, in order to keep away all danger from the dignity of the virginal state, decreed that definitive virginal consecration could not take place before the sixtieth year. At the time of St. Gregory, in order that the bishops might confer the virginal veil on nuns in Sicily, it was required that the candidate should have attained the sixtieth year and that the consecrating bishop should have obtained the special permission of the representative of the Pope, at that time Archbishop Maximian of Syracuse: *"Iuvenculas abbatissas fieri vehementissime prohibemus. Nullum igitur episcopum fraternitas tua, nisi sexagenariam virginem, cuius aetas atque mores exegerint velare permittat."* [11] The jurisdiction which St. Benedict

[11] Bk. III, no. 9.

exercised over the nuns must be considered in the light of the canon law of the sixth century.

In the writings of St. Gregory we find another example, that of Equitius, who, besides presiding, as did St. Benedict, over a congregation of various monasteries of monks, also had under his charge a convent of nuns: ". . . *in monasterio virginum, in quo eiusdem patris cura vigilabat.*" [12] The charge over this monastery was so delicate and so personally reserved to the abbot that, "in the absence of the father, no one of the monks dared to visit the community of virgins." The juridical situation of St. Equitius, like that of St. Benedict, appears exceptional. But St. Gregory attests that he acted under the jurisdiction of the Roman Pontiff. And that explains everything.

[12] *Dial.*, Bk. I, chap. 4.

CHAPTER XXXIII

The Young Monk Who Ran Away

IT befell on another occasion that St. Benedict had to give absolution to one already dead. There was a young monk who had been born in the vicinity of Monte Cassino and who, in accord with the ardent nature of peasants, even after his vows yearned for the folks back home. One fine day the affection for his parents got the better of him. Without permission, without the Abbot's blessing, he left and blithely skipped down the mountain to make a visit to his native village. We can easily imagine the joy of relatives and friends at seeing him again.

To arrive at home in an exhausted condition, to greet his parents, to refresh himself with a drink and to become sick: all of this happened more or less simultaneously. Whatever the cause—congestion, sunstroke, peritonitis, galloping pneumonia, we do not know. But on the very evening of his arrival the young monk took to his bed. A few hours later he was dead. To describe the grief of his family is impossible. According to custom, he was buried in the cemetery adjoining the parish church.[1]

But when the faithful came to their little church on the following

---

[1] A difference must be mentioned here. At Casinum the two noble nuns are entombed inside the church of St. Peter. But this was a "cemetery church," because in other cases canonical legislation did not permit the dedication of oratories or secondary basilicas unless first it was shown that no body had been buried there: "And then . . . if no body has been buried in that place . . . you will proceed to consecrate the oratories" (Gregory, *Epist.*, Bk. VIII, no. 4). The young monk who died at home, on the other hand, is buried in the earth under the open sky. But his body is cast up "unburied," and only after the Patriarch's absolution "the earth received him" (Bk. II, chap. 24). Here undoubtedly the question concerns a small rural cemetery.

morning, they noticed to their surprise that in the cemetery the earth had been moved and that the body was still uncovered. At that time wooden coffins were not yet used. The rich were buried in sarcophagi of baked clay or stone; the poor were simply wrapped in a shroud.

Not knowing what to think, they filled the hole with earth a second time and tamped it down well, so that neither rain nor animals would be able to remove it.[2] All to no purpose! Also the third day the corpse was uncovered, as if mother earth refused to receive into her embrace one who was under the excommunication of St. Benedict. The distraught parents then ran to Monte Cassino, weeping and moaning and tearing their hair—as southern peoples are accustomed to do—and related their sad tale to the holy Patriarch, at the same time beseeching him to readmit the deceased into his favor.

The fault in question was not a slight one, and its punishment was envisaged in chapter 67 of the Rule: "And let him be punished . . . who would presume to leave the enclosure of the monastery and go anywhere or do anything, however small, without an order from the abbot." But there were extenuating circumstances: the youth of the offender and the special character of those peoples, so warmly attached to their parents and their relationship. Softened by their sobs, St. Benedict could no longer delay the absolution of the culprit.

Here a bit of liturgical comment appears apropos. I have already said that in ancient times the absolution of penitents carried with it their readmission to the reception of the Eucharist. St. Leo the Great in his letter to Bishop Rusticus of Narbonne, to the question: "What is to be done about those who are reconciled in their extremity, but die before they can receive Holy Communion?" replies thus: "Their fate must be left to the judgment of God. . . . But those whom during their lifetime we excluded from our communion, we cannot admit to that communion after death."[3] Hence even after absolution, if Mass with the reception of Holy Communion did not follow, the

---

[2] An epitaph from the catacombs of Praetextatus bears witness to the same preoccupation: "Aurelia Marula begs those who bury her to seal well the covering of her grave. If they obey her wishes, may the Lord also seal their prayers," that is, with His grace.

[3] "De hiis qui iam deficientes poenitentiam accipiunt, et ante Communionem moriuntur?—Horum causa Dei iudicio reservanda est . . . Nos autem quibus viventibus non communicavimus, mortuis communicare non possumus" (PL, LVI, 1025 f.).

penitent was not regarded as having been readmitted to ecclesiastical union.

Benedict, then, ascended the altar for the celebration of the Sacrifice. When he reached the point in the Mass where the priest used to detach from the host the particles to be sent to the absent as a sign of union and of participation in the fruits of the Sacrifice, as St. Zachary so well describes, he broke off a fragment, gave it into the hands of the parents, and said: "Go and lay the body of the Lord on the breast of the deceased, and so bury him." [4]

This practice, which was subsequently condemned by several councils,[5] was widespread during the first centuries.[6] It appears to have been the normal thing to place the Eucharist on the corpses of bishops. At Milan, for example, St. Charles found a Eucharistic theca with an engraved dedication to the virgin Dedalia in the altar of the basilica of the Apostles erected by St. Ambrose on the Via Romana. It is possible that this silver capsule contained the Eucharist, which was placed in the sculptured chest enclosing the relics of the apostles which had come from Rome.

[4] The mentality of the Christians of the sixth century regarding the fate of those who died without being able to receive the Eucharist is well illustrated by the deacon Ferrandus of Carthage in a letter to St. Fulgence of Ruspa. An Ethiopian, already sufficiently instructed, had indeed been baptized at the point of death, but, since he was unconscious, he had not been able to receive the Eucharist. What is to be thought of his eternal salvation? The Bishop of Ruspa replies that in such a case the sacrament of baptism, which already incorporates the neophyte into the Church and the mystical body of Christ, and his desire of the Eucharist suffice (Letter 12; *PL*, LXV, 380–92).

[5] Since the custom of placing the Eucharist in the graves of those who had died without receiving Viaticum was so deep-seated and could give rise to grave superstitions, a canon of the so-called *Statuta Ecclesiae Antiqua*, composed at Valencia in the first half of the fifth century, legislated concerning this matter as follows: "Let the Eucharist not be given to the bodies of the deceased. The Lord said: 'Take ye and eat.' But corpses can neither take nor eat. Then, too, care must be taken lest the weaker brethren think that the dead can be baptized when they see the Eucharist given to them" (*PL*, LVI, 421 f.). Notwithstanding the prohibitive legislation of the Gallic episcopate on this point, the custom persisted for a long time, particularly with regard to bishops and martyrs.

A papyrus encolpion in the museum of Berlin, after various scriptural passages, concludes with this Eucharistic invocation: "Body and blood of Christ, be propitious to Thy servant, who wears this phylactery."

[6] St. Leo I had forbidden the reconciliation of the dead with the Church. The Pope was led to this step by the abuse that was then gaining ground of putting off canonical penance until death was imminent (Letter 108; *PL*, IV, 1011–14).

A canon of the Council of Autun in 578 renews the prohibition of giving the Eucharist to the dead: "*Non licet mortuis nec Eucharistiam, nec osculum tradi, nec velo vel palliis corpora eorum involvi*" (can. 12).

I must mention another Eucharistic custom, namely, that of breaking off a particle of the Eucharist at the papal and episcopal Masses in
order to send it by means of acolytes to various parishes of Rome, as
it is described for us in a letter of Pope Innocent I to Decentius,
bishop of Gubbio. This particle was called the *sacrum fermentum*,
because it was placed in the chalice just before Communion, in order
to signify that the one identical Eucharist united the shepherd to his
flock.

St. Zachary in the Greek version of the *Dialogues*, when speaking
of the Eucharist consigned by St. Benedict for the deceased monk,
translates with a paraphrase: "Taking a particle from the Lord's body,
he gave it to them"—λαβὼν ἀπὸ τοῦ δεσποτικοῦ Σώματος μερίδα μίαν
δέδωκεν (chap. 24). The act was entirely liturgical, and it was performed
at Mass.

Furthermore, in the village of the deceased there doubtless was a
church where Mass was celebrated. Hence St. Benedict could well have
ordered that thence be gotten the Eucharistic particle to be placed on
the corpse. But it was not so. The signification would not have been
the same. He himself had to give the Eucharist to the deceased as a
sign of absolution. St. Gregory stresses the point: "immediately . . .
with his own hands."

It must be noted, besides, that in the sixth century not even the
deacon could administer Holy Communion and much less absolve
a culprit from excommunication. In this connection we have a canon
of the Council of Arles, dating from 542: "*In secretario diacono inter
presbyteros sedere non liceat; vel Corpus Domini, praesente presby-
tero tradere non praesumat. Quod si fecerit, ab officio diaconatus
abscedat.*[7]

In Italy the decree issued by Pope Gelasius in 494 and directed to
the bishops of Lucania was in force: "*Diaconi. . . . Sacri Corporis
erogationem sub conspectu pontificis seu presbyteri, nisi hiis ab-
sentibus, ius non habeant exercendi.*"

So the parents of the deceased departed from Monte Cassino quite
resigned. When they returned to their village, with great faith they
placed the sacred particle given to them by St. Benedict on the corpse
of their son, already on the way to decomposition four days after his

---

[7] Labbe, *Summ. Concil.*, IV, 1013.

death. Earth was then heaped on the corpse until the grave was well filled. From that time forth the grave remained undisturbed. The deceased had been readmitted into communion with the Church.

Since we are treating of the Eucharist, we may not pass unnoticed a phrase which the biographer places on the lips of St. Benedict on this occasion: "Lay the body of the Lord upon his breast with great reverence."

This "great reverence" toward the Eucharist expresses an entire program. St. Benedict always shows himself faithful to it. After prescribing in the Rule that the table reader, on Sunday, before beginning his reading, should take an ablution, that is, a bit of watered wine *propter Communionem sanctam,* on the point of death he himself rose from his bed and betook himself for a last time to the oratory of St. Martin in order to receive, standing, the body and the blood of the Lord. St. Charles at Milan tried to repeat the act, but was prevented by reason of the violence of his sickness.

St. Benedict has not written, like other fathers, any treatise on Eucharistic piety. But for him who can understand, the few references preserved for us by St. Gregory suffice to assure us of his "great reverence" toward this Sacrament.

This episode must be placed side by side with another narrated by John the Deacon in the life of St. Gregory the Great. The latter had excommunicated one of the monks of his monastery of St. Andrew for a violation of the vow of poverty, and shortly afterward the culprit died while still under the penalty. Three days later the abbot brought the matter to the attention of the saint, who was greatly saddened thereby, particularly because of the excommunication that still weighed on the poor religious. He drew up a formula of absolution and ordered the deacon to go and read it over the grave of the deceased. This was done.

During the following night, the abbot in a dream saw the deceased monk and asked him where and how he was. He replied that he was truly dead and that he had passed all that time as in a prison. Finally, that he was freed from the excommunication of Pope Gregory and that he was liberated from his bondage.

The author mentions the incident as an example of the holy Pope's power, whose word produced its effect not only here on earth, but even before the tribunal of the world to come.[8] This is an exact parallel of St. Gregory's thought in the case of the young monk who died and was then absolved by St. Benedict.

St. Gregory concludes this episode: "Consider, Peter, in what regard Benedict was held by God, when even the earth refused to receive the corpse of one who did not enjoy his favor."

[8] John the Deacon, *Vita S. Gregorii*, Bk. II, no. 45.

CHAPTER XXXIV

A Dragon at the Gate

ANOTHER young monk at Monte Cassino occasionally manifested to the Abbot his foolish desire of abandoning the monastery in order to lead an easier life with his family in the world. With great patience the saint had several times disabused him of the idea; he had discussed the matter with him, solved his difficulties, absolutely forbidden him to cast his habit into the bushes and to leave Monte Cassino.

For the time being he seemed convinced and promised to remain; but then after a few days, he was back with the same complaints about his health, the rarefied air of the mountain that prevented him from sleeping, his weakened heart and stomach. Finally one day the saint, embittered by this weakness of will, replied that he did not wish to retain anyone by force: let him depart from the monastery and leave the others in peace. The monk, not waiting to be told a second time, settled his affairs, put on the garb with which he had come to the monastery, and got ready to leave Monte Cassino.

But he reckoned badly. He did not think that his good Father, who did not wish to see the devil snatch the youth and draw him to perdition, was praying for him. As the apostate, having passed through the first narrow gate, arrived at that of the external circle of the Samnite walls, behold an immense dragon with jaws distended seemed to come toward him to tear him to bits. We can easily imagine the poor fellow's fear. He began to cry for help. He wished indeed to return to the cloister, but he did not dare to move for fear the monster would follow him. "Help! Help!" he cried. "This dragon intends to eat me!"

The porters at their post heard him and immediately hurried to him, but they could see neither monster nor flames. But the monk, shaking like a leaf, insisted, pointing with his finger at the dragon that was ready to devour him. The porters took him by the arm and led him back up to the monastery. There, at last, the fugitive, somewhat restored, understood that it was the Abbot's prayers that had made him see who it was toward whom he had been going so long without noticing it.[1]

Whoever is conversant with the topography of Monte Cassino, with its double circle of ancient walls, will recognize the exactness of the biographer in describing this episode. After that fright, as we may well believe, the young monk promised from the bottom of his heart never to leave Monte Cassino. And St. Gregory adds that he kept his word: *"Atque ex eadem hora in sua promissione permansit."* [2]

[1] *"Trementem et palpitantem monachum ad monasterium reduxerunt."*
[2] *Dial.*, Bk. II, chap. 25.

CHAPTER XXXV

The Monastic Rule

As is seen in the fioretti of Gregory, the holy Patriarch with a hand mild and paternal but strong laid the basis of the future Benedictine institute of the West. Till his time the monastic life, which consisted essentially in the profession of the evangelical counsels, was left by the Church to the individual initiative of simple anchorites and abbots, who recruited disciples and set up a personal system of spiritual doctrine. Thus had done St. Anthony, St. Pachomius, and St. Hilarion.

Nevertheless, all that luxuriant tropical vegetation that grew so abundantly in the garden of the Church universal was not in a position to serve fully enough the new scope which Rome intended to assign to Latin monachism. In Europe the barbarians must be converted to Christian civilization; episcopal sees had to be supplied with suitable pastors; furthermore, the good tradition of sacred studies had to be preserved, even amid the horrors of the wars that were making Italy desolate.

The clergy of the time was not equal to the task. To whom then could the popes commit an undertaking of such importance and magnitude if not to a specialized corps of "servants of God," like in character to the ancient *scholae* or teaching bodies, extending indeed to the most remote provinces, to all climates and to the most diverse external conditions, but with a single Rule, a definitive and universal authority, proceeding from Rome?

As appears from the Leonine Sacramentary, Rome shied away from the exuberance of Oriental monachism, which in divers ways was insinuating itself on the seven hills, occasionally introducing errors, superstitions, and motives for jealousy on the part of the clergy. It was necessary to discipline this vast movement and lead it into the stream of Catholic asceticism.

St. Caesarius, as I have shown in another study, after imposing a single rule on all the monasteries of his diocese, had desired Pope Hormisdas to place his pontifical seal on the monastic institutions at Arles. At Naples, Eugippius had had recourse to the rule which St. Augustine had written for nuns; he adapted it for monks, adding certain disciplinary norms of his own. About the same time a petition was sent by the synod at Agaun, requesting that the Holy See give the monastery in that city a definitive rule.

These events occurred about 521, precisely at the time when St. Benedict undertook the organization of his thirteen monasteries at Subiaco, focusing upon himself the attention of the Eternal City and enlisting the help of the Roman patriciate.

We do not know what reply was given to the synod of Agaun. Perhaps some light may be shed by a note in the *Liber pontificalis*, stating that Pope Hormisdas, a friend of St. Caesarius and a supporter of his rule, was a native of Frosinone, a city not very far from Monte Cassino. Is there perhaps some connection between this Pope, the monastic foundation at Cassino, and the universal code of Western monasticism? It is absurd to suppose that St. Benedict should have written his Rule on his own initiative.[1]

His new Rule, in fact, strikes us immediately as a common and general law, to which henceforth bishops, abbots, and monks must bow. To depart from it, so it is said, would be acting rashly. For this reason it will not be spoken of as the Rule of St. Benedict or the Rule of Monte Cassino, but simply as the *Regula monasteriorum*.

Now, such a manner of thinking and, above all, the authoritarian and universal character of the language employed are possible only

[1] Also Cassian, the first, one may say, and the greatest legislator of Western monachism, about 420 was induced, at the command of Bishop Castor of Apta, to describe the manner of life of the monks of Egypt and Palestine. "*Poscis praecipisque ut instituta monasteriorum quae per Aegyptum ac Palestinam perspeximus, ita ut ibi nobis a patribus tradita sunt, quamvis imperito digeram stylo*" (*De instit. coenob.*, Praef.). Nevertheless he did not mitigate the excessively austere discipline by adapting it to the climate and the mentality of the Franks. But the one to give the force of law to the work was not so much Cassian, as rather the Bishop, who decided to begin with his own monastery at Apta.

at Rome. Pope John IV attributes to the Patriarch the title of Abbot of the city of Rome: *"Haud procul a nostris temporibus, Benedicti abbatis istius Romae huius urbis."* The fact was known even in Gaul; there, in 623, Venerandus, founder of the monastery of Altaripa, writing to Bishop Constantius of Albi, speaks of the Rule of the Patriarch of Cassino in these words: *Regula S. Benedicti Abbatis Romensis.*

The new Rule is directed generically to the entire class of cenobites in the Latin world. The author intends to and actually does lay down a law for all: *"ad cenobitarum fortissimum genus disponendum"* (chap. 1). He who legislates thus universally cannot be a particular abbot, but one who has general jurisdiction.

The Rule furthermore anticipates its introduction to all places and climes: hence quality and color of the monastic habit are to be adapted to the place; wine may be served if it is found in the region; fasts and hours for manual labor of the monks are left to the discretion of the abbot, but taking into account the local conditions of the monks themselves. But as if to counterbalance this flexibility of the Rule and the spirit of adaptation, so truly Roman, to the various regions of the Western world, the legislator regards his Code as something holy and lays it down that no one may ever deviate from it.

As the Rule is stable, so also the abbot is stable and persevering in demanding its observance, as well as the monk, who in writing [2] will bind himself by the vow of stability to his monastery, where he will have to persevere until death in the service of God. Gone is the time when everyone could make profession of the monastic state on his own account and change residence at his pleasure. Now, if anyone wishes to take the monastic habit, he must first make a year of noviatiate under an abbot canonically recognized and must diligently be formed to the observance of spiritual doctrine.

No longer will it be permissible to pass the monastic life in a sort of penitential nomadism, spending the time in this or that monastery, on a perpetual pilgrimage, after the fashion of the wandering Jew. The monks can no longer withdraw from the obedience of their own abbot, transferring their residence elsewhere, even for the pur-

---

[2] At Arles, as St. Caesarius records, the baptismal formula whereby Satan was renounced was made in writing and signed (*PL*, XXXIX, 2235). The writing of baptismal conversion gave the suggestion for the document of monastic conversion.

pose of greater perfection. He who leaves his monastery will be considered a fugitive, and then the civil law will enter in to seek him out and bring him back by force to his abbot.

The purpose of the monastic life is indeed evangelical perfection through the observance of the counsels given by Christ. But to the daily exercises of the cenobitic life, to prayer and penance in solitude, the Rule adds a new element entirely Roman in inspiration: the organized exercise of the various arts, sacred studies, missions among the infidels. St. Benedict regards the cloister as a guild or *schola,* and the monk as God's workman. He demands that this divine workman place his energies at the service of the Church. Hence the evangelization of the pagans about Cassino and the organization of the Christian life in the surrounding villages. He did the same to convert the pagans and the Jews of Terracina.

Fifty years later, when Gregory the Great wished to undertake the evangelization of England, he did not hesitate a moment in assigning this mission to forty monks of his own monastery. No one saw anything unusual in the choice, since all were convinced that the Rule of St. Benedict precisely prepares and organizes such workmen to labor for the kingdom of God. The apostles had spread the gospel by founding first of all Christian communities, to which they had assigned a local hierarchy.

For a long time the monastic apostolate will preserve this primitive character. The monastery at Cassino together with the neophytes of the surrounding villages will be considered by St. Benedict a single large flock. On the summit of the mountain the evangelical counsels were lived again; at the foot of the mountain and round about the precepts were observed. A priest and a deacon were assigned to the parishes recently organized by him; but the Patriarch from the height of his watchtower retained command of them. If occasionally he sent also his own disciples thither as preachers, he did not, on the other hand, yield the pastoral staff to anyone and reserved to himself the right to excommunicate and to absolve.

Rather than the individuals, it is the entire community that carries out the Christian apostolate, by practicing evangelical perfection by prayer and work, preaching by example before preaching by word of mouth.

Yet the Patriarch attributes great importance to that particular form of the individual apostolate which is exercised when a guest is received into the monastery and the supreme interests of his soul are privately discussed with him. Since the time of his seclusion in the cave at Subiaco, the saint had cultivated this special exercise with good results. Later at Monte Cassino he writes in his Rule that not a day passes with the guesthouse empty.

When St. Benedict founds the monastery at Terracina, into the plans he immediately introduces the building intended for guests. The great abbots of the eighth century will imitate him, and they will develop the idea by constructing hospices and hospitals along the principal roads used by travelers. Thus it appears that monastic tradition attached great importance to this special form of assistance, which interwove Christian charity with the apostolate of the gospel.

Conceiving thus of the monastic life as a school of the Lord's service in the West, it will perhaps no longer allow the divine workmen to practice the rigors so characteristic of Egyptian and Palestinian monachism. If, during the day, the monk must alternate between the psalmody and the exercise of the various crafts and of study, he will need a sufficiency of sleep and of food. In the Campania and Latium he will not even be denied a hemina of wine and an occasional bath.

Similarly the clothes, besides being sufficient, must also be suitable. When they are discarded because the abbot has procured new ones, the old ones must still be in such a condition that they can suitably be given to the poor.

The Romans generally wore footgear according to their income or their social position. The monks likewise will not go barefoot, but will wear on their feet, according to circumstances, either the *pedules* in the house or the *caligae* at work or on a journey. The *pedules*, as the name indicates, bore some resemblance to the *ciocie* of the inhabitants of Latium. The *caligae* may have been *clavatae*, that is, with nailed soles, and served the purpose of our shoes. It would have been impossible to work in the fields or to travel barefooted or wearing only sandals.

The monks are indeed God's workmen, organized for the service of the Church. But they live by the labor of their hands and hence are not and should not be considered mendicants. For this reason they will clothe themselves suitably. The community will possess and administer its own patrimony, which can be increased by the labor of the monks and by benefactors. This patrimony, however, will belong to God and will serve, besides the monks, also for the maintenance of guests and of the poor who every day knock at the gate of the monastery in large numbers.

Contrary to our modern way of thinking, the monasteries of the sixth century in Italy and in Rome possessed slaves. On this point we possess numerous documents, especially from the Register of Gregory the Great. The *Liber diurnus* also contains various formularies for the donation or exchange of slaves between various monasteries. A few examples follow.

Abbot N. of monastery N. in a memorial to the Pope explains that an agricultural servant of his monastery intended to marry a slave belonging to the pontifical patrimony of territory N. and hence asks the Pope's permission to be allowed to give another slave in her stead: *"famulam vicinam."* The Pope agrees and by edict orders the pontifical rector of the patrimony to draw up the documents for the exchange (form. 48).[3]

The *Liber pontificalis* speaks frequently of these slaves used for the cultivation of the lands of the pontifical patrimony. In my history of the Abbey of Farfa, I have treated at length of the slaves of that monastery. The condition of these slaves was inspired by the great principles of the Gospel. Often they were manumitted and declared free Roman citizens. Formulas for this purpose are found in the *Liber diurnus* (form. 49 and 52). Also in his Rule St. Benedict refers to slaves, who at that time commonly constituted a part of the patrimony of monasteries and who performed the heavier work in the fields: "And if . . . their poverty should require that they themselves do the work of gathering the harvest, let them not be discontented, for then they are truly monks" (chap. 48).

This same theme, namely, that the cultivation of the fields, par-

---

[3] Another abbot and priest receives a similar privilege: the Pope gives a slave of foreign origin, taken from patrimony N., in perpetuity to the monastery: *"irrevocabili iure pro monachorum fratrum et congregatione Deo laudes illic canentium sustentatione et stipendii victusque necessitati procurandum."* The slave will remain the property of the monastery, he and the children that may be born to him: *"Ita ut cunctis diebus vitae eorum in eodem deserviant monasterio et omnem obedientiam vobis exhibeant, vel qui ex eo fuerint procreati, sicut certe servi propriae dominationi"* (form. 102).

ticularly in the possessions far from the monastery, be carried out by slaves, is mentioned by the Patriarch in chapter 41: "If they have no work in the fields." In another place the Patriarch refers to the manumission of slaves who then pass over into the category of monks: "Let him not advance one of noble birth ahead of one who was formerly a slave. . . . Whether slaves or freemen, we are all one in Christ and bear an equal burden of service" (chap. 2).

By means of these supernatural principles, Christianity, without provoking any violent social revolution against slavery, on which the life of the Roman Empire was in great part founded, for ten centuries fought for liberty and the right of the human personality and won the battle. Ten centuries indeed were required, but for that length of time, too, the victory has lasted in Europe.

On going forth from the monastery, let there be no show of rigid poverty, because it might argue vain ostentation in one who has lands and slaves at his service. Hence for a journey the monks shall receive better garments and put on drawers (*femoralia*) for riding; on their return to the monastery they shall restore everything in good order to the master of the wardrobe.

We know, in fact, from the Leonine Sacramentary what disgust was provoked in Rome by the groups of Oriental monks, who daily thronged into the Lateran with their theological squabbles—dirty, barefooted, clothes in rags—and who made a living by trafficking in relics of martyrs which they said they had brought from their homeland. "*Nec saltem deforis sunt vel dealbati, vel loti; sed palam, pudore calcato, de pravis conversationibus suis etiam gloriantur, et domi forisque spurcitiam contrahentes, non tam referti sunt ossibus mortuorum, quam ipsi sunt mortui.*" [4]

But above the heart of Benedict, which beats so paternally for all the needs and for the comfort of his disciples, there is also a head, a mind which educates them and forms them according to the norms of the spiritual life, norms which allow of no deviation. The monk by his profession offers himself and consecrates himself to God without restriction. In the simple and the solemn rite of monastic profession, the candidate and the community thrice sing the verse of Psalm 118:

[4] *PL*, LV, 74.

*"Suscipe me, Domine, secundum eloquium tuum et vivam, et ne con-
fundas me ab exspectatione mea."*

It is not exact to say that the poverty of the Friars Minor is more
strict than the vow of St. Benedict's monk. The Patriarch, as a matter
of fact, lays down that the monk can possess nothing at all, depriving
him even of power over his own body. What is necessary for life and
the tasks assigned to him, that he can always expect to receive from
the provident charity of his abbot.

St. Francis dedicated his friars to the work of celebrating Mass, of
preaching here and there in the towns for the welfare of the faithful.
Hence, according to the Gospel, they have the right to gather and to
live from the offerings of the faithful. In ancient times, on the other
hand, most of the monks were laymen who had received no orders of
any kind. For that reason they were not itinerant missioners who had
a right to be maintained by the faithful. The monastery with its
schools and shops for the arts and crafts, with its hospices for the
travelers and the infirm, with its daily doling out of alms to the poor,
absolutely needed landed estates which were administered and sci-
entifically cultivated by the monks themselves.

On this point ecclesiastical legislation was so demanding that Rome
would not even grant permission to open an oratory for worship unless the founder first, by a legal act, gave assurance of a sufficient endowment. But, notwithstanding the fact that the monastery might
own vast estates and even slaves, the monk as an individual could own
nothing: "neither his own body nor his own will," says St. Benedict.
Whatever he receives from the abbot he gets by way of alms, as one
gives to the poor. Similarly the vows of chastity and obedience, now
so common to all religious communities, do not allow of mitiga-
tions of any kind. St. Benedict has made obedience the pivot of monastic discipline, the way by which the monk goes to God and on which
rise those famous twelve degrees of humility, around which the Patriarch groups his mystical doctrine of the perfect union of the soul with
God.[5]

[5] Like Cassiodorus, St. Benedict shows a special predilection for the number twelve.
Hence the degrees of humility must be twelve, though Cassian had only ten. The monastic
cursus is described in twelve chapters (8-19); the penitential code again in twelve (23-30
and 43-46). In his turn, Cassiodorus divides the *Variarum*, the History of the Goths, and

In the sixth century various monasteries already directed their external activity to the service of pilgrims and the sick. In Rome several monasteries had charge of xenodochia; in fact, the *Liber diurnus* in a formula of a privilege for a monastery joins to it also the care and ownership of a dispensary for the poor.

If this is true, then *a fortiori* the monasteries must also have had good infirmaries for the care of the sick religious themselves. St. Benedict treats of them in chapter 36 of the Rule, *"De infirmis fratribus"*; he mentions them also in other places, as in chapters 31, 39, 48. It may be useful to mention the more important prescriptions here.

For the care of the sick a special part of the cloister is set apart, furnished with bathrooms and whatever else may be required. The infirmary is put in charge of a monk possessed of these three qualities: he must be God-fearing, diligent, and solicitous. By diligence the Patriarch means necessary competence. As a matter of fact, later monastic tradition instituted in the great abbeys true schools of medicine for the benefit of the monks. When there is question of the sick, nothing is considered too good. The holy Patriarch orders that the care of the sick receive absolute priority. "Before all things and above all things, care must be taken of the sick, as if they were Christ in person." Let not the sick wait until they ask for help, but let their wants be anticipated by giving them baths, nourishing food, meat dishes.

In chapter 28 the saint describes the cures of the "wise physician," mentioning applications, ointments, medicine, and finally cauterization, cutting and amputation of the diseased member. It is noteworthy that while in the xenodochia in the Eternal City poor slave boys were frequently assigned to the care of the sick, as we find in a formula of the *Liber diurnus*,[6] St. Benedict on the contrary demands for his monastery a monk infirmarian who has the fear of God, is competent and solicitous.

The spiritual descendants of the Patriarch of Cassino, developing the vital principles contained in the Rule, in the course of time founded and encouraged about their abbeys and churches that care

---

the Tripartite History into twelve books. His *De anima* comprises twelve chapters, as does his *De orthographia*.

[6] *"Puerum nomine N. ex iure Xenodochii N. largimus serviendum. . . . pro aegritudinis tuae . . . servitio"* (no. 49).

of the sick in hospitals which constitutes one of the glories of the Church and one of her greatest contributions to society. Also the orders of knights and hospitalers of Palestine drew their inspiration and origin from the Abbey of St. Mary in Jerusalem, where, in the eleventh century, next to the monastery the colony from Amalfi caused to have erected a hospice for assistance to the sick and poor pilgrims.

St. Benedict laid it down that the abbot be chosen by the community and then approved and blessed by the diocesan bishop, perhaps by commission of the Pope. Liturgical insignia of the abbot were rod and buskins.

The Rule demands of the abbot the qualities of teacher, of confessor, of pastor, of physician, of the very vicar of Christ, with such a fund of scriptural knowledge, pastoral experience, maturity of virtue, which gives us to understand that here St. Benedict refers to a monastic superior who has received the sacerdotal dignity. Particularly does this seem to apply to Monte Cassino with the surrounding pagan villages that had been evangelized by the Patriarch.

In the other hypothesis, it would be difficult to see in the Rule how in the daily Office, in which also deacons and priests shared, the more important parts and functions—as the singing of the Gospel on Sunday, the Pater, the Collects and the final blessings—would be reserved to the abbot. It would have been still more strange if St. Benedict had wished to oblige the monks who were guilty of grave sin to make their secret confession to the abbot or the spiritual seniors, if these in turn would have had to send them to a priest to receive sacramental absolution (chap. 46). St. Leo the Great had expressly reserved private and auricular confession exclusively to bishops and priests.[7]

Now, St. Benedict in his Rule treats precisely of the auricular confession of grave faults made to the abbot, and he furthermore demands the observance of the strictest secrecy: ". . . who knows how to cure his own and others' wounds without exposing them and making them public" (chap. 46). St. Leo had said: "Let the sins of the penitent not be brought to the ears of the people." The words and the sense are identical. St. John Climacus on Mount Sinai prescribes a like peni-

7 "*Reatus conscientiarum sufficiat solis sacerdotibus indicari confessione secreta*" (*Epist. Episcopis per Campan.; PL*, LV, 1211).

tential discipline for his monks, but he declares expressly that the abbot to whom the monks confess is a priest. This regulation with regard to abbot-priests seems to have been common in the Orient and even in Constantinople.

To the abbot the Patriarch of Cassino reserves the title of *domnus*, which in St. Gregory's language is regularly ascribed to prominent personages both in the ecclesiastical and in the civil sphere. Thus it is applied to Oriental patriarchs, bishops, high officials of the Court, and noble and titled persons. If St. Benedict on Cassino attributes it indiscriminately also to the abbot, this indicates that he felt it was justified by the hierarchical position which he held.

Among the other prodigies performed by the Patriarch, St. Gregory justly mentions the Rule for monks which he wrote, "commendable both for its good sense and attractive style." Hence admirable both for its contents and literary form. The Rule is a perfect image of Benedict's soul, "because the holy man could not teach otherwise than he himself lived."

It is particularly the monastic Rule which assures the Patriarch an eminent place among the masters of the Church universal: "While the man of God was famous for the many miracles that he wrought, he was no less distinguished for his wisdom in matters pertaining to doctrine." [8] It seems that Gregory here attributes great importance to the heavenly eloquence of St. Benedict, which his knowledge and literary endowments made still more efficacious. I have already said that the principal chapters of the monastic Code were composed according to the classical rules of rhythmic prose. One senses immediately the litterateur who, after long years of schooling, has acquired the habit of writing according to the laws of the *cursus*.

Abbot Butler has made a diligent investigation in order to identify the various sources and citations found in the Benedictine Rule. Besides the Sacred Scriptures, with which the author is well acquainted, he draws upon the monastic rule of St. Augustine, the writings of Eugippius, Ferrandus, Cassian, and the rules of St. Caesarius. He cites several classical and Christian writers, Fathers of the Church and contemporary authors, passages from the letters of Pope Siricius, from the sermons of Leo I, from the monastic writings of Cassian, of

___
[8] *Dial.*, Bk. II, chap. 36.

Faustus of Riez, of Dionysius Exiguus' life of St. Severin,[9] of the deacon Ferrandus' life of St. Fulgentius. A few citations also derive from the Sacramentaries. For this reason in the late Middle Ages the Rule of St. Benedict was simply called *Regula sanctorum patrum.*

Shortly after the Rule was published, about the year 556, when the see of Rome again had a pope, it began its triumphal journey through all the monasteries.[10]

Several decades later Gregory the Great refers to it casually as the *Regula monachorum,* according to which his monasteries in Sicily were governed.[11] The name of St. Benedict passes into the second place before the papal authority which desired it to be the common and universal Rule of all the monasteries. The Pope here takes to task Abbot Urbicus for his ignorance of the Rule and even denies him the title of monk: "You who are called abbot still do not know what it is to be a monk."

When, however, Gregory sends to England the Abbot Augustine with his forty monks, he writes to King Ethelbert this recommendation: "A bishop learned in the Rule of the monastery." [12] In another instance, replying to a letter of the same Augustine, he recalls to his mind the monastic training he had received in Rome: "You who are versed in the Rule of the monastery ought not to live apart from your clerics." [13] By reason of the Rule, even as a bishop, Augustine is obliged to lead a community life with his monks.[14]

[9] To this saint Gregory the Great also was devoted; in 593 he even wrote to his agent in the Campania to send him some of the saint's relics, since he wished to dedicate to St. Severin an ancient Arian church near the *domus Merulana* in the third region of Rome.

[10]   *Simplicius famulus Christi que minister*
          Magistri opus latens propagavit in omnes;
          Una tamen merces utrique manet in aevum.

[11] "*Quod ex quanta amaritudine cordis descenderit, tua poterat dilectio scire, si Regulam monachorum nosse voluisset*" (*Epist.,* Bk. XI, no. 48).

[12] *Epist.,* Bk. XI, no. 66.

[13] *Epist.,* Bk. XI, no. 64.

[14] In his *Morals on Job,* St. Gregory gives a picture of the monastic life, which clearly reflects the *Regula monasteriorum: "Alius, relictis omnibus quae exterius possederat, ut ordinem sublimioris discipulatus apprehendat, etiam intimas frangere voluntates parat; ut rectioribus se alterius voluntatibus subdens, non solum pravis desideriis, sed ad perfectionis cumulum, etiam in bonis votis sibimetipsi renuntiet, et cuncta quae sibi agenda sunt ex alieno arbitrio observet"* (Bk. XXXII, chap. 11 of Job).

Let us now compare St. Gregory and St. Benedict:

ST. BENEDICT	ST. GREGORY
Dominici schola servitii . . .	*Ordinem sublimioris*

In the Rule we see no inkling of the confederation of several monasteries under the central authority of the same abbot general, according to the model set up by St. Benedict at Subiaco. At that time such a government of an extremely personal nature would not have been readily possible, apart from the rare case of exceptional personalities, such as were St. Equitius and St. Benedict.

From the words of St. Gregory it does not appear that St. Benedict, after his departure from Subiaco for Cassino, gave up the government of his communities there. On the contrary, the regulations he lays down at his departure, the penance he imposes on St. Maur, the relations existing between Abbot Honoratus and the monks of Cassino, lead us to the conclusion that from afar the Patriarch continued to rule the communities founded by him. He did the same with the monastery at Terracina.

With excellent arguments Mabillon has maintained the thesis that St. Columban, after writing and propagating his own rule in Gaul, when he came to Italy in 612 and founded the famous abbey of Bobbio, introduced there the *Regula monasteriorum* of St. Benedict. It can be proved from documents that his immediate successors governed the new abbey according to it. Here there is not so much question of preference as rather of ecclesiastical law. Let the Scottish rule be followed in Scottish regions; but when in Rome, do as the Romans do, and Columban had to adapt himself to that principle. At Bobbio the *Regula monasteriorum* was observed from the very beginning.

The journey of St. Maur through Gaul is based on such weak documentation that I shall not discuss it at all. The Benedictine Rule is

St. Benedict (*continued*)	St. Gregory (*continued*)
Discipulus	*discipulatus*
Relinquentes statim	*Relictis omnibus . . .*
quae sua sunt . . .	*quae sibi agenda sunt*
ambulantes alieno	*ex alieno arbitrio*
iudicio et imperio	*observet*
Voluntatem propriam	*Intimas frangere*
deserentes	*voluntates parat*
Cogitationes	*non solum pravis desideriis*
malas . . . ad	*. . . renuntiet*
Christum allidere	*Cuncta quae sibi agenda*
Omnia custodire	*sunt, ex alieno*
et cuncta sibi	*arbitrio observet.*
imperata servare.	

mentioned in France in 637 in the privilege which Pharo, bishop of Meaux, granted to the abbey of Rebais. It was owing to the disciples of St. Columban in the monastery of Luxeuil that about this time the Cassinese Code was propagated in Gaul.

When one considers that St. Columban had left them his own rule and that he had died not long before, with the reputation of a great wonder-worker, it is not easy to explain why his own disciples sub-stituted St. Benedict in place of their founder. The phenomenon can be understood only if one admits that Rome conferred an obligatory character on the *Regula monasteriorum* for all the monasteries of the West. As a matter of fact, about the year 623, the founder of the monastery of Altaripa, Venerandus by name, wrote to Constance, bishop of Albi, regarding the *Regula S. Benedicti Romensis,* certainly a significant title.

We may observe, further, that the Rule served as a basis for those of Isidore of Seville, of Fructuosus of Bracara, of Donatus of Besançon. Besides, Traube has shown that a notable family of codices of the Rule, differing from the Cassinese tradition, belong precisely to the seventh century.

In the past some historians have attributed the rapid spread of the Rule of St. Benedict to its special discretion and to the mildness of the discipline it imposed. These may indeed have been contributing factors; but also in other rules, as those of St. Augustine and of Caesarius of Arles, these same qualities may be found. What especially assured the Code of Cassino its pre-eminence and its victory over the pre-existing monastic rules must have been its juridical character, from the moment Gregory the Great made it current in Italy and even in England as the *Regula monasteriorum S. Benedicti Abbatis Romensis,* which papal Rome promulgated to the world. For this reason, too, the autograph copy of the holy Patriarch was deposited in the library of the Lateran, as was done generally with the originals of the more important documents of the Church.[15] Thence it re-

---

[15] The poem of Arator, *De actibus apostolorum,* dedicated to Pope Vigilius, because of its popularity was deposited in the pontifical *scrinium* where Surgentius was the archivist. But since the cultured class of Rome expressed a desire to hear the poem, a public reading of it was begun on April 6, 544, in the Esquiline church of St. Peter in Chains. The account of this reading is still extant (cf. Moricca, *Storia della Letterat. Antica Cristiana,* III, Part I, p. 211).

In the pontifical *scrinium* were also preserved the *Polypticus* of Pope Gelasius, the

turned to Monte Cassino only during the reign of Pope Zachary.[16]

It was foreign to St. Benedict's purpose to compose the Rule as the expression of his own individual personality. He wished simply to codify the ecclesiastical tradition about monastic discipline; hence it has been easy for recent authors to discover his numerous sources. One senses a man who was master of his material and who, besides the Sacred Scriptures, was also well acquainted with the Fathers.

Apart from St. Caesarius, a contemporary, St. Augustine also exercised a profound influence on Benedict. Not only did the various writings of the doctor of Hippo on divine grace interest him greatly, and he cites them frequently, but through the elaboration of Eugippius of Lucullanum, he made his own St. Augustine's Letter 211 with its so-called rule for a community of female religious. It is found whole and entire in the *Regula monasteriorum* not only in word and in phrase, but above all by that spirit of mild sweetness and of perfect equilibrium which distinguishes the genius of St. Augustine.

Similarly the rules of St. Basil and St. Caesarius were carefully scrutinized by the Patriarch of Cassino, especially the disciplinary sections dealing with monastic government. On the other hand, the spiritual doctrine, the method of prayer, and the mystical ladder of perfection derive in good part from the writings of Cassian, from the monastic writings of Bishop Faustus of Riez, and from the ascetical tradition of the school of Lerins.

The "Romanism" of St. Benedict caused him to reject absolutely

---

Antiphonarium of St. Gregory, his letters, and the collection of his forty homilies on the Gospels. The papal *scrinium* of that time was more than an archive; it took the place of a library to which scholars were admitted to consult documents: "*Homiliae . . . editae autem in scrinio S. Ecclesiae nostrae retinentur, ut si qui forte a tua fraternitate longe sunt, hic inveniant unde in his, quae emendatae sunt, certiores fiant*" (*Epist.*, Bk. IV, 17a, p. 251 Ew.).

[16] The Greek translation of St. Gregory's *Dialogues* by Pope Zachary seems to have been destined for the numerous Eastern monasteries then in Rome, rather than for the Byzantine East, with which relations at the time were neither frequent nor very cordial. There were at least a dozen such monasteries, men's and women's, Greek and Syrian. The Pope himself was Greek. Since these monks lived in an environment both ecclesiastical and monastic that recognized St. Benedict as Patriarch, Pope Zachary, by restoring Monte Cassino and giving back to the place of origin the autograph copy of the *Regula monasteriorum*, desired to popularize also among the Easterners of Rome the figure of the saint.

From a Cassinese text, perhaps of the ninth century, we learn that Abbot Petronax of Monte Cassino had made it a rule that each year, on the feast of St. Benedict, the Greeks should celebrate the divine liturgy in the tower of the saint on a portable altar.

in his monasteries the reading of the apocryphal writings which were then the rage. The so-called *Decretum Gelasianum de libris recipiendis et non recipiendis* is of the time of St. Benedict. Though it originated in northern Italy it perfectly reflects the spirit of the papal Curia, which was absolutely opposed to the apocryphal books of the *Passiones martyrum* or of the acts of the apostles. The principal reason for their rejection was this: "Because even the names of those who wrote them are entirely unknown." Here is also to be found the reason why St. Benedict desires that in choir at the night Office, leaving aside anonymous works, only those patristic writings be read which bear the stamp of authenticity.[17]

It is not to be marveled at that the various Oriental collections of the lives and sayings of the Fathers of the desert should have made their contribution to the Rule, since St. Benedict himself refers to the fact that at his time they were regularly read in communities.

Among the Roman Pontiffs, the saint cites Siricius and St. Leo I, and the references to the so-called Leonine and the Gelasian Sacramentaries are anything but rare. More extraordinary is the dependence of the Rule on the *Syntagma doctrinae*, attributed to St. Athanasius, which in its turn derives from the *Synodicon* of the Council of Alexandria (362). Through these canons we ascend to that precious Christian manual, the *Didache*, that is, to the time of the apostles. If style is a man's expression, then we can say of the author of the *Regula monasteriorum* what St. Gregory predicates of his miracles: "This man was filled with the spirit of all the just." [18]

Almost contemporary with Rome's move to place the vast monastic movement under one Rule, Justinian at Byzantium codified what might be called the *Ius regularium* of the sixth century. Some have thought to discover an influence of St. Benedict on the legislator of Constantinople. A happy thought, but without foundation. It is only necessary to recall that Justinian's work was begun in 528 and completed in 534, while the *Regula monasteriorum* took definitive form at Monte Cassino toward the last years of the holy Patriarch's life.

On the contrary, however, we must maintain that the new monastic

17 "*Expositiones [Scripturarum] quae a nominatis et orthodoxis catholicis Patribus factae sunt*" (chap. 9).
18 *Dial.*, Bk. II, chap. 8.

code of Rome could not prescind from the imperial legislation which was in force, but had itself to absorb it. And here is the proof: Novella 5 commands that no monastery be erected without the consent of the bishop of the place; that profession be preceded by a tyrocinium of three years; that after the three-year novitiate, all can become monks, whether they are slaves or free. If in the case of a slave the master objects, recourse must be had within the first triennium; after this period, no petition will be honored. The ordinary form of the monastic life is the cenobitic. Only the most advanced can obtain permission to retire to the desert. If a monk abandons the monastery, he becomes an apostate before God, but he cannot demand the restitution of his property.

Arbitrary passing from one monastery to another is forbidden; but if the transfer is made legitimately, the new monastery has a right to the property given by the monk to the first monastery. The monks are subject exclusively to the bishop's tribunal.[19] In each monastery five of the most advanced monks are to be ordained priests for the divine service. The burial of women in male monasteries is forbidden. The head of each congregation of monasteries must every year make a visitation of the communities subject to his jurisdiction.[20] It is not difficult to see in the Rule of St. Benedict the application of these established norms of Justinian's civil law.

In the course of this work, I have frequently referred to the *Liber diurnus Romanorum Pontificum,* that is, the formulary of the Pontifical Chancellery from the fourth to the sixth and eighth centuries.

Its 117 documents, for those who know how to interpret them, offer in so many vignettes a living panorama of the life and thought of the Lateran in St. Benedict's century; since they represent formulas of an official and juridical character, they are very valuable. The *Regula monasteriorum* has, quite naturally, left traces of these documents, and that is a rather important consideration.

Formula 96 is entitled *Privilegium monasterii provincia constituti.* The Pope there recommends "a common and sincere life, that the sincerity of the brotherhood be sober"; and he adds: "He labors in vain who submits himself to the yoke of pride, the root of vices. Let

[19] Novella 79.
[20] Novella 133.

there be deep humility in God, because by it the elect have possessed
the heavenly places." Hence the abbot, with the eyes of the mind not
less than with those of the body, will also keep before him the traditional Rule of the Fathers lest the superior exceed in severity with his
subjects and these have to bewail the lack of discretion in the prelate:
"Lest while difficult commands . . . seem to be imposed, they express their contempt at the indiscretion of him that commands." The
monks will walk the way of obedience, and so they will come to God.[21]
The document ends by recalling the mercy of the Savior and the need
of asking for it "with sighs and tears, so that what piety demands the
frailty of human existence . . . by the help of its Creator may attain."

The conformity of ideas and at times also of words between this
papal document and the Rule of St. Benedict is impressive. Where
the *Regula monasteriorum* speaks of the cenobitic life (chap. 1), the
papal bull in a more "Roman" manner calls it *communis vita*.
Reference is made to the ladder of humility (chap. 7), by which the
heights of heaven are attained. Then there is the demand that the
abbot ever keep before his eyes the Rule of the Fathers, conformable
to the precept of St. Benedict: "Especially let him keep this Rule in
all details" (chap. 64).

Similarly the pontifical document 58, *De usu pallei*, should be compared with the two chapters of St. Benedict on the pastoral office. They
manifest an identical mentality, and sometimes the phrases show great
similarity.[22]

[21] *"Per obedientiae lineam . . . ad gaudia caelestis patriae perveniant."*

[22]

De usu pallei	*Regula S. Benedicti*
Qui pastores animarum dicimus, at-tendamus et susceptum officium exhibere . . . ne in die divini examinis pro desidia nostra ante summum pastorem neglegen-tiae reatus excruciet. . . .	Abbas meminere debet quod dicitur. Cum aliquis suscipit nomen abbatis . . . nomen maioris factis implere. In die iudicii ipsarum omnium rationem red-diturus. . . . Timens semper futuram discussionem Pastoris de ovibus sibi creditis . . .
Vita tua filiis sit regula. . . . Benignum te boni sentiant; districtum te maligni cognoscant. . . . Remissum te delinquen-tibus non ostendas, ne quod ultus non fueris, perpetrari permittas. Sit in te et boni pastoris dulcedo; sit et iudicis severa districtio.	Factis amplius quam verbis ostendat. Dirum magistri, pium patris ostendat af-fectum, inquietos debet durius arguere, oboedientes et mites et patientes ut in melius proficiant obsecrare. Neglegentes . . . ut increpet et corripiat admonemus. Neque dissimulet peccata delinquentium.
Ne . . . dum districtus malorum vult iudex existere, transit in crudelitatem cor-rectio.	. . . In ipsa autem correctione pru-denter agat . . . ne dum nimis eradere cupit aeruginem, frangatur vas.

And this prescription is given in order that strictness should not be stressed to excess, but rather that for the monastic life there be preserved that characteristic of wise discretion which St. Benedict had impressed on it: "Bearing in mind the discretion of holy Jacob" (chap. 64). St. Gregory also praises St. Benedict for having written a Rule "outstanding for its discretion."

St. Benedict had promised his monks "that by this road of obedience they would go to God" (chap. 71). The papal document gives the same concept: "By observing well the duties (*lineam*) of obedience . . . may they attain to joys eternal." It is interesting to note that what at Cassino was a *via* becomes a *linea* at Rome.

All this ascetical toil demands assiduous prayer. St. Benedict points that out clearly already in the prologue of the Rule: "And first of all, whatever good work you begin to do, beg of Him with most earnest prayer to perfect it." The same thought is thus expressed in the Lateran: "Before all things, then, let us look forward to the mercy of our Redeemer with sighs and tears." These daily tears are likewise mentioned by St. Benedict in chapter 4: "Daily in one's prayers, with tears and sighs, to confess one's sins to God. . . ."

Evidently the writer of this pontifical bull in the first half of the seventh century was influenced by the *Regula traditionum paternarum*, that is, the Rule of St. Benedict, which he had before him. As a matter of fact, in 628 Honorius I granted to Abbot Bertulph of Bobbio, where hitherto the Benedictine Rule had been followed, a document of identical tenor. The phrase *Regula patrum* in the seventh century was equivalent to the other.

Document 59 of the *Liber diurnus* on the same subject follows the

---

De usu pallei (continued)

Nullius faciem contra iustitiam accipias; nullum querentem iustitiam despicias; custodia in te aequitatis excellat; ut nec divitem potentia sua aliquid apud nos extra viam suadeat rationis audire, nec pauperem de se sua faciat humilitas desperare. . . .

Sed in his omnibus uti salubriter poteris, si Magistram caritatem habueris.

Regula S. Benedicti (continued)

Non ab eo persona . . . discernatur . . . non unus plus ametur quam alius; non convertenti ex servitio praeponatur ingenuus.

Et praecipue, ut praesentem Regulam in omnibus conservet. . . . In omnibus omnes Magistram sequantur Regulam.

concepts and sometimes even the identical words of the *Regula monachorum*.[23]

In these formulas of the *Liber diurnus* it is at times difficult to establish the dependence of various documents, just as it is difficult to trace the influence of the *Regula monasteriorum* on various documents granted in favor of monasteries. Yet it is interesting to note how in the seventh century the mentality of the Apostolic Chancellery was in harmony with the Rule of St. Benedict. This fact helps to explain the work of the popes for the diffusion of the Code of Cassino in the entire Latin monastic world.

[23] Officium sacerdotis assumere . . . exhibeamus ergo quod dicimus, et quibus . . . praeesse nos contigit, prodesse quantum possumus festinemus. . . .

Ut dum Creditor rationes nobiscum positurus advenerit, lucrum nos fecisse reperiat.

Cum aliquis suscipit nomen abbatis . . . meminere debet quod dicitur. . . . Sciatque sibi oportere prodesse magis quam praeesse.

Sciatque . . . culpae pastoris incumbere quidquid in ovibus paterfamilias utilitatis minus potuerit invenire.

CHAPTER XXXVI

The Liturgical Work of St. Benedict

BESIDES the Roman rite, the Oriental rite, and the Ambrosian rite, the Middle Ages also recognize a *Cursus S. Benedicti*, that is, they give the Patriarch's name to the entire liturgy of the Divine Office which the monks day and night chanted in their monastery churches. This special rite of the *Opus Dei*, as the Patriarch usually calls the Divine Office, is described in the Rule in chapters 8–20 and in chapters 43, 47, 52, 58, one of the most complete expositions of the Divine Office left us by the ancients.

As in the rest of the Rule, so also with regard to the liturgy, which he bases on the rite of Rome, the man of God follows the more enlightened tradition of the Fathers, but he casts the practices of the various churches together into a harmonious and wisely balanced whole, in accordance with his Roman character. It would suffice to compare the *Cursus S. Benedicti* with the Office of the Oriental monks and with that of the Irish and the Franks, to bring out immediately that a criterion of discretion inspired the Patriarch in composing his monastic *Cursus*.

When we consider that he divides the longer psalms into two sections; that during the short summer nights, in order not to abbreviate unduly the monks' rest, he shortens and cuts down even the Scriptural reading; that for smaller communities he dispenses from the obligation of singing the antiphons; that between Matins and Lauds he prescribes a brief intermission, so that the old men may retire a moment for the necessities of nature: weighing all these criteria of humaneness, it is impossible not to subscribe to the judgment of St. Gregory regarding the Rule: ". . . outstanding for its discretion." [1]

When the man of God set his hand to compose his liturgical *Cursus,* he found himself face to face with venerable traditions which he could not disregard. Especially there existed a Roman tradition, to which the Apostolic See attached such importance that it obliged all new bishops to swear to conform to it and to propagate it in their dioceses, so that it might become common among the clergy. The formula of this oath is found in the *Liber diurnus.*[2] The new bishop swears and promises that every day, from cockcrow till morning, he will be present in the church with all his clergy for the daily celebration of the morning Office: *"Vigilias in ecclesia celebrare."*

For this purpose the year is divided into two parts, short nights and long nights, summer and winter. The first section runs from Easter to the autumnal equinox (September 24); during this time only three lessons, three antiphons, and three responsories are sung at the Office. There follows the litany customary at the beginning of Mass. At other times, however, because morning comes later, they will say "four lessons, with their responsories and antiphons." On Sundays throughout the year, on the other hand, "nine lessons, with their responsories and antiphons are recited. . . . The litanies twice a month at all times." During the sixth century this constituted the entire Office of the cathedral churches in the metropolitan province of the pope.

Besides this primitive Roman *Cursus,* Italian monachism of St. Benedict's time had before it, too, the ascetical traditions of the great Oriental Fathers, those of the monasticism of Jerusalem, of Cassian, of the abbey of Lerins, and of the Ambrosian Church. But there is this difference, namely, that if, confronted by such varied local customs, St. Benedict felt free to choose the best for his monasteries, this liberty did not extend to the practices of the Church of Rome and to

---

[1] The Ambrosian rite divides and distributes the Psalter into decades, assigning one of them to a night. This division is rather ancient, since it is that followed also by St. Augustine in his *Enarrationes in Psalmos,* as Cassiodorus testifies: *"Uno codice tam diffusa complectens, quae ille [Augustinus] in decadas quindecim mirabiliter explicavit"* (*Comment. in Psalt., Praef.*)

[2] *"Cautio episcopi,"* no. 82.

the ancient ritual traditions of the Catholic Church, to which, without a doubt, he had to conform.[3]

The daily *Cursus S. Benedicti* comprised, besides the night Office, also the prayers of the seven day hours. In them are sung the Psalter, the collection of odes, namely, the hymns of St. Ambrose; there are read the Scriptures with the comments of the most famous Fathers. The chants are taken from the *Liber antiphonalis* or the *Responsoriale;* their execution demands great musical skill on the part of the chanters and the soloists.

According to the Roman fashion the year is divided into two parts: winter and summer. But since the fasts of summer end with the Ides of September, differing in this detail from the *Liber diurnus,* St. Benedict's winter begins with the Kalends of November and lasts till Easter.

In accord with the *"Cautio episcopi,"* there is a difference between the ferial night Office and that of Sunday. To conform as far as possible to the Roman usage, St. Benedict has the Roman Office of the dawn at cockcrow, which he calls *Matutinarum solemnitas,* preceded by another of monastic devotion, which is known simply as *nocturna laus.*

This night Office, peculiar to the cenobites, begins shortly after midnight and, following the practice of the Egyptian monks, twelve psalms are sung in order, with the concluding alleluia. Contrary to the Roman usage, which reserved the scriptural readings for the morning Office, monastic piety anticipated them and inserted them between the psalms of the *nocturna laus.* Thus the morning Office will not be so long and burdensome and will permit the monks to go to their work in good time.

Now, the Roman morning Office enjoys a venerable tradition, which has determined for each day the psalms and the canticles to be used. St. Benedict follows it faithfully ("as the Roman Church prays"). He could not have acted differently; and that is the reason why even today in the *Cursus S. Benedicti* the psalms of the morning

---

[3] An Irishman of the eighth century thus describes the relations between the Roman *Cursus* and that of St. Benedict: *"Est et alius cursus beati Benedicti, qui ipsum singulariter pauco discordante a cursu Romano, in sua Regula repperies scriptum"* (Haddan and Stubb, *Councils and Ecclesiastical Documents,* Oxford, 1869, I, 140).

Office do not follow the order of the Psalter, but are chosen here and there in David's songbook.

As a conclusion to the morning Office, also in the Lateran the custom of Gaul and of Spain was followed, namely, of having the bishop recite the *Pater noster* before dismissing the assembly. St. Benedict introduces this usage into his *Cursus*, reserving the chanting of the closing *Pater* to the abbot, since he holds the place of Christ in the monastery.

On Sundays or feast days the Benedictine rite of the *nocturna laus* is more extended. The Patriarch remains faithful to the Egyptian tradition of twelve psalms each night; but then, after the reading of the scriptural commentary of the Fathers,[4] he introduces, in accord with the custom of Jerusalem and Milan, a special section of chants chosen from the canticles. This extraordinary *nocturna laus* comes to a close with the abbot's chant of the Gospel of the resurrection, preceded by the *Te Deum* and followed by a doxology *post Evangelium*, according to the Ambrosian custom. It is not hard to explain these Milanese elements in the *Cursus S. Benedicti* if we will remember what St. Paulinus says in the life of St. Ambrose, namely, that almost the whole of Italy and the Occident had followed the example of the saint in introducing the night Office into their cathedrals: "At this period for the first time antiphons, hymns, and vigils began to be celebrated in the Church of Milan. Faithfulness to this practice persists until the present day not only in that Church, but throughout almost all the provinces of the West." [5]

Going contrary to Rome, which preserved intact its liturgical traditions—and which for long centuries allowed neither the singing of hymns nor other anticipations of its Office at cockcrow—as St. Benedict had received into his *Cursus* the Ambrosian tradition of hymns, so he also admitted that of the chant of the three canticles which on Sunday precede the solemn Gospel of the resurrection of

[4] In ancient times the faithful stood not only during the divine psalmody, but also during the scriptural readings and the sermon. St. Benedict, however, permits the monks to sit at the night Office during the singing of the lessons and the responsories: ". . . *residentibus cunctis disposite et per ordinem in subsellis*" (chap. 11). At Arles St. Caesarius introduced a similar discipline among the faithful "when longer *Passiones* are read or more extended explanations given." In such a case, the weak and others who found it difficult to stand sat on the floor (*PL*, XXXIX, 2315).

[5] *Vita S. Ambrosii*, no. 13.

Christ. At Jerusalem, as we know from the pilgrim Etheria, this chant
was executed by the bishop in person, standing directly over the entrance of the cave in which the Savior was buried. St. Benedict prescribes that it be done by the abbot, "while all stand in awe and
reverence."

When the reading of the word of God is finished, all must answer
"Amen," precisely as is done at Milan when the Eucharist is received.
There follows the Oriental Trinitarian hymn: *"Te decet laus . . ."*
of the Apostolic Constitutions, which takes the place of the chant *post
Evangelium,* according to the Ambrosian usage.

During the day, the hours of Prime, Terce, Sext, None, Vespers,
and Compline call the monk to choir and to liturgical prayer. The
determination of these hours, which formerly divided the civil day,
came from the Christian tradition which grew out of the Jewish prac-
tice.⁶ According to St. Benedict, who remains indebted to the tradition of Cassian and of Lerins, in each of these hours three psalms are
sung, and they terminate with the litany.

But when the monks are engaged in the work of the fields at some
distance from the oratory, it is not prescribed that they betake themselves to the choir for the individual hours. In this circumstance they
can sing the psalms out in the open, under the vault of heaven and in
the sight of God who looks down upon them from His throne. Only
let them pray with reverence: they "shall perform the work of God
in the place where they are working, bending their knees in reverence
before God" (chap. 50).

The Divine Office constitutes for the monk a daily and a personal
obligation toward the majesty of God. Hence, also outside the choir,
even on a journey, he has to sing the divine praises at the determined
times: "Likewise those who have been sent on a journey shall not let
the appointed hours pass by . . ." (chap. 50).

The day hours of the Office can indeed be sung by the monks while
engaged in work, in the open field. Vespers, on the other hand, like
the Office at dawn, enjoys a special solemnity and is celebrated only
in church, a few hours before sunset.

Since, then, in the monastery the work must be accomplished by

---

⁶ The *Cursus* of Eugippius and Cassiodorus differed from that of St. Benedict in making
no provision for the hour of Prime.

the light of day, because it is not wise to keep the community in the dim light of lanterns, the *vespertina synaxis* of St. Benedict does not at all agree with the *Eucharistia lucernaris,* that is, the chanting of the *Lucernarium,* as practiced at Milan, in Gaul, by Eugippius at Naples. On the other hand, it was not introduced in Rome; and this suffices that St. Benedict should not mention it in the *Regula monasteriorum.* The Ambrosians are accustomed to divide Vespers into several parts, with scriptural readings and distinct orations; but the Vespers of St. Benedict will be adapted to men who are already fatigued after the hard work of the day, who in Lent are still fasting, and at other times have taken their only meal a little before, namely, after None.

The *synaxis vespertina* consists of the daily chant of but four psalms, taken in order from David's songbook. There follows the Ambrosian hymn, *Deus Creator omnium,* with the Magnificat, the Sunday collect sung by the abbot, and the concluding litanies. St. Benedict himself explains what he means by these litanies: ". . . the verse and the petition of the litany, that is, 'Lord, have mercy on us' . . ." (chap. 9). The practice has been preserved in the Ambrosian liturgy, where in the festive Lenten Mass, in the Vespers of the vigil of the greater saints, and in the obsequies of the deceased, these final litanies are sung at the conclusion of the rite.

Differing from the brevity to which they are now reduced in the Benedictine Breviary, these ancient litanies resemble the *Orationes solemnes* of the Roman Missal for Good Friday, where they occur after the afternoon gathering and before the adoration of the wood of the cross. The deacon announces the prayer for the various needs of the Church, for the pope, for the bishop, for the sick, for those imprisoned or condemned to the mines, and people answer: *"Kyrie eleison,"* or *"Domine, miserere."*

St. Benedict carefully distinguished the two parts of the deacon's prayer: ". . . the verse and the petition of the litany, that is, 'Lord, have mercy on us'. . . ."

The Office of *Completoria* seems also to derive from Ambrosian usage, which adds *Completoria* to Vespers. There is question here of three short psalms, always identical, which the monks recited before going to bed, in order to sanctify also the end of the day with prayer and the blessing of the abbot.

Compline is not sung, nor are antiphons interpolated; hence the psalm verses are recited in unison: ". . . three psalms, which are to be said straight through without antiphon" (chap. 17). Compline is treated almost as if it were private prayer; in enumerating the parts of the Divine Office in chapter 15 of the Rule, the Patriarch does not even mention it.

In agreement with the rule of Eugippius, spiritual reading from some work of the holy Fathers or from the Collations of Cassian precedes Compline. Hence arose the medieval custom of abbots granting their monks a light refreshment in the summer shortly before retiring, namely, a bit of watered wine or some fruit to restore them somewhat, and this received the name of "collation."

This, in general, constitutes the *Cursus S. Benedicti,* which together with the *Regula* spread into the entire world and in its turn influenced the Divine Office of the Church universal itself. After St. Benedict has completed his arrangement, he remarks that if his weekly distribution of the Psalter appears unacceptable to some abbot, he should consider himself free, most free, to order it differently, provided always that he remains faithful to the principle of the recitation of the Psalter and Canticles every week, and provided he respects, be it well understood, the liturgical tradition of the Church regarding the Office at dawn *ad galli cantum.*

The holy Patriarch himself reveals to us the measure of his discretion when he notes that the Psalter, which he distributed over the course of a whole week, was formerly recited daily by the ancient Fathers. To whom does he allude? The *Cursus* of Eugippius is exceedingly brief and contains only a few psalms. St. Benedict is aware of that fact, because he consulted Eugippius' rule and used it extensively.

The Ambrosians divided the Psalter into decades, and even to this day employ fifteen days in its recitation. To St. Benedict, however, this distribution does not appeal for his monks; indeed he says outright: "For those monks show themselves too lazy in the service to which they are vowed, who chant less than the Psalter with the customary canticles in the course of a week" (chap. 18). The saint probably was not aware of the fact that the Ambrosians repeat the same psalms in the day hours, so that actually their *Cursus* effectively is much longer than the monastic and runs to about two hundred psalms.

The *Cursus S. Benedicti* represented the true monastic *ratio studiorum* of the Middle Ages. From the moment that in the Benedictine conception the abbey was the "school of the Lord's service," the formative program of this school was supplied by the Divine Office, that is, the *Opus Dei,* as the Patriarch called it. This Divine Office, to which each monk dedicated about ten hours daily, contained everything knowable at that time; for, in a form eminently dramatic, it was at the same time prayer, Scripture study, patristic study, poetry, music, and history of the Church, for the solace of the spirit striving toward heaven.

Standing in choir and assiduously singing the Divine Office, the monk became acquainted with all those varied disciplines. Thanks to this intense higher instruction imparted to Benedictine communities with ability, method and constancy, the Patriarch of Cassino became and remained for more than seven centuries the Master of the Middles Ages.

The celebrated musical *scholae,* the numerous *scriptoria,* the architecture and sacred art, even the various schools of liturgical drama, arose in former times in connection with the *Opus Dei* regulated by St. Benedict, to which he ascribed an absolute primacy when he wrote: "Let nothing, therefore, be put before the Work of God" (chap. 43).

The sacred drama or the *Opus Dei* that is daily celebrated in Benedictine abbeys demands, besides gifts of the spirit, also a true literary and artistic competence. The dispositions of the spirit required for a good understanding of the Divine Office are described in chapters 19 and 20 of the *Regula monasteriorum* and are summed up in the golden principle: ". . . that our mind may be in harmony with our voice," and in the other to which reference has already been made: "Let nothing, therefore, be put before the Work of God."

In order to endow his monks with the suitable cultural preparation for an adequate understanding of the Sacred Scriptures and the songs of David, which go to make up the Divine Office, the Patriarch lays it down that the commentaries on them which are read in public be those "by well known and orthodox Catholic Fathers" (chap. 9). In the last chapter of the Rule he returns to recommend the study of the Bible and the holy Fathers (chap. 73). But since, besides these readings in common, some of the monks had need also of private and personal study, St. Benedict sets apart for this purpose not only the interval between the morning Office and Prime, but also three or four hours of the workday and the entire Sunday (chap. 48).

In choir everything—readings, chants, and ceremonies—must be executed to perfection and according to the rules of art. Whoever is not capable of doing these things in a worthy manner is without further ado excluded from performing such a function: "The brethren are not to read or chant in order, but only those who edify their hearers" (chap. 38).

Father Faber has written a most interesting chapter on the ancient Benedictine school of asceticism. More recently, too, the ancient ascetic tradition of monasticism has received attention, and the conclusion is that all those giants of Catholic sanctity, many of whose lives are contained in the nine folio volumes of Mabillon's *Acta Sanctorum Ordinis S. Benedicti* from the sixth to the twelfth centuries, received their formation in the "school of the Lord's service," thanks above all to the daily *Opus Dei* ordered by St. Benedict. This aspect of the doctrinal apostolate of the holy Patriarch by means of the liturgical *Cursus*, which receives its name from him, generally receives little notice from the historians, despite its decisive effect on ecclesiastical culture during the Middle Ages.

We may observe that the numerous Benedictine abbeys of a former age, spread over Europe, differed greatly from one another in spirit, in nationality, in purpose, in the activity developed by them. Yet all the great saints, apostles, bishops, teachers, and other Benedictine abbots of whom history makes mention possessed an identical spirit and a similar *forma mentis*, that which they derived from the same "school of the Lord's service," by virtue of the efficacy of a common and magnificent liturgy which supplied the place of a regular *ratio studiorum*. For this reason the fathers of the Council of Duzia in 874 placed the *Regula monasteriorum* "among the canonical Scriptures and the writings of the Catholic doctors."

CHAPTER XXXVII

The "Liber Regulae Pastoralis" of St. Gregory
The Writings of Cassian and of Eugippius

ST. BENEDICT devotes two chapters of the Rule, the second and the sixty-fourth, to a description of the nature and the duties of the abbot's pastoral office over his monks. Further, the entire Code is a true textbook of spiritual pedagogy, rich in teachings and norms to help the abbot become a good superior and ruler of souls. In fact, Gregory the Great simply declares that the life of the Patriarch is entirely contained in the Rule, since the man of God could not do otherwise than live in accordance with his principles. Here the teaching becomes identified with the very life of the master.

Thus it came about that from St. Benedict's Code his first biographer, when he in his turn became first an abbot and then Roman Pontiff, drew the material to set up a spiritual norm of life for bishops which he fittingly called, *Liber regulae pastoralis*. Thus the future of the Church will be provided for. If the new world of the Middle Ages is to be reconstructed from the ruins of the old by means of the episcopacy and monachism, the monks will achieve their end through the *Liber regulae monasteriorum*, while bishops will have the *Liber regulae pastoralis* as their guide.

After noting that "the governing of souls is the greatest of all arts," St. Gregory divides his work into four parts: "This book is divided into a fourfold discussion . . . for, when necessity calls for it, a man must consider how he is to attain to the summit of government; when he has rightly reached it, how he is to live; by right living, how he is to teach; by right teaching, let him daily keep his weakness in mind." [1] Similarly St. Benedict begins by distinguishing four kinds of monks.

It is interesting to note that the Patriarch had already written: "Let him [the abbot] understand . . . what a difficult and arduous task he has undertaken: ruling souls and adapting himself to a variety of characters" (chap. 2). Hence he agrees with St. Gregory that "the government of souls is the greatest of all arts." Like St. Benedict, Gregory describes at length the character and the qualities required in the candidate for the pastoral office, employing ideas and phrases that recall the Rule. He desires that he be learned in the law of God, ever mindful of his own weakness, ready to pardon, compassionate with others' infirmities. To him in a special manner Isaias assures the prompt answer to his prayer: "Thou shalt cry, and He shall say: 'Here I am'" (Isa. 58:9). Citing this same text of the prophet, St. Benedict in the prologue to the Rule had commented: "What can be sweeter to us, dearest brethren, than this voice of the Lord inviting us? Behold, in His loving kindness the Lord shows us the way of life."

St. Gregory then passes on to consider the defects that exclude from the pastoral office, and here he develops the same argument touched on by the legislator of Cassino in chapter 64 of the Rule: ". . . a person who will acquiesce in their vices." In the second book of the *Regula pastoralis* St. Gregory explains what kind of life the bishop ought to lead. Above all, it is necessary that he give a good example to the flock. "He [the abbot] should show them all that is good and holy by his deeds even more than by his words," says St. Benedict (chap. 2). But the gentle behavior of the superior must not be allowed to degenerate into weakness with regard to the stubborn. And in this connection St. Benedict as well as Gregory refers to the terrible fate of Heli of the sanctuary of Silo, who was punished by God precisely because he had shown himself too weak toward his sons' vices.

The *Regula monasteriorum* orders that with regard to maladies of

---

1 *Epist.*, Bk. I, no. 24.

the spirit the abbot should act "as a wise physician," using ointments, medicaments, and as a last resort the surgeon's knife. The *Regula pastoralis*, in its turn, calls for the same therapy: "He who has the obligation of healing wounds, let him first cleanse the sores with wine, then let him with the oil also apply the sweetness of sympathy. With the wine the suppuration is disinfected; with the oil healing is hastened."

In the third book St. Gregory describes the various forms of preaching, developing thus the pedagogical principle of St. Benedict, that each one be considered individually and that the abbot must adapt himself to the spiritual psychology of everyone: ". . . threatening at one time and coaxing at another as the occasion may require . . . thus he must adjust and adapt himself to all" (chap. 2). In this manner had acted the Apostle of the Cassinese, when "by continuous preaching he called them to the faith."

Chapter 16 of St. Gregory and chapter 6 of the *Regula monasteriorum, "De taciturnitate,"* in particular ought to be compared. An identical doctrine regarding the time and place to speak and to keep one's peace is proposed, in accordance with the Psalmist's words: "The talkative man is not stable on the earth" (Ps. 139:12). This scriptural quotation is common to both.

As far as pastoral pedagogy is concerned, in the Rule St. Benedict says to the abbot: "In his teaching the abbot should always follow the Apostle's formula: 'Reprove, entreat, rebuke,' threatening at one time and coaxing at another as the occasion may require, showing now the stern countenance of a master, now the loving affection of a father" (chap. 2). Gregory, in his turn, citing as an example the different treatment accorded the ardent Timothy and the timid Titus by St. Paul, makes this observation: "Advising Timothy he says to him: 'Reprove, entreat, rebuke with all patience and teaching.' But Titus he commands: 'Speak and exhort and rebuke with all authority. . . .' To Titus he adds what is wanting to him; from Timothy he takes what is superfluous."

The two final chapters of St. Gregory's third book, "How the lighter faults must be tolerated to uproot graver vices," have their counterpart in chapter 64 of St. Benedict, where he says it is better to tolerate a bit of rust than to scrape too vigorously and thus run the danger of breaking the vessel: "By this we do not mean that he [the abbot] should allow vices to grow; on the contrary . . . he should eradicate them prudently and with charity."

Book IV of St. Gregory, speaking of the interior life of the bishop, contains a chapter that develops this concept of the Patriarch of Cassino: ". . . while by his admonitions he [the abbot] is helping others to amend, he himself is cleansed of his faults" (chap. 2). St. Gregory explains: "It is necessary that the pastor with great solicitude should mortify himself with the discipline of fear, lest it come about that, while he causes others' health to flourish by healing their wounds, he neglect his own through negligence."

These comparisons between the *Liber regulae pastoralis* and the *Regula monasteriorum* could be developed at greater length, but the conclusions would not vary. St. Benedict's book became blood and marrow in the son of St. Sylvia; his spirit became Benedictine.[2]

When he comes to treat of an argument akin to that developed by the Patriarch on the nature of the abbot's government, he does so by revealing a mentality, concepts, and pedagogical methods parallel to those of the monastic Rule. The two books, these two Rules, mutually integrate each other: the first will be for the monks, or rather the abbeys, of the West; the second for the bishops. St. Gregory planned his work from the time he was a simple monk and a deacon

---

[2] Paging through the works of St. Gregory, replete with passages and phrases inspired by the *Regula monasteriorum* or taken from it, we cite the following as characteristic. They come from a letter directed to Conon, abbot of Lerins (Bk. XI, no. 22) and should be compared with chapters 2 and 64 of the Rule:

Epist. ad Cononem	*Regula monasteriorum*
Itaque boni te ducem, pravi sentiant correctorem. In qua videlicet correctione hunc esse ordinem noveris observandum, ut personas diligas, et vitia persequaris. . . .	Dirum magistri, pium patris ostendat affectum.
	In ipsa autem correctione prudenter agat, et ne quid nimis, ne dum nimis eradere cupit eruginem, frangatur vas. . . .
Sic enim vulnus debes abscindere, ut non possis ulcerare quod sanum est, ne si plus quam res exigit ferrum impresseris, noceas cui prodesse festinas. Ipsa enim in te dulcedo cauta sit, non remissa; correctio vero diligens sit, non severa.	Sciatque sibi opportunum prodesse magis quam praeesse . . .
	Oderit vitia, diligat fratres . . .
Sed sic alterum condiatur ab altero, ut et boni habeant amando quod caveant, et pravi metuendo quod diligant.	Studeat plus amari quam timeri . . .
	Sic omnia temperet, ut et fortes sit quod cupiant, et infirmi non refugiant.

apocrisiary at Constantinople.[3] Later, when he became pope and the supreme pastor of the Church, he carried out his plan, composing a work which, like the *Regula monasteriorum*—"outstanding for its discretion, clear in expression"—is the best and most authentic reflection of the holy life of its author: ". . . precise in style, abounding in doctrine, filled with mystery, sweeter than honey, a work for every need." The opinion here expressed is that of a contemporary who was extremely exigent, St. Columban.[4]

St. Benedict's position compared with Cassian is worthy of note. In the *Regula monasteriorum* he assimilates the best of Cassian's monastic writings and in chapter 42 directly indicates the *Collationes* as the book to be used for the public spiritual reading in the evening. Later, in the epilogue to the Rule, he again recommends the two more extensive works of Cassian, the *Collationes* and the *Institutiones*, thus showing that the authority of the author was such that it was not even necessary to mention his name.

How much more reserved is the attitude of Cassiodorus! Like the Patriarch of Cassino, he also praises and recommends Cassian, but with reservations. "Not to be followed in everything indiscriminately," he notes in his commentary on psalm 69. Then, referring to the writings of Victor Mattaritanus, he observes that this African bishop "expurgated the writings of Cassian and supplied what was wanting." [5]

In a word, the learned founder of Vivarium shared the judgment about Cassian which in the Lombard territory had found its way into the so-called Gelasian decree *De libris non recipiendis:* "The works of Cassian, a priest of Gaul—apocryphal." As apocryphal works, they consequently cannot be read in the gatherings of the faithful; precisely contrary to what St. Benedict orders. It has been shown that this so-called decree of Gelasius is a private compilation made in northern Italy in the sixth century. Rome had nothing to do with it. Hence we must conclude that St. Benedict's attitude regarding Cassian was determined by that of Rome, where little interest was shown in the violent polemics of the Frankish theologians for or against the abbot of Marseilles.

---

[3] *Moralia,* Bk. XXX on chap. 3.

[4] *Mon. Germ. Hist., Epist.* III, Karl. aevi. I.

[5] *Inst. divin. liter.,* no. 29.

It is significant that about the year 528, when Caesarius of Arles, in opposition to the Council of Valence, sent to Pope Felix a number of propositions taken from St. Augustine on grace and free will, the Pope, instead of approving them outright, deleted some and added others, thus placing himself outside and above the two parties in conflict about Cassian and his veiled Semi-Pelagianism.

Caesarius, in his turn, here and there retouched the "*Capitula ab Apostolica Sede nobis transmissa*," and forwarded to Rome the definitions of the Council of Orange, together with a special profession of faith, which received the approval of Boniface II in 531. Later, however, St. Caesarius had to recognize that the days in which he enjoyed the unquestioned favor of Rome were over. When he appealed to John II against the contumelious Bishop of Riez, the latter also turned to the Pope. But since the metropolitan of Arles, certain of the guilt of his bishop, had already put his sentence into execution, Pope Agapitus reproved him harshly for his arbitrary proceeding.

In this impartial climate of Rome, the enemies of Cassian had to come to a realization that they could not act in a high-handed manner, and so also St. Benedict did not have to make any reservations regarding the Semi-Pelagianism of the "Collator." He shared the views of Pope Hormisdas who wrote to the African bishop Possessor concerning the works of Faustus of Riez: "Faustus does not, indeed, belong to the Fathers of the Church, and his writings are worth as much as those of any other author; they are, therefore, to be subjected to scrutiny, to discover what in them may not be in accord with the tradition of the Church or what may be contrary to her doctrine. Hence the reading of the theological works of Bishop Faustus of Riez is not prohibited, but certainly anyone sins who follows him also in his errors." [6]

For the past two decades various writers have been attributing exceptional importance to the so-called *Regula secunda Augustini*, which, in an ancient and well-preserved codex of the ninth century (that of Laon, 328 bis), bears this simple title: "*Incipit ordo monasterii. . . .*" Several historians have discovered in this document the first draft of the Rule of St. Benedict; others, with greater caution,

[6] *PL*, LXIII, 489 f.

consider it simply one of the principal sources used by the Patriarch of Cassino. As far as the place of origin of the document is concerned, Dom Morin favors southern Italy and Cassiodorus; others are searching in other directions.

Since it appears evident that St. Benedict had the document in his hands and used it generously, it is opportune to reconsider the problem here. The question concerns a brief treatise on the monastic life; in the tradition of the manuscripts it is also found appended to the so-called *Regula Augustini*, that is, the adaptation for monks of St. Augustine's Letter 221 addressed to virgins.

In the beginning the author describes the *Cursus* of the Divine Office; he mentions the various traditional hours, Prime among them. The rite, especially for Matins, is quite different from the Benedictine and from the Roman tradition and comes close to practices in vogue in northern Italy and in the territory under Milanese influence. For Vespers the term *Lucernarium* is used, after the manner of the Ambrosians; similarly, like them, the author regards both Saturday and Sunday as feast days.

The Divine Office is characterized by its extreme brevity. During the nights of winter no more than six psalms with three lessons are said. In each of the day hours there is one psalm with an antiphon and a lesson followed by the concluding prayer. For the *Lucernarium* only two psalms with antiphons, a lesson and the concluding prayer, that is, Compline. During the intervals between the choir services, the monks study or work. Their physical labors do not engage them more than half of the day in the garden or the shops, from morning till noon; in the afternoon books from the library are distributed to them, and they devote themselves to study for several hours.

In great part the monks live by their own work; the products are sold in the public market of the city. With the money thus received they purchase what is necessary and bring it back to the monastery. It is taken for granted that the monastery is situated near some populous center. At the head of the community stands a *pater* and after him a *praepositus,* who is in immediate charge of the observance when the brethren work as well as when they eat in the refectory. Hence the *pater* takes his meals apart by himself, as is also laid down by St. Benedict. The author of the *Ordo,* in closing his observations, does indeed place himself among the monks, but in a higher category. We may therefore conclude he was an abbot.

Dom Morin has well said that the *Ordo* in question could not have flowered forth in the climate of Rome, where a fast was observed on Saturdays, where the rite of the *Lucernarium* did not exist, where St. Benedict himself had to receive into his *Cursus* the "customary psalms" of the Office at dawn as they were sung in the Lateran. For these reasons it is impossible to consider the Patriarch of Cassino as the author of the *Ordo monasterii.* Along with that fall all the suppositions with regard to a presumed first draft of the *Regula monasteriorum* which St. Benedict was to have made at Subiaco before his departure for Monte Cassino.

According to the *Ordo monasterii,* the monks ordinarily break their fast after None, feast days and the paschal season evidently being excepted. The use of wine, for those who want it, is limited to feast days, that is, the Saturdays and Sundays. This regulation certainly does not apply either to Noricum, Vicovaro, or Monte Cassino, where instead the monks received a hemina of wine at dinner as well as at supper. It is quite possible that southern Italy comes into question; even at the present time gentlemen drink their wine in that region at the end of the meal in dessert glasses. In lower Italy, which differs in this matter from Latium, the hot climate scarcely calls for wine or strongly alcoholic drinks.

The monastery described does indeed admit children; instead of being punished with excommunication for their transgressions, they are, according to the classical custom, whipped or slapped.

I have hinted that the *Ordo monasterii* possibly derives from some monastery of southern Italy. That of Cassiodorus certainly must be excluded, since he did not retire to Vivarium till 540, whereas previous to this date St. Caesarius in his rule for monks already shows acquaintance both with the *Ordo monasterii* and with the rule of St. Augustine in the form in which it was adapted for cenobites.

There arises in my mind the figure of Eugippius, author of the life of St. Severin, who, according to Isidore of Seville, was also the composer of a monastic rule which is now considered lost. Eugippius was abbot of the monastery *ad castellum Lucullanum,* near Naples, and at the behest of a certain Abbot Marinus ("*cohortante domino meo*

Marino abbate vel sanctis coeteris fratribus") made a *florilegium* or collection of excerpts from the works of St. Augustine, 348 extracts containing the marrow of the African doctor's theological teaching. Cassiodorus praises the work for its usefulness; the great number of extant codices testifies to the esteem in which it was held in the early Middle Ages. Consequently no one was better prepared than he to graft the branch of Augustinian monachism on the Italian cenobitic trunk.

The monastery of Eugippius was situated at Pizzoleone, not far from Naples, and had been built by a certain noble lady, Barbara by name, as a shrine for the mortal remains of St. Severin, the apostle of Noricum. Eugippius also hailed from a Roman family, perhaps of African origin, which later settled in Noricum. For a number of years he devoted himself to the monastic life under the guidance of St. Severin; but after his master's death, when the barbarians were invading those regions, he, together with some courageous companions, took the body of St. Severin and after a long and dangerous odyssey finally, with the consent of Pope Gelasius I, settled at Naples. The biography of St. Severin was written between 509 and 511. The *florilegium*, the *Ordo monasterii*, and the *Regula Augustini* belong to a somewhat later date.

The biography of St. Severin does not reveal much concerning the monastic discipline of the master. Even his fatherland remained unknown to all, though his manner of speaking betrayed a Latin origin.[7]

As St. Benedict would do later, so the norms St. Severin laid down for his monks were based on the living tradition of the Fathers: *"Daturus nihilo minus monachis formam, sollicitior admonebat beatorum Patrum vestigiis inhaerere, quibus sanctae conversationis adquireretur instructio."*[8] Generally Severin lived apart by himself in a special cell not far from the monastery, where he also used to recite the canonical day hours. Morning and evening, however, he went to the common choir for Matins and Vespers: *"Cum quibus [monachis] tamen matutinas orationes et propriam noctis principio psalmodiam solemniter adimplebat. . . ."*[9]

---

[7] *Vita S. Severini*, Prol.; *Acta SS.*, Jan., I, 485.
[8] *Op. cit.*, chap. 3.
[9] *Op. cit.*, chap. 10.

It happened one time that when at the hour of Vespers the flint would not produce fire to light the candles, by a miracle the candle which the saint held in his hand lighted up. "By whose light, when the usual evening sacrifice had been offered, thanks were returned to God" (chap. 5). This was the customary rite of the *Lucernarium.* On another occasion, in order to punish the pride of three monks, the saint subjected them to diabolical obsession, that Satan might afflict their bodies and thus humiliate them. Eugippius felt the need of excusing his master: ". . . because these men were handed over to Satan for the destruction of the flesh." But this explanation evidently did not entirely satisfy St. Benedict, who, when quoting in his Rule (chap. 25) the words of the Neapolitan historian, carefully suppresses mention of the devil, thus even leaving the phrase incomplete.

Another time the sacristan of the monastery, Maur by name, contrary to the orders of the abbot, at high noon decided of his own accord to gather fruits in the field. A catastrophe almost befell him, for he would have been carried away as a slave by the barbarians if his abbot had not intervened suddenly to free him by a miracle. When at the point of death, St. Severin gave a final admonition to his monks, reminding them that the name and the habit of a religious would avail them little unless to these externals there was added also a virtuous life. Aided by the matron Barbara, Bishop Victor of Naples, Abbot Marinus, and others, Eugippius built *ad castellum Lucullanum* the monastery of St. Severin, and there can be no doubt that with the saint's veneration he also introduced the discipline which he had acquired from his master and admired in him.

Speaking of the monastic life, the author of the *Ordo monasterii* declares: "We desire to live an apostolic life"; this corresponds exactly to what Eugippius says of St. Severin: ". . . living according to the Gospel and the apostolic teaching."

We know that Eugippius carried on a correspondence with the deacon Ferrandus, the disciple and biographer of St. Fulgence of Ruspa. These relations dated from the time when Ferrandus was under the discipline of the holy Bishop, and they help us to understand better the monastic ideal of Eugippius, which leaned so strongly toward St. Augustine.

The fact stands that in Ferrandus' life of St. Fulgence we find the same spirit of St. Augustine's rule; these elements in their turn will find their way into the monastic statutes of Eugippius and thence into the *Regula monasteriorum*. The life of Fulgence is later than the year 535 and was written by the Carthaginian deacon Ferrandus (d. 546) in order to propagate the saint's virtues and veneration in the Church of Italy: *"in transmarinis partibus longe constituta turba fidelium. . . ."* It interested Abbot Eugippius in a special manner, since he had had correspondence both with the Bishop of Ruspa and with Ferrandus himself. Hence it was quite easy for St. Benedict to have before him the biography of St. Fulgence and to use it for his Rule, as he likewise did with the *Ordo monasterii* of Eugippius.

It is instructive to consider the way the Patriarch of Cassino used his sources, especially St. Augustine. Rarely does he copy outright, but he assimilates the spirit of the various authors, modifies them, completes them, and thus the Rule becomes a kind of anthology of the preceding patristic tradition. Hitherto these relations with Eugippius had been overlooked. Now we have finally discovered the marked Augustinianism exercised on Benedict by the abbot of the Neapolitan monastery.

But even apart from comparisons, the fact that in the manuscript tradition the *Ordo monasterii* and the *Regula Augustini* are always united compels us to recognize Eugippius as the author of both; between the years 511 and 546 he exerted a vast influence on the spread of Augustinianism in Italy. This identification is important for, whereas at first we had merely noted a citation from the life of St. Severin in the Rule, now we can better understand how St. Benedict, the faithful adherent to St. Augustine's doctrines, incorporated into his Code also the monastic norms of his contemporary and fellow citizen Eugippius.

CHAPTER XXXVIII

A Meal Outside the Monastery

AMONG his fioretti Gregory the Great includes some episodes which
in a very lively manner depict the spirit of the primitive community
of Cassino at the time of St. Benedict. Largeheartedness and content-
ment reigned there, as in a group governed by the most sweet laws
of Christian love. "Whoever thou art that dost desire to submit thy
neck to the sweet yoke of Christ, apply thyself heartily to the Rule."
Thus sang Abbot Simplicius or a poet of his century. The saint had
written in the prologue to the Rule that, though the beginning may
be somewhat difficult, yet, "as we advance in the religious life and
in faith, our hearts expand and we run the way of God's commandments with unspeakable sweetness of love."

One day the saint charged two of his monks with a commission in a
certain village in the valley of the Liri. The journey seems to have
been rather long. The descent of the mountain alone requires about
an hour of walking. The business the monks had to transact took
longer than had been anticipated. Thus it came about that at Monte
Cassino the sundial or the clepsydra already indicated the hour of
None, the time for dinner, and they were still in the village without
any hope of returning to the monastery before the evening was far
advanced.

Their stomachs also began to demand their rights, notwithstanding the fact that the Rule forbids dining outside the cloister when the
journey is so short that the monastery can be reached again by evening (chap. 51). There was in the village a certain pious woman, whom

Pope Zachary describes as one of the customary nuns in her own house.[1] At Monte Cassino she was well known, because the monks used to lodge at her house when some business forced them to remain over night in the village.

Here emerges an interesting point that demands our attention, if we are to visualize exactly the life and the practices of the primitive Cassinese community under St. Benedict. We see the two monks knocking at the hospitable door, and we may imagine with what joy they are received. Even though they arrived unannounced, the hostess, bubbling over with friendliness and courtesy, in accordance with the character of the people of the south, brought forth the best she had in her larder and loaded the table with it. No meat, of course!

If the nun wished to honor the monks, these, quite naturally, in their turn reciprocated by doing justice to the local dish of spaghetti, which they washed down with some good wine. "Eat," the nun encouraged them, "the road to Monte Cassino is long." When the meal was finished and the business completed, the two monks set off on their homeward journey as it was already growing dusk.

The verdant valley of the Liri also today is set off by villages and smiling towns. But from every point one sees rising up the great mass of Monte Cassino, which casts its shadow on the valley lying below it. To mount to the summit, the way is not always short or convenient. The path along the side of the mountain is particularly rough. The two monks walked and walked; they reached the town of Cassino and then, taking the mule path dating from the days of the Samnites, they reached the monastery when it was already night.

From his tower above the porter's office, St. Benedict noted who

[1] The ancients recognized as *religiosae foeminae*, besides the consecrated virgins, also the widows who vowed themselves to the service of the Church. This state was looked upon the more favorably if they lived from their own means without demanding maintenance from the Church. The following is an epitaph from the cemetery of Traso:

REGINAE VENEMERENTI FILIA SUA FECIT
VENE REGINE MATRI VIDUE QUE SE
DIT VIDUA ANNOS LX ET AECLESA
NUMQUA GRAVAVIT UNIVIRA QUE
VIXIT ANNOS LXXX MESOR V
DIES XXVI

The deceased, Regina by name, became a widow at the age of twenty and for the space of sixty years *sedit vidua*, probably among the religious or deaconesses. She never was a burden on the treasury of the Roman Church.

entered and who departed. Like good religious, the two monks betook themselves immediately to him to ask his blessing, as the Rule
commands (chap. 67); but the man of God demanded brusquely:
"Where did you dine today?" "Nowhere," they replied. "What!" said
the saint, "you would deny it? Did you not enter the house of that
certain nun and there eat this and that dish? Do you not remember
any longer that you filled the glasses so many times? Did you not
know that my spirit accompanies you and observes you also when you
are far from me?"

Terrified, the monks fell at his feet and confessed their fault. It was
the graver because they had lied. But the good father immediately
pardoned them. Without that pardon they might have had to go to
bed that night without their supper.

In the penitential section of the Rule, fasts, disciplines, and ex-
communications are like a bit of salt and give to the various chapters
a piquant flavor. Nevertheless I suspect that under St. Benedict at
Monte Cassino these penitential canons served the function of the
staff in the hand of the bishop. It is a symbol and a simple warning:
Do evil to no one. As soon as the culprit confesses his guilt, St. Benedict immediately forgives him. Let us note well the word "immediately." It bespeaks a world of goodness.

CHAPTER XXXIX

The Nuns' Presents

IT is strange, but these blessed nuns always get the disciples of St. Benedict into trouble. As at Monte Cassino the Patriarch had established the model monastery for the entire West—and so it was considered in the Middle Ages—so also he propagated the religious life among the women.

Scholastica, the sister of St. Benedict, according to Gregory the Great, was consecrated to the Lord from her infancy, and wore on her head the veil of sacred virginity she had received from the bishop.[1] It is not exact to consider her the first Benedictine nun; because it was possibly the example which his sister exercised on him that decided Benedict to flee from Rome and seek the retirement of Subiaco.

In any case, toward the end of Scholastica's life we discover her in a kind of retreat or cell not far distant from Monte Cassino,[2] in a place subject to the pastoral jurisdiction of the abbey. This dwelling St. Gregory calls a *cella*, and Pope Zachary does the same. Although the word *cella* for the biographer ordinarily signifies a monastery or cloister, from the context we cannot be certain whether other virgins consecrated to God led a common life together with Scholastica. In those times the vicinity of Casinum was studded with such instances of

---

[1] "*Omnipotenti Domino ab ipso infantiae tempore dedicata . . . Sanctimonialis foemina*" (*Dial.*, Bk. II, chaps. 33 f.).

[2] I regard as probable that, in accord with the ancient liturgical discipline, the medieval church dedicated to St. Scholastica near the valley which bears her name to the west, on one of the foothills of Monte Cassino, preserves the memory of the dwelling of the saint (cf. Carettoni, *op. cit.*, p. 14).

Christian virginity. St. Boniface adopts the same means later in the evangelization of Germany.

I have already spoken of the two sharp-tongued nuns who dwelt in their own house not far from the *castrum*. Similarly I have pointed out that the hostess of the two monks who, contrary to the Rule, dined outside the monastery was also a *"foemina religiosa"*; Pope Zachary simply translates this as *"sacratissima virgo."* She lived in a *cella;* hence she was a nun. In another of the villages evangelized by the man of God there was a group of religious women, about whom the holy Patriarch was particularly concerned. The Greek translator speaks of a true monastery: ἀσκητήριον ἐτύγχανεν παρθένων. In a word, Benedictine missionary sisters.

Frequently, when he himself could not go, Benedict sent one of his disciples to give the nuns spiritual conferences, something they appreciated greatly. On their side, the good religious women kept their eyes open for any eventual needs of the monk who spoke to them, in order to send to Monte Cassino boxes of handkerchiefs or other gifts, as was then the custom. Whoever desires more information on this point may consult the narrative of the relations of Venantius Fortunatus with St. Radegundis and her nuns at Holy Cross.

One day, when the conference was over, the nuns in question offered the preacher some linens, the kind permitted by the Rule. The monk out of courtesy at first appeared reluctant, but finally he accepted them and hid them in his bosom. Hardly had he set his foot on the threshold of the monastery, when he met the Abbot, who, with a mien far severer than usual, asked him: "How has this evil thing entered into your heart?" The monk, not remembering the linens, failed to understand. The saint continued: "Did you think that I did not see you from afar, when you accepted the kerchiefs from the nuns and hid them in your bosom?" The culprit, seeing himself discovered, threw the *corpus delicti* away and, acknowledging his fault, asked pardon. It was precisely this the Patriarch was awaiting to readmit him into his favor.

Let not the reader marvel at the harshness of St. Benedict for the infraction of the monastic vow of poverty. He considered this extremely essential, because, as St. Gregory observes in another connection, "if the monks have private property, neither peace nor charity can remain in that community." [3] The guilt of the monk in question became graver because deceit was added to it: "He accepted the linens and hid them in his bosom."

[3] *Epist.*, Bk. XI, no. 24.

CHAPTER XL

The Son of the Procurator

SOMETIMES St. Benedict sent his monks to preach, at other times he himself went, according to circumstances. One day, having gone forth on business of some kind, he returned to the monastery when it was already night and had to take his supper when the others were about to go to bed.[1] Standing before the table, one of his young monks, the son of a certain "defensor," whose father's position gave him an exalted sense of the dignity of his house, held the light.[2]

In St. Gregory's time, there were, it is true, also *defensores Ecclesiae*, among whom we find Gordian himself, the father of the Pope. But this title clearly distinguished them from the civil *defensores*, with whom they had in common a respected position and an extensive jurisdiction within the limits of their offices.[3]

So, while the saint was eating and the other stood before him with the lantern (*"cum lucernae ministerio"*), the youth began to think within himself: "After all, who is this man, that I, while he sits at meat, should stand before him with the light? And who am I, that I

---

[1] *Dial.*, Bk. II, chap. 20.

[2] Of this ancient custom of the Roman authorities having servants with lights precede them and of holding the candelabrum while they sat at table, we find many examples. Gregory of Tours relates that, while Bishop Rauchingi took his meals, a young domestic held the candle. Sidonius Apollinaris describes the wife of Symmacus holding the lighted candelabrum for her spouse (cf. Mabillon, *Annales O.S.B.*, 1, 81 f.).

[3] Also particular churches, at least the more important ones, had each its *defensor*. Thus we find at Nola in 542 a certain *Lucianus defensor:*

HIC REQVIESCIT SC. M. LVCEIANVS. DEFENSOR
QVI VIXIT ANNOS. P. M. XLVIII. DEP. DIE
V. KAL. DECEMB P. C. BASILI V. C.

should debase myself to so lowly a task? If my father would know of this!" It is well known that before the great lords and the authorities, especially after the reform of the ceremonial introduced by Diocletian, servants carried lighted candelabra, as is still done by the acolytes in the churches to this day. At Monte Cassino the Patriarch had not suppressed the forms then current, also as far as prelates were concerned.[4] In democratic times such as ours, we would set the light on the table, in order to eat in peace without disturbing anyone. St. Benedict did not think that way, and the whole Roman world thought with him.

Like St. Augustine, he felt that superiors, in the interests of the community, could not abrogate certain external forms of behavior which serve so well to recall to the minds of the subjects the divine character of the principle of authority which descends from God. To put head and member on the same level would be to empty of its sacred character the obedience of the subject.

Between the anchorite of Monte Taleo and the Abbot of Monte Cassino, who is served at table as a "lord and abbot," we note a great difference, which supposes a notable change in St. Benedict. Now we know what this change was: at Subiaco the saint is simply a hermit; at Monte Cassino, on the other hand, he is the apostle and the ecclesiastical chief of the Cassinese region.

The son of the *defensor* stood, then, thinking of his father's position and the lowly duty to which he was assigned, when the man of God, who till then had remained silent, suddenly said to him: "Brother, make the sign of the cross on your heart. What are you thinking of? Make the sign of the cross."

Immediately he called some monks, ordered that they should take the light, and send the other to bed. The disciples, urged by curiosity, sought from the young monk the reason why he was sent away. The youth was truly humble, and openly told his companions how the Abbot had discovered the thoughts of pride he was harboring in his mind at the moment. What generosity, familiarity and openheartedness among the members of the primitive Cassinese community!

---

[4] Even today this *lucernae ministerium* in the liturgy of Milan cathedral is carried out by the canons of the order of subdeacons. They carry the candles at the Gospel, in processions, and at the intonation of the Magnificat.

CHAPTER XLI

A Medieval Guide to St. Benedict's Monastery

AT this point in our story, let us follow the example of the tourist, who, armed with his Baedeker, visits the monuments of European cities. Occasionally he stops, reads the guide, and looks at the attached map. In the Cassinese manuscript 175 (al. 353), next to a commentary on the Rule, is found a topographical description of Monte Cassino. This has been several times edited and commented upon by Mabillon, Della Noce, Gattola, Tosti, Morin and others. The manuscript is of the tenth century, but the writing may have been done at a later date. The style of the document in any case indicates the period between the eighth and tenth centuries.[1]

1
In turre iusta sanctum martinum
in fenestra alta que est
contra capuam vidit sanctus B.
anima germ. cap. epi. et ibi
in fenestra que est contra plumbar.
vidit animam sancte scol.
ibi resanavit severum contritum
et lecprosum. et ibi cunctas
virtutes fecit. in fundo turris
fecit miraculum de labello olei.
et ibi supra arca tridecim sol
de auro ceciderunt. per fenestra
unde vidit anima sce scol
iactata est ampulla de vitro.
ibi resuscitavit mortuum
ad pede de turre extra porta.
ibi scs maurus claudum esten

I shall translate and somewhat explain the "Latin" of the Cassinese annotator.

"From the upper story of the tower near St. Martin's, through the window which faces toward Capua, St. Benedict saw the soul of Bishop Germanus. From the other, looking toward Piumarola, on the floor beneath, he viewed the soul of St. Scholastica. In this same room he restored to life Severus, who had been crushed under the walls; there also he cured the leper and worked other miracles.

"On the ground floor of the tower took place the miracle of the pot of oil, and there on the chest rained from heaven the thirteen pieces of gold.

"The glass cruet with oil was thrown from the same window whence the saint saw the soul of St. Scholastica ascending to heaven.

"Outside the gate of the monastery, at the foot of the tower, St. Benedict restored the dead man to life; there likewise St. Maur healed a lame man.

"Opposite the door of the tower, from the balcony of the dormitory, the saint broke the bonds of the peasant; thence also he spoke to Totila.

"In the refectory, near the dormitory, he prophesied the fate of Rome and spoke of the lack of bread.

"In the tower he wrote the Rule.

"At the foot of the ramp which leads to the oratory of St. John, he freed the obsessed monk.

---

dit. in poio qui est in dormitorio
ante porte de turre solsit
rusticu et ibi carrivit ad
totila. in refectorio qui est
iusta ipsum dormitorium profeta
vid de Roma et de pani.
in turre ipsa scipsit regla.
in pede de rabe que vadit a scu
ianne fugabi demone. in fron
de ipsu dormitorio et de scu mart
fecit cerbenera. da foris porta
a pede de turre inbeni c moia
de farina. altare de scu M. . .
fuit sub corona de rame. in ipsa
turre omni anno sci (benedicti
altare biariczo faciebant officium
greci et latini sicut praecepit pe
tronax abbas).

"The miracle of the elephantiac was worked on the slope near the dormitory and in front of St. Martin's oratory.

"Outside the gate, at the foot of the tower were found the hundred measures of flour.

"Over the altar of St. Martin was a round lamp of copper. Within the tower itself, on a portable altar, on the feast of St. Benedict, Greeks and Latins celebrated the liturgy, as Abbot Petronax had commanded."

On what sources is this document based? The context gives the impression that the topography of the monastery had remained unchanged since the days of Petronax, under Pope Gregory II. The author seems to be ignorant of the great transformations of Monte Cassino wrought by Abbot Desiderius. The monastic structure still is pictured as being grouped about the tower and the oratory of St. Martin; the church on the summit of the mountain preserves its original title of St. John the Baptist. Similarly the portico, uniting St. Martin and St. John the Baptist, which was pulled down under Desiderius, still exists. This description of the primitive arrangement of the buildings gives the impression that the document was written not very long after the time of Petronax, when St. Zachary at Rome was translating the life of St. Benedict into Greek.

Several precious particulars seem to be independent of St. Gregory's story, which, however, they serve to illustrate in a marvelous manner. Thus the monk crushed under the ruins was called Severus. When St. Benedict terrified and brought to terms both Zalla and King Totila, he stood on the balcony which projected from the dormitory, situated before the tower in the neighborhood of St. Martin's. The refectory was situated near the dormitory and opposite the tower. The cistern near which the saint cured the obsessed monk was in the court at the foot of the Roman arcade that joined the sanctuaries of Jupiter and Apollo.

Of interest is the mention of the corona, or liturgical lamp of copper, which formerly hung over the altar of St. Martin. This altar had already been moved by Abbot Petronax when he lengthened the small basilica by about twenty feet. The naos of Apollo evidently must have been rather small since, even after its reconstruction by

Abbot Desiderius in more ample proportions, it was scarcely over sixty feet in length.

Quite possibly when, toward the end of the tenth century, St. Nilus of Valleluce was asked to come to Monte Cassino to celebrate there the festive Greek liturgy of St. Benedict, this invitation followed upon the rule set up by Petronax and mentioned by the anonymous author. The question still remains: Why this Byzantine Mass at Monte Cassino? We must not forget that in the eighth century Oriental monks were not rare in Rome and in Italy; as a matter of fact, Pope Zachary himself, the translator of St. Gregory's *Dialogues,* was an Oriental.

I have the impression that the Cassinese document of the eleventh century depends on local sources that are older, going back to the times of Petronax. For the study of the life of St. Benedict, these simple notes help to localize the incidents related in the *Dialogues,* by giving us a topographical sketch of Monte Cassino as it was between the eighth and eleventh centuries. For various reasons I would exclude a later date.

Neither the anonymous Cassinese writer nor the life of St. Maur explains whether and when the latter followed his master to Monte Cassino. Perhaps there was no need of an explanation. Taking into consideration what St. Gregory says, namely, that from the beginning St. Maur was the principal assistant of St. Benedict at Subiaco, we are hardly able to see how he could have remained away from the much more difficult mission at Monte Cassino.

Prudence dictates that I should not quote here the Acts of St. Maur, where they describe his departure for France and the gifts given to him by the Patriarch. Mention may be made, however, of the ivory box containing the following relics: "Three particles of the wood of the Holy Cross, relics of the holy Mother of God, of St. Michael the archangel, namely, from the altar-covering of his church, also of Stephen the protomartyr, and of the blessed confessor of Christ, Martin." Here the archaeologists make no difficulties. The altar-covering of St. Michael comes from the sanctuary on Monte Gargano; the altar-cloth of the Madonna, as also the relic of St. Stephen, probably from Constantinople.

The reference of the anonymous author to St. Maur, who healed the cripple at the foot of the tower, must not be forgotten. This miracle is described at greater length in the *Acta Mauri*, worked over by Odo of Glanfeuil in the ninth century, but the Cassinese reference seems to be independent and anterior. It is difficult to come to any conclusion regarding the authenticity of the Acts of St. Maur. In any event they beautifully frame the scene of the miracle before the tower at the entrance to Monte Cassino; wherefore they merit mention here. They contain some gold nuggets buried in a large quantity of earth and sand.

One day St. Benedict had gone to bless a puerpera who was said to be possessed by the devil. Her husband was a noble of those parts, and the monks of Cassino owed him gratitude for the many favors he had granted them. St. Benedict honored him with his friendship and, since he sympathized with him, he easily allowed himself to be induced to go to his house to bless the sick woman. To make matters worse, the devil, it seemed, had taken possession also of the newborn child.

While Benedict was absent from the monastery, there arrived at Monte Cassino the parents of a deaf and dumb child, and with great insistence they begged Maur, who was taking the Abbot's place, to restore the child by a miracle. At first Maur refused, saying he was unworthy and a sinner. But since the poor folk insisted, he finally placed his diaconal stole on the head of the boy, blessed him with the sign of the cross, and immediately the child was cured.

Mabillon cites various documents to prove that in ancient times priests and deacons wore the stole or orarium in public as a sign of their dignity. Then, from the *Ordines Romani* we know that the stoles of the deacons of Rome were taken from above the tomb of St. Peter, as is done to the present day with the palliums of the archbishops. This may explain why St. Maur placed his stole on the head of the boy.

CHAPTER XLII

A Meal in the Open

ABBOT VALENTINIAN, who governed the community in the Lateran for a long time and whom I mentioned in the beginning, had a brother who was a pious layman.[1] He must have dwelt in the vicinity of Aquino, Atina, or Ciociaria, because St. Gregory tells us that he used to make an annual visit to Monte Cassino, either to see his brother or to receive the blessing of St. Benedict. Out of respect for the Patriarch, he used to make the journey fasting till evening, as was done on the days of Lent or on the more solemn vigils.

One year he met on the road another traveler who was going the same way and who was carrying a basket of provisions. They began a conversation and talked about this and that. The brother of Valentinian said he was going to Monte Cassino; the other did not disclose his destination.

They walked and walked, over hill and dale. At a certain point the unknown traveler stopped and, observing that the hour was already late, said that unless they ate—after all the heat and the dust of the Via Latina—it would be impossible to go on. A rest and a bite of lunch would refresh them for the rest of the journey. "Oh, no," replied the other, "it is my custom to go fasting to the venerable Father Benedict just as one does on a pilgrimage to the sanctuaries of the martyrs." It may be noted that he spoke of the man of God as of a personage universally known. He gave him the title "venerable Father" just as

---

[1] Bk. II, chap. 13.

we now call priests "reverend," and the pope calls the bishops "venerable brethren."

Satan—for he was the unknown traveler—when he heard the servant of God named, turned away, so that his companion might not see the anger in his face. "Very well, very well," he interjected brusquely, "then let us get along." From then on the conversation languished. The matter of the fast and, worse still, this business of visiting St. Benedict had so gotten on the nerves of the unknown traveler that thenceforth speech was limited to an occasional monosyllable.

Meanwhile the day was passing. The white dust of the road and the sweat made traveling uncomfortable. At a particular point the pair entered a green valley shaded by several rows of trees. The unknown companion, apparently more fatigued than ever, insisted that they take lunch. But he received the same reply as before. Finally, when the sun was already low in the sky, they entered the valley of the Liri. From the edge of the dusty road extended a thick green carpet with flower designs. A small fountain splashed in the shade of a row of trees; from afar could be seen Casinum with its large amphitheater and on the heights the fortress surrounded with the green crown of its groves. The spot invited the wayfarers to halt and refresh themselves before undertaking the ascent.

"Look at this meadow," said the unknown, "behold the fountain. What a delightful place to take our meal together before we part. Come, my brother, do not wrong me by refusing."

Even more than to the persuasive words of the devil, the brother of Valentinian listened to the argument of his stomach, which was registering its protests. Anyway, the customary hour when he arrived at the monastery other years was already passed, and here he was still on the road and fasting. Penance and devotion are well enough, but a gesture of courtesy toward his companion would also be an act of charity. To put it briefly, he allowed himself to be persuaded, and so, reclining on the thick grass of the meadow in the shade of the trees, the two took a bite of lunch together. Pity it is that St. Gregory does not tell us what the devil had in his basket.

As God willed, toward evening the brother of Valentinian finally arrived at the monastery, after a hard day of travel. Never before had he been so fatigued as this time. But before anything else, he wished to be presented to St. Benedict to receive his blessing.

The saint, with an air of reproof, said: "What, O my brother, has happened? The devil, after failing a first and second time to ensnare you, finally at the third attempt overcame you, and you yielded to his temptation to gluttony." The man was stupefied. True, during the journey the company of the unknown wayfarer and his ceremonious manner of acting had not pleased him. But then to think that it was the devil himself in flesh and bone—in appearance, be it understood—was quite a jump.

Immediately he threw himself at the feet of the servant of God, begging him to pardon his weakness. The saint, who looked upon him as a son or one of his disciples rather than as a mere guest, gave him his blessing. After they had prayed together and the wayfarer's feet had been washed, St. Benedict sat down at table with him and the other guests, as the Rule prescribes.

I leave it to the reader to imagine how the pilgrim felt after the experiences of the day. A few hours before he had lunched with the devil, eating the sandwich that was offered him. It tasted like ashes and would hardly go down. Good reason! Now, instead, he was supping with the Patriarch of monks, and the food that was served him, besides having the seasoning of Christian charity, must have appeared to him still tastier because it had been blessed by a saint.

To this incident the biographer adds no comment whatever. But we may make some of our own. This good man, who out of devotion makes the pilgrimage to Monte Cassino fasting and then, immediately upon his arrival, throws himself at the Abbot's feet to ask his blessing (*orationem dari*) was carrying out a liturgical practice of the time. The phrase *"orationem dare"* was equivalent to the phrase "to bless," because at the end of every liturgical function the priest pronounced over the faithful a brief concluding prayer.

Even today, in the ferial Masses of Lent, before the priest recites the blessing, that is, the so-called "Prayer over the people," the deacon invites those present to incline the head: "Bow down your heads before God." In the Ambrosian rite the diaconal formula is: "Bow for the blessing." Also in his Rule St. Benedict prescribes that at the end of each hour of the Divine Office, the litany together with the

Lord's Prayer be recited as a formula of blessing: "Lord, have mercy on us, the blessing and the concluding prayers" (chap. 17).

For the pilgrim to Cassino, his action did not mean simply that he recommended himself to the prayers of St. Benedict, but that he requested his priestly blessing. He received it fasting, as was then the custom with liturgical rites of special importance.[2]

Another observation. St. Gregory directly refers to this luncheon by the roadside as a fault: ". . . *reatum infirmae suae mentis agnoscens.*" The pious pilgrim himself is convinced of his guilt; he throws himself at the feet of the saint, weeps, and asks pardon for it. It is difficult to see a sin where we should only suspect some weakness in keeping a good resolution.

To understand the nature of the fault, we must keep in mind the liturgical customs of the times. The brother of Valentinian undertook the annual journey principally to receive the blessing of St. Benedict. This is the reason for the prolonged fast. One year, fooled by the devil, he failed in his resolution, yet dared to present himself to the saint to ask the customary blessing without making mention of the violated fast. He tried to deceive St. Benedict. But the father immediately discovered the fraud, and the other learned at his expense that, even when absent, the eye of the Patriarch followed him.

---

[2] "*Ad venerabilem Patrem Benedictum ieiunus semper pervenire consuevi.*" Pope Zachary describes him as kneeling at the feet of the saint, soliciting this signal favor: Πεσὼν ἐπὶ τὴν γῆν εὐχὴν ᾐτήσατο λαβεῖν.

CHAPTER XLIII

The Flour of the Angels

AFTER the meal of the devil's bread made out of husks follows the story of the flour of the angels. Benedict, in his tower 1,500 feet above the sea, was in a kind of observatory from which he could follow in the plain of the Liri lying below him the advance of the Goths, who continued their conquest of the southern part of the Peninsula.

On October 2, 534, King Athalaric died, a victim of his vices. His mother, Amalasunta, to prevent the Gothic kingdom from breaking up married her former enemy and cousin, Theodatus, who, to show his gratitude, had her strangled. Justinian intervened to avenge her; thus in 535, began the Gothic war in Italy. In 536 Theodatus was slain in his turn; while Ravenna returned to the Empire, the barbarian soldiery acclaimed as their king the strong warrior Witigis.

In vain were attempts made to work out an agreement between Goths and Greeks. Even Pope Agapitus was forced to go to Constantinople to plead the cause of peace. But instead of peace, he found death there, and toward the end of 536 his corpse was brought to the Vatican.

In the preceding spring, St. Benedict, from his vantage point, had observed on the Via Latina the gleam of lances advancing toward Aquino in a sea goldened by the sun and by fire. They were the troops of Belisarius, who, departing from Sicily for the reconquest of Italy, by an advance so rapid that it resembled a triumphal march across lower Italy, took Naples, crossed the Campania, and now was moving decisively on Rome. The occupation of Cassino gave into his hand the key to Latium.

The chair of St. Peter at that time was occupied by Pope Sylverius. Unfortunately, the understanding between him and Belisarius did not last long. The Byzantine leader, having become master of the capital, began to suspect that the Pontiff was secretly favoring Witigis, who at that time was besieging the city with a force of 150,000 men.

Thanks to the secret manipulations of the Empress Theodora, one day the Byzantine general seized the Pope, who was regarded as friendly to the Goths, took away his pontifical pallium, threw a monk's cloak on him, and sent him to Patara in exile. On the following March 29, 537, the Byzantine court set up as Sylverius' successor the intriguing deacon Vigilius of the party of nobles.[1] In the meantime, by reason of the siege, the famine steadily continued to grow more terrible. One can easily imagine what effect was produced on the whole of Italy by the sad plight of Rome and of the papacy.

Belisarius, who envisioned the reconquest of the entire Peninsula, could now set himself up as representing the ancient imperial ideal of the Romans. In reality his army was composed of Italians, Greeks, and even of Huns, a heterogeneous mass that sowed devastation and misery wherever it passed. Especially during these years of war and want St. Benedict's monastery served the poor as an asylum to which all fled for help.

Several contemporaneous sources (Procopius, the *Liber pontificalis*, and Cassiodorus) describe the horrible famine afflicting Italy about the year 536. A rumor reported that at Milan a woman had gone to the length of roasting her own child to satisfy her hunger. Bishop Dacius obtained a rescript from King Theodatus which authorized him to draw upon the granaries of Pavia and of Tortona for a determined quantity of grain for distribution to the most desperate of his episcopal city.[2]

[1] Discussing the moderation to be observed by the abbot, St. Benedict declares: "Let the abbot always bear in mind that at the dread judgment of God, there will be an examination of these two matters: his teaching and the obedience of his disciples" (chap. 2).

In the Leonine Sacramentary a formula for the anniversary of the coronation of Pope Vigilius reads as follows: "Grant us, we beseech Thee, O Lord, the observance of a holy discipline, that through Thy grace may come about both the moderation of those who govern and the obedience of the subjects." It is noteworthy that this formula, so much akin to the mentality and the language of the *Regula monasteriorum*, was composed precisely between the years 537 and 545, while St. Benedict was still living.

[2] Evidently the sad conditions of the times even left their imprint on the liturgical formulas of the so-called Leonine Sacramentary. In 538 Easter fell on April 4. Witigis

St. Benedict did his share to mitigate the misery of the period. He considered himself the steward of divine Providence for all the faithful of the rural area depending on him, and he decided to continue giving to the poor until there was nothing left at the abbey. The good God would have to care for his disciples.[3]

One day the cellarer went to inform him that his generosity toward outsiders had almost exhausted the stores. For the community there remained but five loaves of bread, as in the Gospel narrative, but without any salted fish. When the time for the meal came, the man of God observed that the faith of his monks did not measure up to their vocation. Standing before the closed door of the refectory, without indeed murmuring against the prodigality of the Abbot, yet with long faces and sad countenances, they let it easily be seen that the chapter about perfect Benedictine joy even in times of privation was still rather difficult for them to understand.

In vain the saint strove to strengthen their weak faith. Finally he had the five loaves distributed among the most famished, and when he entered the refectory, he said: "Why are you saddened at the lack of a little bread? Why do you not rather put greater trust in God? He treats us according to the measure of our faith. Today your faith is small and bread scarce. But console yourselves; tomorrow you shall have in abundance." [4]

Meanwhile the bell for Compline sounded, and all went to choir. The following morning, after the Office, the porter entered St. Martin's to report that outside the gate he had found two hundred sacks

---

had lifted his siege of Rome shortly before, in the month of March. We find the following Secret for July 28: "We offer to Thy name, O Lord, these gifts with thanksgiving; grant that we, who have been freed from the violence of our enemies, may receive the paschal Sacrament with a safe mind."

In the preceding year (537), the besieging Goths had harvested the abundant crops of Latium, while the Romans who had cultivated them suffered extreme want. A reminder of this fact is contained in the following Preface: "We recognize, O Lord, that it is part of the sinners' lot that the things sought by the labor of Thy servants should be snatched from before our eyes by the hands of our enemies, and that what Thou didst grant to nature by the labor of Thy faithful Thou dost allow to be carried off by others" (Mass of July 6).

Also St. Benedict on Monte Cassino must have prayed in those days, if not with the same words, certainly with the same sentiments as those expressed in the Leonine Sacramentary.

[3] "*Vir Dei diversis indigentibus monasterii sui cuncta tribuerat, ut pene nihil in cellario . . . remaneret*" (*Dial.*, chap. 28).

[4] "*In refectorio . . . prophetavit de Roma et de pani.*"

of flour. We may imagine how astonished the monks were at this announcement. They gave thanks to the Lord with all their hearts. But
at the same time they were curious to know whence this great gift had
come and who had sent it. They scoured the mountainside in all directions, to see if they could hear the creak of a cart or if they could discover the tracks of the mule drivers. No luck!

Then they bethought themselves of the promise made by their
father the preceding evening: "Today indeed you are in want, but
tomorrow you will have in abundance," and they were convinced that
this great quantity of flour did not come from any mill of the state
—there were none such at the time anyway—but that it was a gift
from heaven. Their conviction regarding this miracle of Providence
was so deep-seated, that they decided to keep at least some of the sacks
as a souvenir of the prodigy.

When, in 589, the Cassinese were attacked at night by the troops
of Duke Zoto, they were constrained to flee from the monastery to
save their lives. Among the treasures they brought with them to Rome
were the autograph copy of the Rule, the authentic weight of the daily
pound of bread, and several of the famous sacks.[5] Unfortunately, in
the fire of the monastery of Teano in 896 both the Rule and the sacks
were destroyed.[6]

[5] Paul the Deacon, *History of the Lombards,* Bk. IV, chap. 17.
[6] *Chronicon Cassinense,* I, 48.

CHAPTER XLIV

The Oil That Was Multiplied

On another day a poor subdeacon, Agapitus by name, ascended to Monte Cassino. His wretched clothing and his pale and emaciated face were good evidence that in his church, perhaps in Cassino or in Aquino,[1] famine was making itself felt. We are still in the period of the great want (535–36). He begged for merely a bit of oil with which to season his tomatoes, and thus carry him along a bit. Seeing him in such a pitiable condition, the sympathetic Abbot, whom Zachary in

---

[1] In ancient times the subdeacons had principally administrative functions in the episcopal sees and they assisted the deacons in serving the bishops. They used to reside in rural parishes.

An epitaph in the basilica of St. Agnes in Rome records:

LOCVS IMPORTVNI SVBDIAC REG QVARTAE

Between St. Mary Major and St. Praxedes in Rome was found the epitaph of a certain Serinus, subdeacon of the fourth region of the city:

LOCUS SERINI SUBD REG
QUEM COMPARAVIT AB IS
PECIOSA ABBA CON TV
TA CONGREGATIONE
SUA SI QUIS AVTEM LO
CUM ISTUM BIOLABE
RIT PARTEM ABEAT C
VM IVDA TRADITOR
EM DNI NOSTRI IHV
XRI AMEN.
(Cf. Fabretti, *Inscrip. Antiq.*, p. 110, no. 272)

In the disappearance of so many episcopal sees that followed upon the invasion of the Lombards, we can scarcely marvel at St. Gregory's description of the subdeacon Quadragesimus, who was reduced to pasturing his sheep near that section of the Via Aurelia which passed the ancient episcopal see of Buxentum.

his Greek version calls: χριστοῦ πιστὸς καὶ φρόνιμος οἰκονόμος—"the wise and faithful steward of Christ," desired him to remain for supper. After all, there would be a good bowl of soup for him too. Meanwhile he called the cellarer and gave orders that the poor man's request be filled.

The cellarer remarked that only a bit of oil remained in the bottle for the needs of the community. All the rest had been given away. Benedict replied that his order was to be carried out exactly; God would then provide for the monks. To argue with the saints is always a losing venture. The prudent cellarer then made a deep reverence to the Abbot and withdrew; meanwhile the guest was doing justice to his meal in the xenodochium. But as far as giving him the oil, that was farthest from the cellarer's thoughts.

Even now the bottle was almost empty. The Abbot was generous, too generous. If he had been obeyed, how could the meal of the monks have been prepared? Perhaps the monks would not have dared to dispute with the superior; their criticisms and the bitter looks would be directed against the innocent cellarer. A little later, the Abbot met him and inquired if he had taken care of the guest and given him the oil. The cellarer began to make excuses, asserting that if he had been obliged that day to give away the last remnant of oil, he could not have taken care of the meal for the community.

This disobedience of the disciple, the fruit of a weak faith, saddened the Patriarch greatly. "What! Are we going to keep that bit of oil in violation of obedience? Never!" While the poor cellarer stood there trembling at this reproof, the saint commanded the monks to bring the bottle and to throw it out of the window. The order was given so peremptorily that it allowed of no delay. But God immediately made known how pleasing to Him was this energetic act of faith. The bottle, falling from the height upon the rock, neither broke nor overturned, so that not even a drop of the oil was lost.

While the amazed monks observed this miracle from the window, Benedict ordered one of the younger men to go down with the subdeacon to pick up the unbroken bottle, so that the latter might at once carry it home. When the guest had departed and the community remained alone with the Abbot, he decided first of all to go to the pantry to see if really not a drop of oil remained in the round-bellied terra-cotta jars, such as are still used in Latium. Unfortunately it was as the cellarer had said.

Since human aid was wanting, the saint asked for divine assistance. After reproving the cellarer's lack of faith, he knelt down in the *cellarium* to pray with his monks. And while they were praying, they heard the oil bubble, as if it were coming from the bottom and filling the jar. The more they prayed, the higher the oil rose in the container, until it passed over the brim, began to lift the wooden cover and flowed forth on the floor. We can easily picture the amazement of all at this contact with the supernatural world. Most likely the deepest touched was the poor cellarer.

The saint took occasion of the prodigy to encourage the monks anew to obedience and to a humble trust in the Lord. Of this he had an excellent example before his very eyes. For a cup or a little more of oil in the bottom of the bottle given to the subdeacon Agapitus, divine Providence had filled the oil jar to the very top.

Both St. Gregory and Pope Zachary apparently take delight in sketching the picture of the monks standing about St. Benedict, who, after the miracle, gave a well-merited paternal admonition to the cellarer: "My son," he tells him in the words of St. Zachary, "have a firm faith and a humility worthy of your monastic state." With these two virtues the Patriarch of monks in the name of God worked his miracles. It is always profitable to remember that secret.

We have already intimated that, if our figures regarding the foundation of the Lateran monastery are correct,—in any case it can not be later than 560—we feel it must be placed in the first years of the pontificate of Vigilius, before he was sent into exile on the Bosphorus. This Pope had indeed much for which to be pardoned by the Romans, who remembered the shameless manner in which, to please the Greeks, he had confined his predecessor Sylverius on the island of Ponza. As if to make amends, Pope Vigilius then dedicated himself to prayer and works of piety; and since the Goths in their occupation of Rome had devastated also the cemeteries of the martyrs,[2] the aristocratic Pontiff undertook the vast labor of repairing the tombs

---

[2] *"Ecclesiae et corpora martyrum exterminata sunt a Gothis"* (*Liber pontificalis in Sylverii vita*).

and of restoring in marble the ancient inscriptions that Pope Damasus had placed there.[3]

He also carried out new constructions in the Lateran, where the dining hall, called *Basilica Vigilii,* for a long time preserved the memory of his name. For the Lateran he had a special predilection. When he was deported to Constantinople, he delegated Bishop Valentine of St. Rufina "to the guardianship of the Lateran." The banqueting hall was an imposing structure. Later St. Gregory the Great made it the reception room of his private apartment.[4]

If, then, one of the popes of this period has the merit of having the foundation of the Lateran monastery attributed to him, the most likely candidate is Vigilius.[5] He was the pope of the Roman aristocracy, which was all devoted to St. Benedict, whom it considered as belonging to the nobility. We know, besides, from St. Gregory that, at the request of King Childebert, he granted a diploma of pontifical protection to the new monastery which the monarch had erected within the city of Arles.[6]

Those who are familiar with the Scriptures will find pleasure in recognizing in St. Benedict's miracles analogies with those of the patriarchs and prophets of Israel. St. Gregory himself points this out: "In the water drawn from the rock, I recognize Moses; in the recovery of the iron implement, Eliseus; in the walking on the waters, the apostle Peter; in the obedience of the raven, Elias; in the grief for

[3]   DIRUTA VIGILIUS NAM MOX HAEC PAPA GEMISCENS
            HOSTIBUS EXPULSIS OMNE NOVAVIT OPUS.

[4] *"In basilica quondam doctissimi papae Vigilii, iuxta quam consuetudinaliter habitabat"* (John the Deacon, *Vita S. Gregorii,* Bk. II, no. 30).

[5] Is there a relation between the Lateran monastery dedicated to St. Pancratius and the cemetery of the martyr on the Via Aurelia, whose protection Vigilius retained? The following epitaph of 537 seems to point that way.

            HIC REQUIESCIT SEVERUS TINCTOR
            Q. V. ANN PLUS MINUS LXII EX QUIB
        XVII CUM IUGALE SUA QUIETA PACE TRANS
        EGIT CUIUS CORPUS NE ALIUD UMQUAM SUPER
        PONATUR PROHIBENS BEATISSIMO PAPA VI
        GILIO CONCEDENTE IN HOC LOCO SITUM EST DPST

Regularly the administration of this cemetery belonged to the priests of the title of St. Chrysogonus. If, then, Vigilius is mentioned here instead, it is a sign that the Pope for some special reason had reserved to himself the granting of burial there.

[6] *Epist.,* Bk. IX, no. 111.

the death of his enemy, I recognize David. In my opinion, that man was filled with the spirit of all the just." [7]

This observation holds true not only for the miracles themselves, but also for the way they were worked. Thus, when reading that the Patriarch immersed the handle of the axe in the lake of Claudius, who does not recall a similar gesture on the part of Eliseus? When he shuts the door of the cell, and there recalls the dead boy to life, who does not think of a like scene in the life of Elias? When he multiplies the oil, how can we be unmindful of an identical episode in the life of Eliseus? When, finally, near the threshold of the monastery, Benedict stretched himself on the little corpse, to warm it and to restore it to life, does it not recall the gesture of Elias who stretched himself on the dead child of the woman whose guest he was, in order to bring into the cold members the vital spark of a new life?

Thus St. Benedict meditated upon and carried out the teaching of the Sacred Scriptures, in accordance with the recommendation he himself gives in the Rule: "What page. . . . of the divinely inspired books of the Old and New Testaments is not a most unerring rule for human life?"

[7] *Dial.*, Bk. II, chap. 8.

CHAPTER XLV

The Adventure of Exhilaratus

IF God deigned miraculously to fill the empty oil jar, why should he fail to bless also the granary and the breadbox? During these years Monte Cassino was like a port of refuge: some went and others came; some ascended the mountain to bring something thither, others to beg for help. All wished to say the same thing. They all went to the Patriarch, "to the venerable Father Benedict" as they said, as to the common father of the poor, as to the faithful steward of Christ.

One day a certain servant, Exhilaratus by name, was sent by his master to bring to the saint on Monte Cassino two containers of that generous wine which the residents of the Castelli and of Latium are so proud of. All recall the verses of Leo XIII of Carpineto in honor of the wine of Frascati. "Wooden containers, ordinarily called flagons," says St. Gregory. Now, the glass flasks, covered with straw, are something else. The wooden containers are still in use and are known as *cupelle*. Each holds about a gallon and a half.

The road to Monte Cassino was long, and the burden of the two containers made the way still more fatiguing. The youth had a sudden inspiration. He was called Exhilaratus, and this he was both in name and in deed. Somewhere along the path he hid one of the containers in the grass of a meadow, and with the other, whistling and singing snatches of songs, he continued his journey. Well, after all this work there would be a good drink also for him on his way back home.

When he reached the monastery and was presented to the Abbot, he carried out his commission and gave over the container to be emptied. Benedict thanked him humbly and quite naturally invited him to have a bite to eat. After such a long journey, the boy could not be sent back to his village fasting. Afterward, when the youth had received the Abbot's blessing and was about to leave, St. Benedict called after him: "Take care, my son, and do not drink out of the container you hid in the grass; but open it cautiously and see what is inside."

Exhilaratus blushed for shame at being discovered and taken for a thief, but he did not reply or even turn his face. He descended by leaps and bounds down the mule path. When he reached the meadow in the valley where he had hidden the wine, he found the receptacle intact in the thick grass. But he opened it carefully, as had been suggested to him, and then suddenly dropped it when he saw issue from it a large serpent, of the kind that is plentiful in that region during the summer. I do not know which frightened the boy more: the serpent instead of the wine, or the fact that the Patriarch, though absent, had discovered this trick of Exhilaratus. Certainly he never forgot that lesson. Many years later, when he had become a monk in St. Gregory's monastery in Rome,—and Peter the Deacon knew him there already as a novice—he used quite frankly to tell all this rather unhappy adventure of his young days.

This same Exhilaratus, whom Gregory was accustomed generously to call "our Exhilaratus," later on held several offices of trust under the Pope. In the Epistolary [1] we find a letter to the apocrisiary Sabinian, in which Gregory tells him of his intention to send Exhilaratus to Constantinople. From another letter [2] to the priest Anastasius we learn that the same Exhilaratus became *secundicerius*, and that, when he returned from Constantinople, he presented the Pontiff with some gifts from the Holy Land. [3]

[1] Bk. IV, no. 47: *"Exhilaratum autem nostrum pro ea re dirigi volui."*

[2] Bk. XXXII, no. 32.

[3] *"Benedictionem vero quam et prius per Exhilaratum secundicerium et postmodum per Sabinianum transmisistis, cum gratiarum actione suscepi."*

CHAPTER XLVI

Gold from Heaven

THE boyish prank of Exhilaratus recalls to the biographer another marvelous event, which one of the Cassinese monks who later transferred to the Lateran monastery was accustomed to relate. This monk was called Peregrinus, and in the manner of good old men who live on the memories of their youth, when he was prodded by his companions, he very willingly for a hundredth time repeated the story of the miracle he had witnessed.[1]

One beautiful summer's day, while the monks were working on the threshing floor, a man arrived all out of breath and asked to speak with the Abbot. He was not one of the ordinary poor who came every day to receive an alms. He was well dressed and had distinguished manners. Apparently he was a man of affairs, a merchant perhaps, or the manager of some business. Evidently things had been going ill with him.

Just at that time a note of his was coming due, and he saw no possibility of meeting it. But one hope remained for him, the charity of St. Benedict. Indeed, the amount was rather large, twelve solidi. Cassiodorus states for that time that the gold solidus was equivalent to no less than six thousand denarii.[2]

The good man called into play all his eloquence—and it is well known that Neapolitans are born lawyers—to prove to the wonder-worker the danger to which he and his family were exposed by the

---

[1] *Dial.*, Bk. II, chap. 27: *"Narrare consueverat."*
[2] *Variarum, Epist.*, 10: *"Sex millia denariorum solidum esse voluerunt."*

demands of the hardhearted creditor. If he could not pay at the stipulated time, he would have to go to prison, and even his children would be sold as slaves. The Roman law was inexorable with debtors, and precisely in the writings of St. Gregory we read of persons being sold into slavery because they were not in a position to pay into the Byzantine treasury the heavy taxes with which the Greeks at that time were squeezing out the lifeblood of the Latins.

Similarly the letters of Cassiodorus give us information on this matter. The degree of devastation to which the wars had reduced many parts of Italy made still more difficult the payment of debts to the treasury and to others. In some cases Cassiodorus himself had to intervene; for example, he declared a moratorium of two years on the debts with which the association of merchants of Sipontini was burdened.[3]

St. Benedict tried to encourage the unfortunate man and exhorted him to have confidence in God. Since at the moment he did not have on hand the large sum requested, he told the debtor to return in three days. Who knows? Perhaps in the meantime the bank of divine Providence would advance to both of them a substantial loan.

The debtor departed with hope in his heart, and St. Benedict spent almost two days continuously in prayer. *"In ipso autem biduo, more suo, in oratione fuit occupatus"* (chap. 27). On the morning of the third day the man was on the spot to inquire if the promised money had come. Perhaps the merchant thought that the Abbot had relations with the bankers of Rome or of Ravenna and that in the interval some messenger had brought him the sum required. What was his surprise when the Patriarch, instead of coming to him with a purse of shining gold pieces, calmly sent one of his disciples to see if perchance money had fallen into the granary as the dew had descended on Gideon's fleece in the days of old.

At the moment the merchant thought that they were fooling him. But then the monk returned with the news that on the mass of grain, spread here and there, he had found new, shining coins. He gathered them up: precisely thirteen solidi of the mint, which he brought to the saint. In his turn Benedict graciously gave them to the worried debtor, and informed him that twelve solidi were to be used to pay

[3] Bk. I, no. 37.

the debt, and that he might use the thirteenth as he best saw fit for the needs of his family.

I cannot omit making two observations at this point. St. Gregory, in narrating this incident of the money that rained from heaven, tells us that on the two preceding days St. Benedict "according to his custom, gave himself over to incessant prayer." Here we have revealed another secret of supernatural power. Often the biographer describes the Abbot engaged in prayer in the silence of his cell, while the monks are occupied in various tasks of the monastery. One might almost assert that he prays uninterruptedly, and that the spiritual majesty that shines forth from his face, so as even to bring terror to the barbarian kings, comes to him, as it did to Moses, from the divine familiarity of his colloquies with God.

On the basis of St. Gregory's words it would not be difficult to show how St. Benedict was elevated by God to the most sublime degrees of mystical prayer, even to ecstasy and rapture. The man of God first put into practice himself what he taught his disciple in the very prologue of the Rule: "First of all, whatever good work you begin to do, beg of Him with most earnest prayer to perfect it." And among the "instruments of good works" (chap. 4), he repeats: "To devote oneself frequently to prayer." As he taught, so the holy Patriarch lived, and he continued praying to his last breath.

The efficacy of his prayers was experienced also on another occasion. Even till the present time, there is no water on Monte Cassino, and it is necessary to drink the rain water collected in cisterns. But St. Benedict with consideration for his monks, since he had reduced the daily portion of wine to a hemina, desired that they should at least have good, fresh, healthful water. Mark the Poet assures us that at his prayer, as formerly at Subiaco, *"Siccaque mirandas terra reteit aquas."* Hence it was a miraculous spring; hence the "wonderful waters" which flowed forth at the prayer of the wonder-worker.

CHAPTER XLVII

Healing of a Bewitched Man

On another occasion a poor wretch was brought to St. Benedict. He was sick, and his entire body was covered with sores as if he were infected with leprosy. He said that he had been bewitched by his enemy, who had given him poison in his drink. Sorcery or no, the poor man was miserable and suffered considerably; merely looking at him was nauseating. St. Zachary says that he was afflicted with elephantiasis. The wonder-worker, however, regarded him with particular compassion. Recalling to mind that Jesus in the Gospel had touched the leper, he wished to imitate Him. At the touch of the saint's holy hand, the malady disappeared, and the skin recovered its former color (chap. 27).

The miracle became the talk of the surrounding country: St. Benedict healed all sorts of ailments, and occasionally even snatched some victims from death. One day a good man—whose son, the "illustrious Anthony," later told St. Gregory of the occurrence—sent one of his slaves to Monte Cassino, so that the Abbot might bless him.

This man likewise suffered from elephantiasis; he had lost all his hair and his head was covered with boils and sores. He was a miserable sight to behold. St. Benedict met him near St. Martin's, gave him the requested blessing, and encouraged him to hope in the Lord. When the poor boy returned home, he discovered that he was healed.[1] The anonymous Cassinese author of the time of Abbot Petronax records

---

[1] *"Ad virum Dei ab eodem patre eius missus est, et saluti pristinae sub omni celeritate restitutus"* (chap. 26).

this miracle. *"In fronde ipsu dormitorio et de sanctu Martino fuit cerbenera."*

Of this "illustrious man" we have no other record. He must have been a personage of some importance in one of the villages not far from Casinum, because the title "illustrious" was at that time reserved to prefects of the pretorium, certain military officers, and so on. The title was conferred by the sovereign, and in his epistolary Cassiodorus gives the formulary.[2] As may be seen, St. Benedict also had relations with the aristocracy of the province, and not only with the poor.

[2] *Variarum*, Bk. VI, chap. 2.

CHAPTER XLVIII

The Possessed Cleric

IF the fame of so many miracles drew to the monastery a continuous pilgrimage of the poor and the afflicted who sought comfort and aid, the episcopate of the Campania also directed its attention thither. Besides his relations with the Apostolic See, which, as John IV attests, numbered St. Benedict among the abbots "of this city of Rome," we learn from St. Gregory's biography that the Patriarch stood close to three bishops in particular: Constance, the bishop of Aquino; Germanus of Capua, which was regarded almost as a metropolitan see; and finally with the distant bishop of Canosa, Sabinus by name. Both Germanus and Sabinus were well known in diplomatic circles because of very important missions they had carried out at Constantinople and at Ravenna.

At that time the diocese of Aquino evidently did not amount to much. When in 573 Constance came to die, thinking perhaps of the prophecy of St. Benedict about the Lombard invasion and himself divining the future, he announced that after him would come a stableman, then a laundryman, and then—then no more. As a matter of fact, when the Lombards arrived about 589 and occupied Monte Cassino, the city of Aquino also was destroyed. Thenceforth, as St. Gregory well observes, episcopal elections became impossible, since both the flock and the electors were wanting. Of Aquino scarcely even a few ruins remained standing.[1]

[1] When the enemy arrived, the Bishop of Aquino was an old laundryman, by name Jovinus.
It is noteworthy that during the invasion of Zoto, just as the monks of Cassino, so also

Some are of the opinion that Bishop Victor of Capua wrote a letter to this Bishop Constance to accompany a scriptural work requested by the latter. The book in question is a liturgical lectionary, with scriptural pericopes assigned to the various feasts of the ecclesiastical year. It is noteworthy that in Lent, in accordance with the custom still followed in the Ambrosian rite, there are added biblical excerpts of a moral character for the instruction of the catechumens.[2]

This attempt of the bishops to attain liturgical unity in the territory about Monte Cassino and Capua is interesting. St. Benedict could not remain apart from this movement, the more so since this trend toward unification was part of the vast pontifical plan to bring about unity also in the religious life in Italy by means of an identical monastic Rule.

St. Gregory gives us to understand that the most cordial relations of friendship and service existed between Constance and the monks of Cassino. Those "religious and truthful men" who described to the Pope the last hours of the holy bishop were none other than the Cassinese monks who had betaken themselves to the Lateran. Earlier I hinted that St. Benedict must have been tied to Constance by special bonds of charity and canonical subjection, for it was by his action that the Patriarch received the mission to work among the pagans of Casinum. The juridical practice of the sixth century allows of no doubt in the matter. When the episcopal see of Casinum became widowed, the Apostolic See united it to the neighboring diocese of Aquino, according to formula 20 of the *Liber diurnus.*[3]

Among the clergy of Aquino, there was at the time a poor cleric, who for several years seemed to be possessed by the devil. Constance, his bishop, without attempting a cure himself, had sent him on pilgrimage to various churches of martyrs—Pope Zachary says "cemeteries," and thus brings us directly to Rome—that he might be healed.

---

the metropolitan of Capua, Fuscus, went to Rome, where he died. Part of the clergy withdrew to Naples. The city of Capua remained so abandoned that St. Gregory had to give over its government to the neighboring bishop of Nola (*Epist.,* Bk. V, nos. 13 f.).

[2] *PL,* XXX, 501–4; cf. G. Morin, *Rev. Bénéd.,* VII, 416–23.

[3] St. Gregory sings the praises of Bishop Constance in Book III of the *Dialogues* (chap. 8). His informants at Rome had told him of many wonderful deeds performed by him, among others that he was endowed with a prophetic spirit. He was much beloved by his people; when his last hour drew nigh, they shed tears as they stood about his bed: ". . . *discessurus pater amabilis plangeretur.*"

But the poor man, instead of being cured, became worse. Finally, not knowing any longer to what saint in heaven to turn, the bishop decided to have recourse to those still on earth. Accordingly he had someone accompany the youth to Monte Cassino, so that the Abbot, who had healed so many others, might do the same for this cleric, who would then be in a position to render valuable services to the diocese.

When the cleric arrived at the monastery, the saint pronounced the customary exorcisms—"*Iesu Christo Domino preces fundens*"—and forced the devil to leave. This time Satan did not wait for a second injunction, because he had not forgotten the blows and slaps he received on former occasions. Then St. Benedict said to the cleric: "Go, but beware of eating flesh and of ascending to holy orders. Should you ever dare to ascend to the Lord's altar, you will immediately fall back into the power of the devil." Already a canon of Gelasius I of the year 494 forbade those who had been possessed from receiving the sacred orders.[4]

The cleric promised, and for many years he forgot neither his former condition nor the papal prohibition of which his spiritual physician had reminded him. But with the passage of time, since at Aquino occasionally some younger man was promoted to orders and passed him by, he finally appealed to his bishop and succeeded in having himself ordained. Benedict was dead by that time, and probably also Constance, who was aware of the situation. The cleric felt that now, after twenty-five years and more, with a new bishop, Andrew—a gentle soul, formerly a stableman—the papal veto had ceased in the general confusion and upheaval of the period. But the devil did not seem to think so. He afflicted him worse than ever before and tormented him to such an extent that finally the unfortunate man died impinged on the horns of that dragon. At Aquino some recalled the words of Benedict, and the cleric's horrible death made a deep impression upon the faithful. Now let us seek to draw a bit of moral teaching for ourselves out of this brief story of Gregory.

Evidently God did not desire this cleric for the service of the altar; and, in order that worse things should not befall him, He had allowed that the devil, like a snarling dog, should stand at the entrance to the

---

[4] "*Illicita . . . ut demoniacis, similibusque passionibus irretitis, ministeria sacrosancta tractare tribuatur*" (*Ad episc. Lucan.*, no. 21).

sanctuary, lest the other should rashly attempt to enter. A man warned is half saved. The cleric, unfortunately, chose to neglect the admonition and he lived to regret it. Certainly if St. Benedict, a priest himself in the diocesan territory of Aquino or Casinum, gave him a strict command not to intrude himself into the sanctuary, it was because by a light from above he had read the cleric's heart and had perceived that he was unworthy and not called to become a priest. For this very reason God had permitted the affliction of possession, which in the canon law of the time constituted a permanent impediment for holy orders.

The word "rashly" which the biographer puts in the mouth of the saint here supplies the key to a better understanding of the mystery of this vocation gone awry. The man of God, then, forbids the cleric of Aquino lest he ascend to profane holy orders. This injunction seems to be an indication that, besides the diabolical affliction, there was some occult fault in his preceding life which made him perpetually unsuitable for the sacred ministry. We should not pass over this lesson lightly. The Church has profited well from it and as a result has drawn up a list of irregularities that exclude definitely from the service of the altar.

St. Benedict was so impressed with the necessity that the ministers of the sanctuary should bring to the altar the purity and the sanctity befitting their position—"*qui dignus sit sacerdotio fungi*"—that he devoted one entire chapter of the Rule to this subject (chap. 62). Monks may indeed be elevated to the dignity of the priesthood. This calls for a pure spirit in a chaste body, a spirit that is zealous for discipline and, above all, humble.

That is precisely what Pope Gelasius I had demanded in writing to the bishops of Lucania half a century earlier. The Pope does, indeed, shorten the canonical interstices in favor of the monastic state, and permits monks to receive all the orders up to the priesthood within the course of a single year. But he insists that their preceding life must be without blemish and he desires that the holiness of their monastic discipline should supply for what the observance of the interstices, required of other clerics, would have conferred on them.[5]

---

[5] "*Cui tamen quod annorum interstitia fuerant collatura, sancti propositi sponte suscepta doceatur praestitisse devotio*" (loc. cit., no. 3).

According to St. Benedict, sacred ordination in no way must diminish the obligation of claustral observance; but the monk, in order to be truly worthy of the priesthood, must "ever more and more progress toward God."

This short chapter in St. Benedict's rule on the sanctity required for the priestly state has brought forth for the Catholic Church that galaxy of popes, bishops, and priests who for fourteen centuries and more have been formed for the sacred ministry in "the school of the Lord's service."

CHAPTER XLIX

Raising a Child to Life

UNTIL its recent destruction, there used to be a small niche with a statue of St. Benedict, dating from the fifteenth century, near the entrance to the abbey of Monte Cassino. Into the base of this niche was incorporated a piece of the rough rock of the mountain, respectfully covered with a wooden guard. Perhaps that was the only stone of Monte Cassino that remained in its primitive position after all the changes and reconstructions the monastery underwent. The reason for the respect shown this stone is that fourteen centuries ago St. Benedict knelt on that rock to call a dead child back to life.

Here is Gregory's simple account of the incident. One day, when the Patriarch had gone forth with his monks to labor in the fields, an exhausted peasant arrived at the monastery, carrying his dead child in his arms. He asked where the Abbot was. Upon learning that he was in the field, the man deposited the corpse on the threshold and ran to seek him. When he espied St. Benedict from a distance as he was returning from the labor with his monks, he began to cry out in an anguished voice: "Give me back my son! Give me back my son!"

When Benedict heard these words, and still more when he saw that face, bronzed by the sun, on which, however, were traced the lines of great sorrow, not grasping what the peasant meant, he said: "Have I taken your son?" Most likely he was thinking of the depredations of the Goths.

"No," replied the poor man, "but he is dead. Come, you must restore him to life for me."

Here, reader, pause to consider. In the lives of the saints we do not often find that someone came to them and said simply: "Raise this corpse to life," as one might say to a priest: "Here is a dollar. Celebrate a Mass for my deceased relative."

If the peasants of the territory of Cassino dared so much with St. Benedict, we must conclude that their faith in the Patriarch was as great as the faith of the Canaanite woman of the Gospel; this faith was based on such virtues and prodigies as to justify the belief of these good people that St. Benedict was the master of life and death. The man in question made his demand with such vehemence as not even to allow of discussion about the possibility of the miracle.

The monks were touched; they readily took the part of the afflicted father and begged the saint to console him. This was too much. They expected him to repeat the deeds of Peter, of Paul, of Martin of Tours, and to call the dead back to life. It is true that on another occasion he had restored the young monk Severus whose bones had been crushed by a falling wall. But then there was question of overcoming the devil, who did not wish to see the monastery built. The man of God in his humility was greatly perturbed and he attempted to dissuade his disciples, but to no purpose.

"Leave us be, leave us be, my brethren," he said. "These things are not for us, but for the holy apostles who rest in Rome. Why do you wish to impose on us a responsibility which is beyond our strength?" It is to be noted that here as well as in the Rule, St. Benedict always uses the majestic plural "we," as was done by persons in authority in the fifth and sixth centuries.

The poor peasant, who by reason of the bitterness of his sorrow scarcely knew what was going on, stood there like a stone, without grasping this humility. Then he began in his simple but efficacious jargon to protest and swear that he would leave the place only with his son restored to life.

"Where is the dead boy?" asked St. Benedict.

"The corpse is lying on the threshold of the monastery," replied the father.

When St. Benedict arrived at the gate, he saw the frail, cold little body and he knelt down to pray. The monks hardly breathed, awaiting the miracle. Imitating the action of the prophets Elias and Eliseus, the Abbot stretched himself over the cold corpse as if to melt the ice of death with the warmth of his divine love. Then, raising his hands and eyes to heaven, he said: "O Lord, look not upon my sins, but consider the faith of this man, who desires to see his son alive, and give back to this little body the soul which Thou has called to Thyself." Scarcely had he finished this prayer when the dead boy began to tremble and to breathe; he opened his eyes and finally moved sluggishly as if awaking from a deep sleep.

The father and the others were amazed. They seemed to be present at some scene of the Gospel, when, for example, after restoring to life the young man at the gate of Naim, Jesus took him by the hand and gave him back to his mother. The wonder-worker did the same. While the poor peasant looked on in stupefaction, scarcely daring to believe his eyes, the saint took the hand of the boy and ordered him to rise. The boy immediately threw himself into the arms of his father. Naturally they were both invited to remain at the monastery for dinner. On the way back to their village, the father and son everywhere spread the news of the marvelous happening. Instead of being carried to the cemetery, it was necessary only to go to Monte Cassino to have life restored!

This is already the second miracle of the kind worked by St. Benedict of which the biographer has left a record. Contrary to the case of the young monk Severus, who was called from death to life in the secrecy of his cell, the Patriarch worked the new miracle in the presence of the community and other witnesses, as Christ did with Lazarus. The fame of the miracle left such a deep impression that, even apart from St. Gregory's narrative, its memory remained localized in the rough stone of the mountain with the altar erected over it by the faith of our medieval ancestors.

It is not out of place to call attention to the circumstance in which the miracle was performed. St. Benedict had gone to work in the fields with his monks. On other occasions the biographer pictures the saint as living more or less apart from the community, engaged in prayer or meditating on the Sacred Scriptures. Chapter 48 of the Rule, "Of the Daily Manual Labor," thus receives its most authentic confirmation. The hands that penned the immortal pages of the Rule, the hands that at their mere touch healed lepers, were also hardened and cal-loused from using the spade and guiding the plow in the task of clearing the wooded fields of Italy. *"Ora et labora."* That prayer and that work gave the world the civilization of the Middle Ages.

CHAPTER L

The Death of Germanus of Capua

GERMANUS OF CAPUA was one of the most famous men of his time; indeed, in 519 Pope Hormisdas sent him to Constantinople in the quality of a legate to work for the reconciliation of the East with the Roman See. St. Benedict and he must have understood each other very well, as is customary with saints. Furthermore, the Bishop of Capua acted as the metropolitan of the territory, though he did not have the title, and the apostolate of the Abbot of Monte Cassino of necessity fell under the hierarchical jurisdiction of Germanus. Also patrimonial interests of the monastery of Monte Cassino in the territory of Capua brought the two into contact.

In the autumn of 540, on October 30, one of those splendid days a person finds so often in Latium and in the Campania at that time of year, the deacon Servandus arrived at Monte Cassino. He was the abbot of the monastery of St. Sebastian, which I have already mentioned. Several monks of that monastery accompanied him. It is quite understandable that they wished to sanctify this beautiful season by a trip to Monte Cassino. The deacon was a saintly man; he was wont to visit Cassino; and St. Benedict, who delighted in conversing with him on the attainment of the heavenly fatherland, had a deep affection for him. St. Gregory explicitly tells us that Servandus was outstanding for his spiritual doctrine.[1]

We can easily understand the friendship binding these two great souls together. It was not only the simple, the Goths, the poor peasants

[1] ". . . idem quoque vir doctrina gratiae caelestis influebat."

of the villages about Casinum, who flocked to the abbey. At times there were also persons of distinction, ecclesiastical dignitaries. The names of some of them have come down to us.

For these periodic visits to the Patriarch of monks, St. Sabinus journeyed all the way from Apulia. Servandus with his monks came from Alatri; the Gothic king, Totila, not so much invited Benedict to approach him, but rather he himself requested an audience in order to converse with him. Evidently we are here dealing with an extraordinary person who exercises a profound influence on the world of his time. His authority, backed up by the gift of miracles, became far greater than that which the hierarchical degree of abbot—missioner of Casinum—would have conferred on him. Every time Pope Zachary mentions him, he finds occasion, in the Greek manner, to attribute some beautiful title to him. Most frequently he calls him "the wonder-working father."

Speaking of paradise and of the Blessed Trinity, the two abbots spent that mild autumn day in a holy manner. And at Monte Cassino this season is wonderful. When evening came, Benedict had the beds for the monk guests prepared in the common monastic dormitory, but the deacon Servandus he lodged in the room on the ground floor of the tower. It was the private study of the saint, whence a simple ladder led to the cell above, where he had his couch. Gregory, who in his customary manner describes the most minute topographical details of Monte Cassino, again here reveals the pen of the scholar, who, before writing the story of St. Benedict, perhaps went to study it and to reconstruct it on the spot.

In the deep of the night, while the monks slept profoundly in their large hall opposite the entrance to the monastery,[2] the holy Patriarch had already anticipated the hour for the common night prayer. In accordance with the deep appreciation of nature which the great friends of God possess, he enjoyed praying at his window; thence on a moonlit night with the heavens full of sparkling stars he could see a goodly portion of the *Campania felix*, watered by the Rapido and the noisy Liri. Several times while at Monte Cassino, I have enjoyed the same vast panorama by the light of the moon. It was indeed beauti-

[2] ". . . *ante eamdem vero turrim largius erat habitaculum in quo utriusque discipuli quiescebant*" (chap. 35).

ful; but to grasp it more fully, something was lacking to me—the spiritual esthetic sense of St. Benedict.

Little by little as, with his eyes fixed on the stars above, he sank into divine contemplation, the saint felt the fire of love grow in his heart. He stood at the window, since by now the narrow cell seemed to suffocate him. For him the starry firmament was like an embroidered curtain that veiled the holy of holies. Suddenly his mind felt itself transported beyond the other side of the curtain in order to contemplate, face to face, Him who dwells in light inaccessible and sits above the thrones and cherubim.

Here the mystical writers, beginning with St. Gregory, treat at length of the nature of this elevation of the holy Patriarch. St. Bonaventure asserts that the seer at that time contemplated God and saw all things in Him: "The world was not concentrated in one ray of the sun, but his spirit became enlarged, because he saw all things in Him, in comparison with whose greatness every creature is narrow and small." [3] The Angelic Doctor does not express himself clearly on the point; [4] but Pope Urban VIII in a bull treating of the Patriarch says that the saint, while still living on earth, merited to see his Creator and all other things in Him. [5]

This mass of knowledge infused into the saint from above gives a great authority to his monastic Code, so much so that the biographer numbers it among his greater miracles. While leaving the mystic doctors to dispute whether or not St. Benedict had the divine essence revealed to him, I wish to observe that, unfortunately, we lack the necessary data to treat of this question. [6]

According to Gregory's narrative, St. Benedict merely related that he had seen the entire earth as it were immersed in the sea of light of the Creator. To contemplate this vision, it was not creation that was, so to speak, seen from the wrong end of a telescope, but his soul was apparently immersed in God and enlarged in such a fashion that in one glance and in a single ray of light he was able to contemplate the entire work of God in the created world.

---

[3] *De luminar. eccl.*, Serm. 20.

[4] IIa IIae q. 180, a.5 ad 3.

[5] "*Deum ipsum et in ipso Deo adhuc mortalis, omne quod infra Deum est videre meruerit*" (Tamburin., Vol. II, disput. XXIV, quaest. 5).

[6] Cf. A. Stolz, *Doctrine of Spiritual Perfection*, pp. 73 f.

Gregory wished to explain the mystic nature of this elevation to Peter the Deacon and he put it thus: "For the soul that sees the Creator every creature becomes small." On that night a twofold light illumined St. Benedict: first the sensible vision which disclosed to his eyes the work of the Creator in the world; then the intellectual light that snatched up the Patriarch in God and showed him, in part, the divine beauty (". . . animae videnti Creatorem").

The Scholastics have variously commented on Gregory's narrative of the vision, explaining this kind of duplication of the ecstatic, which rises above itself to see in God all earthly things beneath it. But let us beware of putting into Gregory's mouth words he did not say. The great Pope wisely spoke of "some little part of the light of the Creator" and not of the divine essence. Further, the biographer learned of this vision from two series of witnesses de auditu, and we must not seek in their words the absolute precision of language which modern mystical theologians would demand.

Gregory simply tells us of a mystical rapture, in which, to a first sensible vision of an intense illumination which dispelled the darkness of the night and which partially could also be seen by the deacon Servandus, was added a great intellectual light in which Benedict was lifted above himself to the contemplation of the attributes of God.

It is to be noted that St. Benedict was so well prepared and strengthened for this highest kind of mystical communication with heaven that his organism did not fall into an ecstasy or a faint. He remained standing at the window, fully conscious of himself; as a matter of fact, he repeatedly and with a loud voice called to the deacon, who slept in the room below him, to come so that he, too, might see the vision.

The excited voice of the holy Patriarch awakened Servandus and caused him to marvel; he had always known the Abbot as a calm man, completely master of himself. Understanding that something truly extraordinary must have happened, he was disturbed ("insolito tanti viri clamore turbatus"), rose, and hurried up the ladder to the saint's side. Benedict at the window pointed out to him the light that was still shining in the sky in the direction of Capua and told him what he had seen. He added that at that very time the angels were bearing to heaven the soul of Bishop Germanus in the form of a fiery sphere.

Without waiting, St. Benedict during that same moonlit night which illumined the path down the mountain, decided to send a messenger to the good monk Theoprobus, who lived in the town below to see after the affairs of the monastery, instructing him to dispatch a courier immediately to Capua to get news of the Bishop.[7]

Most likely the courier was one of the slaves belonging to the monastery; they were used for the cultivation of the monastery's lands, as we learn from the letters of St. Gregory. That is the reason why St. Benedict, from the summit of the mountain, orders Theoprobus to take care of the matter of sending a messenger.

The distance from Cassino to Capua is about sixty-three miles. If there had been only a question of checking the news about Germanus, such haste would hardly have been required. After all, it would have sufficed to note the day and the hour and then at some convenient time obtain the necessary confirmation. If, then, the holy Abbot desired a slave to ride posthaste to Capua that very night to inquire about Germanus, some other reason must be sought for his anxiety and concern. At that time it was customary for ecclesiastics to hasten to give the last honors to their proper bishop or metropolitan. Indeed, usually a bishop was not buried until all the other bishops of the province had gathered to celebrate the obsequies.[8]

In fact the messenger sent to Capua by Theoprobus learned that Germanus had indeed died at the hour indicated.

The declaration of St. Benedict on the heavenly glory of the Bishop of Capua was equivalent in those days to a bull of canonization. Our present Martyrology for October 30 mentions the feast of St. Ger-

---

[7] Regarding the administration of the abbey's property in those early times, we have no knowledge. Both the Rule and the biographer refer to land holdings, but they do not give any details. The impression arises, however, that the patrimony was already extensive, if for its better administration Benedict kept the monk Theoprobus stationed at Casinum and Formosus at Capua.

[8] Regarding this custom, see Martène, *De antiquis ecclesiae ritibus*, III, 1037 ff. In 524 the Council of Valence ordered: "*Si quis autem Antistes obitu repentino discesserit, et conlimitanei sacerdotes de longinquo minime adesse potuerint, uno die tantum cum nocte exanimatus corpusculum sacerdotis maneat . . . et mos antiquus in sepeliendis sacerdotibus servetur*" (can. 4). Similarly the second Council of Orleans laid down: "*Nullus episcopus ad sepeliendum episcopum conficta occasione dissimulet, ne cuiuslibet corpusculum diutius inhumatum, negligentia interveniente, solvatur*" (can. 5).

manus, basing itself simply on the authority of the seer of Monte Cassino.

Quite likely St. Benedict hastened to the funeral, and on this occasion saw the colleagues of St. Formosus, namely, those few monks
who in the vicinity of Capua looked after the interests of the monastery.

What spiritual relations bound together the Apostle of Casinum
and the deceased Bishop of Capua? If Benedict took such a great
interest in him and called Servandus two or three times to come to
see the light which illumined the sky toward Capua, this is an indication that some contact existed, though we do not know the details.
Noteworthy is the point that St. Benedict saw Germanus ascending
to heaven in the form of a fiery sphere, while later on he will contemplate St. Scholastica going to her divine Spouse in the guise of
a white dove. Both of these symbols are appropriate. It is well that the
virgin should wing her way to heaven "like the doves called by desire"; and it is fitting that the Bishop of Capua should go to his eternal
reward in the form of a fiery sphere since, by his zeal and his preaching, he had inflamed the hearts of the multitude.

I have already hinted at the influence which this chapter of St.
Gregory's narrative exercised on the mystical literature of the Middle
Ages. Without doubt the vision worked still more powerfully on the
soul of the seer himself. As St. Paul after being raised to the third
heaven must have felt profoundly changed in mind and will, so the
Patriarch of Cassino, after contemplating in a single and simple ray
of divine light whatever is below the infinite Good, had to begin a
new life. Henceforth he saw all human affairs in their one and simple
cause, God Himself.

His soul was enlarged in God, as St. Gregory well explains: "The
spirit of the seer was dilatated; enraptured in God, he was able to comprehend without difficulty whatever is below God." The vision, indeed, was transient, but its effects could no longer be blotted out of
the prophet's soul.

After being raised to the third heaven, the apostle Paul declared
that he could in no way express in human language what he had been
privileged to see, that he found in this world neither concepts nor
words that were suitable for the purpose. No doubt the same thing

happened to St. Benedict. In the Rule he alludes precisely to this impossibility of translating into human idiom what he felt in his heart: "For as we advance in the religious life and in faith, our hearts expand and we run the way of God's commandments with unspeakable sweetness of love" (Prol.). It may not be out of place to mention that St. Gregory, after narrating this sublime rapture of the Patriarch, follows with chapter 36, concerning the quasi-miraculous composition of the *Regula monasteriorum;* as if to insinuate that it was precisely in this heavenly light that the monastic Code was first conceived and then put down on parchment.

After this time St. Benedict's longing for heaven increased. During the seven years of his life that remained, he spoke of and sighed only for paradise. Other saints, his contemporaries, amid great perils undertook the journey to Monte Cassino merely to have the satisfaction of tasting beforehand the joys of heaven by discoursing with St. Benedict. When, in the Rule, among the instruments of good works he mentions, "To desire eternal life with all the passion of the spirit," it was because in reality during his last years here below he continued to repeat with the Apostle: "I desire to depart and to be with Christ" (Phil. 1:23).

From that night on which he contemplated the divine light in heaven, he underwent also bodily changes, as did Moses when he descended from Mount Sinai. This is how the liturgy of the Church describes him: "The man of God had a serene countenance and an angelic behavior. An atmosphere of heavenly light enveloped him, so that, though still living on earth, his dwelling was in the heavenly places."

In his *De anima* (chap. 12), Cassiodorus traces the portrait of a monk who, after struggling against his vices in the desert, has become a master of the spiritual life and an apostle among the faithful. "His countenance is always cheerful and serene, while its pallor and emaciation give it a certain majesty. It is tranquil, though always bathed in tears. A long beard confers reverence, while he appears, without any affectation, most neat in his garb. Indeed, virtue is wont to render men more beautiful even in the midst of troublesome affairs. His eyes are joyful and mild in their modesty. His word is truthful, penetrates the hearts of those who are well disposed; he seeks to infuse into all the love of God with which he himself is filled. The very tone of his voice is controlled, so that, while it cannot be said to be so low as almost to approach silence, on the other hand it is not so loud as to become strident. Adversities do not cast him down; prosperity does not make him giddy.

"His external behavior and his life are in agreement; he might be said to be the temple and the dwelling of all the virtues. His appearance never changes, thus showing forth a constancy of spirit. His step is neither halting nor hurried. In his relations with others he does not seek his own advantage and he does not use personal bias in reproving others. His counsel is righteous, however he teaches without arrogance. Despite all his humility, he knows how to preserve his independence; even in severity he is charitable. To be separated from him is as difficult as to depart from this life.

"While he was yet in his beloved solitude, no sensuality ever conquered him, no persecution succeeded in making him bitter. He is not blown up with pride, envies no one, speaks no word to his brethren that he must afterward regret, nor does he allow others to speak harsh words in his presence. When he was in solitude, as a valiant warrior he overcame the call of his carnal passions with the help of God. His tunic—and he has but one—just like his skin, gives forth a sweeter fragrance than all the perfumes of India, thus proving that the human body can have its own good odor, provided it be not defiled with surfeiting, by reason of which it gives forth a stench.

"It can easily be seen that divine Omnipotence deigns to visit such a man, when we ourselves are delighted by his presence. There is no need to learn further details concerning him, since divine inspiration directly makes him known to us. . . . After treating at length of the soul, we have also put down with regard to the human body what we ourselves have seen."

Thus far Cassiodorus. It is an accurate portrait, though the artist left it anonymous, since it was made of a person during his lifetime. But the details are extremely concrete: he is a monk, indeed an abbot who wears a single tunic. The long beard,[9] the gait, grave and

9 In the letter of the clergy of Milan to the Frankish legates on their departure for Constantinople about the year 551, reference is made to the beard of Pope Vigilius: "*Postea vero ipsum sanctum Papam alii a pedibus, alii a capillis et barba tantum crudeliter abstrahebant*" (Mansi, *Summa concil.*, IX, 154).

measured, the grace which the solitary life conferred on him, make him the more venerable. His teaching, modest and without arrogance, the attraction he exerts on others, so that no one ever wishes to depart from him; intolerance of words that are scurrilous and useless; the perfume that is given off by his person and his very garments: these are all details that coincide in a marvelous manner with so many phrases of the Rule of St. Benedict, particularly where are described the higher degrees of the ladder of humility regarding the posture of the body, the tone of the voice, and so on.

Cassiodorus asserts that he speaks of what he himself saw and gives the assurance that he knew such a man—*"non admonitus intelligit, quem caelesti inspiratione cognoscit."* Noteworthy is the detail regarding the love of cleanliness and the fragrance given off by the garments. More interesting still, the reference to the carnal temptations overcome in the solitude and to the persecutions there suffered.

Cassiodorus wrote his *De anima* shortly after he retired from the court of Ravenna (about 540) and before he settled down at Vivarium. St. Benedict was still living at that time, and this fact explains why the author, after painting his portrait, left it anonymous, lest he offend the saint's modesty. I seek in vain in the hagiography of the period for some other personage to which this selection from *De anima* might apply: one who was so endowed with heavenly gifts; one who exerted so powerful an influence that people preferred to die rather than be separated from him; or one whose very garments diffused a chaste odor. The author further affirms that he had relations with this man, whom he knew by divine inspiration (*"cum charitate districtus"*).

I ask who this extraordinary personage was whom the author met about 540, not at Ravenna, but probably in Rome. At first glance one might think of Dionysius Exiguus, with whom Cassiodorus had intimate scientific and spiritual relations and whose eulogy he wrote in chapter 23 of *De institutione*. But the picture he draws there does not at all correspond to the portrait we find delineated in his *De anima*.

Dionysius is a famous writer and professor in Rome; although a monk, he lives in the midst of the world and often takes part in banquets together with the matrons and aristocracy of the capital. He is Scythian by birth, but Roman in outlook and behavior. Naturally, Dionysius also has his enemies, who censure his doctrine as being not

THE DEATH OF GERMANUS OF CAPUA

entirely orthodox. But Cassiodorus testifies that, notwithstanding the calumnies of the envious, Dionysius is truly a saint, that he died in the peace and communion of the Catholic Church. Hence his books can be assiduously studied.

We are, then, far from the ascetic described in the *De anima,* who wears only a tunic, has a beard, loves solitude, and edifies all by his holy life. Who can it be? If it is not Dionysius Exiguus, in Rome there is but one other name: that of St. Benedict, "the abbot of this city of Rome," as John IV calls him.

CHAPTER LI

Bishop Victor of Capua

―――――――

TOWARD the end of February, 541, Victor succeeded to the see of Capua; he occupied it for thirteen years and enjoyed the reputation of a saint. Quite possibly Benedict had close relations also with him. Victor was above all a scholar; he has left several writings. To him is ascribed a scriptural lectionary for the various feasts of the liturgical cycle, with a prefatory letter addressed to a certain Constance, who is readily identified as the bishop of Aquino (527–73). In it the author declares that the work was composed at the instance of Constance himself.

The use of lectionaries was widespread in all the churches at that time. Since, however, the texts varied from place to place, the metropolitan of Capua undertook to edit one which was to become common, to be received and spread in the entire Campania, so as to bring about a certain degree of uniformity in the liturgy. It is more than likely that St. Benedict immediately had a copy of the new lectionary of Capua made for use in his monastery.

This selfsame Victor, during the first years of his episcopate, caused to be transcribed the so-called *Codex Fuldensis* of the Sacred Scriptures, which he then corrected with his own hand. During those years of wars and repeated occupation of the territory—now by Totila, now by the Greeks—the copyist, with a truly Benedictine patience, persisted in his transcription of the famous codex. Was he perhaps a monk of Monte Cassino?

Interesting to note is the fact that the Gospels are presented in a kind of "harmony," recalling to a certain extent the *Diatesseron* of Tatian. In all probability also at Monte Cassino the monks used this "harmony" of the Gospels of the church of Capua. A faint allusion to it may be seen in the terminology used by St. Benedict in the Rule: *"lectionem de Evangelia, canticum de Evangelia,"* and so on, always using the plural form (chaps. 11, 13).

When the Patriarch commands in chapter 9 of the Rule that in the night Office the Sacred Scriptures be read together with "the explanations of them which have been made by well-known and orthodox Catholic Fathers," he doubtless was referring to an extensive collection of excerpts from the Fathers which at that time was preserved in the library of the monastery. Victor of Capua manifested the same preoccupation when he published the translation of the biblical scholia of Polycarp of Smyrna, of Origen, of Basil, of Diodorus of Tarsus, of Severianus of Gabala. Here then are "explanations of the Scriptures by well-known and orthodox Fathers," collected for the region of the Campania by the Bishop of Capua himself. Such a similarity between the liturgical work of Victor and the ordinances of the Rule is very meaningful.

The metropolitan Victor jealously guarded the codex of the Gospel "harmony," today known under the title of *Codex Fuldensis*. At the end of the Acts of the Apostles and of the Apocalypse, we find in cursive script some autograph annotations, from which we learn that he collated the manuscript for the first time in Constantine's basilica on April 19, 546, and again a second time on April 12, 547. It seems that he made an annual journey to Rome, even when no pope was there. On the way thither, no doubt a stop was obligatory at Monte Cassino.

CHAPTER LII

Among the Pagans and Jews at Terracina

It is incredible that, while St. Benedict propagated the monastic life by founding twelve monasteries at Subiaco, he should have remained inactive at Monte Cassino, not attempting to spread the discipline of the Rule in that vast region. I have already spoken of the erection of the Lateran monastery of St. Pancratius; at the latest this foundation was made about 545.

Quite naturally St. Gregory, all intent on weaving together the *fioretti*, tells us nothing of the relations of the Abbot of Monte Cassino with the Pope and the Lateran court, just as he has furnished us with no details about the Roman aristocracy, which from the beginning of the sixth century flocked to St. Benedict and entrusted its children to him, so that they might be formed to a virtuous life in the school of St. Clement's monastery.

The biographer does, indeed, mention the *Monasterium Later-anense*, but he presupposes that the Roman reader is already well acquainted with the story of that foundation. Pope John IV in 641, some forty years after St. Gregory, also makes a reference to this Roman undertaking of St. Benedict, and speaks of him as the Abbot "of this city of Rome." Pope John IV likewise takes it for granted that the facts are known to all, and hence he abstains from giving any further details.

Among the various monasteries founded by the Patriarch in the

Campania is that of St. Stephen at Terracina. The land and the money for it were furnished by an anonymous donor. At Terracina, or rather, as St. Gregory says, in the *castellum* of Terracina, besides a strong group of pagans, still compact and very active till the end of the sixth century, there must have been a large and influential colony of Jews. Their synagogue was situated only a few steps from the parish church; frequently the voices of the Jews, as they sang their psalms in the synagogue, were mingled with the psalmody of the faithful in the sanctuary dedicated to Christ.[1] A strong monastery of missionary monks was, therefore, an opportune means of paralyzing in that town the twofold deleterious influence of the non-Christian folk. In a word, also at Terracina bishop and authorities had recourse to the same expedients that had so well proved their worth at Casinum.

It must be admitted, however, that the fruit produced was not very abundant, since half a century later St. Gregory wrote to Bishop Agnellus of Terracina: "News has reached Us that certain men there . . . worship trees and perpetrate many other forbidden deeds against the Christian faith." [2] In agreement with the episcopal authority, St. Benedict accepted the offer and sent thither a small group of monks, at whose head was an abbot, assisted by a prior or *praepositus*.[3] There was no need to speak of deans at this point, because the community was so small.

When he sent off his disciples, St. Benedict said, "Go and await me on that day," mentioning it to them. "I myself will come and draw the plan for the new monastery: where the oratory is to be, where the refectory for the community, the guest house, and whatever else is necessary for the regular life of a monastery." After receiving the Abbot's blessing, the little colony departed from Monte Cassino, and during the first days of their sojourn on the hill, whence the eye could reach the blue waters of the sea of Anxur, the monks consoled themselves with the thought that the Patriarch would soon come to visit

---

[1] *Epist.*, Bk. I, no. 10.

[2] *Epist.*, Bk. VIII, no. 18.

[3] To be exact, once Gregory calls him *praepositus* and once *secundus*. In practice, the δευτεράριος of the Greeks assisted the abbot particularly in the material management of the monastery; hence, the cellarer.

In the Council of Constantinople, held under the presidency of Patriarch Menna in the absence of Pope Vigilius, we find, among others, the following signatures to the acts: Φλαβιάνος πρεσβύτερος καὶ δευτεράριος, Ἀναστάσιος πρεσβύτερος καὶ δευτεράριος.

them. But God watched over him. Possibly that trip to Terracina was not opportune, because Jews and pagans had some old accounts to settle with him.

In the meanwhile the small group of monks at Terracina prepared to the best of their ability to receive the Abbot and the monks who would accompany him. What was their disappointment when St. Benedict did not put in his appearance on the appointed day! They awaited him in the forenoon; they looked for him in the afternoon; even during the following days they watched for his coming. When he did not arrive and no news came from Monte Cassino, they did not know what to think. Merely living in that environment of Jews and idolaters made their stay rather unpleasant. The fact that they were apparently forgotten at Monte Cassino increased their dislike of the place.

Then one night the new abbot had a dream. It seemed to him that St. Benedict had visited the spot where the community was to be established and that he had examined the old structure in his presence, had explained the plans of the building, indicating very carefully what parts were to be remodeled so that it might be adapted for monastic uses. When the abbot related this dream to the prior in the morning, the new abbot learned to his surprise that the prior, too, had had a dream very like his own. At the time they thought no more of the coincidence. It is well known that not rarely dreams reflect one's waking thoughts of the previous day.

After a few more days had passed in aimless waiting, the two superiors, not knowing what to think, returned anxiously to Monte Cassino and complained to the Father that he had failed to keep his promise.

Benedict listened to them with a quiet smile and then replied: "Why, O my brethren, why do you speak thus? Did I not come as I had promised?"

The others, thoroughly confused, asked: "But when, O Father, did you come?"

The saint made answer: "Is it not true that while you two were sleeping, I came thither and explained the entire work to be undertaken? Go now and build according to what was shown to you in the dream."

With such a man it was useless to argue. If he chose not to go to

Terracina, he doubtless had a good reason for it. Marveling at the holiness of the master, whose spirit broke the bounds both of space and of time, the two disciples returned to the new monastery and undertook the work of remodeling according to the plan they had seen in their dream.

The Cassinese monastery of St. Stephen at Terracina is mentioned in a bull of Agapitus II of 995 and in a document of Leo IX of 1052. In 1641 the monks sold it to a Roman patrician, Giacomo Filonardi, who made an agricultural project of it. By the year 1706 scarcely the ruins of the monastery of St. Stephen remained.[4]

Here again St. Gregory adds a bit of comment to explain to Peter the Deacon this case of bilocation of the holy Patriarch. The prophet Habacuc, he observes, was carried in a moment from Judea to Babylon to provide a meal for Daniel. So also Benedict, in order to provide for the spiritual needs of the new foundation at Terracina, betook himself thither by night in spirit, appearing to the two superiors in a dream.

Among the monks sent to the new monastery at Terracina were two good brothers, Speciosus and Gregory; they were of noble extraction, were well gifted by God, and had acquitted themselves well in the customary course of the trivium and the quadrivium.[5]

Their retirement from the world created a bit of a stir among the people, because the two fervent novices, following the counsel of the Gospel, began by giving to the poor their considerable patrimony; then they handed themselves over to St. Benedict that he might make saints of them through the observance of the Rule. After spending some time at Terracina, Speciosus was transferred to the landed property near Capua, the better to look after the interests of the monastery.

It happened that one day, while standing at table with his companions, Gregory fell into what appeared to be a faint; but when he recovered his senses, he said he had seen his brother Speciosus die at that moment. In those days, the atmosphere of the disciples of St. Benedict was so saturated with the supernatural that it entered the mind of no one to question Gregory's statement.

[4] Cf. Contatore, *De historia Terracinnensi*, Rome, 1706; Moricca, *Gregorii Magni Dialogi*, Rome, 1924.
[5] *Dial.*, Bk. IV, chap. 8.

The vision was regarded as authentic. In fact, the abbot, taking into account the intense love which had united the two brothers in life and in death, allowed Gregory to set out immediately for Capua in order to be present at his brother's funeral. Unfortunately, when he arrived there, he discovered that Speciosus was already buried. But Gregory, inquiring about the details of his brother's death, ascertained that he had breathed his last at the very moment when he himself received the heavenly admonition. This phenomenon of telepathy by which the one brother perceived the other's death at a distance made a deep impression on the community. St. Gregory tells us that he learned of this incident from the first disciples of the Patriarch, those, namely, who succeeded him in the government of the monastery.

The authority of the Pontiff, who narrates the rare virtues of the two brothers, was so great in the Middle Ages that the name of Speciosus was inserted without hesitation in the Roman Martyrology on March 15.

On this occasion I cannot pass over in silence a circumstance which shows us the good-heartedness of St. Benedict. The two noble brothers loved each other holily in the Lord. The spiritual teaching of their master is not so rigid as to desire to tear the bonds of nature, sanctified by the grace of a vocation. For this reason Gregory and Speciosus are sent to Terracina together. Later Speciosus is temporarily assigned to the grange near Capua. But when he dies, the abbot immediately sends Gregory so that he may at least assist at the last rites of his beloved brother and thus pay nature its due. What humaneness there is in the Rule! The words of the Psalmist come to mind: "How good and pleasant it is for brethren to dwell together in unity" (Ps. 132).

The church of St. Stephen at Terracina recalls that other sanctuary dedicated to the saint, which from the eighth century stood outside the gate of Monte Cassino. Here, about the year 1103, during the remodeling of the old structure, were found the graves of the monks Paulinus and Augustine, together with two anonymous skeletons. The tradition that they were among the first disciples of St. Benedict found a ready confirmation on the lips of a possessed man who, according to Peter the Deacon, began to cry out: "Paulinus and Augustine, the disciples of Benedict, together with their two companions, are casting me out." When this event had been reported to Abbot Oderisius, he gave orders that the four bodies be buried "in the wall of the Church of St. Andrew the Apostle," behind the apse of St. Benedict and the infirmary of the monastery.[6] Near their grave was buried also Abbot Seniorettus: "He was entombed on the right side at the entrance to the cemetery, near the steps where the four disciples of the Blessed Benedict rest." [7]

[6] *Chron. Casin.*, Bk. IV, no. 23; *PL*, CLXXIII, 849.
[7] *PL, loc. cit.*, 927.

CHAPTER LIII

King Totila at the Feet of Benedict

WHILE on the heights of Monte Cassino even the angels stopped off to behold the marvels of that house of God, down below in the world the Goths and Greeks continued to do the work of the devil. The decrepit Roman Empire went tottering along, and now the Gothic kingdom also was beginning its meteoric decline.

After Uraias and Ildebald had been slain and Eraric had disappeared without much noise, the valiant Badwilla, more commonly known by the name of Totila, was proclaimed king. Like Theodoric, this sovereign in his government manifested certain qualities which would have been worthy of admiration if occasionally passion had not gotten the upper hand, bringing to the surface the atavistic tendencies of the former barbarian.

Scarcely had Totila succeeded to the throne, when he proposed to carry out the program of Theodoric with regard to the peaceful fusion of the two races. At the same time, however, he did not give up the plan of conquest. About the year 542, after recapturing a number of the cities of Emilia, the king moved on to the reconquest of Naples, going thither by the Via Latina at the head of his troops. The terror of the people in the villages about Casinum may be easily imagined.

In the Gothic army, be it said to Totila's credit, there reigned a sense of discipline. The soldiers never dared to begin sacking a town until the king first gave them the signal. To the poor peasants Totila presented himself as the avenger of the proletariat against the exactions of the fat Byzantines; in fact, Procopius writes of him, "Throughout Italy he did no harm to the peasants." [1] Once, in southern Italy, disregarding the petitions of his followers, he had one of his body-guards executed because he had raped the daughter of a Calabrian; he further ordered that the soldier's goods be given to the outraged woman. On that occasion Totila averred that by rendering justice the kingdom of the Goths would become strong, as the avarice of his predecessors had weakened it. Animated with such sentiments, Totila, putting off to a more favorable time the retaking of Rome, went down the Via Latina toward Naples.

From every spot of *Latium adiectum,* the eyes were directed to Monte Cassino and looked for safety from the prophet who com-manded on the heights. This hope was bruited abroad, and as a result the barbarian king conceived the desire to see the giant and to put his prophetic powers to a test. Therefore, while passing through Casinum, roughhewn and superstitious as he was, he decided to play a trick. First he sent a messenger to the saint announcing his visit, and when the reply came that he was welcome, he commanded a certain Riggo, his shieldbearer, to impersonate him. So, resplendent as a king, wear-ing the royal buskins,[2] clothes, and arms, he was given a noble escort, which included Counts Wult, Ruderic, and Blindin, that they might assist in the performance of this farce of a simulated royal visit.[3]

Laughing and guffawing, these Gothic magnates came to the sum-mit of the mountain, where St. Benedict sat quietly reading on the balcony of the dormitory. Scarcely had they passed the gate of the first circle of walls and were going ahead, when he called from a distance to the king of the comedy: "Put off, O son, put off those garments, be-cause they do not belong to you." Here Gregory is so specific, that only

---

[1] *De bello Gothorum,* Bk. II, 259, 282, 310.

[2] St. Gregory expressly mentions these buskins (*"cui calceamenta sua praebuit,"*) be-cause in ancient times the kind of footwear served to point out a person's dignity, among laymen as well as among ecclesiastics. For this reason abbots, in the ceremony of their blessing, received the buskins and the staff from the hands of the bishop.

[3] Singular that St. Gregory should have preserved for us the names of these Gothic leaders. Thus, in this instance, beside the king, the *spatharius* Riggo, and the *comites* Wult, Ruderic, and Blindin ascend to Monte Cassino. On another occasion it is the captain Zalla, who has the poor manacled peasant lead him thither. In Book I of the *Dialogues,* the author mentions *Darida Gothorum dux* (chap. 3) and Bucelin with his Franks. In Book III we find Gummarith (chap. 11) and the *comes* Pronulphus (chap. 19). It is rather difficult to believe that Gregory kept the names of all these barbarians filed away in his mind. No doubt, for some of the *fioretti* he had recourse to cards or written records.

he who is acquainted with the ancient topography of Monte Cassino with its twofold circle of walls, can understand him. Let the reader imagine the reaction of the Goths at that cry of the prophet.

Utterly surprised at being discovered and terrified by the superhuman majesty that shone forth from the face of the Patriarch, Riggo, the puppet king, fell to the ground in a faint. The same happened to the three counts and the soldiers of the escort, who too late learned at their own cost that attempting to trick saints can be a dangerous business.

When finally their strength returned, they arose. But as to approaching closer to salute the man of God: none of that! He was a wonderworker who reminded them too much of Elias, when the prophet called down fire to consume the troops who had been sent to arrest him. If on the first occasion Benedict threw them to the ground, who knows but that, if they would come nearer to him, he might cause lightning to strike them. You could never tell.

This carnival cortege of frauds prudently decided to retreat. In haste they descended by the mule path to report to their master, who awaited them at Casinum, how the prophet had without any ado unmasked them. The Goths, who never trembled before the armies of Belisarius and of the Romans, on this occasion, in spite of themselves, no longer able to remain upright before Benedict, had fallen to the ground and trembled. "*Ad suum regem reversi nuntiaverunt trepidi in quanta velocitate fuerunt deprehensi*" (chap. 14). These marvels did but add to Totila's desire to see the Patriarch. The king was indeed an Arian, but he had not given up his religious beliefs entirely. Later, immediately after taking Rome, he will betake himself for a visit to the basilica of St. Peter and will show due deference to the deacon Pelagius.

These counts, he thought within himself, may well have trembled in the presence of this man; but the King of the Goths does not tremble even in the face of the devil. With such thoughts revolving in his mind, the sovereign ascended the mountain and passed the gate of the first circle of walls of the fortress. He was already commanding his legs not to fail him, when, scarcely seeing St. Benedict from a distance as he sat near the balcony of the dormitory opposite the tower, he felt himself weaken. Fear enveloped him and he fell on his knees. What is fear? It is something that cannot be described, says Manzoni, and only he understands it who experiences it. That is precisely what happened to Totila. *"Quem cum longe sedentem cerneret, non ausus accedere, sese in terram dedit"* (chap. 15).

Lifting his eyes from the book he was reading, St. Benedict made repeated signs for him to rise and to come through the inner circle of walls, but to no purpose. Terror in the presence of the divine had apparently paralyzed the barbarian king, who basically was not a bad sort. Then St. Benedict rose and—as a mark of great condescension, remarks St. Gregory—went to Totila, lifted him up, and led him into the building.

The Patriarch who does not even move when a king approaches, who remains sitting near the balcony and makes a sign to Totila to come to him, rather startles us moderns, accustomed as we are to an entirely different procedure. But the man of God follows his own usage and the Roman customs. When receiving inferiors, the Roman authorities habitually remained seated as a symbol of their office or dignity. Thus, when St. Augustine, the apostle of England, at one of the councils received the Breton bishops, he, as the metropolitan and legate of Pope Gregory I, had them presented to himself while he was seated on his throne. At this gesture the Bretons took such umbrage that they almost refused to take part in the conciliar sessions.

Quite justly, then, St. Gregory stresses the fact that St. Benedict's rising to go to lift up King Totila was an act of true condescension on the part of the man of God toward a humiliated monarch.

When the two were alone, the guest began to make his excuses for the trick he had intended to play; but St. Benedict straightway gave him his paternal admonition: "In the past you have committed many crimes. Also at present your road is strewn with misdeeds. Now is the time to give up this impious life. You will indeed take Rome; then you will go on to conquer Sicily and you will reign for nine years; but in the tenth you will die."

It appeared as if at Monte Cassino was being repeated the biblical scene of Isaias announcing to King Ezechias his impending death, or the episode of St. Ambrose disregarding the power of Theodosius the murderer and making him prostate himself in the dust.

The thought of death inspired Totila with a salutary fear. The conquest of Rome and his victorious campaign in Sicily gave every promise of a happy future. But what would all these ephemeral triumphs avail if at an early age death would catch up with him, prematurely precipitating him into the grave? Nevertheless he threw himself at the saint's feet and begged his blessing and a prayer for himself.[4]

Then, as if the earth were burning under his feet, he hastily departed from the monastery, thinking along the way of the threat of death which, like the sword of Damocles, thenceforth hung over his head. St. Gregory assures us that after this conversation with St. Benedict, Totila's conduct improved. Certain contemporary historians confirm this observation.[5] When Totila took Naples, he treated it generously. On his return from that city, he passed below Monte Cassino and, perhaps recalling the prophecy of the Abbot, moved on toward Rome.

What fate awaited Riggo? This shieldbearer of Totila is mentioned in another connection by St. Gregory, when he speaks of the capture of Narni, shortly before 546. Unable to offer any resistance, the citizens decided to surrender, and Bishop Cassius went out to meet the conqueror to beg mercy for his flock.

At Monte Cassino, Totila had found in St. Benedict a pale and thin man. Since Cassius, on the contrary, was of a ruddy complexion, the Goths made fun of this fat bishop, regarding him as a tippler and a good trencherman.

The shieldbearer Riggo, the star of the company, thought he had to call attention to himself by caricaturing the unfortunate prisoner behind his back, but this time the play came out badly; for St. Gregory narrates that he was immediately invaded by a demon so furious that his very appearance called forth pity. The Goths themselves recognized the hand of God in the incident; they led the madman to the Bishop and asked that he should pardon and heal him. In the presence of all, St. Cassius, after a brief prayer, drew the cross on Riggo, and at that sign the devil fled.

Only too late the royal shieldbearer learned to his sorrow that it

---

[4] "*Quibus auditis rex, vehementer territus, oratione petita, recessit.*" St. Zachary translates this: ἔρριψεν ἑαυτὸν ἐπὶ τὴν γῆν καὶ εὐχὴν αἰτήσας ἀνεχώρεσεν τῆς μονῆς.

[5] Pope Zachary attributes it entirely to the reprehension of St. Benedict: διὰ τῆς τοῦ ὁσίου διδασκαλίας.

is good sense to follow the proverb that says: "Joke with infants, but leave the saints in peace."

On November 22, 544, Pope Vigilius had been sent to the vicinity of Constantinople, a victim of the theological abstruseness of Justinian. During his journey the Pope, unmindful of his own misfortunes, sent a great cargo of grain from the possessions of the Church in Sicily to succor the starving city of Rome. But when the vessels arrived at Porto Romano, they were sequestrated by the Goths, whose king caused the hands of the bishop of Silva Candida to be cut off because he was accused of having shown some disloyalty.

The besieged, constrained by a famine that was growing rapidly worse, induced the deacon Pelagius, who was at the time considered the most influential and esteemed personage after the Pope, to go as an ambassador to Totila, in an effort to secure a truce of a few days. If within that time the help promised by the Greeks had not arrived, the gates of the city would be thrown open to him without further ado.

Totila, who had not yet forgotten the recommendations of the Abbot of Monte Cassino, received the deacon with great honor and gave him the kiss as a sign of peace. He declared, however, that, while he might spare the city, there were three things he could never grant: pardoning the Sicilian traitors who had gone over to the side of Belisarius; returning the slaves who had deserted and passed over to the Goths; sparing the Aurelian walls of Rome.

When this proud reply of the king was reported, the citizens were greatly alarmed. But Pelagius, conscious of his evangelical mission of peace and pardon, had the fortitude to declare to Totila that, since these negotiations for peace had failed, he would turn to the King of kings, who humbles those who despise the petitions of the oppressed.

Among the various captains of Totila's army, the first place in cruelty was held by a certain Zalla, who seemed to derive a special satisfaction from the death of priests and monks. Whoever fell into his grasp he slaughtered. One day as he was going through the country about Cassino, plundering the houses and granaries of the peasants—requisitioning, we would say today—he entered the dwelling of a certain man and in a rough voice commanded him to bring forth his well-furnished chests. The peasant said he had no money, but only a few kitchen utensils and some agricultural tools. Zalla, however, chose not to believe him, accused him of having a large quantity of money hidden away, and had him put to torture that in this way he might learn the secret of his treasure. The other persisted in his denial for a time, but finally, overcome by pain, he had recourse to a lie: he asserted that he had given over all of his goods to the Patriarch Benedict on Monte Cassino.

Calling a halt for the time being to the proceedings, the savage Zalla forced the peasant to go before his horse, his arms tied behind his back, to act as a guide to the monastery. I do not know how pleased Zalla was to make this visit to the wonder-worker, who had caused even the king to tremble. Quite likely Totila had even given orders that the monastery be respected. "Very well," thought the captain, "we shall leave the prophet and his followers in peace; but they will give over to the troops the goods of the civilians, which the king has consigned as a prize to the soldiers."

It cannot be denied that the law of Theodoric favored the demands of Zalla. In the *Edictum Theodorici* (art. 71) we read: "If anyone owes anything to the government and seeks asylum in a church, the archdeacon shall compel him to leave in order to settle his accounts with the state. If he is unwilling to do this, he shall immediately turn over the goods which the other had offered to the church. If he refuses, the archdeacon shall pay out of his own pocket." [6]

Hence the laws of the Goths were not to be trifled with: either hand over the deposit or satisfy out of one's own purse. With what a heavy heart the poor man must have gone his way! He was walking to his death, because in a short time Zalla would discover the deception and kill him on the spot.

When they arrived before the entrance of the monastery, they saw Benedict sitting and reading quietly. The unfortunate peasant immediately pointed him out to Zalla: "There is the Father Benedict, of whom I told you." The captain cast a cruel look of contempt at the saint and, with the hope of cowing him by the brutal methods which had worked with many others, he bellowed at him: "Get up, get up and hand over the belongings of this man." At this unusual dis-

[6] *"Si quis in causa publici debiti ad ecclesiam quamlibet convolaverit, archidiaconus eum compellat egredi ad edenda legibus ratiocinia sua; aut si hoc facere noluerit, eius substantiam, quod (!) ad ecclesiam distribuit, sine mora contradat. Quod nisi fecerit, quanti interest utilitatis publicae archidiaconus rogatus exsolvat."*

turbance, the Patriarch lifted his eyes from the book, and saw before him the bound peasant and behind him the ferocious Zalla on his horse, his eyes bulging as if he wished to devour Benedict alive.

To see the farmer, to cast his eyes on the rope that bound his arms, and to tear those bonds with his gaze was the work of but an instant. When Zalla perceived the broken cords, only one thing remained for him in the face of this power of holiness. He leaped from the saddle, prostrated himself at the feet of the saint, and asked for his prayers. With this ruffian St. Benedict decided to go the limits of courtesy. Without rising from his seat—for it was necessary to preserve the dignity of the sacred ministry before the Goths—he called some monks and gave over this new kind of guest into their hands. He commanded them *"ut benedictionem acciperet,"* that is to say, to prepare a sumptuous meal for him and to treat him with all charity.

A bit of God's gifts or of a blessing, I think, was also kept for the miserable peasant. Perhaps he and Zalla even sat at the same table and thus made their peace in the name of God and of St. Benedict. When the meal was over, the Gothic tribune was brought again to the Abbot, who awaited him to read him a well-merited lecture. What did he say to him? More or less he gave him the same admonition that the King had received earlier: that the time had come to end the brutalities inflicted on the Italians, because otherwise, in its own good time, the hand of God would reach also the Goths, as it was now afflicting both the Romans and the Greeks.

Zalla appeared touched. He had learned that there existed the divine power of faith which was greater than that of arms, and he knelt at the feet of the father to ask his blessing, while St. Benedict counseled him to abate his cruelty in the victory which the Lord had granted his nation.

The peasant, who was still present, was stupefied to see the barbarian ask pardon. The fact stands that the Goth, *"fractus recedens,"* departed from the monastery with such salutary fear in his heart that henceforth he was careful not to let his savagery run riot against the lambs of so powerful a shepherd, who loosened bonds and sent forth lightning by the mere glance of his eyes.

All these miracles which God was working in the Campania during those months must have made a deep impression on the Goths. Totila's ascent to Monte Cassino and his enforced prostration at the feet of St. Benedict could not remain without effect on the minds of the invading troops. That may be seen even in the attitude of that priest-eater Zalla. Indeed he shows his worst side with the poor peasant whose money he could not find; but he refrains meticulously from doing any harm to the monks on Monte Cassino.

At that time God surrounded holy bishops and abbots in Italy with such an awful majesty, because supernatural power was the only means of taming the young German generations and thus fashioning them with a view to the desired fusion of the two races.

CHAPTER LIV

Rome without a Pope

WHILE at Monte Cassino St. Benedict was engaged in giving a definitive form to the new *Regula monasteriorum,* which in the mind of the
Pope who had commissioned him was to bring about unity of discipline in the whole of Latin monachism, the affairs of the Church
and its head were going from bad to worse. At Constantinople the aged
Justinian, now passionately enamored of Theodora, had returned to
the old concept of emperor-pontiff, master of the earth and of heaven,
arbiter of the Churches as well as of his subjects' consciences. "His
principal care," says a contemporary, "was directed to the true teachings of God and the good behavior of ecclesiastics." [1]

Having in mind to draw together the separated factions, he determined to root out of the Church even the least vestiges of Nestorian-
ism. Hence he issued a threefold anathema against certain writings
of Theodore of Cyrus, Iba of Edessa, and Theodore of Mopsuestia,
even though the Council of Chalcedon, after hearing them explained,
deliberately abstained from condemning them. Quite naturally the
rift became wider than ever. The Latins generally, unacquainted with
the dialectic of the Greeks, suspected a trick in the imperial anathema
and saw in it nothing less than an attack upon the authority of the
ecumenical Council of Chalcedon.

St. Benedict seems to betray a similar diffidence in the face of all
these state theologasters. Twice in the Rule he commands that the
scriptural commentaries that are read in public shall be those written

---

[1] Cf. Saba, *Storia dei Papi,* Turin, 1936, I, 184.

"by well-known and orthodox Catholic Fathers" (chap. 9), and he ends his code with the same prescription, "the book of the holy Catholic Fathers" (chap. 73).

Here also we find the reason for the vacillation of Pope Vigilius. To overcome his resistance, as we have said, Justinian had him snatched by the soldiery from the very altar of St. Cecilia in Trastevere on November 22, 545, and brought him by force to Constantinople. It may be added, however, that Vigilius was very unpopular with the Romans, who bore in mind the machinations through which he had attained the papacy.

Hence, when the Pontiff gave his final blessing from aboard the vessel in the Tiber that was to carry him to the East, the popular party, that was opposed to him, did not refrain from saluting him with catcalls and unbecoming jibes: "Take with you the famine you have caused. You loved the Greeks. May they treat you well."

No one has recorded the impressions which these most unfortunate events made on St. Benedict. If in the Rule he speaks to us of apparently hopeless situations, it is only that he may immediately correct this attitude and exhort us to greater trust in God: "Never to despair of God's mercy" (chap. 4). He must readily have understood that the situation created by Vigilius rendered ever more difficult the old papal plan of using the institution of monasticism to prepare the future apostles of the new peoples of Europe.

In the meantime he was engaged in making the final draft of the Rule and, at the request of the priest Mareas, he sent to the new monastery of St. Pancratius a colony of his monks with Valentinian at their head as abbot. Quite likely they were instructed to distribute help to the victims of the war, as they had done previously at Monte Cassino.

Unfortunately, the succession of events during the pontificates of Silverius and Vigilius did nothing to raise the prestige of the papacy in the minds of the faithful. In the Empire and in Italy there existed a political crisis as well as a religious crisis; a crisis especially of authority and prestige. Indeed the Lateran monastery, quite contrary to Roman usage, was never mentioned in connection with Pope Vigilius, who was looked upon as being barely this side of excommunication.

What could St. Benedict do in this predicament? It is symptomatic of his character that in the Rule, to which in those days he was putting the finishing touches, he does not in any way betray a disturbed or, at the least, a sad state of mind. When the earthly City was going to rack and ruin, he followed the example of St. Augustine proposing to Christians the conquest of the eternal City, "that we may deserve to see Him who has called us to His kingdom" (Prologue).

Unperturbed, as if the fire which was devastating Italy did not lift its smoke and its odor of burning to the heights where his monastery was perched, he does not reveal any preoccupation in the Rule; there is not the least reference to the political conditions then existing in Italy. It almost appears that he knows he is the universal master of the centuries to come, and for that reason he need not take into account the special contingencies of a particular moment in the Peninsula's history.

Rather than a political genius, the Patriarch of Cassino is an ascetic and a missioner; only from a distance he follows the theological controversies of his day. Far more than the Greek questions about the Three Chapters, which never agitated the Romans, we observe in the Rule that its author interested himself in the Pelagian constroversy on grace, which two centuries before called forth in the Latin episcopate, especially in Africa and in Gaul, such excitement.

St. Benedict nourished a profound respect for the school of Lerins and particularly for Cassian, whose ascetic medulla he incorporated into the Rule. But this admiration for the abbot of Marseilles did not blind him so much that he overlooked what was not entirely orthodox in his teachings on grace. From such errors he desired, in the Rule, to keep his monks absolutely immune.

His relations with the abbot of Lucullanum, who was one of the strongest champions of St. Augustine in the sixth century, induced the holy Patriarch resolutely to declare himself opposed to every form of Pelagianism and Semi-Pelagianism. He does so at the very beginning of the Rule, where he admonishes his disciple not to glory because of the good he has accomplished, since it is a gift of divine grace: "They . . . do not pride themselves on their good observance; but, convinced that the good which is in them cannot come from themselves and must be from the Lord, they glorify the Lord's work in them. . . . Thus also the apostle Paul attributed nothing of the success of his preaching to himself, but said, 'By the grace of God I am what I am' " (Prologue).

Frequently in the course of the Rule the man of God returns to the great theological principle that, in order to do any good work, we need the help of divine grace. Thus he says: *"Bonum aliquid in se cum viderit, Deo applicet non sibi. Malum vero semper a se factum sciat et sibi reputet"* (chap. IV, 42, 43). This grace must be asked for by insistent prayer: "And first of all, whatever good work you begin to do, beg of Him with most earnest prayer to perfect it." Human nature alone, weakened by original sin, has not the power to persevere in good: "Let us ask God that He be pleased to give us the help of His grace for anything which our nature finds hardly possible" (Prologue). When St. Benedict wrote these words, perhaps in his mind were the words of a preface of the Leonine Sacramentary: "Truly it is meet and just. . . . Because, since it is clear that every good deed by Thee is begun and perfected, we are certain that we shall be able to obtain what we ask, namely, this perseverance in prayer which you grant. Through Christ our Lord. . . ." [2]

We could not understand this insistence in the Rule on the necessity of divine grace, if we did not keep in mind that precisely in those years, in Gaul as well as in Constantinople and Rome, the theologians were quarreling about this doctrine.

About July, 529, St. Caesarius summoned the Council of Orange and there published the *Capitula ab Apostolica Sede nobis transmissa.* Hence there was question of a papal decision. What had happened? The metropolitan of Arles, in order to vanquish the difficulties proposed by his colleagues in the episcopate regarding the doctrine of grace, had some time before sent extracts from the writings of St. Augustine on this subject to Rome. They are the nineteen *Capitula S. Augustini in Urbe Roma transmissa.* Pope Felix IV revised this sylloge and eliminated the texts relating to the Manicheans; of the fourteen canons that preceded he retained only eight, but added other

---

2 *"Vere dignum . . . Quia cum omne opus bonum a te inchoari constet et perfici, hanc ipsam quam nobis tribuis perseverantiam supplicandi, certi sumus impetrare nos posse quae poscimus. Per Christum. . . ."*

Probably St. Benedict was also inspired by a celebrated collect from this Sacramentary: *"Actiones nostras, quaesumus, Domine, et adspirando praeveni, et adiuvando prosequere; ut cuncta nostra operatio a te semper incipiat, et per te coepta, finiatur."*

opinions of St. Augustine. After the Council of Orange, Caesarius insisted anew that the Pope confirm its acts; this was later done by John II on January 25, 531.

It is impossible to prove any literary dependence between the writings of Caesarius on grace and the corresponding doctrine of St. Benedict. The Patriarch rather depends on Eugippius and, through him, on Ferrandus and St. Augustine. Nevertheless, between the years 528 and 531, the papal consistory had undertaken another complete investigation of the question, as the metropolitan of Arles had proposed it.

God—so teaches St. Caesarius in the *Capitula* sent to Rome—prepares the good will in us; on Him depends the beginning of faith, and none of our works can be perfected without grace. Also the beginning of a good work comes from God and from His grace: "In every good work we do not begin and are afterward helped through God's mercy"; but there are required prevenient grace, concomitant grace, and that which leads to a successful ending.

In his turn the Patriarch of Cassino, positing the general principle that we carry out all good works by the help of divine grace, insists again and again on the gratuitous nature of our call to the faith: "Behold, in His loving kindness the Lord shows us the way of life." Hence God works the good in us: "Convinced that the good which is in them cannot come from themselves and must be from the Lord, [they] glorify the Lord's work in them" (Prologue).

In St. Benedict's time the Mariological questions had been settled. By reason of the Christocentric plan on which the Holy Rule is conceived and executed, the Patriarch never finds occasion to mention the Blessed Virgin. The same is true of the author of *The Imitation of Christ*. It may be well to recall that for the inhabitants of Nursia devotion to the great Mother of God was traditional; in fact, they had dedicated to her the old Roman temple, called to the present day Sancta Maria Argentea. As a result of this Marian piety, which he imbibed at Nursia with his mother's milk, St. Benedict, as legend would have it, dedicated to the Blessed Virgin one of his twelve monasteries at Subiaco, that of S. Maria in Primorana. This special worship of the Virgin, traditional with the monks of Subiaco, in the ninth century inspired them with the thought of decorating the very cave of St. Benedict with a fresco depicting Mary as Queen between SS. Stephen and Lawrence.

Now the new barbarian peoples are busily overturning in Italy the entire ancient Roman civilization, and the Church herself feels the effects. But precisely for this purpose, namely, to reconstruct still more wonderfully the *civitas Christiana* on the ruins of paganism, St. Benedict establishes in his monastery what he calls "the school of the Lord's service." [3] In that school will have to be formed the popes, the doctors of the Church, the apostles of the various countries of Europe, the bishops, the genial craftsmen of the medieval civilization, which was essentially Christian and essentially monastic.

Contemporaneously Justinian at Constantinople was busied with codifying the laws of imperial Rome. The work was promulgated on April 7, 529, with a constitution that determined it should go into effect April 16. This first compilation was then replaced in 533–34 by a new collection, made under the supervision of Tribonian. In this manner the Roman juridical tradition was safeguarded for the centuries to come. During these same years on Monte Cassino St. Benedict was codifying the preceding ecclesiastical legislation regarding religious life in the West.

---

[3] The word *"schola"* used to have a twofold meaning; in ancient times it also signified "association" or "guild." The portico where the public awaited their turn at the baths was called *"schola."* The Middle Ages had its associations or guilds of the various arts and crafts and called them *"schola fabrorum, schola sutorum, schola S. Mariae,"* and so on.

In the Rule, *"Dominici schola servitii"* can be taken in either sense. The monastery, besides being an institution of learning, is also an association of "the servants of God."

CHAPTER LV

St. Benedict Foretells the Destruction of Monte Cassino

I HAVE already mentioned the monk Theoprobus, who probably had charge of a monastery grange in the *castrum Casinum* and, together with several colleagues and slaves, saw to the business of the abbey on the mountain. Since at that time the ranks of the clergy of Aquino were much depleted, it is almost certain that the monks administered the sacraments to the faithful of the countryside. In any case, Theoprobus appears as the right-hand man of the saint, and his administration must have called for a certain degree of ability since on the night of St. Germanus' death Benedict without further ado ordered him to send a courier to Capua posthaste to get news about the Bishop.

Two centuries later, when Monte Cassino was being restored under the Lombards, the need was felt of building another monastery at the foot of the mountain to receive the pilgrims on their way to Rome and also to give the abbey a foothold in the *castrum*, situated halfway between Rome and Naples. Even until recent years, after so many centuries, conditions in this regard were regarded as unchanged, and a part of the community resided near the former monastery of St. Savior, in order to take care both of the spiritual needs of the populace and of the material business of the abbey.

In the eighth century, St. Willibald, before being sent to Germany as a missionary bishop, spent some time as porter at Monte Cassino and then was transferred to the monastery in the valley. In the series of procurators of the abbey in the city of Cassino, the monk The-oprobus, then, heads an honored list. This Theoprobus, as St. Gregory tells us, came of a noble family, and after being called to the monastic life by the admonitions of St. Benedict, acquired his full confidence.

To understand the character of the monastic family governed by St. Benedict, we must not overlook the importance St. Gregory at-taches to the houses from which these fervent novices came. Maur and Placid belonged to the Roman patriciate; the brothers Gregory and Speciosus had possessed great wealth; Theoprobus came of noble stock; Mark the Poet was a scholar; Severus was the son of a state official; the father of another monk was a *defensor*. Hence in general they came from select surroundings, a circumstance which must have given to the community a special tone of spiritual aristocracy.

The charge of the peasants and the slaves, together with carrying on the business of Monte Cassino in the city, called for frequent con-tact between Theoprobus and the holy Patriarch. One day as The-oprobus, with his customary familiarity, entered the cell of the saint, he found him lying prostrate on his mat, so deep in prayer that he did not notice the entrance of Theoprobus. Contrary to what had happened before, that is, instead of his eyes being moist with tears, as was usual when St. Benedict prayed, on this occasion the Patriarch was shedding copious tears, as if overcome by some mighty catastrophe.

At this unusual sight, Theoprobus waited for a long time in order not to disturb the saint. But since the lamenting did not cease, he in-quired into the reason for it. The Patriarch did not hide from his trusted disciple the cause of his tears. He replied immediately, *"vir Dei illico respondit."* Note the force of that *"illico."* It seems that he had reached the limit and that his heart was breaking. "Behold, Theoprobus, this entire monastery with its churches, its buildings, its shops, mills, baths, gardens, which have cost us so many years of toil and struggle. We have snatched this place from the jaws of the devil; we have brought about the conversion of these poor pagans and gathered together monks for the Lord's service. Now, by the just and holy will of God, what we have so laboriously built up will fall into the hands of the heretical barbarians. By all my prayer I have scarcely been able to save the lives of the monks from becoming victims of their cruel swords." And he began to weep anew.

I do not know how Theoprobus was affected by this prophecy or what impression it produced on the minds of the few monks who shared knowledge of this incident. By good fortune Mark did not learn of it. Little trust can be placed in the secrets of poets. Chronological indications were not given in the prophecy; hence the impending disaster remained suspended over the monastery like the sword of Damocles. One thing, at any rate, was a solace to the monks who knew the secret: it was the hope that, as their Patriarch's prayer had succeeded in averting the danger of death, so it would likewise protect and help them in the hour of trial.

The prophecy was not fulfilled till about forty years later, namely, during the interregnum which followed the murder of King Clefi at Pavia in 574. At that time the various restive Lombard dukes threw off the yoke of a sovereign and began to war each on his own account. Zoto of Beneventum decided to besiege Rome while Pelagius II was pope. The citizens of the city had to endure some terrible days. The Pope speaks of the swords of the Lombards set at the throats of the Romans and preserves a memorial of the fact in the mosaic inscription on the great arch of the basilica of St. Lawrence.

Abandoned, alas, to its fate by the emperor of Constantinople, Rome finally had to consent to a treaty of peace with the Duke of Beneventum, who then retired beyond the river Liri, to the vicinity of Casinum. A short time earlier the region had been ravaged by pestilence,[1] but it is well known that famine, pestilence, and war go together like three sisters.

Monte Cassino, standing on the other side of the river, remained in the hands of the Lombards, who saw to it that they lost no time in occupying this border position of great strategic importance. Not to excite the faithful unduly, the invasion came by surprise at night. But the Lombards on this occasion had no intention to kill or to destroy; they simply wished to convert the fortress to military uses. The monks in their dormitory were terrified at the sudden appearance of the soldiers. In the confusion of arms and armed men, while the Lombards were concerned above all with finding quarters or perhaps went directly to seek some strength in the wine cellar or the kitchen after their exertions, the poor monks, under cover of darkness, succeeded in flee-

[1] *Dial.*, Bk. III, chap. 8.

ing into the mountains and thus saving themselves. Nevertheless, in abandoning their home, they took time to carry away with them the autograph copy of the Rule, the authentic weight of the daily bread ration, a number of manuscripts from the library, and several of the two hundred sacks which had contained the marvelous supply of flour. The soldiers allowed them to depart. It was the year 589.

The prophecy of St. Benedict had been fulfilled to the letter. While in the neighboring city of Aquino the Lombards put a considerable number of the citizens to the sword, at Monte Cassino all were spared.[2]

Later the monks, after they had crossed the boundary, withdrew onto the territory of the Empire and joined their colleagues in the Lateran monastery. This small political detail must not be overlooked. The bishop and the leaders of Milan had done something similar: they fled to Genoa, which was in the hands of the Greeks.

I should like to add that on this occasion God drew good out of evil. By thus transplanting the community of Monte Cassino to Rome, the first disciples of St. Benedict were in a better position to make known the work of the holy legislator. Otherwise there might have been danger that the Rule would remain simply the spiritual patrimony of the Cassinese family. But when it was carried to Rome and deposited in the papal library, which was situated only a short distance from Gregory's home, it became, thanks to that outstanding Pontiff, the universal code of Western monasticism.

When the Lombards took Monte Cassino, Bonitus was its abbot; curiously, St. Gregory does not mention his name. However, he relates that he was on intimate terms, almost certainly in Rome, with his immediate predecessors, Abbots Simplicius and Constantine, from whom he learned in great part the details of the Patriarch's life. Possibly already at that time they gave to the future biographer some notes they had carefully written. The exactness with regard to the least structural and topographical details about Monte Cassino can scarcely depend exclusively on the youthful memories of Gregory. More is demanded.

Gregory had left Constantinople in 585 to seek peace in his monastery. The years that followed were most precious for the future historian of St. Benedict, because the nearness of the monastery of St.

---

[2] *Dial.*, Bk. III, chap. 8; Bk. II, chap. 17.

Andrew to that of St. Pancratius in the Lateran put him in the best possible position to complete the collection of the historical material required for the literary monument he intended to compose to the glory of the Patriarch of Latin monachism.

Very likely St. Gregory commenced the work of writing the *Dialogues* while he was still living on the Clivus Scauri, before he became pope. Indeed, a historical work, so varied and complex as are the *Dialogues*, requires a long period of preparation to gather the material and the documents. How the new Pontiff could have worked on this project and completed it during the first months of his troubled reign is hard to see. No, this gracious and idyllic collection of biographies of saints betrays a prolonged and calm period of preparation in surroundings that were quiet and religious.

I should also like to point out that among the sources for the story of St. Benedict, Gregory cites some witnesses who, with the exception of Honoratus, had been dead for many years. Now it is difficult to conceive that this Pope, worried and suffering from gout, should draw his numerous *fioretti* with all their details solely from the storehouse of his memory. If, besides, we take into account that Gregory's narratives are embellished with local descriptions, including at times minute particulars about the buildings of Monte Cassino, the conclusion seems justified either that the author used written sources or that several years before his elevation to the papacy he began to gather material by visiting Subiaco and Monte Cassino.

The descriptive importance that Gregory attaches to all these topographical details point him out as a person who describes scenes in places well known to him, where the events narrated actually occurred. A simple historian, who is not personally acquainted with the environment of his accounts, keeps to general remarks; he does not descend to describe details of a building.

At the time Gregory the Great laid down the insignia of the urban prefecture to put on the monastic garb in the monastery of St. Andrew, which had been the residence of his ancestors, he and his mother Sylvia no doubt were acquainted with St. Benedict and his miracles. Hence the Rule of the Patriarch of Cassino was introduced into the new monastery at the very outset. The first contacts of the Pontiff with Abbot Constantine began in his early youth, about the year 555. Quite likely the excursions of Gregory to Subiaco and to Monte Cassino, inspired by these spiritual conversations, date from the time when he was a civil functionary, when he was obliged to travel by reason of his office. Later on, when he had become a monk, he had neither the occasion nor the desire to travel.

In the *Dialogues* the Pope attributed a particular importance to his former acquaintanceship with the Cassinese abbots, most probably in Rome. If, then, the first successors of the Patriarch appeared from time to time in the capital of the Christian world, we may be certain that also in this regard they continued the tradition of the master. Thus God disposed that the future biographer of Western monachism should prepare himself for the task that proved decisive for the spread of the Benedictine Order.

CHAPTER LVI

The Siege of Rome

ALMOST simultaneously St. Benedict received extremely bad news both from Rome and from Constantinople. While Pope Vigilius, a prisoner in the imperial city, was subjected to such violence that he had to seek asylum in a church near the tomb of St. Euphemia at Chalcedon, King Totila was tightening his siege of Rome. But the man of God calmly abided in his trust in the Lord.

For the moment the manuscript of the Rule was placed in the archives, awaiting a more favorable moment. In the light of God the Patriarch read the future like a book. Had he not, about five years before, foretold to Totila his success in war, promising him even the capture of Rome? It must be noted that at that time, as far as the barbarian peoples were concerned, the occupation of the metropolis of the world, far from representing a triumph, was rather considered a sort of fate to which they had to submit. These foreign kings had a foreboding that the conquest of the *sacra Urbs* meant incurring the divine displeasure, meant death.

Thus it had befallen Odoacer, thus Alaric, thus Genseric, and more recently Theodoric. To a monk who begged him not to march on Rome, the last-mentioned, according to the historian Socrates, replied: "I am not setting out on my own accord. But I do not know who it is that daily tempts me and urges me on, saying: 'Go, lay waste the city of Rome.' " [1] It was a cruel fate that drew down simultaneously both conquered and conqueror.

[1] *"Ego sponte non proficiscor. Sed nescio quisque quotidie solicitat ac stimulat dicens,*

There was no doubt that a similar end awaited Totila. "You will take Rome," St. Benedict had told him, "you will pass over into Sicily, you will reign nine years, but in the tenth you will die." Indeed these foreign kings, moving on Rome with their armies, felt that they were, despite themselves, the instruments of divine justice, which in a burst of fire wished to purify the shameful deeds of pagan Rome, of the hands dripping with the blood of the martyrs. "Man of God," Attila had said to a holy anchorite who, grasping the bridle of his charger, wished to turn him from his design of going into Italy, "man of God, let me go. It is not I who am making this resolve, but it is as if someone were guiding me and urging me on with the command: 'March on Rome.' "

After the fall of the city, the walls were dismantled and large numbers of the inhabitants, in chains, were sent along the Via Latina past Casinum into the Campania. From his eminence St. Benedict could witness the sad spectacle, and perhaps he attempted a second time to induce the conqueror to abate his cruelties. Procopius relates that "Totila led the Romans into captivity in the Campania, and Rome remained deserted for forty days, so that in the depopulated streets wild animals freely wandered about." This state of affairs is also reflected in the pages of the Rule where it is said that the poor cry habitually at the gate of the monastery,[2] and that every day the guest-house of Monte Cassino is not without an abundant quota of guests and pilgrims.[3]

However much Totila may have tried to restrain the Goths from their accustomed excesses, he did not always succeed. By good fortune, God sometimes sent his saints to temper the wrath of the invading army to a certain extent. Of this the story of St. Sabinus is an example. Gregory the Great tells us that, about the year 543, King Totila, after capturing the city of Naples, likewise made himself master of Apulia and Calabria and occupied the city of Canosa. Sabinus, by this time old and blind, mindful perhaps of the King's reception on

---

perge, urbem Romam vastaturus" (Socrates, III).

[2] The phrase *"pauper clamavit"* perhaps had a very precise meaning at Monte Cassino, where the poor, entering through the gate of the first external circle of walls, had to cry aloud to make themselves heard by the porter, who sat farther up near the tower that guarded the entrance to the fortress.

[3] *"Hospites qui numquam desunt monasteriis. . . . Pauperum et peregrinorum maxime susceptionis cura sollicite exhibeatur"* (chap. 53).

the part of St. Benedict a year before, invited the sovereign to table in the hope of inducing him to deal gently with the populace. The King was extremely pleased with this mark of deference paid to him by one so universally esteemed as Sabinus.

But he had been told that the Bishop, owing to cataracts, could no longer perceive the light of the sun, but with the eyes of the soul he could clearly discern the things of the spirit and read in the book of the future. Totila decided to put him to a test, as he had done with Benedict on Monte Cassino.

Whether moved by superstition or diffidence, he would not join the others at table, but preferred to sit at the right of the Bishop in order to observe him. It so happened that during the banquet, the cupbearer came to Sabinus to prepare his drink. The barbarian king, as soon as he perceived him, with a rapid gesture took the cup from his hand and presented it himself to the blind man. He hoped that he would not be recognized. Sabinus, however, in receiving the drink, with a smile turned to Totila and, showing clearly that he knew the hand of the improvised Ganymede, said: "Hail that hand." [4]

Totila, seeing himself discovered, blushed; but the good augury easily made him swallow the disappointment of the trick that did not come off. *"De quo verbo rex laetatus erubuit."* "All the saints apparently are alike," he must have mused. "They read the present and the future like a book. The prophet whom I visited last year on Monte Cassino did the same. He, like this blind old man, foretold for me a series of victories. 'Hail that hand,' he had said. Who knows? Perhaps this word of the Bishop of Canosa rescinded that of the prophet of Cassino, who foresaw my death after only nine years of rule."

Drawing new impetus from the Bishop's words, he went on from triumph to triumph until, in the summer of 548, near Rossano in Calabria he inflicted such a bloody defeat on the Greeks that Justinian recalled Belisarius to the East in disgrace. Then, after a succession of rapid advances, the Goths took Rome. From there, again descending through the Campania and Calabria, Totila in 549 sailed over to Sicily, precisely as St. Benedict had foretold. But the intoxication of victory made him forget the wise counsels given by the Patriarch.

[4] *Dial.*, Bk. III, chap. 5.

With the Sicilians the King had some old scores to settle, dating from the time they had not informed him of the arrival of the fleet of Belisarius and thus had supplied the Greeks an excellent base of operation. Consequently, when Totila had taken the island, he avenged himself on it by giving free reign to the brutality of his soldiers, who, indeed, conducted themselves as savages.

The arrival of Narses finally constrained the Goths to retreat toward Ravenna, which was looked upon as the second capital of the Greeks. In July, 552, the two armies met near Gualdo Fadino, and this time Narses won the victory. Totila, after fighting valorously, at last died in a stable of the village of Caprara as the result of a mortal wound. It was the tenth year of St. Benedict's prophecy. Perhaps his last thoughts went back to the heights of Cassino. Reconsidering the examination of conscience which the Abbot had made for him when he was kneeling at his feet, in his dying moment, as ten years before, he begged of him a prayer and a heavenly blessing.

CHAPTER LVII

Sad Prediction about Rome

In the autumn of 546, during the long weeks of the siege of Rome, among the refugees that came to Monte Cassino was also Sabinus, the aged Bishop of Canosa. From personal experience he was acquainted with the cruelty of the Goths, because in 525 he had accompanied Pope John I to Constantinople and at his return to Ravenna had witnessed the Pontiff's incarceration by order of Theodoric. The holy bishop was now bent with the weight of years; besides, his eyes had been blinded by cataracts.

But since from time to time, while going to Rome for ecclesiastical business [1] he used to visit with St. Benedict on Monte Cassino, to whom he was united by the closest bonds of friendship, so again in thi year of wars and sieges he did not wish to deprive himself of the con solation of visiting his friend for the last time. I suspect that Victor of Capua did the same, since we learn from the *Codex Fuldensis* that on April 19, 546, and on April 12 of the following year he was in Rome. To go to the capital from Capua, a stop at Casinum is, as it were, obligatory.

In a few but telling words St. Gregory here describes for us a kind of idyl of Christian friendship. He tells us that the Bishop of Canosa "was accustomed to visit the servant of God." This is not something small, considering the dignity of Sabinus. Furthermore, at the time

---

[1] Boniface II celebrated a Roman Council in the *consistorium* of St. Andrew's to judge the cause of Stephen, bishop of Larissa (530–32). Among the bishops attending we find Sabinus of Canosa. The same Sabinus was sent to Constantinople in 535 by Pope Agapitus I in the interests of the same case.

he was old and blind, travel was both difficult and dangerous. Such was the reputation of Benedict, however, that even the most famous men of his day flocked to him.

"The man of God loved him dearly for the merit of his life." [2] These are all significant details, and we must bear them in mind in order to understand the scene that follows. The Patriarch treated Sabinus with a certain familiarity, because, as an ancient Cassinese tradition has it, instead of having him dine in the guest quarters, he admitted him directly into the common refectory of the community, as if he belonged to the family. But perhaps this was the practice followed with high ecclesiastical dignitaries, who could not be served together with laymen.

At Monte Cassino the Bishop breathes easily. Here no one will try to poison his wine, as, indeed, his own archdeacon had attempted to do at Canosa.[3] During the meal, after speaking of spiritual things for the edification of the monks, the talk turns to the happenings of the day and the siege of Rome.

Unfortunately the Romans were deluding themselves. In the spring of 544, the papal subdeacon Arator, during a poetical reading in the Esquiline basilica of St. Peter-in-Chains, had given the assurance that the Goths would never destroy the walls of Rome, because these walls had been placed under the protection of St. Peter. The entire audience applauded since to have thought differently would have been regarded as an act of distrust in the patron of Rome. But the proverb says: "God helps those who help themselves." Both government and citizenry did absolutely nothing to defend Rome and the Empire against the relentless power of the barbarians.

At Monte Cassino, on the contrary, a far more realistic attitude was taken.

"I think," said St. Sabinus, "that when the King of the Goths enters the city, he will raze it to the ground, so that it can no longer be inhabited."

"No," St. Benedict interrupted, "no; the sovereign of the Goths, though he is a heretic, will not dare to expose himself to divine vengeance by destroying the capital of the world. I told him this

---

[2] *Dial.*, Bk. II, chap. 15.
[3] *Dial.*, Bk. III, chap. 5.

privately when he was up here four years ago. Alas, paganism has so honeycombed Rome that, festering from its own moral corruption, it will collapse under a stroke of divine justice, which will lash it with its lightnings and destroy the city's buildings with storms and numerous earthquakes."

St. Gregory sadly adds that in the course of half a century this prophecy was fulfilled to the letter, and he attests to the spectacle of seeing the Aurelian walls pulled down, the churches fired by lightning, the ancient buildings falling into ruin, because no one was any longer in a position to repair them.[4]

As I have already remarked, the Cassinese tradition of the tenth century asserts that this conference with Bishop Sabinus took place in the monastic dining room. The papal biographer informs us, in his turn, that he learned of the incident from Abbot Honoratus of Subiaco, who, however, is careful to state that, although he did not hear the conversation himself, he had it from one who was actually present. Such meticulousness in handling his historical sources does great honor to Gregory.

On December 17, 546, the defending Isaurian soldiery opened to the Goths the Porta Asinaria near the Lateran; the cowardly Byzantine leaders and those members of the patriciate who were able, profiting by the darkness of the night, fled ignominiously from the betrayed city. Recalling St. Benedict's prophecy, Totila did not permit the glory of this victory to inflate his pride. Indeed, his first act on entering Rome was to give thanks to God and, at the head of his troops, to pay his homage to St. Peter. Into this basilica, mixed among the people, had fled also the patricians Maximus and Orestes. All hoped that in this sacred place they would enjoy the right of asylum, as they had done under Alaric.

When the King of the Goths arrived at the great entrance, he saw

---

[4] In his first homily on the Gospel, the Pope again describes the extensive damage caused to the city of Rome at that time by the elements: *"Nudiustertius, fratres, agnovistis quod subito annosa arbusta eruta, destructae domus, atque ecclesiae a fundamentis erutae sunt. Quanti ad vesperum sani atque incolumes, acturos se in crastinum aliquid putabant, et tamen nocte eadem repentina morte defuncti sunt, in laqueo ruinae deprehensi?"* The cloudburst came at night. In the same homily the saint mentions some other atmospheric phenomena that were observed soon after St. Benedict's death: *"Priusquam Italia gentili gladio ferienda traderetur, igneas in caelo acies vidimus, ipsum qui postea humani generis est, sanguinem coruscantem."*

the deacon Pelagius, with the cross and Gospel in his hands, approaching him anew to conjure him to spare the populace. At first the monarch replied to the excited Levite with a sneer: "Deacon, is it you who stand before me now and beg with such a suppliant voice?"

"It is indeed," replied Pelagius; "but God himself this day has given us all into your hands. Spare what is yours."

He begged so insistently that the King promised to save the lives of the Romans and to respect the honor of their women. But he could not be induced to spare the city the horrors of pillaging; in particular he inveighed against the rich and the senators. "What evil have the Goths done you that you refused to grant them even a piece of desert land? See, the Isaurians have opened to us the gates of Spoleto and Rome. For that reason they will receive the principal posts, and you will obey them." Finally the deacon Pelagius soothed the conqueror to the extent that he was sent to Constantinople to negotiate a peace in the name of the King. As we see, the exhortation of the Patriarch of Cassino now produced its effect.

Later on the varying fortunes of war brought it about that Rome was alternately occupied by the Goths and by the Greeks. We can hardly say which side conducted itself worse. If Totila from time to time murdered bishops and dukes, the Romans also, in their turn, conceived such a hatred for the Byzantines that one day they slew outright their general, Conon, who was starving the populace, and they forced the court to declare an amnesty, under threat of handing them all over to the Goths if they did not comply with the demand.

We know absolutely nothing about the fate of the monasteries at Subiaco when that territory was occupied by the barbarians. By order of Totila, the inhabitants of Tivoli together with their bishop were butchered in such a shameful manner that Procopius refrains from describing the slaughter. Perugia, too, was sacked by the Goths, who then beheaded Bishop Herculanus and cast his corpse over the wall.

The holy bishop Cerbonius of Populonia had hidden some Greek soldiers who were passing through the city. For this crime Totila threw him to ferocious bears near the gates of Rome.

Not far from Monte Cassino, Darida, one of the conqueror's captains, met the monk Libertine, superior of the monastery at Fondi. The soldiers stopped and threw him off his horse in order to rob him of his beast. The monk, recalling the words of the Gospel, "If anyone . . . take thy tunic, let him take they cloak as well," gave them even the whip.

In another spot, about thirty miles from Rome, not determined more exactly, but one which some have tried to identify with the monastery of the deacon Servandus, there lived another holy monk, who bore the name of Benedict. Though young in years, he was strong and mature in virtue. He lived in a slight shelter not far from a baker, outside the village. One day the Goths, truly bestial fellows, sought some diversion at the expense of the holy hermit; they shut him in his cell and set fire to the fields round about. The trees and bushes indeed burned, but the cabin of Benedict remained unharmed, to the wonderment and exasperation of the butchers, who on the following day found their victim quite calm, lost in prayer. Not even this miracle softened the hearts of the savages. Since they had not succeeded in cremating him in his hermitage, they drew him forth by force and thrust him into the baker's heated oven and shut the door. A little later the soldiers became curious to know if at least the bones remained. What was their surprise when they espied the monk reclining in the oven, immobile as if he were in a little cell, intent on prayer! Not even his garments were singed.

Gregory [5] compares this prodigy to that of the three youths in the fiery furnace in Babylon and states that he received the information from one of his monks of St. Andrew's, a man who was very learned in the Sacred Scriptures. Evidently it must have been one of the monks of Latium or of the Campania, whom the Gothic and Lombard wars forced to flee to Rome.

[5] *Dial.*, Bk. III, chap. 18.

CHAPTER LVIII

More Powerful than Her Brother

I HAVE already told how St. Scholastica from childhood was consecrated to the Lord by the veil of holy virginity and how her example
influenced her brother to abandon Rome and seek the solitude of
the desert in the flower of his youth. Throughout the life of St. Benedict, the biographer tells us nothing more about her, only to have
her suddenly reappear on the scene three days before her death.

Conjectures about a residence of St. Scholastica in Rome, at Subiaco, or at Cassino, within the sphere of her brother's spiritual influence, can be made at will; St. Gregory seems to intimate something of
the kind.[1] But history, given the complete lack of documentation,
cannot confirm it. We know only that Scholastica, like other virgins
of the vicinity, dwelt not in her own house, like the sharp-tongued
nuns, but in a *cella,* that is, a small convent, perhaps in company with
another religious woman who assisted her and served her.

Some historians speak very positively of a convent of sacred virgins
over whom Scholastica presided as abbess. True it is, the word *cella,*
used on that occasion by the biographer, according to his manner of
speaking can be applied even to Monte Cassino, which he calls *cella*
in another connection. But from the context of St. Gregory's story one
does not get the impression that Scholastica lived with a community
of nuns. It must have been a kind of hermitage with a few religious;
there were others like it on the mountain of Casinum.

Hence it is impossible to speak of the office of abbess in connection

---

[1] *"Quorum mens una semper in Deo fuerat"* (*Dial.*, Bk. II, chap. 34).

with the Rule of St. Benedict, though true abbesses already existed at that time, not only at Capua, but even in Rome, at the tomb of St. Agnes.

Further, if St. Scholastica in her early years followed her brother to Rome, she may easily have been acquainted with the abbess Serena, who lived at the second milestone on the Via Nomentana and whose epitaph is still extant.[2]

A Cassinese tradition, whose origin is lost, places the *cella* of St. Scholastica at *Plumbariola,* not far from Aquino. In that spot, through the efforts of King Ratchis, in the eighth century, a former monastery for men, which had been dedicated to St. Petronilla, was remodeled to serve as a convent for virgins. The first nuns were Queen Tasia and her daughter Ratrudis, to whom Pope Zachary himself gave the veil. This happened about 750.

The dedication of the church to St. Petronilla convinces me more and more that St. Scholastica had nothing to do with the place. As we learn from the *Liber diurnus,* in the early Christian era there existed in that place a monastery of men with a basilica dedicated to the Blessed Virgin. Indeed we possess a papal document granted "to the abbot of the venerable monastery of St. Mary, Mother of God, at *Plumbariola,* in the territory of Aquino." We can ascertain neither the date nor the name of the recipient of the papal letter; but from the context we know that the monastery, before being turned into a convent for noble Lombard virgins, had been occupied by male religious and went under the title of the great Mother of God.

The cult of St. Scholastica, thanks to the Benedictine nuns, appears much later in that place. I do not even understand how the tradition of Piumarola can be harmonized with the other represented by the author of the metrical life of St. Scholastica, who assures us that she went to Cassino and there established her residence in the plain at

---

[2]   † HIC REQVIESCIT IN PACE †
SERENA ABBATISSA S. V.
QVAE VIXIT ANNVS P. M. LXXXV
DEP. VII ID MAI SENATORE
VC CONS

The inscription is of the year 514, when Flavius Magnus Aurelius Cassiodorus was consul. A *"soror Benedicta,"* a nun in the Vatican convent of St. Stephen kata Galla Placidia and a contemporary of St. Benedict, is mentioned in Book IV, chapter 13, of the *Dialogues.*

the base of the valley. It is true that Piumarola also is in a plain; but it does not belong to Cassino, since it is in the territory of Aquino and is about three miles distant from the abbey.[3]

At the base of Monte Cassino, however, is an ancient church dedicated to St. Scholastica; its location corresponds rather well with the topographical indications of the old documents. Recent excavations behind the so-called Chapel of the Conversation have brought to light the remains of a small basilica with an apse, which was later enlarged.

The floor of this second oratory in its turn was laid over an earlier one and shows traces of successive restorations. This stratification of floors and especially the great importance attached to this church from the early Middle Ages make me look for the residence of the Patriarch's sister in the village, in whose midst, already at an early period, rose the chapel dedicated to her. At that time churches were dedicated only to martyrs or to a few confessors who enjoyed universal veneration.[4] Hence St. Scholastica must be considered an exception.

Rome used to dedicate to the saints the residences they had occupied, as, for example, those of St. Clement, St. Felicitas, St. Cecilia, SS. John and Paul, St. Hippolytus, St. Eusebius, and so on. The monks of Cassino did the same.

Peter the Deacon relates how in 1134 a certain lady of Frosinone,

[3] The anonymous Cassinese author, who in the tenth century points out to us the window through which St. Benedict saw St. Scholastica's soul rising to heaven, tells us that this window looks toward *Plumbariola*, as, on the other hand, that through which he perceived the soul of Germanus going heavenward looks toward Capua. It is quite possible that here the author speaks of *Plumbariola*, since at that time it was regarded as the place where the saint dwelt. But considering the matter strictly, the author may have indicated the well-known Roman *vicus* merely as a point of orientation. The small medieval basilica of St. Scholastica at the foot of the mountain does, in fact, lie in the direction of *Plumbariola*. As a result, the mention of *Plumbariola*, not rightly interpreted, gave rise to the belief that this *vicus* was the place where Scholastica spent her last years.

[4] On the spot in question artifacts of many generations of inhabitants and of ancient civilizations have been uncovered. I have already mentioned arms of the Iron Age and small clay vessels used for votive purposes. Did another temple stand in this place, or do the votive offerings have some connection with the *"antiquissimum fanum"* of Cassino?

As far as the medieval basilica is concerned—possibly a successor to a pagan shrine— mention of it occurs in a Cassinese calendar of the eighth century (*Codex Parisinus*, no. 1530). For June 19 we read:

Sancti Gervasii et Protasii, et Dedicatio
Sce Scholasticae

after being healed from an ailment through the intercession of St. Scholastica, went to make her thanksgiving, not at Piumarola, but in this oratory; at the same time she offered a band of silver all round the chapel. She also undertook to pay the expenses for the annual celebration of the titular feast of the saint at that place.

St. Gregory relates that Scholastica, all intent on heavenly things, scarcely once a year left her *cella* to go up the mountain to visit her brother. By reason of the monastic enclosure, Benedict used to receive her at a little distance from the first circle of the ancient walls on a piece of property belonging to the monastery, to which reference has already been made. Attached to this land was a small house, supplied with the necessary conveniences for spending the day there, for taking meals, and for sleeping as well. The building was a little more than two hundred yards down from the monastery. It was an easy matter for one in good health to make the ascent by day; but for an aged man, perhaps suffering from a weak heart, and particularly in the dark of night, during a violent storm, with the rain coming down in torrents, that was an entirely different matter. To understand St. Gregory's story which follows, these circumstances must be borne in mind.

The last time St. Scholastica went up the mountain to see her brother must have been in the first days of February about the year 547. Doubtless the virgin could not go alone, but took along some companions. If the chronological data supplied by ancient writers are exact, February 7, 547, fell on the Thursday preceding the first Sunday of Lent. It was customary for religious and pious souls to anticipate the beginning of the solemn Lenten fast during the week of Quinquagesima. But, according to the Roman tradition prior to Gregory II, Thursday was always a non-liturgical day on which no stational Mass was celebrated. I repeat, if the traditional chronology is correct, then it is easily understandable that Scholastica wished to visit her brother before beginning the strict Lenten retreat.

Earlier mention was made of the fact that St. Radegundis in her monastery of the Holy Cross at Poitiers used to pass the whole of Lent without leaving her cell. During the first year Benedict resided at Casinum, he did the same. According to his custom, then, the Patriarch went down to meet his sister. Since his strength was declining, he was accompanied by a group of monks who also spent the entire day in the little house. From the context of St. Gregory's story it becomes clear that the monks of Cassino were well acquainted with the Abbot's sister, and hence her annual visit on the mountain was a bit of a feast for all. They could not help being edified by her conversation!

It is superfluous to say that these two great souls discoursed of that which filled their hearts. Since their spirits could not yet soar to the heavenly fatherland, they consoled each other by speaking of it, as saints who suffer homesickness for paradise are accustomed to do. The intimacy of this sweet converse between brother and sister was not at all disturbed by the presence of the monks. Quite naturally they shared St. Benedict's spiritual confidence, and they also knew of the treasure of virtue hidden in his sister's heart. This spiritual conversation continued throughout the day. It seemed as if Scholastica hung on every word that fell from her brother's lips. The longer St. Benedict spoke of God and of paradise, the more ardent became the fire of divine love burning in Scholastica's soul.

An echo of these pre-Lenten conferences can be perceived in chapter 41 of the Rule, "On the Observance of Lent." There the holy Patriarch speaks insistently of the joy of the Holy Spirit and of the salutary desire with which we ought to pass that season in the joyous expectation of the eternal Easter: "Let each one look forward to holy Easter with the joy of spiritual desire." On that day, who adverted to the needs of the body? Who remembered that they had not eaten?

But when it began to grow dark, St. Benedict at last had the table prepared, so that he might sup with his sister. It was understood that Scholastica would spend the night in the hospice. They desired to imitate Jesus, to make this a true last supper. Like the divine Master, during this meal on the pre-Lenten holy Thursday, Benedict quite likely spoke of the infinite love of the heavenly Father in sending His own Son into the world as a Savior. The man of God was not in any hurry, since the monastery was but a few steps from the guesthouse of the women. Perhaps also Scholastica at a certain point of the supper interrupted her brother to repeat the petition of the apostle Philip: "Lord, show us the Father, and it is enough."

The supper and the sweet fraternal conversation went calmly on, while outside night had fallen, and the monks of St. Martin's were reciting Compline. Perhaps the two saints purposely waited till night-fall on the occasion of that final meeting so that even the hour of their last supper might coincide with that celebrated by Jesus in the upper room. No doubt this circumstance was mentioned, and St. Bene-dict, the wonder-worker, could not help recalling the promise of the Savior that those who would believe in Him would work miracles like His, or even greater ones. Scholastica listened and prudently kept her peace.

Suddenly she said to the Abbot: "Please, brother, do not leave me tonight, but let us speak of the delights of heaven till dawn."

The Patriarch replied with great astonishment: "What are you ask-ing, my sister? I may not spend the night outside the monastery."

The weather at the moment was exceedingly beautiful, as it usually is in the Campania toward the approach of spring. When she heard her brother's refusal, the sacred virgin put her thin and almost diaphanous hands up to her face and then bowed over the table. It seemed as if she were trying to hide her tears, when in fact she was praying. A few moments later she raised her head, and her eyes were bathed in tears; and in the distance, from behind Monte Cairo, could be heard the low rumble of an approaching storm.

Benedict looked at Scholastica in amazement, without yet compre-hending what she was about.

"Now, brother," she said with a happy smile, "go back to your monastery if you will, and leave me alone here this night."

While she was saying these words, suddenly an extremely violent spring storm broke upon them with lightning, thunder, and tor-rential rain. To go outside in those circumstances was simply impos-sible.

"What have you done, my sister?" St. Benedict asked with a re-proachful voice.

"I asked a favor of you, and you refused to hear me," she replied sweetly. "I turned to my Lord, and He, more generous than you, granted my request. Leave me now, leave if you can, and return to your monastery."

What was to be done? The miracle was manifest. For a moment a holy fraternal love had been in conflict with the regularity of dis-cipline. But God Himself had declared in favor of love, so that, contrary to St. Benedict's will, Scholastica, as the biographer remarks, turned out to be stronger than her brother, because her love was greater (*"plus potuit quia plus amavit"*). The rain continued to pour down with such violence that neither the aged Abbot nor any of his disciples, as St. Gregory points out, succeeded in setting foot outside the house. Perhaps they, too, were impressed by the miracle. They had to reconcile themselves to the need of spending the night there; and indeed it passed very rapidly, for, after the psalms of the night Office had been said, the two saints continued their pious colloquy. Friday dawned, and since in Rome the stational Mass consecrating the beginning of the fast was being celebrated, we may justly suppose that St. Scholastica assisted at the Mass celebrated by her brother and from his blessed hands received her last Communion. Otherwise, why should St. Benedict have arranged for his sister to spend the night on Monte Cassino instead of sending her back to her residence? [5]

Finally, when day had come, brother and sister said farewell to each other. Scholastica's eyes were red with weeping, because in her heart she knew that this was the last time she would see her brother. The Abbot's troubled gaze followed her for a while as she descended the

---

[5] I wish to emphasize that I am here expressing a simple conjecture, though it is not entirely unfounded. In a guesthouse having a number of rooms (a kitchen and dining room, bedrooms for Scholastica and her companions), why should we not find a chapel for singing the Office and celebrating Mass for the convenience of the guests, "who are never lacking" (Rule, chap. 53) at Monte Cassino?

In various medieval monasteries, at Farfa, for example, since the early eighth century there existed a building for guests outside the walls surrounding the monastery, and the women were received outside the clausura in the little church of St. Mary. At Monte Cassino there must have been a similar arrangement. Guests there were every day, as St. Benedict himself writes: men, women, ecclesiastics, and so on. It was not always possible for all of these, after a long journey and the fatigue of the ascent, to return to Casinum the same day. On the other hand, the monastic enclosure and even the Cassinese basilicas remained inaccessible to women throughout the Middle Ages.

For the convenience of the guests, ever since the eighth century, we find at Monte Cassino near the gate the little church of St. Stephen *de foris portam*, whose dedication is assigned to June 8 in the Cassinese calendars of the *Codex Cavensis* (23) and the *Codex Parisinus* (7350):

Dedicatio oratorii Sancti Stephani.

To conclude, an *oratorium* or a *sacellum* for the celebration of the Divine Office was a constituent part of the plan of a medieval xenodochium. This the Rule itself seems to indicate, where it commands that guests, immediately upon their arrival, be "taken to prayer, and afterward let the superior . . . sit with them" at table. Both the liturgical prayer at their reception and the meal took place in the guesthouse, that is, in the *"cella hospitum"* (Rule, chap. 53). Hence the place also had a chapel.

mountain by the circuitous path. Then, with the other monks, he went up to the monastery.

With a heart that was overflowing with the fire of love that was devouring her, the virgin, with considerable fatigue, went down the rocky mountainside and returned to her convent. If the labors and the weight of years were burdening her brother, in whose veins already was beginning the fever that would destroy him, the fire of divine love was consuming her, too, and prevented her from living longer here below. At the end of the journey she was tired. She spent the following day lost in the recollection of that last supper. Suddenly she was seized with such a mighty longing for paradise that her heart could stand it no longer. Without any apparent illness, under the powerful influence of love alone, she breathed her last, and her soul, like a white dove, winged its way upward to heaven. It was the tenth day of February.

At that selfsame moment, probably before the night Office, Benedict was engaged in prayer. He stood at the window of the tower, because thus he could breathe easier, and his spirit readily soared beyond the starry vault of heaven. Suddenly, in the direction of *Plumbariola*, he noticed a great light, in which he seemed to detect the soul of Scholastica rising upward under the symbol of a dove. He beheld the embrace which her heavenly Spouse gave her, saw the immense glory which she shared in the choir of holy virgins, and recognized how God wished to glorify also on this earth the most chaste body which for so long a time had harbored that pure soul.

What effect this vision created in St. Benedict no human mind can grasp. If the affection of the sister three days earlier seemed more tender, his love for her was stronger, more virile, because into it entered spirit, mind, and heart. St. Gregory says simply that the two possessed but one soul, which united them in the Lord. For this reason the holy Patriarch decided that after death their bodies should repose together in the peace of the grave. "Whose souls were always one in God, were not even separated by the tomb" (chap. 34). When he came out of the ecstasy, the man of God began to sing psalms and hymns with all his heart, to accompany Scholastica into heaven, thanking the infinite goodness of God for reserving to her such a sublime degree of glory.

On the following morning, when the community gathered in the chapter room after the Office of Prime, the Patriarch, in terms that still betrayed deep emotion, told of the vision he had enjoyed and described the glory that was his sister's in paradise. *"Tantae eius gloriae congaudens . . . eiusque obitum fratribus nuntiavit."*

Since in Scholastica's convent [6] there was no one who could vindicate to himself the right of giving her the final honors of burial,[7] Benedict claimed it for himself. It is true that a novella of Justinian (133) forbade the burial of women in the monasteries of men. But since this was a case of brother and sister, it was considered as not falling under the prohibition. Therefore the Patriarch sent some monks to bring the angelic remains to the monastery, so that they might be placed in his own tomb.[8]

The command was carried out, and we can reconstruct the moving scene without much difficulty. While the cortege of monks sang psalms as they ascended the mountain by its winding path and slowly drew nearer, the Patriarch, surrounded by the community, most likely awaited Scholastica not far from the outer circle of walls, in almost the very spot where four days before they had spoken their last farewell. The monks, with the Abbot at their head, sang hymns and psalms to the Lord with a full heart. Those who were coming up with

[6] I have already mentioned that this *cella* or convent of St. Scholastica was situated in a very ancient *vicus* to the west of Casinum. We do not know whether, after Theodoric had dismantled Cassino, also the old Samnite settlement in which Scholastica lived remained deserted. In any case, it appears improbable that this *sanctimonialis foemina* should have lived alone, *in loco proprio*. If she resided in a *cella* or convent, she had to lead a religious life with other virgins. And the fact that Benedict should claim the body to bring it up to Monte Cassino for burial in his own grave causes no difficulty. The laws of the time reserved to the nearest relative the charge of paying the last honors to the deceased. Thus also St. Ambrose did with his brother Satyrus.

[7] About half a mile from the medieval church of St. Scholastica we find the remains of a rectangular building resting on the slope of the hill. It measured about 46 x 15 feet and was built of large blocks of stone.
The structure appears isolated, but Carettoni advances the hypothesis that it may have been an observation post, depending on the fortress of Casinum, for the protection of the inhabitants of the region. Hence also the spot where St. Benedict established St. Scholastica's residence must have been state property (cf. Carettoni, *op. cit.*, p. 106).

[8] As monasteries had their own chapels, so they had their proper cemeteries. Therefore Gregory I reproaches John, bishop of Orvieto, because he forbade the monks of the monastery of St. George to bury their dead in that place: *"In eodem monasterio Missas prohibeatis celebrari, sepeliri ibidem mortuos interdicatis. Quod si ita est, a tali vos hortamur inhumanitate suspendi"* (*Letters*, Bk. I, no. 12) .

the bier replied, and the mountain echoed with the joyous strains of sacred song.

When the corpse had been deposited in the basilica of St. Martin, the brother most likely presided at the customary rite of Christian burial. St. Jerome, in describing how St. Anthony buried St. Paul in the desert, relates that first he sang the psalms which were customary on such occasion "by Christian tradition."

The virginal body of Scholastica lay for a whole night in St. Martin's. The next day the *"Sacrificium pro dormitione"* was celebrated for her.[9] I do not know if, following the example of St. Ambrose at the burial of his brother Satyrus, Benedict likewise pronounced a funeral eulogy. But the praises of Scholastica were already in the hearts and on the lips of all, while they bore in mind the miracle worked by her only four days before, when through her prayers and tears she had brought it about that even the heavens should weep, shedding a deluge of water on Monte Cassino.

After the Mass and the final farewell to the deceased ("*In pace spiritus Scholasticae. Amen*"), they proceeded to the entombment. The veil of virginal consecration was arranged about her head, as is expressly stated in a Milanese epitaph of another virgin who was buried "*cum capete velato.*"

Already some time previously St. Benedict had had his grave prepared in the little building dedicated to St. John the Baptist, which stood where formerly the oracle of Apollo had given its replies. In that place, removed from the residence, where a thick votive grove had surrounded that sanctuary of a dying idolatry, the Patriarch laid out the cemetery of the community.[10] The chapel of the Baptist

[9] A Roman inscription from the cemetery of SS. Processus and Martinian clearly states that the corpse was buried only the day after it had been brought to the place of burial:

PECORI DULCIS ANIMA BENIT IN CIMITERO VII IDUS IVL DP POSTERA DIE MARTIRORUM.

The body of Pecorius was carried to the cemetery on July 9, but was entombed only the following day, which was dedicated precisely to the memory of the Seven Brothers.

[10] Of this *coemeterium fratrum*, in whose center rose the oratory of St. John the Baptist, whither St. Benedict at times betook himself to pray, mention is made in the anonymous *Translatio S. Benedicti*, edited by Mabillon (*Analecta*, IV, 451). This account, which is of the eighth century, states that the tomb in which the bodies of the holy twins reposed was divided horizontally by a marble slab that separated the remains. This circumstance helps to explain how St. Benedict, according to St. Gregory's account, could order his grave to be opened six days before his death (*Dial.*, Bk. II, chap. 37).

stood in the center; round about it were arranged the graves of the monks, naturally lying under the open sky and dug out of the rock of the mountain.

Just as Ambrose at Milan had yielded the right side of his tomb to the martyrs Gervase and Protase, so that after death he might rest with them and close to his brother Satyrus, so also did Benedict act. He placed his sister in the lower part of the grave, so that even in the sleep of death he might be near her with whom he had been spiritually united throughout his earthly life. Thus it came about, observes St. Gregory, that these two great souls, who lived but for each other, were not separated even in death. For a century and a half their bodies lay together in the tomb on Monte Cassino before the cult of the two saints flowered out in churches and chapels throughout Europe.

Of this tenderness of St. Benedict for his sister, however surprising it may appear to us, history furnishes us with other famous examples. When, as a youth, St. Benedict visited the catacombs of St. Callistus on the Via Appia, he must have paused frequently to read the long eulogy in marble which Pope Damasus placed over the grave of his sister Irene. This consecrated virgin, confided by her dying mother to the care of the brother, had been the inspiration of Damasus' whole life. For her alone he lived; when she died at a mature age, it seemed to the Pope that life had lost much of its meaning. Later, when he himself was on the point of leaving this world, he preferred burial near his mother and sister in the catacombs of Callistus rather than in the official tomb in St. Peter's among his predecessors.[11]

It is hard to see how the Patriarch could have been ignorant of this perfumed page of chaste fraternal love in the life of St. Damasus. Indeed, the spiritual relations between St. Benedict and St. Scholastica, in Gregory's narrative, seem to be inspired by those of Damasus and Irene.[12]

If this had been the usual double grave, with a vertical dividing slab, its opening would not have been possible, since for a whole week the air would have been contaminated by an exposed corpse in an advanced stage of decomposition. But the circumstance of the horizontal slab between the corpses clarifies the situation described by St. Gregory and gives greater authority to the account of the anonymous author of the *Translatio*. It is true that, generally speaking, Christians did not favor the superimposition of corpses. But several examples of it are extant.

[11] ". . . iuxta matrem suam et sororem suam," as the *Liber diurnus* puts it.

[12] I cannot resist the temptation of setting down in this place the beautiful verses of

The eulogy which Damasus composed for the virgin Irene reads as follows: "In this tomb the remains of the sister of Damasus, Irene by name, a virgin consecrated to God, have found their final resting place. When not yet twenty years of age, she dedicated the flower of her life to Christ. Her holy modesty showed forth the maturity of her virtue. With outstanding good works she anticipated her years, since the deep piety of youth guaranteed the firmness of her resolutions, which in later years brought forth wonderful fruits. Our mother, the only witness of our fraternal affection, when on the point of leaving this world, entrusted you to me, O my sister, as the earnest of her love for us. And when at last heaven snatched you away, death did not frighten me, since I knew you would go straightway to paradise; but I wept, I confess, because I had lost my life's companion. Now that the Lord is about to come, remember me, O virgin, so that God may grant me light in the brightness of your lamp." [13]

---

the Pope on the grave of his sister. They serve as a commentary on the epitaph of St. Gregory on the tomb of brother and sister of Monte Cassino:

VT QVORVM MENS VNA SEMPER IN DEO EVERAT, EORVM QVOQVE
CORPORA NEC SEPVLTVRA SEPARARET.

(. . . that the bodies of these two, whose souls were always one in God, might not even be separated by the tomb.)

[13] HOC TVMVLO SACRATA DEO NVNC MEMBRA QVIESCVNT
HIC SOROR EST DAMASI NOMEN SI QVAERIS IRENE.
VOVERAT HAEC SESE CHRISTO CVM VITA MANERET,
VIRGINIS VT MERITVM SANCTVM PVDOR IPSE PROBARET.
BIS DENOS HIEMES NECDVM COMPLEVERAT AETAS
EGREGIOS MORES VITAE PRAECESSERAT AETAS
PROPOSITVM MENTIS PIETAS VENERANDA PVELLAE
MAGNIFICOS FRVCTVS DEDERAT MELIORIBVS ANNIS.
TE GERMANA SOROR, NOSTRI TVNC TESTIS AMORIS
CVM FVGERET MVNDVM DEDERAT MIHI PIGNVS HONESTVM
QVAM SIBI CVM RAPERET MELIOR TVNC REGIA CAELI
NON TIMVI MORTEM CAELOS QVOS LIBERA ADIRET
SED DOLVI, FATEOR, CONSORTIA PERDERE VITAE.
NVNC VENIENTE DEO, NOSTRI REMINISCERE, VIRGO,
VT TVA PER DOMINVM PRAESTET MIHI FACVLA LVMEN.

CHAPTER LIX

Stars That Set

THE Patriarch was growing old, and round about him a void was developing. Gone were the happy days of those popes from whom Benedict had received the authorization to construct the first group of twelve monasteries at Subiaco, the confirmation of the missionary endeavor at Casinum, the invitation to send a colony of his disciples to the Lateran, and finally the task of drawing up a new and universal Rule for monasteries.

Pope Felix IV, a relative of St. Gregory who calls him "my ancestor," died in 530, when the Patriarch was just beginning his missionary work at the *castrum* of Cassino.

Pope Agapitus, who had so fully shared the views of Cassiodorus about the foundation of a monastic school of graduate studies in theology in Rome, passed away at Constantinople in the spring of 536.

Pope Silverius was a native of Frosinone, and better than any other was in a position to be well acquainted with the affairs of the neighboring abbey of Monte Cassino. But, alas! he perished the victim of the theologaster Justinian and of Theodora, the former circus performer. The sick who at his tomb on the island of Ponza recovered their health were among the very few who dared to proclaim the merits of the tormented Pontiff.

On March 29, 537, while Silverius was going into exile, the intriguing deacon Vigilius, not the least responsible for the woes of his predecessor, mounted the papal throne. We know absolutely nothing of the relations of St. Benedict with the new pope, but the founda-

tion of St. Pancratius in the Lateran dates from that time. Certain it
is that, however much the Pontiff tried to redeem himself by restoring
the smashed inscriptions of Damasus and by erecting the church of
SS. Stephen and Lawrence near the Forum, the Roman people never
could bring themselves to have any love for Vigilius, whom they were
to know only for a few years and in a decidedly unfavorable light.

We must, however, mention Vigilius' relations with Bishop Dacius
of Milan. When, during the Pope's long exile at Constantinople, we
find the Milanese bishop sharing with him the hardships of his lot,
his flight and his refuge near the tomb of St. Euphemia, it will help
to keep in mind that Dacius' influence on Vigilius derived from a
long-time aquaintance and from family connections. In fact, before
being elevated to the see of St. Ambrose, Dacius had been a monk
and the abbot of a monastery called "Romanum" in the plains of
Milan, today known as Romano Banco.

When in 544 the subdeacon Arator read his poem *De actibus apostolorum* in honor of Vigilius in Rome, the manuscript had first been
submitted to the censorship of Abbot Florian, Milanese by birth, a
monk and successively a disciple of Dacius and then of Caesarius of
Arles. This last name is important because of the influence he exercised on the *Regula monasteriorum*.

In 537 Bishop Dacius went to Rome to plead with Belisarius for
troops to defend Milan. Later on Reparatus, brother of Vigilius and
pretorian prefect, fled to Dacius to escape the ire of Witigis, who was
furious at the election of the new pope, a *persona non grata* with the
Goths. When Uraias took Milan in 539, he had Reparatus cut up and
threw the pieces to the dogs. Later still, Dacius was deported to Constantinople. As soon as he learned that Pope Vigilius was about to
arrive at the capital of the East, he went immediately to meet him at
Syracuse and to instruct him concerning the theological controversies
that Justinian was fomenting in Constantinople. When the time came,
Dacius exerted a decisive influence on Pope Vigilius in the question
of the Three Chapters.

These intimate and continued relations of the former abbot of
"Romanum" with the exiled Pope help to explain better the interest
which Vigilius took in monastic affairs.

Vigilius assumed the pontificate in 537 and eight years later was deported from Rome. Confined in Constantinople, he lived on there for ten years and finally died at Syracuse on June 7, 555. His body was carried to Rome, but the citizens, who had known little of him during his lifetime, cared for him even less after his death. Contrary to the tradition followed in the case of his predecessors, the corpse of Pope Vigilius, instead of being buried in St. Peter's, was carried outside the gates for interment in the catacombs of Priscilla on the Via Salaria. The Roman clergy and a good part of the Latin episcopate regarded him as a traitor to the beliefs of the fathers of Chalcedon by reason of the condemnation of the Three Chapters.

St. Caesarius had died already on August 27, 543. St. Benedict who, together with the majority of the Roman patriciate, might have become acquainted with him in the capital, in any case was well versed in his thought and used his writings copiously in composing the Rule.

At the age of seventy-one, when the Bishop of Arles felt his death approaching, he had himself carried in a chair to the monastery of St. John, there to see for the last time his sister Caesaria and the choir of two hundred consecrated virgins serving Christ in that place. He gave them a final instruction, blessed them, and amid the weeping of the nuns returned to his own church, where he died on the vigil of the feast of St. Augustine. This incident of a saintly brother and sister meeting for the last time before death recurred four years later in the life of St. Benedict.

A considerably longer span of life was granted to a veteran in the new crusade for the restoration of monasticism in Italy. This was Cassiodorus, who at the age of seventy laid down the highest honor in the Gothic kingdom in order to become the founder of a monastery at Vivarium on his possessions in Calabria.[1] There the former minister

---

[1] Historians are not agreed about the true reasons for Cassiodorus' retirement from political life. Probably his sense of "Romanism" induced the prime minister of the Goths to resign his office when his government decided to declare war on the Greeks.

Under identical circumstances, the poet Arator, *comes privatarum*, at the outbreak of hostilities, abandoned the court of Ravenna to seek refuge in Rome. There Pope Vigilius gave him a cordial reception, ordained him subdeacon, and in every way seconded his literary studies. As a mark of his gratitude, Arator dedicated to him the poem *De actibus apostolorum*, which, at the request of the clergy, after April 6, 544, he declaimed in the basilica of St. Peter-in-Chains on the Esquiline.

Contrary to St. Benedict's prophecy, Arator gave the Romans the assurance that the Goths would not enter Rome, defended as it was, so he maintained, by the sacred chains of St. Peter: no barbarian horde would ever succeed in battering down its walls.

of state spent almost another half century (from 543 to 583) engaged in directing his "school of the Lord's service." After his ninety-third birthday he was still occupied in writing, gathering books for the library of the monastery, hoping against every hope to see the fulfillment of his golden dream, the religious renascence of Europe by means of monachism.

I have already related the juridical affairs which doubtless brought St. Benedict into contact with the court of Ravenna and with Cassiodorus, namely, obtaining the fortress of Casinum and converting the temples into Christian churches.

Apart from the chapter of *De anima* in which Cassiodorus paints the word-portrait of a holy monk, who, from the iconographic features, can, in my opinion, be no one else than St. Benedict, we find no reference to the Patriarch in the writings of the abbot of Vivarium, though he mentions other famous personages of his time. In the *De institutione* divinarum litterarum, however, he is concerned exclusively with the great Fathers and writers of the Church. Nevertheless it is interesting to find so close an affinity of thought and sometimes of words between him and St. Benedict that apparently a literary dependence exists between the two writers.[2]

[2] The following excerpts will suffice:

St. Benedict	Cassiodorus
Constituenda est ergo nobis Dominici schola servitii (Prol.). Exaltatione descendere et humilitate adscendere (chap. 7).	In schola siquidem Christi cor indocile non potest inveniri. . . . Ad te . . . nemo se erigendo pervenit sed potius humiliatus adscendit (*De anima*, chap. 19).
Actibus nostris ascendentibus scala illa erigenda est, quae in somno Iacob apparuit, per quam ei descendentes et adscendentes angeli monstrabantur (chap. 7).	Divina Scriptura. . . . Ista est enim fortasse scala Iacob, per quam Angeli adscendunt atque descendunt, cui Dominus innititur.
Codices autem legantur in Vigiliis Divinae Auctoritatis (chap. 9).	Hunc debemus lectionis ordinem custodire, ut primum tyrones Christi, postquam psalmos didicerint, Auctoritatem Divinam in codicibus emendatis iugi exercitatione meditentur (*De instit.*, I, 1).
Sicut psallit Ecclesia Romana dicatur (chap. 13).	Quod hodie usu celeberrimo Ecclesia Romana complectitur (Bk. X, chap. 23).
Obsculta, o fili, praecepta Magistri . . . et admonitionem pii patris libenter excipe et efficaciter comple (Prol.).	Omnes quos Monasterii septa concludunt, tam Patrum Regulas quam Praeceptoris proprii iussa servate et libenter quae vobis salubriter imperantur efficite;
Sed haec ipsa oboedientia tunc acceptabilis erit Deo . . . si quod iubetur non trepide . . . aut cum murmurio . . . efficiatur (chap. 7).	quia magnae remunerationis praemium sine aliquo murmure praeceptis salutaribus oboedire.

This affinity of words and of ideas is rather impressive; indeed, it becomes certain, if the anonymous prelate of the treatise *De anima* with the white beard and the single tunic, perfectly clean and giving off an angelic perfume, is St. Benedict. Who else can this person be? The perfect correspondence between the sketch of Cassiodorus and the portrait of the monk which St. Benedict draws, particularly in describing the mystical ladder of humility (chap. 7), lends greater credence to the supposition.[3]

St. Benedict *(continued)*

De generibus monachorum. . . . His ergo omissis, ad coenobitarum fortissimum genus disponendum . . . veniamus (Prol.).

Ita et [abbatem] ipsum condecet cuncta disponere (chap. 2).

Abbas timens semper futuram discussionem Pastoris de creditis ovibus (chap. 2).

Pauperum et peregrinorum maxime susceptionis cura solliciter exhibeatur (chap. 53).

Ecce, haec sunt instrumenta artis spiritalis (chap. 4).

Necnon et Collationes Patrum et Instituta et Vitas eorum . . . quarum observatio perducat hominem ad celsitudinem perfectionis (chap. 73).

Balnearum usus infirmis quotiens expedit offeratur (chap. 36).

Anachoritarum qui . . . monasterii probatione diuturna didicerunt contra diabolum . . . pugnare . . . Deo auxiliante pugnare sufficient (chap. 1).

Cuius infirmitati in tantum compassus est, ut eam in sacris humeris suis dignaretur imponere (chap. 27).

[3] A few citations will suffice.

Regula monasteriorum

Undecimus humilitatis gradus est, si cum loquitur monachus leniter et sine risu, humiliter cum gravitate, vel pauca

Cassiodorus *(continued)*

Coetera vero genera monachorum vehementer accusat (*De div. lect.*, XXIX).

Vos autem sanctissimos viros Abbates Chalcedonium et Gerontium deprecor, ut sic cuncta disponatis quatenus gregem vobis creditum, praestante Domino, ad beatitudinis dona perducere debeatis.

Peregrinum igitur ante omnia suscipite, eleemosynam date.

. . . Praesto sunt vobis Sanctarum Scripturarum instrumenta dogmatica . . . Vitas Patrum, Confessiones fidelium, Passiones Martyrum legite constanter . . . ut sancta imitatio ad caelestia regna perducat (*De div. lect.*, chap. 32).

Balnea quoque congruenter aegris praeparata corporibus iussimus aedificari (*op. cit.*, chap. 29).

Nam si vos in monasterio Vivariensi . . . divina gratia suffragante, coenobiorum consuetudo competenter audiat, et aliquid sublimius delectos animos optare contigat, habetis montis Castelli secreta suavia, ut veluti anachoritae . . . feliciter esse possitis. Quapropter optatum vobis erit eligere exercitatis iamque probatissimis illud habitaculum, si prius in corde vestro fuerit praeparatus adscensus (*loc. cit.*).

Oremus . . . ut ovem perditam reportare suis humeris dignaretur (*De div. lect.*, chap. 32).

De anima (chap. 11)

Hilaris illi semper vultus est et quietus. Vox ipsa mediocris, nec debilis vicina silentio, nec robusto clamore dilatata.

Rather impressive is the circumstance of the pure monk's single tunic, whose fragrance exceeds the finest perfumes of the East; he diffuses it about his virginal body, which has become the very temple of God and the receptacle of all virtues. This extraordinary charism which cannot be missed by anyone [4] well accords with the other grace of freedom from carnal temptations with which, by St. Benedict's own testimony, he was endowed by God after the spiritual combat in the thicket of thorns at the Sacro Speco.[5]

He was subjected to no more carnal temptations, and hence, as happened with St. Philip Neri, St. Catherine of Siena, and several other saints, his very body gave off a sweet odor.[6] Moreover, the circumstance of the tears with which his eyes are always moistened corresponds to the Rule, where it is said: "we shall be heard . . . in purity of heart and in tears of compunction" (chap. 20). In two chapters (1 and 17) St. Gregory mentions the charismatic gift of tears with which St. Benedict was endowed.

It is impossible to show how Cassiodorus, *"homo novus,"* could show forth so much monastic experience and such close affinity to the Benedictine idea, unless one admits his dependence on the *Regula monasteriorum,* which had already attained its place of pre-eminence in Rome. Perhaps Cassiodorus himself refers to this contact, when in different words he repeats what St. Benedict had taught, namely, that

Regula monasteriorum	*De anima* (chap. 11)
verba et rationabilia loquatur, et non sit clamosus in voce.	Gradus quoque ipsius nec tardus conspicitur, nec velox.
	Cum humilitate liber, cum charitate districtus. Superbia non inflatur, invidiam non habet. Nulli fratrum loquitur quod poeniteat, nil audit absurdum.
Duodecimus humilitatis gradus est, si non solum corde, sed etiam ipso corpore humilitatem videntibus se semper indicet . . . inclinato sit semper capite, defixis in terram aspectibus.	Lacrymis assiduis decoratus.
. . . Verba otiosa aut risum moventia . . . ad talia eloquia discipulum aperire os non permittimus (chap. 6).	Oculi laeti et honeste blandi.
Sufficit enim monacho duas tunicas et duas cucullas habere (chap. 55).	Tunicam postremo suam, quamvis more cutis una sit, suavissimis implet odoribus.

[4] *"Facile est advertere quem superna potentia dignatur invisere."*

[5] *"Ita in ea est tentatio voluptatis edomita, ut tale aliquid in se minime sentiret"* (*Dial.,* Bk. II, chap. 2).

[6] *"Agnoscitur in illo humanum corpus habere aromata sua."*

the cenobitic class of monks fight for God "under a rule and an abbot" (chap. 1), whose teachings are to be received "willingly" and carried out "effectively." Thus the holy Patriarch. The abbot of Vivarium
writes in his turn: "Wherefore all you who dwell within the confines of the monastery, observe both the rules of the Fathers as well
as the commands of your superior . . . and willingly . . . carry
them out." [7]

We can scarcely conceive that the phrase "rules of the Fathers,"
which are to be carried out "willingly," designates generically the
vast Patristic production; rather it seems to indicate a specific compilation or summary, which constituted the monastic code also for
Vivarium. How could it happen that Cassiodorus would found so important a monastery for studies and the spiritual life, whose library
was an encyclopedia of all the learning of his day, and that only a
Regula monasteriorum should be missing from its shelves? I believe
that, in its absence, Cassiodorus himself would have written it, just
as in fact he did compose various scientific manuals that were to serve
for the formation of his monks. If he did not write a rule, this seems
to indicate that he could not do so, namely, that Rome had already
taken care of this matter. Indeed, under the name of "the rules of the
Fathers" the ecclesiastical jurisprudence of the seventh century regularly understood the *Regula monasteriorum.*

Similarly the chapter of Cassiodorus, "*Commonitio abbatis,*" shows
forth such a verbal affinity with St. Benedict's corresponding chapter
"*Qualis debeat abbas esse,*" as to demand a close affinity of thought
between the two founders. [8]

---

[7] "*Quapropter omnes quos monasterii septa concludunt, tam Patrum regulas quam praeceptoris proprii iussa servate, et libenter . . . efficite*" (chap. 32).

[8] The liturgical *cursus* introduced by Cassiodorus at Vivarium has been the object of recent research and discussion. It contained all the canonical hours of St. Benedict, both day and night, with the exception of Prime.

"*Psalmi sunt denique qui nobis gratas faciunt esse vigilias, quando silenti nocte psal-lentibus choris humana vox erumpit in musicam, verbisque arte modulatis ad illum redire facit a quo pro salute humani generis divinum venit eloquium. Cautus qui aures oblectat et animas instituit fit vox una psallentium . . . Unde merito eis Patris et Filii et Spiritus sancti una Gloria sociatur.*

"*Ipsi diem venturum matutina exultatione conciliant; ipsi nobis tertiam horam con-secrant; ipsi sextam in panis confractione laetificant; ipsi nobis nona ieiunia resolvunt; ipsi diei postrema concludunt; ipsi noctis adventa ne mens nostra tenebretur efficiunt*" (*In Psalt.,* Praef.; *PL,* LXX, 10 f.).

Commenting on Psalm 76, Cassiodorus explains: "*Dicit enim oculos suos anticipasse Vigilias, quas in Dei laudibus solemniter exhibebat. Istas usus noster consuevit vocare*

The fact that Cassiodorus never alludes to St. Benedict by name can be explained. When he wrote his treatise *De anima* in 540, the Patriarch was still living; in the work *De institutione* he barely gives more than a list of the doctors of the Church.

We do not know whether St. Benedict and the Lateran community fostered relations with Dionysius Exiguus, himself a Roman monk, at least by choice. In the Rule his Latin translation of the life of St. Pachomius is indeed cited; Cassiodorus informs us that this great scholar, who earlier had studied dialectics with him, for a number of years occupied a teaching position in Rome. Bede and Paul the Deacon give him the title of abbot; whence Abbot Amelli concludes that Dionysius spent his last years in the monastery of Squillace, in company with his friend and protector, Cassiodorus, who, in fact, after Dionysius' death, writes that he looks upon him as a protector in heaven, after they had so many times prayed together "*hic*," that is, at Vivarium.

Again the reason for the departure of this famous monk from Rome, after his outstanding work in behalf of the Apostolic See, is not very clear. Did he leave during the absence of Pope Vigilius? On the banks of the Tiber this is explained in a ready manner: "What one pope makes, the next unmakes." Stars that rise and stars that set. . . .

In St. Benedict's time, the priest and abbot Eugippius, founder of the monastery of Lucullanum near Naples and author of a rule which the Patriarch used in writing his own, enjoyed great renown. Cassiodorus asserts that he knew him barely by sight, but he praises his writings. Eugippius, however, corresponded with Proba Anicia, daughter of the consul Symmacus, with Dionysius Exiguus, with St. Fulgence, and with the Roman deacons Paschasius and Ferrandus. This man was destined to exert great influence for the spread of the monastic ideal in his territory.[9] He it was who adapted St. Augustine's

---

Nocturnos" (col. 547). He likewise stresses the number seven in connection with the daily Office. Contrary to St. Benedict, however, in order to include the vigils, the founder of Vivarium has to omit Prime. "*Septies in diem laudem dixi tibi super iudicia iustitiae tuae. Si ad litteram hunc numerum velimus advertere, septem illas significat vices quibus se monachorum pia devotio consolatur, idest matutinis, tertia, sexta, nona, lucernaria, Completoriis, nocturnis.*" Cassiodorus never quotes Caesarius, but he was well acquainted with Cassian.

[9] The abbey of Eugippius in the Castrum Lucullanum was famous for its scriptorium, mentioned by Fulgence of Ruspa and in several ancient manuscripts (cf. *Dictionnaire d'archéologie chrétienne*, Vol. V, Part 1, col. 703).

Letter 211 for monks, thus offering St. Benedict a new basis for his Rule. Through Eugippius, too, the Patriarch of Cassino became acquainted with the life of Fulgence by the deacon Ferrandus, and he used it in composing his work.

Another literary effort of Eugippius is entitled *Excerpta ex operibus Sancti Augustini,* undertaken at the behest of a certain Abbot Marinus, which, as Cassiodorus affirms, in its 348 selections contained what would otherwise have had to be sought in an immense number of books. It would be most interesting to be able to verify whether the extensive use which Benedict in his Rule makes of Augustine's writings derives directly from the original sources or rather from the anthology of Abbot Eugippius. In any event, it appears certain that the Patriarch's Augustinianism, particularly in questions regarding divine grace, proceeds from the books of the *scriptorium Lucullanum* and from his relations with the founder.

To understand fully the times and the environment in which St. Benedict lived, one must take into account the representative ecclesiastical thinkers of the day and these founders of monasteries. No one can, for example, understand how St. Benedict came to codify the pre-existing rules of the monastic life for the Latin world, unless he recalls that only a few years before, by commission of Pope Hormisdas (514–23), the monk Dionysius Exiguus gathered the Greek conciliar canons into a Greco-Latin collection, of which, however, only the preface is extant.

CHAPTER LX

The Glorious Departure

THUS we arrive at the early spring of 547. When the tomb was closed into which the body of his sister had been placed, St. Benedict announced that in a short time also his corpse would be deposited there. During the preceding winter months he had spoken of death more often than usual. To a few of the monks who, like Theoprobus, enjoyed his special confidence, he even foretold the day and the hour of his departure. Nevertheless, not to sadden the community unduly the man of God had imposed silence on these confidants. In this interval, too, Benedict was bidding farewell to his dearer disciples who were absent; he sent them, as it were, funeral announcements before his death. In these he clearly indicated by what marvelous sign God would inform them of his passage from earth to heaven.

For a long time already he had contemplated created things in the uncreated light; for him death no longer held any mystery. Benedict knew when it would come and was even in a position to foretell to his disciples by what means God would let them know of it. Meanwhile in prayer and retirement in God, to a greater degree than before, he went on preparing for the great step.

It is well known that the sickness which carries off the great saints is ordinarily the fire of divine love. The Abbot has described this illness in the Rule where he explains the twelfth degree of humility, when he speaks of a perfect love that casts out of the heart all human considerations of fear. The soul, instead, is fully possessed by the holy fear of God. Under the influence of the golden rays of faith, the performance of the most heroic acts becomes, as it were, natural for the spirit: "For as we advance in the religious life and in faith, our hearts expand and we run the way of God's commandments" (Prol.). The heart enlarges, the soul expands in God, while the world contracts: "When the soul sees God, it understands how insignificant all creatures are."

On the night of the storm, when the man of God was in the little house not far from the outside gate of the fortress and by reason of the rain could not return to the monastery, an acute observer might have noticed that it was not so much the downpour of water that prevented him, as rather a declining condition of health, which did not permit him to go outside during such an atmospheric disturbance. Similarly, on the morning of the following tenth of February, when he sent his disciples to fetch the body of Scholastica and did not himself go to compose her corpse on the bier, many at Monte Cassino must have divined that their dear father's strength was declining rapidly. In such a condition a man cannot long survive, and he suffers an acute homesickness for heaven.

After the first week of March, to the Patriarch's general weakness was added a cold, which is always dangerous for the aged and feeble. He was now approaching his eightieth year.[1] The season was favorable for colds and particularly for pneumonia, as medical statistics show. About the middle of the same month, while nothing yet indicated his imminent death, he ordered his tomb opened, perhaps to convey to his disciples the certainty that now his days were numbered. They must have called to mind the words of the liturgy of the dead: "*Aperite mihi portas iustitiae; ingressus in eas confitebor Domino.*"

After studying St. Gregory's narrative, a certain physician has come

---

[1] We have already mentioned the traditional chronology which gives 480 as the year of St. Benedict's birth and assigns the founding of Monte Cassino to 529. If we suppose that he retired to Subiaco about 500, he employed only about twenty-four years (505-29) to found twelve monasteries—one every two years. In our opinion that appears a bit too brief.

In the ordinary way, the development and organization of those first twelve monasteries, the necessary increase of vocations, presuppose at least again as many years. Since the usual date of birth in 480 is not based on documentary evidence, I would lean toward anticipating it by at least a dozen years, in order to allow the Patriarch sufficient time to develop the Subiaco congregation: a good thirty years, no less. When the saint died after 546, he must have been close to eighty.

to the conclusion that pneumonia was the immediate cause of St. Benedict's death. This diagnosis is based on the following clinical data supplied by the biographer.

First, there is a fever that rises rapidly. The sick man is in a state of grave prostration which culminates with a difficulty in breathing (the *"faticari"* of St. Gregory). The sickness grows worse, until on the sixth day the crisis is reached.

On this same sixth day, as the biographer is careful to note, the fever abates, preceded almost always by an increase in gravity of all the symptoms. In this condition, after the fever lessened, St. Benedict has himself carried to the oratory, because he feels he is about to die. The circulatory system and the heart are weakened to the extreme.

If the Patriarch died on March 21, 547, then, as Dom Mabillon observes, his death occurred on Maundy Thursday of that year. According to the custom of many bishops of that time, Benedict, too, desired that the last act of his apostolic life should be a Eucharistic function, that he should breathe his last in the sacred place which he had snatched from Satan and dedicated to the worship of Christ. Sustained by the arms of his disciples, toward evening he went to the basilica of St. Martin, and there ordered that the Mass *in Coena Domini* be celebrated. Perhaps he recalled the words of Vespasian, a fellow citizen of his, who declared that an emperor ought to die standing up (Suetonius, *Vita*).

For St. Benedict the Easter solemnity always was distinguished by some great event. At Subiaco it was the visit of the priest of Monte Praeclaro who drew him from his hiding place and made him known to the people. In 529, while in his new home at Casinum he was preparing for the apostolate among the pagans, which he intended to begin precisely with the paschal alleluia, the mountain folk of the vicinity of Subiaco came knocking at the door of his cell, demanding that he return to them immediately. But the saint, like Christ in the desert, calmly continued his Lenten retreat.

Now, finally, the Easter of 547 will mark the beginning of the holy apostle's Easter of eternity. The celebrant, trembling with emotion, after his own Communion approached the dying man and gave him the body of the Lord, exchanging with him also, according to custom, the kiss of peace. The deacon followed, holding to the Abbot's lips the chalice with the precious blood, and received his last kiss. During the Postcommunion, while the congregation stood, the saint likewise rose and extended his arms for the common prayer. The monks supported him and prayed with him. Finally the deacon announced that the Sacrifice was over and that the assembly might disperse. St. Benedict lifted his eyes and his hands toward heaven and, perhaps again murmuring the prayer of the Psalmist: "*Suscipe me, Domine, secundum eloquium tuum et vivam*," breathed forth his spirit.[2]

According to the custom two of his intimate disciples spread a kerchief over his face in order to hide his last breath from those present.[3] As he had written in the Rule: "With the joy of spiritual desire let him look forward to holy Easter" (chap. 49), so in very deed for him had come the Easter of glory, the Easter completely holy.

According to an ancient tradition of the Roman Church, so well illustrated by Cardinal Rampolla in his notes on the life of St. Melania, persons who were dying were given the Holy Eucharist to show forth in this manner the price of their redemption as well as their perfect union with the Catholic Church. Of this liturgical custom mention is also made in the life of St. Ambrose. When he entered upon his agony, Bishop Honoratus of Vercelli, who had retired to an upper room of the episcopal residence for a little rest, was called by a voice from above: "Behold, he is about to die." Rising up, he went to the bedside of the saint and "offered to him the body of the Lord. When he

---

[2] St. Gregory's account of St. Benedict's death recalls that of the passing of the holy Abbot Spes of the monastery of Cample, about five miles distant from Subiaco. Spes also received a premonition of his approaching end. For the last time the Abbot makes a visitation of the monasteries under his jurisdiction and preaches to his disciples. Fifteen days before his death, "*ad monasterium suum . . . reversus est, ibique fratribus convocatis, adstans in medio, Sacramentum Dominici Corporis et Sanguinis sumpsit, namque cum ipsis mysticos Psalmorum cantus exorsus est. Qui illis psallentibus, orationi intentus animam reddidit. Omnes vero fratres qui aderant, ex ore eius exiisse columbam viderunt, quae mox aperto tecto oratorii egressa, adspicientibus fratribus penetravit caelum*" (*Dial.*, Bk. IV, chap. 10). Hence his death—like Benedict's at Monte Cassino—took place in church.

It is not too farfetched to suppose that St. Benedict knew of the manner of death of this saintly contemporary and desired to imitate it.

[3] St. Gregory, in describing the death of St. Cassius, bishop of Narni, after recalling his final discourse to the clergy, writes: ". . . *clamavit dicens: Hora est. Mox assistentibus ipse suis manibus linteum dedit, quod ea more morientium sibi contra faciem tenderetur. Quo extenso, spiritum emisit*" (Hom. 37).

had received it, he gave forth his spirit, bearing with him a goodly Viaticum." [4] It was the eve of Easter.

From what has been said, the same usage obtained at Monte Cassino. St. Gregory says expressly: "He strengthened himself for his departure by receiving the body and blood of the Lord" (chap. 37). Since outside the Mass the precious blood was not given to the sick and to those dying—not even Honoratus presented the cup to his metropolitan Ambrose, but the Viaticum was administered only under the species of bread—the Patriarch of monks, who employed his final moments in receiving the body and blood of the Lord, shows us that, as if he were not aware of his end, he wished to participate once more with his monks in the Mass of Maundy Thursday. He appears like an aged and robust oak which, standing upright in the plain, despises the fiercest storms.

That Maundy Thursday of 547 was truly an Easter of glory. Even some of the absent disciples perceived its rays. This happened, for example, to a monk who lived in a distant monastery—some believe it was St. Maur in Gaul—and to a good cenobite near Monte Cassino. Both of them, though separated, nevertheless had an identical vision. They seemed to see a triumphal way, gleaming with lights and beautifully carpeted, a kind of Via Appia which from Porta Capena appears in the distance to rise above the Alban Hills and to lose itself in the blue skies of Latium.

Like this was the path which the two good disciples of St. Benedict contemplated, except that the one they perceived surpassed in light and glory anything they had ever seen, and from Monte Cassino it went toward the east directly into heaven. At the top of this rising path or stairway stood a venerable personage, splendidly robed, who asked the two monks if they knew for whom this triumphal way had been prepared and adorned. When they replied in the negative, he said: "This is the way by which Benedict, the beloved of the Lord, now ascends into heaven."

What consolation the two religious derived from this manifestation may be easily imagined. When they beheld this symbolism, so typically Roman, of an ascending path, with its carpets, lights, and so

[4] ". . . obtulit sancto Domini Corpus. Quo accepto ubi glutivit, emisit spiritum, bonum Viaticum secum ferens" (Paulinus, Life of Saint Ambrose, no. 48).

on, they must have called to mind the words of their father who, in the Rule, when interpreting the patriarch Jacob's vision of the symbolical ladder, makes this application: "The ladder thus set up is our life in the world, which the Lord raises up to heaven if our heart is humbled" (chap. 7). God had kept His word.

The corpse was first anointed on the breast with chrism, as the prevailing liturgical custom then required for monks.[5] We cannot doubt that this usage was observed at Monte Cassino. After the Mass *pro dormitione*, which coincided with the Easter Mass, as happened also in the case of St. Ambrose, the body was placed in the double grave where Scholastica already reposed. For a century and a half brother and sister remained undisturbed in the peace of the tomb.[6]

Sometimes misguided devotion or lack of space led to the burying of a second corpse over the first in the same tomb. To prevent this, especially among strangers, a special papal prohibition was invoked in Rome.[7]

After the dispersion of the monks of Monte Cassino, as a result of Zoto's occupation of the monastery, since the place remained unguarded and almost deserted, about the year 703, while Gisulph was duke of Beneventum, some Frankish monks arrived to steal the relics, which were then carried off to Fleury, where they enjoyed a very great veneration throughout the Middle Ages. Today no vestige remains of that once famous abbey.

[5] *"Secundum Romanam Ecclesiam mos est monachos vel religiosos defunctos in ecclesiam portare et cum chrismate ungere pectora, ibique pro eis Missam celebrare"* (Theodore of Canterbury, *Poenitent.;* PL, XCIX, 929 f.).

[6] Besides the example of St. Simplician who at Milan buried the virgin St. Marcellina near her brother Ambrose, we find in the catacombs of St. Agnes in Rome, flanking the tomb of the priest Celerinus, that of his sister with the following epitaph:

HEMILIANE SE VI(va comparavit . . .)
SOROR PRESBYTERI CEL(erini)

[7] The following is an epitaph of the year 537, where the veto of Pope Vigilius is mentioned:.

HIC REQVIESCIT SEBERVS TINCTOR
Q. V. ANN. PLVS MINVS LXII EX QVIB
XVII CVM IVGALE SVA QVIETA PACE TRANS
EGIT CVIVS CORPVS NE ALIVD VNQVAM SVPER
PONATVR PROHIBENS BEATISSIMO PAPA V
IGILIO CONCEDENTE IN HOC LOCO SITVM EST DEPST
. . . IDVM IVLIARVM PC V VILISARII VIRI EX
CELLENTISSIMI CONS ADQVE PATRICI

From an almost contemporary document, edited by Dom Mabillon, we learn how the tomb was disposed: "They found a marble slab. When the stone had been broken, the bones of St. Benedict the Abbot were discovered, and underneath, in the same tomb, but separated by another slab, lay the remains of the blessed Scholastica, his sister." [8] This manner of imposing bodies one over the other did not meet with popular approval,[9] particularly when there was question of strangers. Nevertheless Rome itself supplies us with some examples. Thus, in the Coemeterium minus on the Via Nomentana, we find the following epitaph:

(benemer)ENTI SABINAE ALUMN(e quae)
(vix an)N P M XX D XXIII SUPER PATRO(nam)
DEC III IDUS

Because of the ties of affection, the little girl was buried with the body of her protectress, just as, at Monte Cassino, the brother rested over the corpse of his sister.[10]

At the time of the restoration of Monte Cassino through the efforts of Popes Gregory II and Zachary, the monks, as legal heirs of the former monastery, demanded, but in vain, that the bones of the Patriarch be restored to them. The monks of Fleury as well as the Frankish bishops turned a deaf ear to the letters of Pope Zachary. Indeed, during the same century Paul the Deacon had to admit that in the

---

[8] "Invenerunt lapidem marmoreum perforandum. Destructo vero lapide, invenerunt ossa sancti Benedicti abbatis, et in eodem monumento ossa beatae Scholasticae sororis eiusubter iacere, marmore tamen inter posito" (Mabillon, Vet. Analect., pp. 211 f.).

[9] Already a synod of Auxerre had forbidden "mortuum super mortuum ponere" (can. 10). Baronius quotes an epitaph with the same prohibition: "Nemo suum vel alienum cadaver super me mittat; quod si praesumpserit, sit maledictus et in perpetuum anathemate constrictus" (Anal. Eccl., I, c. 26).

[10] An ancient tradition decreed that bishops and priests be buried near the altar of Sacrifice. Well known is the case of St. Ambrose, who justified his choice of a tomb below the altar of the church that now bears his name with these words: ". . . dignum est ut ibi requiescat sacerdos ubi offerre consuevit." Similarly at Constantinople, the Arian bishop Eudossius was buried beneath the altar. Gregory of Tours states that the holy Bishop Valerius was entombed before the sacred mensa. The same is related of Bishop Adalbert of Metz.

St. Benedict prepared his grave not directly beneath the altar of the chapel of John the Baptist, but near it. Indeed, two altars are mentioned in the basilica as restored at the time of Abbot Petronax: one in the center of the apse; the other near the first, over the original tomb of St. Benedict. Leo of Ostia assures us that the tomb was about nine feet deep. Perhaps this indicates that it was one of the holes whence the pagan oracles used to give their replies.

original tomb at Monte Cassino scarcely the residual dust of the flesh of the two bodies remained.[11] In the early Middle Ages such abstractions of saints' bodies were frequent; consequently it is not unusual for some of them to have several tombs. Thus some of St. Benedict's remains are in France; other bones and ashes at Monte Cassino. But his spirit, thanks to the Rule, filled and dominated the whole of medieval Europe.

[11] *"Franci eiusdem venerabilis Patris pariterque eius germanae Scholasticae ossa auferentes, in suam patriam adportarunt"* (*Hist. Longobard.*, VI, 2).

CHAPTER LXI

The Social Contribution of St. Benedict

SCHOLASTIC manuals quite generally salute St. Benedict as the savior and protector of the ancient Roman culture, which he then, by means of the monachism formed by him, transmitted to the Middle Ages. Many historians have treated of the contributions of monasticism to the improvement of Europe and have come to the conclusion that one of the chief sources of national wealth in Italy, in France, and in Germany derives in the last analysis from the labor of the Benedictines.

Various monographs have dealt with the medieval origins of some Italian communes and have shown that they arose in consequence of the colonizing action of a neighboring abbey. We have some outstanding histories of individual Italian abbeys; but a comprehensive study on this social activity of Italian monachism still is wanting, and possibly, for a variety of reasons, such a work presents great difficulties.

Immediately there arises a question which I admit is prejudicial. Does all this external activity of monachism of former times represent the genuine thought of St. Benedict? To what extent can it be ascribed to the Patriarch? Precisely this problem I intend, if not to solve, because of its vastness, at least simply to illustrate.

That St. Benedict did in fact carry out a religious and social mission in the Latin sphere where he worked cannot be doubted; St. Gregory himself alludes to it: "Almighty God wished . . . to show forth the life of His servant Benedict as a pattern for men, that, being set as a light upon a candlestick, he might shine unto all that dwell in the house of God." [1]

This external work begins at Subiaco with the doctrinal instruc- tion of the shepherds; it develops with the school set up in St. Clem- ent's for the noble youths intended for the religious life; it culminates finally on the heights of Monte Cassino with a revitalizing of a dormant Christianity in an old diocese, which had pretty well gone to seed and been without a bishop for several decades. I have already mentioned the missionary work of the Patriarch when "by continuous preaching . . . he called to the faith"; when he periodically sent out his disciples to the towns in the vicinity of Cassino to give con- ferences; when, in fine, with a wise but firm hand he governed the churches of his recent converts, seeing also to their physical needs during the years of want and famine that then tormented Italy. He also sent the monastic colony to the Lateran.

If divine Providence placed Benedict in contact, not only with popes and bishops, but also with government officials and with King Totila himself, the holy Abbot employed these opportunities for the wel- fare of the people. If in December, 546, Rome was not razed by the conqueror, no small part of the merit belongs to St. Benedict, who, under threat of sudden death, had implored mercy for the poor capital of the Roman world. *"Roma a gentibus non exterminabitur."*

All this is well known and can be deduced from the narrative of Gregory the Great. My question, however, is slightly different. The theocratic concept of the *"polis,"* actuated by the great Italian abbeys of the Middle Ages, around which, in fact, little states developed, with towns and villages belonging to the abbeys, with their own armies, the abbots functioning both as sovereigns and bishops of the people subject to them: to what extent does this fit into St. Benedict's plan?

We must distinguish. It is true, most true, that certain external factors in the early Middle Ages contributed to the formation of ecclesiastical states, among them those of the Benedictine abbeys. Indeed these political factors found in the Benedictine abbeys a suitable environment in which to develop, together with the best conditions to help protect the Italian people, abandoned by the gov- ernment to their fate in the face of the barbarian invaders.

---

[1] Bk. II, chap. 1.

When in the early Middle Ages the government in Italy had practically ceased to exist, because it resided only ideally on the banks of the Bosphorus; when the Lombards laid waste the country by fire and sword, destroying cities and churches, devastating whole provinces, pulling down public buildings and aqueducts: at this juncture divine Providence disposed that the barbarians, though they feared neither St. Peter nor his successors in the Lateran, should nevertheless respect and fear St. Benedict and his social institutions. King Totila must have given precise and strict orders in this regard.

Gregorovius has described the power of the abbot of Monte Cassino, likening him to a little thundering Jupiter, who from the heights on which he lived struck fear into the Lombards with the spiritual bolts of his anathemas. We read the same about the abbot of Subiaco. In the eleventh century his own subjects complain of his immense power, describing him in a document still extant in the archives as a kind of god: "He looses, he binds; he saves, he damns." At Farfa, the power of the abbot was so great that at the beginning of the eleventh century, when the castle of Bocchignano in the Sabine Hills rebelled against the monastery, Henry II, upon being urgently called to Germany, simply charged Pope Benedict VIII to carry on the siege of the village and then turn it back to Abbot Hugo of Farfa.

This historical development of Italian monachism is, without doubt, the effect and consequence of diverse factors of the early Middle Ages; but the principles go back to the patriarch St. Benedict. The abbatial state is the historical development of the monastic citadel organized by St. Benedict in the *Regula monasteriorum*.

As if divining the later days of the Middle Ages when the Byzantine emperor would abandon Italy to its fate, the Patriarch of Monte Cassino conceives of his monastery as an autonomous city, entirely sufficient unto itself: "If it can be done, the monastery should be so established that all the necessary things, such as water, mill, garden, and various workshops, may be within the enclosure" (*Rule*, chap. 66).

By reason of this concept of autonomy on which the saint founded the government of his monastic citadel, it followed naturally that a monastery might have vast land holdings, proportioned, that is, to its needs and the number of its members. St. Gregory mentions the monk Theoprobus who looked after the affairs of the abbey in the city of Cassino, while other monks resided near Capua *"pro neces-sitate monasterii,"* probably to superintend the administration of certain lands in that vicinity. This situation was quite normal at the time. Almost all the episcopal sees had their own landed endowment, and this consisted of numerous farms in Italy, in Sicily, in Africa, and even in the Orient, all with their groups of slaves to cultivate the fields.[2]

Cassiodorus, for example, had given in gift to his monastery of Vivarium the entire *Castellum Scyllacium,* for which reason all the inhabitants held their lands in emphyteusis from the abbey, to which they paid an annual canon. This is still St. Benedict's century, and we are scarcely at the portals of the Middle Ages.

In the Rule we find but a single reference to the lay workers of the monastery, to whom was reserved the harder work in the fields, the performance of which did not fit in well with the monks' schedule. "If the circumstances of the place or their poverty should require that they themselves do the work of gathering the harvest, let them not be discontented" (chap. 48). Hence, in the ordinary course of events, others performed such tasks, and more particularly slaves (*servi*). Every monastery, even the smallest, had some of these. St. Gregory's letters preserve for us the inventory of a small convent of nuns. Their beds number not more than ten; but in the document, besides their lands, explicit mention is made of "two slaves, that is, Maur and John, and two yoke of oxen only."[3]

It would have been impossible for the monasteries not to follow the traditional economic forms of Roman society. Indeed the registers of Italian abbeys show that as late as the eleventh century the ancient institution of slavery was still in vogue: a slavery, be it understood, mitigated according to the spirit of the Gospels and the dictates of the Rule. Very fittingly St. Benedict had reminded his disciples that,

---

[2] The administration of these monastic properties necessarily brought with it occasional recourse to the government, lawsuits, dealings with lawyers and judges. Frequently enough, the religious showed themselves incapable of carrying on such business or suffered harm to their souls because of the dissipation of spirit. Among St. Gregory's letters is one (Bk. I, no. 69) addressed to Peter, a subdeacon and administrator of the papal patrimony in Sicily, instructing him that a certain Faustus be given the power to handle the affairs of the monastery of St. Lucy in Syracuse, for which service he is to receive an annual salary (*"constituto salario"*).

[3] ". . . *cum servis duobus, idest, Mauro et Iohanne, et boum paria duo tantum"* (Bk. VIII, no. 4).

"whether slaves or freemen, we are all one in Christ and bear an equal burden of service in the army of the same Lord" (chap. 2).

About twenty-five years ago I published the results of my studies on the patrimonial conditions of the monasteries of the Lombard era, with special reference to the celebrated abbey of Farfa in the Sabine Hills. I there pointed out how that monastic patrimony, little by little and under the pressure of political events, ended up by becoming an important buffer state between the duchy of Rome and the Lombard kingdom. Both Pope and monarch were concerned with maintaining and protecting it. The territory of this abbatial state extended almost from the gates of Rome to Fano and the March of Ancona; the privileged vessels of the abbey plied the Adriatic and Tyrrhenian seas undisturbed, importing and exporting oil, grain, and wine.

The abbot's government extended over several hundred churches and towns; he had his own governors, maintained an army, and, in the midst of the chaotic political life of Italy during the first few centuries of the Middle Ages, he assured his subjects at least a minimum of peace and sustenance. That the abbot of Farfa, and like him, many other Benedictine abbots, with one hand grasped the pastoral staff and in the other held the scepter was owing to political necessity, not greed for power. This becomes evident when, for example, in the eleventh century the Saracens succeeded in taking Rome and sacking the basilicas of the Princes of the Apostles, Peter and Paul. Peter I, abbot of Farfa, at the head of his army for seven years successfully prevented the barbarians from invading the Sabines; when he finally realized that his enemies were gradually obtaining a strangle hold, by an able strategic retreat he saved his monks, his soldiers, and the treasure and archives of the monastery from the Saracens.

Worthy of note is this detail: among the things regarded as most precious, which under no circumstances were to fall into the enemies' hands, were the papers and the parchments of the monastery. We possess the eleventh-century register of the vast administration of this entire state of Farfa, which went under the title of the Blessed Virgin, whose property it was considered.

At the head of each district was a monk who superintended the right administration, both religious and economic, of his area and who maintained frequent contact with the central government at

Farfa. This last was made possible by a well-organized post, that is, couriers and messengers, who despatched the abbey's correspondence on horseback.

Armies of workers were assigned to the cultivation of the fields. Many of these were freemen, but others were slaves, "slaves of St. Mary." This slavery was not at all degrading or harsh. Indeed from the register of Farfa for the eighth and ninth centuries we learn that a number of freemen of their own accord gave themselves over to the monastery as slaves "because they could not continue living otherwise." Liberty, so they reasoned, is not a thing that helps support life. Among these "slaves of the Blessed Virgin" were also some priests, that is, sons of slaves of the monastery, to whom the abbot had first given a scientific training; then, after having them ordained, he gave over to them the administration of one of Farfa's churches, together with the annexed care of souls.

In the monasteries the Roman concept of slavery had been so spiritualized and diluted that the "slaves of the Blessed Virgin," whether priests or laymen, were regarded more or less as oblates, consecrated to the service of the Mother of God in her sanctuary at Farfa. Generally speaking, the people preferred the abbot's staff to the heavy yoke of the feudal lords. "The nobles take everything; you want but a little." Thus a group of inhabitants of the Marches wrote to Abbot Berard I when they offered themselves to the abbey of Farfa to obtain its protection.

At the same time one must not be deceived by this extremely large number of donations of lands which were made to the more important Italian abbeys during the first half of the Middle Ages. Rather it represented a kind of game with the players going in a circle.

Since the state was no longer able to protect the citizen, he gave his property to a monastery, thus making it something sacred, something that could not be touched either by private individuals or by the civil power. But it was understood that the abbot would grant it to the donor under title of emphyteusis. The usufructuary gave to the monastery a pound of wax for the feast of the Assumption or a couple of chickens at Shrovetide. That was all. At the same time he and his family were enjoying the protection of the Church.

St. Benedict had attributed great importance to the hospice attached to every monastery, whither the poor, the sick, the aged, travelers of all kinds flocked daily. He knew that in those centuries of political turbulence people of every sort would come to the monastery: rich, poor, ecclesiastics, laymen, exiled monarchs, like King Harduin, and popes deprived of all their territory, like Hildebrand and Victor III to Monte Cassino. Hence the Rule ordains that there shall be a respectful and adequate reception corresponding to the varying social positions of the guests: "Let due honor be shown . . . for as far as the rich are concerned, the very fear which they inspire wins them respect" (chap. 53).

These guests depend on the cellarer and form the object of the special care of the abbot, who daily must take his meals with them. The kitchen for the visitors is distinct from that of the community, with a special and skilled personnel. The guests are received within the sacred walls of the abbey with liturgical ceremonies deriving in part from the East. They are met in procession. First they are brought to the oratory for prayer; then their feet are washed, and, while they refresh their bodies at table after the fatigue of the journey, their souls receive the food of the Sacred Scriptures.

In the eighth century this ebb and flow of guests at Farfa, at Monte Cassino, at St. Vincent's on the Volturno, and at some of the other more prominent Italian abbeys became so great that, in order not to disturb the monks and to maintain the spirit of monastic recollection, the great abbots of the Lombard era instituted, parallel with the monks but distinct from them, a special category of clerics or oblates, who were known as "canons." These had their own quarters near the guesthouse; night and day they recited the Divine Office in the church of the hospice and, subject to the abbot's orders, they carried out the work connected with the reception of guests. They developed into the *conversi*, that is, the lay brothers of the more recent orders. In Palestine they were transformed into hospitalers or knights, as, for example, the Templars.

If we take into account the special concept of the autonomous monastery-citadel, with its farm laborers, its slaves, its workmen practicing the different crafts, we see that inevitably, once the old Roman *"polis"* had disappeared, it had to be reconstituted anew about the Benedictine abbeys. It does not correspond entirely to the truth to assert that Christian democracy in Italy originated in the communes of the Franciscan era.

No; considerably before the twelfth and thirteenth centuries the Christian proletariat, the laborers, the peasants dispersed by war and deprived of everything, were gathered and regrouped in villages, thanks to the activity of the sons and successors of St. Benedict. Various statutes of these abbatial settlements are extant, in which, as early as the year 1000, we can perceive the dawning of the later communal liberties.

We could easily show that all these villages of the former abbatial states of Farfa, of Monte Cassino, of St. Vincent's on the Volturno, of Casauria, of Subiaco, and so on, were the result of monastic colonization on lands on which were accumulated the age-old ruins of war. As far as the state of Farfa is concerned, this condition is still shown by names of the following places: Castelnuovo di Farfa, Monte Santa Maria, Montapoli (Mons Operis), San Donato, Santa Vittoria, and so on.

The extensive state of the Campania, over which during the early Middle Ages the abbot of Monte Cassino exercised complete jurisdiction, bore a significant name: it was called "*Terra Sancti Benedicti.*" But this title might be extended to all the vast holdings of monasteries in medieval times, because it was in the name of the Patriarch and according to the principles laid down in his spiritual code that his sons and successors possessed, administered, and rightly governed them.

On Monte Cassino St. Benedict had given his institute the form of an autonomous citadel or state, with a monarchical form of government and a double chamber of counselors (chaps. 2 f.). Round about the abbey was the territory of the ancient diocese of Cassino, whose pagans were converted to the faith by the Patriarch. Over this region he exercised pastoral jurisdiction, like a kind of chorepiscopus. Now let us transport this autonomous mode of government and let us multiply it a hundred times, a thousand times, several thousand times, not only in Italy but throughout Europe, and then we shall understand what a decisive influence St. Benedict exercised over the whole life of the Church.

CHAPTER LXII

St. Pancratius in the Lateran

SEVERAL times mention has been made in these pages of the Lateran monastery which received the refugee disciples of St. Benedict when the soldiers of Zoto invaded Monte Cassino. I shall now speak of it more at length. In the early Middle Ages four monasteries arose successively about the basilica of St. Savior (Lateran). The oldest, founded by Pope Hilary (461–68) in honor of St. Stephen, stood near the baptistery, but rapidly went into decline. Gregory the Great transformed it into a musical school for the young singers who served the cathedral of Rome.

A second monastery, dedicated to St. Pancratius, arose in the vicinity of the sacristy of the basilica; in 593 Gregory refers to it as having existed already for many years. Its traditional location is certain; the beautiful cosmatesque cloister beside the basilica is all that now remains of it.

A third monastery had as its founder Pope Honorius I who, in imitation of Gregory I, transformed his paternal house into a residence for monks. It was dedicated to the apostles Andrew and Bartholomew; the tiny church at the gate of the hospital of St. John is a remnant of it.

A fourth monastery stood near the aqueduct and is mentioned in the life of Leo III. It had the Oriental martyrs Sergius and Bacchus as patrons. First nuns dwelt there, but later Paschal I gave it over to monks.

From its very foundation, the monks of St. Pancratius sang the

Divine Office in the basilica of St. Savior. But at the time of Gregory III, when the monastery had declined, he reorganized the administration of its property and placed a new community there under the government of an abbot charged with the duty of regulating the daily Offices in Rome's cathedral and presiding over them. Later on Hadrian I decided that Pope Honorius' community should have the left side of the Lateran choir, thus obliging the monks of St. Pancratius to remain on the right side, in such a manner that the two choirs would alternate in the divine psalmody. Still later the monks of St. Sergius and Bacchus were joined to them.

The history of the monastery of St. Pancratius is shrouded in complete obscurity because of lack of documentation. Contrary to the later assertions of Cassinese historians, the monastic colony recruited by Abbot Petronax at the behest of Gregory II for the re-establishment of Monte Cassino did not proceed from the Lateran monastery, but was drawn from various other abbeys, notably from St. Vincent's on the Volturno and from Farfa. The monks of St. Pancratius, instead of helping others, were themselves in need of aid from Gregory III.

Here is a surprising detail. Generally speaking, all the Roman monasteries have their "birth certificate," if we may call it such, in the *Liber pontificalis,* where their foundation by popes or other benefactors is recorded. Further, occasionally they take their name from these founders: Monasterium Honorii, Xenodochium Valeri, Monasterium in Formoso, Monasterium kata Pauli, Monasterium kata Galla Patricia, Monasterium S. Salvatoris in Dompni Campo, and so on. Singular is the fact that only concerning the origin of St. Pancratius not a word is said, nor is its founder ever mentioned. And yet it stood at the very flank of the papal residence, and even for that reason enjoyed a certain importance. But the contrary seems to be true.

In 589, when the monks of Cassino fled to Rome, the Lateran monastery had already been in existence for a long time under the government of Abbot Valentinian. Thus we arrive at the first half of the sixth century; because, besides the silence of the *Liber pontificalis* with regard to Pelagius I, we may well suppose that, owing to the inimical attitude of the Roman clergy and monks to his religious policy, he must have had worries enough without erecting another monastery, and that precisely in the Lateran.

In any event, his official biographer would certainly have mentioned the fact, as he did, for example, with regard to the basilica constructed by this Pope at the foot of the Quirinal. Concerning the Lateran monastery we find not a word, either in the biography of Pelagius I or in that of Vigilius. On the other hand, we know that Vigilius erected a splendid hall in the Lateran, where in the early Middle Ages the great receptions of the papal court were held. Contiguous to it Gregory the Great chose his private apartments where, together with a group of monks from St. Andrew's, he continued to lead a monastic life according to the Rule of St. Benedict.

The custody of the Lateran buildings was a matter of so great importance to Vigilius that in the spring of 546, while in Sicily, he appointed Bishop Valentine of Silva Candida and the priest Ampliatus *"ad custodiendum Lateranis."* Of this we have already spoken. The priest Mareas functioned as the pope's vicar in the city; perhaps it fell to his lot to set up the Lateran monastery, conceived before by Vigilius, and to introduce there a small colony of monks under Abbot Valentinian. Later on, under Pelagius I and his immediate successors, this community so declined that finally Pelagius II gave the buildings over to the refugees from Monte Cassino; it must have been half empty.

Noteworthy, too, is the fact that Gregory mentions none of the Lateran monks except Valentinian. Indeed, when about the year 575 he laid aside the insignia of an urban praetor to assume the monastic cowl, instead of turning to the monks of the Lateran, he preferred to found a new monastery on the Caelian, in his own house. One might almost say that in the history of Christian Rome the monks of St. Pancratius lived in the shadows and disappeared without anyone to grieve for them.

We notice, in fact, that in the second half of the sixth century all the better Benedictine vocations go, not to the Lateran, but to St. Andrew's on the Caelian Hill. From among the monks of this abbey, and not from St. Pancratius, Gregory selects the monks who will lead a common life with him in the papal apartments. The bishops of Ravenna and Syracuse as also Augustine and his forty companions were all monks of St. Andrew's. It seems that the foundation of St. Pancratius was and remained a small affair, the monks exclusively engaged in the chanting of the Divine Office in the pope's cathedral.

It did not bear the name of its papal founder, perhaps because it was inaugurated during the period when Mareas was vicar, when, namely, Vigilius was residing on the Bosphorus.

In the *Liber diurnus Romanorum Pontificum,* which contains the oldest collection of formularies of the papal chancellery, we find a very interesting document (no. 95). To a community of monks, driven from their home and seeking refuge in Rome, the Pope grants perpetual possession of a monastery in the city, with the obligation of chanting the Divine Office in honor of the Savior. Naturally one thinks of Bonitus and his refugees in the Lateran. The document reads thus: "Out of sympathy for your sad lot, this monastery is granted to you. And just as We order that you may not leave it, so also We decree and establish that no one of Our successors shall eject you therefrom. It is always to be a monastery in which daily the community shall sing the praises of our Lord Jesus Christ, the Savior of mankind."

The "monastery N. of our holy Church, established in this city of Rome, Region N.," together with other details in the document fit so exactly to the historical situation of the Cassinese monks under Abbot Bonitus that I cannot imagine to what other monastic migration the papal decree might refer.

When in the year 614 the Arabs took Jerusalem, the monks of the Laura of St. Saba, after much wandering, finally found a home in Rome on the (lesser) Aventine; they called it Cella Nova and dedicated it to St. Saba. But the document of the *Liber diurnus* cannot have reference to this second case; because, whereas before the time of the Oriental monks' arrival no monastery existed there (the region was simply a field belonging to St. Gregory's family), the papal decree speaks of a monastery as already established and dedicated to a saint, who, we suppose, is St. Pancratius.

The document makes no mention of the state of the monks already residing in the monastery which then was turned over to the abbot of the refugee monks, because in fact they must have been the disciples whom St. Benedict earlier sent to make the foundation in the Lateran. One gathers that in the mind of Pope Pelagius II and of Abbot Bonitus the hope of returning to restore the monastery of Monte Cassino, once the buffeting of war had ceased, burned rather dimly.

The papal decree then lays down the obligation contracted by the two parties: that the monks would never leave the Lateran monastery and that the successors of Pelagius II would never revoke the donation that had been made. History gives us the assurance that they kept their word.

Thus we see that the exodus of the Cassinese community to Rome in 589 did not at all have the importance which some historians attribute to it, as if on that fact depended the diffusion of the Benedictine Rule in the whole of the West. This tiny monastery, almost lost among the vast conglomerate of the papal buildings, never attained any fame in the history of Rome. No one ever speaks of it; no one ever mentions either its abbots or its possessions. At the time of Honorius I, that is, scarcely half a century later, it must have been so reduced in men and means, that the Pope only a matter of a few yards away erected a new monastery in his own house, called for that reason Monasterium Honorii.

The diffusion of the Benedictine Rule in the world dates back to a time prior to the assault of Zoto on Monte Cassino; as a matter of fact it was introduced by St. Gregory into his new monastery on the Caelian at least fifteen years before the refugee Abbot Bonitus arrived in Rome.

Of the four immediate successors of St. Benedict (Constantine, Simplicius, Vitalis, and Bonitus), Gregory refers only to the first two; they supplied him with the information on the life and work of the master. At that time Gregory was still an urban praetor. Later, after 574, he became a monk; then he was sent as apocrisiary to Constantinople, and his contacts with Vitalis lessened and became unimportant. When Gregory finally undertook the writing of the *Dialogues*, Bonitus and a group of his monks were living only a short distance from him in the Lateran; but already this community represented a second generation which knew the Patriarch only by reputation. This is the reason why the Pope does not even mention Bonitus; but he refers to Abbot Honoratus of Subiaco, who in his advanced age still represented the first generation of St. Benedict's disciples.

With the arrival of the refugee monks in Rome, the history of Monte Cassino is interrupted for 137 years, after which Paul the Deacon continues it with the abbatial tenure of Petronax. This new start has nothing in common with the declining Lateran community, if this still existed; perhaps it disappeared during the Lombard wars.

Strange that the Cassinese tradition should have preserved the series of its abbots from St. Benedict to the year 580 and then afterward have continued with Petronax and his successors, without transmitting so much as the name of a single Lateran abbot who came after Bonitus. Is not this perhaps an indication that the new community which on the heights of Monte Cassino came together under Abbot Petronax did not, in fact, consider itself a successor to the Roman community?

In the Roman Council of 595 St. Gregory promulgated a statute by which he excluded all laymen from the private service of the pope and assigned clerics and monks to this duty. The saint himself explains the reason for the change: he desired to have continuous witnesses of his private life, whom on his side he might benefit by good example. This reason is not very convincing, because also the laity have eyes with which to observe their masters. Probably he had some other reason which he did not wish to divulge officially.

What strikes us as strange is the fact that John the Deacon, in giving the first list of ecclesiastics assigned to the pontifical apartments, mentions the names of several monks of St. Andrew's, but not one of the Cassinese monks of St. Pancratius in the Lateran. The Pope, then, wished to have his former disciples about him, leaving Bonitus in peace among his refugees. Why? We do not know. History has its secrets.

CHAPTER LXIII

The Posthumous Cult of St. Benedict

By way of epilogue St. Gregory adds a final chapter, the thirty-eighth, to the second Book of the *Dialogues* concerning the miracles of the holy Patriarch. St. Zachary speaks of "outstanding" miracles that made St. Benedict famous throughout the Christian world. As a matter of fact, however, the Pope relates only one that happened at Subiaco; but he lets it be clearly understood that other miracles were worked at the tomb of the saint.

There was a poor insane woman, who, finding no relief from her spasms by day or by night, had gone out into the country, wandering through the mountains as if pursued by hounds. Where the dark of evening came upon her, there, exhausted from her ceaseless gadding about, she stretched out on the ground and passed the night. It so happened that one day she came upon the grotto of St. Benedict and, without knowing where she was, entered and went to sleep. From this narrative it is clear that at the time, about the year 570, the Speco was still open to all, in complete solitude. On the following morning, after a restful sleep, the woman came forth from the cave quiet and composed, to the marvel of all. She was completely cured.

Almost certainly Abbot Honoratus must have been the relator of this incident. But the chronological sequence is not so clear. St. Gregory affirms that the miracle happened "lately" ("*nuper*"). But this adverb must be taken in a wide sense, because shortly after the biographer informs us that this woman was already dead and that the cure was lasting. Apparently the miracle had happened some twenty-five years earlier.

At this point Peter the Deacon, the interlocutor in the *Dialogues,* asks: "Why is it that the martyrs regularly work more miracles in oratories dedicated to them, where some of their relics are preserved, than where they themselves repose?" The Pope replies that this happens by divine disposition and to show to simple minds the efficacy of the martyrs' intercession.

Among the other *fioretti,* St. Gregory in Book Four of the *Dialogues* (chap. 47) recounts a miracle which happened in his own monastery on the Caelian, which easily might be attributed to St. Benedict. In those years of epidemics and pestilences a young monk by the name of John, who by reason of his intellectual ability and spiritual fervor was one of the best men in the community, became deathly ill. The physicians held out no hope for his recovery. Then, while preparations for the funeral were already under way, one night a venerable old man, bearing in his hand a rod, which was at that time the insigne of abbots, appeared to him. Touching the dying youth with the rod, the aged man healed him instantly and then said: "Rise, you are healed; this time you will not die. But prepare yourself better for death, because your life here below will not be long."

Who was this aged wonder-worker, bearing the insigne of an abbot? Gregory, in his haste to get to another subject, says simply: "In a vision at night an old man appeared to him and touched him with his rod."

In the monastery of St. Andrew on the Caelian Hill two names rose up spontaneously in the monks' minds: either it was St. Andrew, titular of the monastery, or St. Benedict, the monastic lawgiver. St. Gregory's description better befits St. Benedict, by reason of the rod mentioned.

When the vision disappeared, the young monk felt completely cured; with renewed fervor he returned to the customary exercises of the regular observance and excelled even the oldest monks in virtue. Two years passed. Then one day a monk was buried in the cemetery of St. Andrew's. Gregory, then a deacon of the Roman Church, also was present.

After the community had retired, the fervent monk remained behind to pray at the new grave, when he suddenly seemed to hear the dead man calling to him from below: "Brother John! Brother John!"

At first the youth was frightened; but then he understood that it was a warning and immediately mentioned it to his superiors. Indeed ten days later he was seized by a fever and died shortly thereafter. This happened at the time when an inguinal pestilence was afflicting the whole of Italy.

St. Gregory assures us that this incident occurred "three years back," hence in 590. Both the Roman and the monastic Martyrologies have given a place of honor to this St. John, monk of St. Andrew's on the Caelian, and mention him on January 17.

Other copious collections of St. Benedict's miracles have been made by Adrevaldus in the ninth century and by Desiderius of Monte Cassino in the eleventh century. The first tended to glorify the saint's tomb at Fleury; Desiderius, on the other hand, when he had become pope with the name of Victor III, wished to imitate Gregory the Great by narrating more recent miracles in the Patriarch's basilica on Monte Cassino and in various other filial abbeys.

After the publication of St. Gregory's *Dialogues,* the cult of St. Benedict rapidly spread to the whole Latin world. The great doctor heaps titles on the Patriarch: ". . . that, being set as a light upon a candlestick, he might shine unto all that dwell in the house of God" (chap. 1); "the man of God . . . the holy man . . . the venerable Benedict" (chap. 3); "the venerable Father" (chap. 8); "Benedict, the servant of Jesus Christ" (chap. 15); "the blessed man Benedict" (chap. 38); "the man of venerable life" (Bk. III, chap. 16).

In the hundreds of times the biographer mentions Benedict, he never fails to accompany his name with some title of veneration.

The Greek translator of the *Dialogues,* who wrote for the Greek communities of Rome and for the many Byzantine monasteries of Italy, likewise is not sparing in his praises of St. Benedict. St. Zachary does not hesitate to liken him to "the morning star in the midst of a cloud." And the encomia rise in a continuous crescendo as the translation progresses.

Historians generally reject as spurious the acts of the Roman Synod supposedly celebrated in 610 under Boniface IV, which speak of "the blessed Benedict, the genial master of monks." No one, however, doubts the fact that the first forty missioners sent by Gregory the Great to England introduced the Rule of St. Benedict as well as devotion to its author into that land. St. Aldhelm (d. 705), who from being an abbot became bishop of Chichester, sings his praises.

During this time, too, the Rule of St. Benedict found its way into various formulas of the *Liber diurnus Romanorum Pontificum,* where it was referred to as the *Patrum Regula* or the *Paternarum Regula Traditionum.* The Ambrosian codex of the *Liber diurnus,* edited by Ratti (Pius XI), even though it belonged to the monastery of Bobbio since the tenth century, seems to derive from a Roman scriptorium. We find there also an ancient rite of monastic profession with this interesting prayer: "O God, who through the blessed Benedict hast laid down a norm of human life, particularly for those who renounce the world. . . ." The entire rite breathes the spirit of great antiquity and brings us back rather close to the times of Gregory I.

Other writers have treated of the introduction of St. Benedict's name into the Canon of the Mass and into various Martyrologies from the eighth century on.

The theft of the Patriarch's remains and their translation to Fleury show how esteemed St. Benedict was in Gaul; this great repute owed its origin to the universal adoption of his Rule. In 623, a document of Venerandus, founder of the abbey of Altaripa, mentions the "Rule of St. Benedict, Abbot of Rome (*Abbatis Romensis*)." Similarly Pope John IV in a privilege of the year 641 refers to the saint thus: "Not far distant from our times, Benedict, the Abbot of this city of Rome . . ."

St. Gregory was dead only a few decades at that time, and, notwithstanding his biography, both in France and in Rome St. Benedict was looked upon and called "a Roman abbot." The saint's mission in Rome and in the Lateran was receiving more attention than his work at Monte Cassino.

Traube has shown [1] that an entire family of manuscripts of the Rule of St. Benedict, in widespread use during the sixth, seventh, and eighth centuries in Italy, Gaul, Germany and England, before the time when Charlemagne received his copy of the original of Monte Cassino, descends from an archetypal text Σ, which was in circulation already in the sixth century. So soon, then, Abbot Simplicius of Monte Cassino "propagated the hidden work of the master everywhere."

[1] Cf. Butler, *S. Benedicti Regula Monachorum,* 3rd ed., Freiburg, 1935, p. xv.

We discovered recently a confirmation of a widespread cult of St. Benedict in former times in Rome, in the catacombs of Hermes on the Via Salaria. There, in the subterranean basilica of the martyr, in an apse with frescoes dating back to about the eighth century, perhaps made during the reign of Pope Hadrian I, flanking the Madonna with the Child, who sits between the archangels Michael and Gabriel, we find the figures of St. John the Evangelist, St. Hermes, and St. Benedict. Up to the present time this appears to be the oldest representation of St. Benedict.

The place of distinction reserved to the Patriarch, namely, to the left of Mary the Queen, while at her right there are, not one, but two persons, of itself bespeaks the importance attached to this image of St. Benedict. The Patriarch is shown standing, a capuche on his head, which is surrounded by a nimbus, garbed in a long white tunic with a black cucullion placed over it. While he blesses with his right hand, in the left he holds a book of the Scriptures. On the right-hand page, after a Greek cross, the following words of the Psalmist are inscribed: *"Initium sapientiae timor Domini"* ("The fear of the Lord is the beginning of wisdom"); on the opposite page we read: *"S. Benedictus Abbas."* He has gray hair, moustache, and beard; the beard is short. What I have called a cucullion is a kind of tight-fitting penula, shortened in front, akin to the modern chasuble. This form of cowl is not without interest, since it shows how from it the later scapular of the monastic orders derived.

It was characteristic of ancient sacred iconography to represent a saint in a habit proper to the liturgical office he was to fulfill in church. This is the reason why the painter of the catacombs of St. Hermes dressed St. Benedict in the white tunic adorned with a row of crosses about the neck, and over this placed the cucullion in the shortened form then in use.

I wish to mention here that what is called in the Rule "a scapular for work" (chap. 55) was something entirely different from the shortened cucullion. St. Benedict's scapular served a purpose analogous to the workman's apron and tended principally to keep the loose tunic, which otherwise would have hindered the free movement of the arms, close to the body.

Noteworthy is the fact that, instead of a copy of the Rule, the

Patriarch is holding the Psalter opened at Psalm 110. The quotation given by the painter of the catacombs of Hermes is not found in the Rule, where, however, we find something akin to it in the Prologue: "And what does He say? 'Come, My children, listen to Me; I will teach you the fear of the Lord.' "

Perhaps the Roman painter, who has given us this portrait of St. Benedict, with the alb and with the embroidered crosses around the neck, wished to emphasize not so much the monastic activity of the saint as his apostolic and doctrinal work among the people. Not without reason the liturgy salutes him thus: "O God, who through the blessed Benedict hast sanctioned a norm of life, particularly for those who give up the world . . ."

A word must be said, too, about the "eyed" alb (*alba oculata*), worn by the saint as a member of the higher clergy. Of this kind of ornamentation with stripes of purple or lace we find mention from Tertullian and the ancient authors down to the ostiary Beroldus of the cathedral of Milan. St. Germain of Paris informs us that the liturgical alb of his time was trimmed with silk or wool. These tunics reserved for the sacred functions had purple galloons or binding worked into them, as is done to the present day in the cathedral of Milan with the sacred shirts and the cloths of the high altar. The archbishop and the sacred ministers wear "eyed" albs, having a lace collar with crosses about the neck.

Very similar to the representation of St. Benedict just described is another of the Patriarch of monks in the church of the monastery of St. Peter at Civate, not far from the Lake of Lecco. The picture is found in a secondary apse of the church and dates back to the ninth century. Represented is a choir of martyrs, of popes, and of anchorites, among whom St. Benedict stands forth wearing a black cowl, with a nimbus about the head deep in the capuche. With the right hand he appears to be gesticulating; in the left he holds a writing-style and a copy of the Rule. According to the Roman fashion the figure is beardless, of mature age, not yet aged. Above the head, in characters of the Carolingian renascence, appears a fragmentary inscription: MARTI(*res pontifice*)S A(*nac*)HORETE. Next to him is St. Anthony in a white tunic, a rule in his hand, while behind, in a second row, appears another group of monks and the blessed.

On one of the side walls, on a rich background, the figure of the legislator catches the eye. He is standing and somewhat bearded; in the right hand he grasps the pastoral staff, while in the left he holds open the book of the Rule. On the pages we read: *"Ego sum Benedictus abbas."* Over the long tunic the saint wears a black cowl with rather narrow sleeves. The head is tonsured and is not covered with the customary capuche. To the right and left at the height of the knees are the words: *"Benedictus sanctus."* Both pictures are important, because they were made at the time of Hildemar, who in that abbey at Civate, after Paul the Deacon, wrote one of the first commentaries on the Rule of St. Benedict.

As I am about to lay down my pen at the end of this book, inspired by the filial love I have borne from the years of my early youth toward the Patriarch Benedict who received me into his abbey of St. Paul in Rome, it gives me pleasure to close with the decree of the bishops gathered in the second Council of Duzio in 874: "We decree that this Rule, promulgated by the Holy Spirit and under the authority of the blessed Pope Gregory, be numbered among the canonical Scriptures and the writings of the Catholic doctors." [2]

Today the world, so many centuries after the Redemption, is returning violently to those remote ages that preceded the Italian civilizations of the Etruscans, the Sabines, and the Quirites. Matter contends against the spirit; brute force takes the place of right and makes itself arbiter. When the Lord, who is "always rich in mercy" (Rom. 10:12), will sound the hour to rise from this immense ruin, together with the Gospel it will perhaps be necessary to return to a study of the Benedictine Rule, which in another day, after the universal deluge of the barbarian invasions, begot for the Church the new offspring, which under Charlemagne finally succeeded in reconstructing the Empire of the West. Will thus perhaps be fulfilled the dream of the Calabrian Abbot Joachim, who, endowed with a prophetic spirit, foresaw a new era of the Paraclete, in which Benedictine monachism would again undertake the Christianization of the world?

---

[2] *"Eadem Regula Sancto Spiritu promulgata et laudis auctoritate beati Papae Gregorii in Canonicas Scripturas et Catholicorum Doctorum scripta teneri decreta est"* (cf. Mabillon, *Annal. O.S.B.*, I, 608).

APPENDIX

The Ruins of Monte Cassino

AMONG the greatest victims of the late war must be numbered the abbey of Monte Cassino, which was bombarded by the Allies on February 15, 1944. So much of the structure was destroyed that the expense of removing the rubble was estimated at fifty million lire.

The Germans and the Allies mutually blame each other for the destruction, and perhaps both are right. The Germans, though declaring that they respected the monastic enclosure, nevertheless had transformed the hilltop into a first-class fortress, whence day by day from a hundred rocky caves they poured a fire of death upon the Allied army, which at all costs were determined to open a way through Cassino in order to get into Latium.

After so many centuries, the Cassinese fortress still served the military purpose of protecting the road to Rome and effectively to prevent the Allies from getting through. The fact stands that for four months American and Polish troops tried to force the pass, but in vain; their corpses were strewn over the area. The Germans from their vantage point were able to note the Allies' every move and succeeded in quashing every attempt to open a way there toward Rome.

The exasperation of the Allied and Polish troops reached such a pitch that finally the commanders decided on the desperate gesture of getting at the Germans from the air and therefore bombed Monte Cassino. Otherwise, so they thought, they would have to give up hope of taking Rome.

The abbey of Monte Cassino of our times did not resemble very much the structure of the Lombard era, which I have described in the preceding pages. Historians count at least five or six partial destructions of the monastery at the hands of the Lombards, the Saracens, the Normans, the Spaniards, the sans-culottes, and others. But every time the structure was either rebuilt or restored; and until recent times only the expert eye of the archaeologist could recognize in that vast Benedictine conglomerate the remains of the ancient Samnite fortress and the buildings put up by St. Benedict.

Yet Monte Cassino until its recent destruction represented a real continuation, both historically and artistically, of the ancient sanctuary of the Samnites, and its churches which were still *in situ* were the very ones that St. Benedict had transformed into Christian basilicas. The twofold circle of walls with the Roman tower over the entrance to the fortress, the covered passage and the stairway that connected the two sanctuaries of the god still existed more or less, though in a Bramantesque garb. When the rubble is removed, we shall see what has been saved.

The two primitive Samnite sanctuaries, namely, the temple and the oracle at the summit of the mountain, divided Monte Cassino into two distinct sections of buildings.

The original monastery of St. Benedict at the terminus of the ancient mule path was built about the tower and the temple of Apollo, and did not amount to much. In the eighth century Abbot Petronax enlarged St. Martin's by sixteen cubits, about twenty-five feet. In 1880, on the occasion of the fourteenth centenary of the holy Patriarch's birth, excavations were made in that area, but with meager results. Nevertheless, near the tower which Desiderius had built for the new entrance to the monastery, a basilica was discovered which was readily identified as that of the Savior. The recently founded artists' school of Beuron decorated its walls with pictures; and this turned out to be one of the best attempts in modern times by a completely Christian school of artists.

The continuing development of the abbey's power in the duchy of Beneventum toward the end of the eighth century decided Abbot Gisulph (797–817) to undertake a reconstruction of Monte Cassino. Before him, the majority of the monks dwelt at the foot of the mountain, because on the summit no more space was available. At that time the thing that drew the faithful of all Catholic Europe was the original tomb of St. Benedict, which in the beginning was outside the inhabited area, in the middle of the sacred grove.

This narrow structure Abbot Gisulph transformed into a large basilica with three columned porticoes, round which he then built the new monastery; the necessities of the times demanded that it have the aspect of a fortress. The chapel of the Baptist thus became the *Basilica Sancti Benedicti*, while the little church of St. Martin remained but a pious souvenir of the saintly founder.

After the destruction of Monte Cassino at the hands of the Saracens in 883 and after the long abandonment of the abbey during the residence of the monks at Capua, the great restorer of Monte Cassino was Abbot Desiderius, who later on added the keys of the blessed Peter to the abbatial staff. His rule (1055–87) coincided with the period of the greatest splendor of the monastery, whose civil jurisdiction under the Normans extended far and wide in southern Italy and even to Sardinia. Leo of Ostia in his *Chronicon Cassinense* describes the reconstruction of the basilicas of St. Benedict and of St. Martin with precious materials, shining with gold, marbles, and mosaics. The chapter room, the refectory, the long and spacious dormitories, the kitchens, the stairway leading to the *paradysus* before the large basilica: all these were the work of Desiderius. Although remade later on with a touch of Bramante, they defied the ages to come right down to our own days.

Until a few years ago, the monumental entrance to the monastery was through "the strong tower sustained by four large columns," as Leo of Ostia says; this new entrance stood out about forty feet from the primitive Roman tower. Thence by a sharp ascent a ramp led to a second entrance, almost before the church of St. Martin. Here, on a level space, Antonio and Giovanni da Sangallo in the sixteenth century built their cloister, at the right side of the stairway leading to the basilica of St. Benedict.

An examination of the drawing of the abbey of Monte Cassino which was made by the Sangallos between the years 1507 and 1512 and preserved in the Uffizi at Florence, shows that by and large, despite several earthquakes, wars, sieges, and sackings, the work of Desiderius has been preserved to a remarkable extent. The following centuries, rather than knocking down the old structures and building new ones, limited themselves to refurbishing and adding to the old giant, dressing him in the style in vogue at the time.

Thus it was that the abbey buildings, beginning with the splendid basilica, appeared in their ornate and baroque form, that baroque, so judicious and discreet, concerning which Abbot Tosti very acutely observed: "From the purely artistic point of view, the baroque basilica of Monte Cassino was a mistake; but what a great and beautiful mistake!"

I have already mentioned the art school of the Benedictines of Beuron. It needed all the daring, so truly revolutionary, of Abbot Krug to erect and deck out a new subterranean chapel in the Beuronese style and to set it over against the work of Luca Giordano, the painter of the baroque basilica of Monte Cassino. The crypt, as it was called, extended below the choir of the abbey church and surrounded the original tomb of St. Benedict, which remained invisible below the high altar consecrated by Pope Benedict XIII. For the Italians of the Campania several more decades would have been required to habituate themselves to and to comprehend the exquisitely spiritual art of Father Desiderius Lenz, founder of the Beuronese school, which went back to the ancient art of Egypt, the esthetic canons of the Greeks, to the style of the paleo-Christian artists of Ravenna and of Constantinople, to the ingenuous simplicity of the primitives of the fourteenth and fifteenth centuries. I shall leave it to others to determine if Dom Lenz really succeeded in fusing these various artistic currents into a single and vital whole.

Certain it is, before the spiritual void of baroque art, this crypt of Monte Cassino, with its bas-reliefs and its mosaics, which so exquisitely echoed the same mystical poem of faith which the melodious psalmody sang in the choir above, called forth meditation and, let us admit it freely, admiration.

Without doubt, under the azure skies of Monte Cassino something better was demanded; yet the Beuronese school with all the orthodoxy of its esthetic rigorism represented the best modern artistic interpretation of the ancient Benedictine spirituality.

I do not know what plan will be followed in the reconstruction of Monte Cassino—whether the abbey will be modernized on the architectonic lines of Bramante or whether, instead, Abbot Desiderius' plan for the superstructures, as they existed from the eleventh to the eighteenth century, will be adapted to present-day exigencies. A great student of the history of Monte Cassino, Dom Morin, favored the latter idea.

But however Monte Cassino will be rebuilt, whether with walls of gold and floors of jasper, the treasures of ancient art are gone forever. The basilica with its inlaid marbles and the gold of its stuccoes framing Luca Giordano's pictures will never be seen again. The cruciform crypt, sparkling with the best masterpieces of the Beuronese school will remain only a memory, because now both Abbot Krug and Dom Lenz, the only men capable of conceiving and executing this great poem of faith, are dead. From this standpoint, the destruction of Monte Cassino represents an irreparable loss for the whole of Christian civilization.

LAUS DEO

Index